MW00653108

On the Road to Vatican II

On the Road to Vatican II

German Catholic Enlightenment and Reform of the Church

Ulrich L. Lehner

Fortress Press
Minneapolis

ON THE ROAD TO VATICAN II
German Catholic Enlightenment and Reform of the Church

Cover image: Closing session of Council of Trent in 1563, by Nicolo Dorigati (active 1692-1748), 1711. Detail. Italy, 16th century. / De Agostini Picture Library / A. Dagli Orti / Bridgeman Images

Cover design: Laurie Ingram

Library of Congress Cataloging-in-Publication Data
Print ISBN: 978-1-5064-0898-9
eBook ISBN: 978-1-5064-0899-6

The paper used in this publication meets the minimum requirements of American National Standard for Information Sciences — Permanence of Paper for Printed Library Materials, ANSI Z329.48-1984.

Manufactured in the U.S.A.

This book was produced using Pressbooks.com, and PDF rendering was done by PrinceXML.

Dedicated in Gratitude to the
Hochschule für Philosophie, Philosophische Fakultät SJ,
Munich, Germany

Contents

Part III. Church Reform

Series Preface

Renewal

Conversations in Catholic Theology

Edited by Lewis Ayres and Medi Ann Volpe

Continue your search without tiring and without ever despairing of the truth. Recall the words of one of your great friends, St. Augustine: "Let us seek with the desire to find, and find with the desire to seek still more." Happy are those who, while possessing the truth, search more earnestly for it in order to renew it, deepen it and transmit it to others. Happy also are those who, not having found it, are working toward it with a sincere heart. May they seek the light of tomorrow with the light of today until they reach the fullness of light. But do not forget that if thinking is something great, it is first a duty.

For this purpose, without troubling your efforts, without dazzling brilliance, we come to offer you the light of our mysterious lamp which is faith. He who entrusted this lamp to us is the sovereign Master of all thought, He whose humble disciples we are, the only one who said and could have said: "I am the light of the world, I am the way, the truth and the life."

These words are from the Second Vatican Council's closing message to Thinkers and Scientists, delivered on December 8, 1965. While they were addressed first to those beyond the Church, they can—and should—speak to us all. These words remind us well of the importance and the duty of thinking as a bringing toward the light of reason that which may be known and a showing to reason of the resources we have received in faith. In this call to those beyond the Church's boundaries is hidden one of Vatican II's great charges to those within the Church: the charge to think for renewal, using all the resources we can appropriately bring to bear.

"Renewal" is a series of books offered in aid of contemporary Catholic conversation, although readers of theology across the ecumenical spectrum will, hopefully, find them stimulating and rewarding. This series will offer resources that seek to further the work of the Council, exploring, excavating, explaining aspects of the faith that we have inherited. Some volumes in the series will have a strongly historical focus, excavating old treasures in order to aid us now—these may concern figures from our Patristic or Medieval heritage—while others will focus on figures more proximate in time. Some books will bring a treasure that is new, that is primarily in a constructive mode. Theologians or themes well-known and under-studied, those who shaped the distinctive emphases of Vatican II, as well as those whose theologies represent different moments in modern Catholic thought, all will be welcomed—as long as their concern is the constant search for the flourishing of the Catholic conversation.

Acknowledgments

I acknowledge, in gratitude, the support of the Humboldt Foundation, Germany, and the hospitality of the Hochschule für Philosophie, Philosophische Fakultät SJ (Munich), without which I could not have assembled the current volume. It was particularly delightful to come back to the place where I began my academic training in philosophy.

Moreover, I am grateful to have received outstanding research support from my academic home, Marquette University in Milwaukee, Wisconsin—in particular, Dean Dr. Richard Holz and Vice-President Dr. Jeanne Hossenlopp.

I would especially like to thank Prof. Dr. Harald Schöndorf SJ, who has been a friend and mentor since my undergraduate days; Prof. Dr. Bernhard Schneider (Trier), who has been a most gracious conversation partner on the Catholic Enlightenment and host for my Humboldt Fellowship; my doctoral student Shaun Blanchard; and Dr. Lewis Ayres and Dr. Medi Ann Volpe for accepting the current volume for their book series.

March 25, 2016
Milwaukee, WI

1

Introduction

When Jorge Mario Bergoglio was elected pope in March 2013, many wrote about the significance of the choice of his papal name—Francis. Commentators insisted that this symbolized his indebtedness to the ideals of St. Francis of Assisi and St. Francis Xavier, the famous Jesuit missionary. He himself explained his choice of name by his profound veneration of St. Francis of Assisi. But there may be an overlooked "third" Francis: St. Francis de Sales (1567–1622), the great master of spirituality, doctor of the Church, and bishop of Geneva. For both Pope Francis and St. Francis de Sales, reform is central: St. Francis de Sales studied theology and worked as a priest and preacher in the wake of the Council of Trent (1543–65). Reform was in the air; attempts were being made to retrieve the spiritual power sources of faith and to eliminate sources of scandal from within. De Sales called this the "cutting of the aqueducts." Pope Francis, likewise, emphasizes reform. Yet, for both men, "reform" has not been primarily a political matter: it is the constant struggle to let the church be the salt of the earth and light of the world. Both have realized that a self-contented church that is not dynamically reaching out beyond the pews is doomed to wither away. The Catholic Church is always in need of reform, of weeding its theological and ecclesiastical garden, and updating its methods of evangelization. The Tridentine reform ideas of de Sales, Charles Borromeo (1538–84), and others were, therefore, adapted to the needs of the time and complemented by new concepts, which lived on in the eighteenth century and merged with Enlightenment ideals to forge a Catholic Enlightenment that was to rejuvenate a complacent church.

These Tridentine reform ideas heavily influenced the Second Vatican Council. Giuseppe Roncalli (1881–1963)—later, Pope St. John XXIII (1958–63)—had studied the Tridentine reforms in depth and even edited Borromeo's records after visiting the parishes of Bergamo. In the introduction to the edition of 1937, he wrote:

> The Council of Trent offered the spectacle of a vigorous renewal of Catholic life [in] a period of mysterious and fruitful rejuvenation and, what seemed still more marvelous, of efforts by the most remarkable individuals of the Church to implement the new legislation. The pastoral ardor burning in them drove them to realize as perfectly as possible the conciliar mandates aimed at the perfection and spiritual elevation of the clergy and people. . . . [It was] a time of potent reawakening of energies that has no equal in any other period of church history.[1]

One cannot overestimate the last sentence of the future pope's statement. If the Tridentine period had, for him, no equal in church history in regard to the "potent reawakening of energies," then it must have been his guiding star for a rejuvenation of Catholicism too in the twentieth century. And indeed, when he was appointed patriarch of Venice in 1953, Roncalli emulated Borromeo by regular visitations of the parishes in his diocese and performing the role of "shepherd and father" for the faithful entrusted to him. In his diary, he explicitly referenced his pastoral ideas to "the spirit of the Council of Trent."[2] This became even more obvious when, in 1957, he called for a diocesan synod, just as Trent had advised. He envisioned another Tridentine moment in the Church's history, a "reestablishment of Catholic life."

---

1. Jared Wicks, "Tridentine Motivations of John XXIII before and during Vatican II," *Theological Studies* 75 (2014):847–62, at 852.
2. Ibid., 849.

It was in the announcement of the synod that he first used the term *aggiornamento* (updating), which became the crucial terminological key to understanding the Second Vatican Council:

> Have you not heard the word aggiornamento repeated many times? Here is our church, always young and ready to follow different changes in the circumstances of life, with the intention of adapting, correcting, improving, and arousing enthusiasm. In summary, this is the nature of the synod, this is its purpose.[3]

Could there be a better description of what Vatican II tried to realize than the description Roncalli gave of a Tridentine synod? Even the often-invoked pastoral style of Vatican II has its roots in the Tridentine role models of Borromeo and de Sales, albeit not in the documents of the Council of Trent. Yet, despite the importance of the Tridentine reform, and especially, its application in the eighteenth century for understanding the event and meaning of Vatican II, it has been completely marginalized by theologians because the twentieth-century roots of the Council have been overemphasized as its *only* roots.

Trent's Aftermath

The Council of Trent not only addressed the Protestant Reformation, but also its homemade problems of corruption and decay. It identified what was necessary to reform—for example, it determined that future priests should be properly educated and guided to become authentic pastors—but it also codified what Catholics believed, in contrast to Protestants. Thus, for example, the Council stressed that human freedom is a crucial feature of theology. This particular teaching was part of a new, more optimistic view of the human person: one could do good deeds without faith or divine help, and could freely reject God's grace. While this prepared the ground for ongoing controversies over the question of predestination, most importantly, it became the foundation of the Enlightenment belief in individual freedom and the

3. Ibid., 850.

natural capacities of the human person. It was the beginning of Catholic reform.

One of the most important products of the Council was the *Roman Catechism*, a handbook that allowed parish priests to teach doctrine intelligently and with clarity. A new edition of the Bible followed later. The Church emerged, as Roncalli correctly stated, stronger from the shock of the Reformation than it had ever been before.

Yet, just as the implementation of Vatican II took time, so the reforms of Trent were not embraced overnight. In fact, the Council faced a massive problem virtually unknown at the time of Vatican II: many early modern states, where sovereigns enjoyed strong influence over the Church, perceived Trent as a threat because it called old privileges into question. The Council insisted on the freedom to choose one's own spouse, and declared that no one could force a Catholic to legally marry another person. This undermined the rights of the French kings, who openly opposed the publication of the decrees of the Council for a long time. As a consequence, generations of bishops and priests passed until the Council's decrees were accepted in France, and even then, only partially. Similar things could be said of other states. While in the midst of the seventeenth century, the zeal for reform had weakened in many places, largely because of the devastating effects of the Thirty Years' War in Central Europe, it was again rekindled in the eighteenth century. Now, however, it faced another problem—namely, that of modern philosophies and a mindset that made faith only one option among many others. The South American Catholic Enlightener Pablo de Olavide (1725-1803) astutely realized the danger of the "secular option" (two hundred years before Charles Taylor). He lamented that as long as theologians did not understand this, until they produced a catechism that addressed this change in mentality, there was no hope for a religious revival.[4] Reform Catholicism in the eighteenth century—as one could call the movement that tried for a rejuvenation of the Church in the spirit of Trent—could not ignore

---

4. Pablo de Olavide, *Triumph des Evangeliums. Memoiren eines von den Verirrungen der heutigen Philosophie zurückgekommenen Weltmenschen*, trans. J. des Echelles (Regensburg: 1848), 4:322–79; cf. for the "secular option," Charles Taylor, *A Secular Age* (Harvard, MA: Belknap Press, 2007).

Enlightenment thinkers and ideas if it wanted to remain an intelligent and alternative worldview. The result was the Catholic Enlightenment—a movement that tried to reform the Church, rearticulate its dogmas in modern language, and update and correct its teachings. At the same time, this movement was so diverse that it is impossible to describe it as a unified program, apart from encompassing these broader ideas.

It is here that the importance of eighteenth-century Catholicism and Catholic Enlightenment for the Church today lies: like today, the Church faced the staunch opposition of leading thinkers, and for the first time, the faithful had to answer for themselves the question: "how can I remain faithful to the faith and be part of the modern world?"

What Enlightenment Project?

Some might wonder why they should care about the Enlightenment. After all, is it not conventional wisdom that "the Enlightenment project"—a phrase invented by Alasdair MacIntyre and Jürgen Habermas in the 1980s—has failed?[5] Not so fast. Intellectual and cultural historians of the past three decades have shown that it would be overly simplistic to state that the project of modernity, namely "relentless development of the objectivating sciences, of the universalistic foundations of morality and law, of autonomous art," which results in "releasing the cognitive potentials accumulated in the process from their esoteric high forms and attempting to apply them on the sphere of praxis, that is to encourage the rational organization of social relations" was solely created by Enlightenment philosophers.[6] In other words, Habermas (and MacIntyre) state the existence of a unified Enlightenment that divinizes reason so that it can rationalize

---

5. James Schmidt, "What Enlightenment Project?" accessed May 18, 2015, https://persistentenlightenment.wordpress.com/2013/05/15/revisiting-the-enlightenment-project-inspired-by-anthony-pagden-and-armed-with-some-ngrams.
6. Jürgen Habermas, "Modernity: An Unfinished Project," in *Habermas and the Unfinished Project of Modernity: Critical Essays on The Philosophical Discourse of Modernity*, ed. Maurizio Passerin d'Entreves and Seyla Benhabib, trans. Nicholas Walker (Cambridge: Polity Press, 1996), 44–46.

misogyny, colonialism, racism, and beliefs in the limitless pursuit of human perfection.

There are many problems with such a view, one of which is that there never was a homogenous Enlightenment. By going beyond the established literary canon of Enlightenment writers, historians have found that it is impossible to determine the distinctively common themes, arguments, or ideas of these Enlighteners. Only broad concepts, such as the fight against conceptual opacity or superstition, could be discerned—but it has been questioned whether these qualify as a unified "project." Many have, therefore, looked at the overall cultural process of Enlightenment with its correspondence networks and publishing ventures as a way of defining the Enlightenment more broadly. Although some still hold up the flag for a unified vision of Enlightenment, most historians have moved on, and now, accept a variety of Enlightenments and even families of different Enlightenments.[7] The biggest revision in the historiography of the eighteenth century, however, was the realization that there was a religious Enlightenment, which was more widespread than that of the elitist propagators of the "objectivating sciences" that was of such concern to Habermas. God was not pushed out of the equation during the Enlightenment, as Peter Gay had thought,[8] but put back in. Religious Enlighteners in Judaism and Christianity thought about how to articulate the faith under new premises. Christopher Dawson gets it exactly right: "The age of Voltaire and Bolingbroke and Frederick the Great was also the age of Wesley, Tersteegen and St. Paul of the Cross."[9]

Enlightenment theology is still conceived by many as rationalist, with a naïve belief in human perfection. It is as if a nuanced view of eighteenth-century theologians is not possible without polemics. This is only all the more so in Catholicism. Since the Catholic Church felt embarrassed by its dialogue with modernity, it felt the need to

---

7. The most prominent voice in favor of a unified Enlightenment is John Robertson, *The Case for the Enlightenment. Scotland and Naples, 1680-1760* (New York: Cambridge University Press, 2005); Robertson, *Enlightenment: A Very Short Introduction* (Oxford: Oxford University Press, 2015).

8. Peter Gay, *The Enlightenment: An Interpretation*, 2 vols. (New York: Knopf, 1966–69).

9. Christopher Dawson, *The Gods of Revolution* [1972] (Washington, DC: Catholic University of America Press, 2015), 30.

denounce it as a deficient form of Catholicism. How could a rationalist and obsolete theology have influenced Vatican II, the "most important event in the history of modern Catholicism after the Council of Trent"?[10] Already on the defensive against conservative critics of Vatican II, who claimed that heretical modernists had undermined the bishops' gathering,[11] historically traceable contributions to the Council's theology—like those of Catholic Enlightenment, Febronianism, Conciliarism, and Jansenism—were downplayed or eclipsed. Theological debates today are oblivious to Vatican II's indebtedness to the Tridentine zeal for reform and its eighteenth-century application. Yet, how profound can an understanding of Vatican II be if, as often happens, its own roots and theological forerunners are denied, as if it was an entirely twentieth-century invention? Trent and Vatican II are taught to theology students as contrasting (even conflicting) councils without consulting the history of Trent's practical implementation. It is as if one compares two different wines and judges them simply from the labels, without opening the bottles and tasting the results of the fermentation process.

Was the Catholic Enlightenment Rationalist or Reactionary?

How do Catholic Enlighteners fit into the historiography of theology? They (at least most) were neither rationalists nor reactionaries. Most are best classified as moderates, favoring a modernization that compromised with tradition and reigning authorities. Their aims were: (a) to use the newest achievements of philosophy and science to defend the essential dogmas of Catholic Christianity by explaining them in a new language, and (b) to reconcile Catholicism with modern culture. If anything held these diverse thinkers together, it was their belief that Catholicism had to modernize if it wanted to be a viable intellectual alternative to the persuasive arguments of the anti-clerical

---

10. Massimo Faggioli, *A Council for the Global Church: Receiving Vatican II in History* (Minneapolis, MN: Fortress Press, 2015), 1.
11. Dietrich von Hildebrand, *The Trojan Horse in the City of God* (Chicago: Franciscan Herald Press, 1967); Ralph Wiltgen, *The Rhine Flows into the Tiber. The Unknown Council* (New York: Hawthorn, 1967); Roberto de Mattei, *The Second Vatican Council: An Unwritten Story* (Fitzwilliam, NH: Loreto, 2012).

Enlighteners. Catholic Enlighteners differed among themselves as to how such a modernization should be brought about, but all agreed that Aristotelian scholasticism could no longer serve as the universal foundation for theology. Not only did the philosophical approaches to theology and faith change and vary, but the styles did so even more. Some still wrote in Latin, many in the vernacular, while a few even tried to put their thoughts in prose form and wrote theological novels.[12]

This sounds all too familiar: in the decades before the Second Vatican Council, many identified neo-Thomism as a stumbling block for the Church in continuing her journey through the twentieth century. It was overhauled by engaging and appropriating the philosophies of Kant, Heidegger, and others to create transcendental Thomism. Others preferred a more phenomenological approach. The debates about the reform of theology from the 1940s to 1960s restored diversity in thought—last seen to such extent and vigor in the eighteenth century. Although the core of the debate is the same—namely, the alleged insufficiency of scholasticism to deal with the problems of the modern world—twentieth- and twenty-first-century theologians have ignored the attempts of their eighteenth-century predecessors to address this question. If they actually read their works, they would discover that a number of recent syntheses of thought sound dramatically similar to those of the Catholic Enlightenment. Let us take Jean-Jacques Rousseau (1712–78) as a simple example: he argued that religious education should be withheld from children so that they are not brainwashed into a religion and can freely make up their minds when they are of age. Men such as Cardinal Gerdil (1718–1802) rejected such a notion, and instead developed a Catholic vision of education—a work that has been ignored by modern scholars although it was widely read two hundred years ago. For Rousseau, an adolescent was incapable of distinguishing between good and evil until at least the age of fifteen. Gerdil, a close follower of John Locke

12. See, for example, the works of Jeanne-Marie Leprince de Beaumont, Stéphanie de Genlis, but also (usually forgotten) Lorenz Westenrieder, *Leben des guten Jüngling's Engelhof,* 2 vols. (Munich: 1782).

(1632–1704), did not think so: "Children distinguish the evil that was done inadvertently from that which was done by design. They excuse the one, but not pardon the other."[13] For Rousseau, a child of ten years did not need reason to make judgments, because reason was a "bridle of strength" a child does not need; instead, he should follow his instincts. Gerdil, however, saw that while animals were immediately ruled by natural instincts, in humans, such immediate authority was the role of reason:

> Why then should reason be entirely useless to a child of ten years old? This interior propensity that stirs and agitates him, which prompts him to continual action and keeps him always out of breath—does it not need some restraint? It is true that at this age reason is too weak to suffice by itself. It needs to be assisted and fortified by precepts, examples, and appropriate practices. "We are born weak . . . we need judgment . . . , [and it is] given to us by education."[14]

Gerdil also rejects Rousseau's denial of objective teleology on epistemological grounds: "Man is naturally a friend of order, and wherever he finds it he approves it and delights in it."[15] Humans are dependent in their understanding of the world on finding order; without discerning order via sensory perception, humans could never gain any knowledge at all. Gerdil argues, however, that it is through society that such order is further advanced and enables the progress of the sciences; without having established rules and order, the business of scientific endeavor would be impossible. Consequently, society is not the root of all evil and man's corruption, as Rousseau taught, but the seedbed of his perfection.

Or, take the discussion about the possibility of salvation for members of other religions, or the idea of revelation in the works of the great Nicolas-Sylvestre Bergier (1718–90). Instead of realizing that Bergier

---

13. Sigismond Gerdil, *The Anti-Emile: Reflections on Theory and Practice of Education against the Principles of Rousseau* (South Bend, IN: St. Augustine Press, 2011), 48.
14. Ibid. The quotation is contributed to Eugene of Savoy. The best, and to my knowledge only, history of teleological thought is Robert Spaemann and Reinhard Löw, *Natürliche Ziele. Geschichte und Wiederentdeckung teleologischen Denkens* (Stuttgart: 2005). A translation of this important book into English would be highly desirable.
15. Gerdil, *The Anti-Emile*, 35.

had articulated important insights that refute the simplistic view that the Catholic Church never dealt with the challenges of Enlightenment thought until 1962, many theologians still cling to this old tale.

The Catholic Enlightenment also teaches a valuable lesson with regard to the perception of Catholics in academia: in the eighteenth century, Catholic intellectuals felt uneasy with how their Protestant or secular peers perceived them. Old prejudices against their faith were still alive, but the charge that Catholics had fallen behind the natural sciences during the eighteenth century was correct. Nobody outside the Church cared much for enlightened Catholic thought, unless it could be proven that Catholics were also receptive to modern science. After all, the natural sciences had opened up so many fields of new research that the old university curriculum became obsolete. With admirable vigor, Catholic scientists tried to catch up—some, quite successfully. Against the resistance of conservatives, Catholic Enlighteners urged the Church not to bind itself to outdated science, and instead introduce the sciences into the curriculum of its universities. The Benedictine University of Salzburg in Austria was the first European institution of higher learning to introduce the discipline of experimental physics in the 1740s. Lectures in this field focused on demonstration experiments in hydrostatics, electricity, mechanics, pneumatics, and optics, and often, attracted a wide public. Roger Boscovich (1711–87), one of the greatest astronomers of the century and a Jesuit priest, said that "the greatest harm that can be done to religion is to connect religion with the things in physics which are considered wrong.... The youth then ... say that such and such a thing in physics is wrong and consequently religion is wrong."[16] Instead, the Church had to be, according to the Jesuit, in a dialogue with scientists, and it had to abandon disproven theories from the past, such as the pre-Copernican worldview.

I suggest that Catholic theology is trapped in a similar perception as it was three hundred years ago. Our sophisticated attempts to preach

16. Marcus Hellyer, *Catholic Physics: Jesuit Natural Philosophy in Early Modern Germany* (Notre Dame, IN: University of Notre Dame Press, 2005), 178.

the message of Christ will fall on rocky ground among those who believe that Catholicism is premised or connected to outdated science, or is simply anti-scientific or anti-intellectual altogether. By studying the eighteenth century, contemporary theologians can learn how their predecessors approached the same problem, often with the same methods—and often, encountering the same misfortunes. From eighteenth-century theology, Catholic theologians can learn how to be open to discussion, to science, to new philosophies, to everything—just as long as the truths of faith are not undermined. Moreover, the Catholic Enlightenment reminds us that it was not Vatican II that invented the celebrated "embrace" of the modern world summarized by *Lumen Gentium*, namely that "whatever good is in the minds and hearts of men, whatever good lies latent in the religious practices and cultures of diverse peoples, is not only saved from destruction" by the actions of the Church, but "also cleansed, raised up and perfected."[17] Such "exchange between the Church and the diverse cultures of people,"[18] as the document *Gaudium et Spes* calls it, had always been practiced by Catholic theologians, but in particular by Catholic Enlighteners, for whom this practice was simply called "eclecticism."

The Lost Quest for a Biblical Hermeneutic

Catholic Enlighteners, however, also faced an internal battle: how far could the philosophical insights of Enlightenment be applied? Some radical and moderate Enlighteners pushed Church teachings—some of which were not yet defined—to their limits and uncomfortably questioned the established status quo of some theological disciplines. This is an important task in theology: to help the church to think. A good example of this is the engagement with historical criticism in exegetical questions. Spinoza's (1632–77) radical claim was that the biblical books were the product of a long process of editing and development. The French Oratorian Richard Simon (1638–1712) productively engaged with this charge and attempted to defeat it, but

17. *Lumen Gentium*, ch. 17.
18. *Gaudium et Spes*, ch. 44.

not without reinforcing his own theology with what we today call "historical criticism." Likewise, Johann Lorenz Isenbiehl (1744–1818) used his historical training to suggest a new way of reading Isaiah 7:14 and the prophecy about the virgin who will bear a child. He did not have in mind a rejection of the virgin birth, but simply an honest reading of Matthew 1 where Isaiah is quoted. In his arguments, he showed that the original text of the Hebrew Bible likely referred not to a virgin, but a young woman. A firestorm of criticism silenced the young researcher; his book was censored and his career as an academic destroyed. Isenbiehl's case, which we discuss in this collection, was similar to many others over the course of the eighteenth, nineteenth, and even, early twentieth centuries.

If we fast-forward the history of Catholic exegesis to the 1960s, we suddenly find Bible scholars slowly coming out of their defensive corner as they try to implement the research of their (mostly) Protestant peers. Yet, almost none of them were (and are) aware of the initial discussion about historical criticism in the eighteenth century. The attempts of someone such as Simon in the seventeenth century to proffer a biblical hermeneutic that is conscious of history and criticism—but also of the rule of faith—has been passed over by conservatives because they believed him to be a Spinozian, and by progressives because they believed he could not have anything insightful to offer because he was a thinker of the Tridentine era.

Has Catholic theology really achieved anything over the last decades when it comes to reconciling historical criticism and theological exegesis? Some, such as the German exegetes Marius Reiser and Klaus Berger, think not.[19] While scholars and church leaders have no problem with labeling biblical accounts as "poetic tales," which, two hundred years ago, brought Johann Jahn (1750–1816) into serious trouble, "we still have not established what this means for their theological interpretation and the truth of their story," Reiser laments.[20] Looking,

19. Klaus Berger, *Die Bibelfälscher wie wir um die Wahrheit betrogen werden* (Munich: Pattloch, 2013).
20. Marius Reiser, "The History of Catholic Exegesis, 1600–1800," in *Oxford Handbook of Early Modern Theology*, ed. Ulrich L. Lehner, A. G. Roeber, and Richard Muller (New York: Oxford University Press, 2016).

in particular, at historical figures of the Catholic Enlightenment, such as Richard Simon and Aloysius Sandbichler (1751–1820), would demonstrate that both perspectives could stimulate a renewed attempt to bring historical and theological exegesis into dialogue.

Would it not be time, then, to ask the witnesses of early modernity how they dealt with the challenge of historical criticism as they tried to reconcile tradition and history? The work of Sandbichler could serve as a lesson in how to take philology and history seriously without setting aside the theological dimension of a text. I think it is here, where perhaps the greatest importance of the history of modern exegesis lies: while a number of contemporary theologians rediscover patristic and medieval exegesis in a "resourcement" movement, they usually dismiss early modern interpreters in almost total ignorance of them. However, it is precisely these early modern exegetes—in particular, those wrestling with theological interpretation in the face of historical criticism—who offer the best lessons in how both approaches can be mutually inclusive. These theologians were, after all, much closer to the questions that haunt us today than were the medievals, and to dismiss them is tantamount to downplaying the need for theology to constructively wrestle with modernity, instead of romanticizing the past or giving in to mere rationalism or fideism. Furthermore, ignorance of the past usually produces pride; one boasts of achievements such as the allegedly radically new twentieth-century concept of divine inspiration espoused in *Dei Verbum* (chapter 11) without realizing its roots in Richard Simon's works.[21] How seriously is one to take such a theologian who forgets that he stands on the shoulders of giants and is just one link in a long line of men and women searching for truth? If Catholic exegesis refuses to acknowledge such indebtedness to the past and is unaware of its own more recent history, how can it really claim to be a critical enterprise? After all, the core meaning of criticism is the ability to discern truth from error. Without knowledge of earlier scholarly achievements and erroneous journeys,

---

21. Marius Reiser, "Richard Simons biblische Hermeneutik," in *Bibelkritik und Auslegung der Heiligen Schrift*, ed. Marius Reiser (Tübingen: Mohr Siebeck, 2007), 185–218.

one deprives oneself of necessary knowledge and catapults one's discipline into an ivory tower. How would one perceive a biologist who redid Gregor Mendel's (1822–84) basic genetic lab tests, and afterwards, published his findings in a peer-reviewed journal as "new" and original research? This might seem like an extreme example, but we cannot deny the parallels if one reads seventeenth- and eighteenth-century literature in consort with the exegetical literature of the present.

Likewise, twentieth-century theology is often credited with correcting a Catholic theological view that left out the dimension of salvation history in the revelation of God. While historians have tried to show that the Catholic Tübingen School dealt with the idea of the kingdom of God as a basic theological term right after the turn of the eighteenth century, and others have pointed to its roots in the Catholic Enlightenment, systematic theology has hitherto ignored such findings. A close reading and integration of late-seventeenth- and eighteenth-century theology may retrieve a theology willing to be simultaneously original and faithful.[22] A good example of such faithful creativity is the work of Aloysius Sandbichler, whose concept of salvation history from the 1790s we outline in this volume. The fact that not all exegetical literature was open to dialogue, but actually sometimes fits the caricatures painted by critics can be found in the exegetical commentary on the book of Revelation by Alphonsus Frey of 1762.

Going back to the sources of the past will enable Catholic theologians to better understand the shortcomings of their own approaches to biblical hermeneutics: like their predecessors, they are walking a fine line between rationalist flattening of the Bible or theological eisegesis. By taking the work of Catholic Enlightenment scripture scholars seriously, we can pick up where the conversation about a biblical hermeneutic has stopped (very much due to papal censorship).

22. An insightful criticism of "salvation history" is provided by Martin Hengel, "Heilsgeschichte," in *Theologische, historische und biographische Skizzen. Kleine Schriften*, ed. Martin Hengel (Tübingen: Mohr Siebeck, 2010), 7:1–34.

Ecclesiology and Ecumenism

The Catholic Enlightenment not only initiated a retrieval of the biblical sources of the faith, but also led to the realization that the Church lacked a theology of the episcopal office. Not yet equipped with the proper theological vocabulary, the discussion about the role bishops should play in the Church used concepts that had been developed a few hundred years earlier by the Conciliarist movement. Nevertheless, it also adopted ideas of French Gallicanism and Jansenism, especially in regard to the role of the papacy. It has been widely forgotten that the understanding of the pope as the "center of unity" had been stressed so much by Gallican thinkers (even though it did not originate with them), that by the eighteenth century, no supporter of papal primacy would use it. By 1763, it had become the programmatic term for a new ecclesiology by way of the Trier auxiliary bishop Nikolaus von Hontheim and his manifesto *Febronius*: instead of a monarchical papacy, the Church should be governed in a more collegial way by the authority of local bishops, while the pope should remain a spiritual center of unity without real jurisdiction. Because of its connection to Febronianism, the term "center of unity" was avoided in the Catholic restoration of the early nineteenth century and only revived at the end of the century, before it was reinterpreted at Vatican II.[23] Febronius's (1701–90) main theological problem, however, was that he built his criticism of the papacy on the claim that the papacy built its primacy of jurisdiction solely with the help of the pseudo-Isidorian decretals. As the eminent law historian Georg May has pointed out, this is incorrect: the decretals were not the reason for the increasing authority of the papacy, but a symptom of it.[24] Would not a more sincere look into the history of the term also help current ecclesiologists understand and appreciate better the Conciliarist tradition, as Francis Oakley has

---

23. Peter Frowein, "Primat und Episkopat," *Römische Quartalschrift für christliche Altertumskunde und Kirchengeschichte* 69 (1974): 227–29; Klaus Schatz, *Kirchenbild und Päpstliche Unfehlbarkeit bei den deutschsprachigen Minoritätsbischöfen auf dem I. Vatikanum* (Rome: Universita Gregoriana Editrice, 1975), 460; Bernward Schmidt, *Die Konzilien und der Papst* (Freiburg: Herder, 2013), 182, 278.

24. Georg May, *Die Auseinandersetzungen zwischen den Mainzer Erzbischöfen und dem Heiligen Stuhl um die Dispensbefugnis im 18. Jahrhundert* (Frankfurt: Peter Lang, 2007), 45–46.

pointed out?[25] Yet, a look at the sometimes selfish intentions of the German Febronian bishops and their failures to withstand the onslaught of Napoleon's attack on the Church should also remind us that neither a romantic view of the early church as "authority-free" nor a romanticizing of Ultramontanism help, but only a sincere look at the historical fact that local churches and papal leaders can fail miserably.

That the ecumenical dimension of Vatican II was prepared by a thorough discussion of the Christian churches, even and especially under the pressure of the Nazi regime,[26] is a well-known fact. But it is almost forgotten that the Catholic Enlightenment produced serious ecumenical projects worth remembering. The first one is a project that evolved between Protestant and Catholic theologians and has been called the Fulda- or Piderit-Böhm-Plan for a reunification of the churches. Its core idea was to overcome confessional polemics and come to a mutual appreciation of doctrinal differences and possible solutions. It was not the plan for "lowest common denominator" ecumenism, but a sincere attempt to overcome schism by searching for truth. The failure of the project, in large part due to papal censorship and the disinterest of most Protestant theologians, poses an important question: do academic societies dedicated to ecumenism, such as the one Piderit and Böhm envisioned, help to obtain the goal of reunification if the majority of the guild is disinterested in it? Is the feeling of shame and scandal about the separation of the churches that these early ecumenists felt not something worth rediscovering? The Piderit-Böhm plan was based on prayer and the willingness of the participants to suffer for the truth of Christ. By consciously following in the footsteps of previously failed ecumenical attempts through a process of historical appropriation, we begin to develop more empathy, and perhaps, feel the pain of separation more strongly, and hopefully, begin the journey with fortitude that does not shy away from suffering. But paying attention to the ecumenical discussions of

25. Francis Oakley, *The Conciliarist Tradition* (Oxford: Oxford University Press, 2003).
26. Jörg Ernesti, *Ökumene im Dritten Reich* (Paderborn: Bonifatius, 2007).

the past also reminds us how easily the desire for union can result in a compromise of the truth, and ultimately, relativism or syncretism.

Another article in the section on ecumenism follows the insight that true ecumenical theology grows out of prayerful reflection. An example of this is the Bavarian Benedictine Beda Mayr (1742–94), who not only came up with a plan for an academy dedicated to ecumenical questions, but also with a remarkable ecumenical methodology: nothing that was not dogmatically defined should stand in the way of a reunification of the churches. This included hotly debated issues such as papal infallibility—a good one hundred years before it became a dogma. Mayr did not dislike the papacy or distrust the popes, as one might assume. Instead, he saw in the monarchical office of the papacy, as it was exercised in the 1780s, a stumbling block for Protestants and Catholics coming together in one Church. Consequently, he developed the concept of a limited and essentially negative infallibility. For him, infallibility could not extend beyond the *necessary* elements of faith and morals:[27]

> I call *infallibility* the privilege which Christ gave to his church: to teach everything without the danger of falling into error and to teach what is necessary or useful for the faithful to achieve eternal blessedness. This also includes that she cannot teach anything that leads the faithful away from the order of salvation.[28]

Consequently, the Church was fallible when it came to the formal aspects of dogmatic facts; for example, if the Church were to declare an unrevealed doctrine to be revealed. Such a formal error would not affect the holy order of salvation, even if the doctrine in question was useful for the advancement of saving one's soul.[29] Therefore, even an "erroneous" teaching—that is, a wrong proposition about the revelation status of a doctrine—would not be completely wrong, because the Church can never err in teaching something helpful for

---

27. Cf. Beda Mayr, *Apologie seiner Vertheidigung der katholischen Religion; eine Beylage zu seiner Vertheidigung der natürlichen, christlichen und katholischen Religion* (Augsburg: 1790), 210–11.
28. Beda Mayr, *Vertheidigung der natürlichen, christlichen und katholischen Religion,* (Augsburg: 1789), 3:269.
29. Ibid., 3:270–71.

achieving eternal bliss. Certainly, such a view contains the theological contradiction, as Giovanni Sala pointed out, that the Holy Spirit would assist the Church in formulating fallible teachings,[30] but the value of Mayr's work lies elsewhere: he offered his ideas to the Church and was willing to accept her final judgment over them. Moreover, he engaged with Protestant peers to answer theological problems that had arisen for the Christian message through Enlightenment thinkers such as Rousseau and Lessing (1729–81). Openness to new ways of thought, an ecumenism based on prayer and reflection, and the willingness to recant if the Magisterium orders obedience, are, in my view, the three most valuable insights we can gain from his work.

How Enlightened Can a Catholic Be?

The most daunting question is surely: "How enlightened can we be?" or to what extent can a Christian theologian engage positively with the cultural process of Enlightenment, its philosophies, its new ways of life and thought. Some Catholic Enlighteners were radical in their approach: rather than slow, gentle, pastoral, and theological reforms, they tried to restructure the entire Church overnight. This gave their projects an elitist patina, which the masses of the faithful rejected. By "radical," I refer to the original meaning of the word, deriving from the Latin "radix," or root: radical Catholic Enlighteners tended to uproot central tenets of the faith and central traditions, or in the case of the liturgical Enlighteners, their attitude lacked roots among the faithful.

A good example of how to study the extent to which Christian theology and lifestyle can adapt to the Enlightenment world is the microcosm of monasticism. After all, monasteries were (and still are) a vital part of the Church's life; they strive for a dedicated imitation of Christ, or in St. Benedict's words, to be a "school of the Lord." By sanctifying community life by prayer and work, religious men and women sought to become transformed by Christ. The Enlightenment culture, however, also infiltrated monastic life. It permeated the walls

---

30. Giovanni Sala, "Fallible Teachings and the Assistance of the Holy Spirit," *Kontroverse Theologie* (Cologne: Nova & Vetera, 2005), 237–58.

of the cloister and inspired many to question old forms of obedience and traditional life. In communities, this was social dynamite. In the study on Benedictine monks, it is demonstrated how helpless superiors looked upon the new resistance to their commands, wondered how they could restructure traditions intelligibly, or how they simply abandoned them without replacing them with untested or unproven innovations. A good example of the latter is the abolition of the holy silence during meals in the cloister of Melk in favor of small talk in order to create a "community atmosphere." In my book *Enlightened Monks*,[31] I traced the mostly bad influence Enlightenment culture had on monasteries as an assimilation to the world. Lawrence Cunningham wrote in a review: "These German Benedictine reforms anticipated so many later changes in religious life that it is hard not to think of the period covered by Lehner's book as a kind of dress rehearsal for the period after Vatican II."[32] Adoption of contemporaneous cultures is nothing bad, to be sure, but it can be a sign of weakness and failure if such assimilation is done without much reflection about the value of traditions or beliefs.

This, of course, brings us to the bigger question of how enlightened Catholicism can be today and how much it can adapt to contemporaneous culture; that is, how can it modernize itself? Consequently, the cultural history of the Catholic Enlightenment and its theology poses the question: to what extent Catholic thought and life should adapt to "worldly" expectations. Some theologians point to Romans 12:2 as a verdict against any such assimilation, yet most read only the first seven words, "Do not conform yourselves to this age." They fail to recognize that the sentence continues: "but be transformed by the renewal of your mind, that you may discern what is the will of God, what is good and pleasing and perfect." It is, after all, Paul himself who established new forms for his own message and theology—so, it cannot mean a complete denial of interaction with culture and

31. Ulrich Lehner, *Enlightened Monks: The German Benedictines, 1740-1803* (Oxford: Oxford University Press, 2011).
32. Lawrence Cunningham, "Review of Ulrich Lehner, *Enlightened Monks*," *Commonweal* 139 (September 3, 2012): 26–27.

thought. Instead, it seems to point to a careful discernment of spirits and a theological eclecticism: whatever is good in a culture can be adopted if it is pleasing to God's will. This reminds us of the perennial question of how to be in the world, and yet, not of it. Yet, the Catholic Enlightenment teaches us a lesson more valuable than, perhaps, other periods in history, because it also faced the daunting questions of modernity that were alien to antiquity and the Middle Ages. The eminent German sociologist and philosopher Hans Joas rightly stated that the academic consensus is that modernization as envisioned by Catholic Enlighteners does *not* necessarily lead to secularization. Moreover, he successfully questions whether there are homogenous concepts of modernization and secularization.[33] If this is true, it complicates our questions even more: can we even identify expectations as "merely worldly" or could it be that some have religious roots? If that is the case, both the historian and the theologian must be careful not to interpret the past through teleological lenses, but rather abstain from value judgments as much as possible.

Research on Catholicism in the eighteenth century shows that much of what we consider contemporary problems (even the question of divorce and remarriage) was already discussed at that time. Even questions about the state's expectations of religion, such as the acceptance of divorce and remarriage, echo contemporary political concerns. Likewise, the question of tax exemption for religious entities was on the agenda of Catholic Enlightenment thinkers. By not listening to these intellectual controversies, historians and religion scholars not only deprive themselves of a vast amount of learning, but also silence several generations of thinkers, believers, and skeptics, and therefore, arrive at a caricatured view of the Enlightenment world.

Almost no history or religion university department in the United States has an expert on early modern Catholicism or Catholicism between the Middle Ages and Vatican II. Even in thriving doctoral programs, this historical period is marginalized. It is treated as though

33. Hans Joas, *Faith as an Option: Possible Futures for Christianity* (Stanford: Stanford University Press, 2014).

it is a blip on the screen and played no part in the becoming of the modern world. Theology department curriculums joined the bandwagon of those who jump from the Council of Trent to Vatican I as if nothing happened in the intervening four centuries. How can this be anything but a-historical? The "unfinished business and trailing ends"[34] of the Catholic Enlightenment are still with us: how do we post-Vatican II Catholics address the faithful and demonstrate that faith is an intelligible option worth pursuing? How do we overcome the lethargy to reform and begin trying out new things after sincere discernment? I believe the eighteenth century offers some invaluable insights: not necessarily recipes for how to solve problems, but rather a model for how to intellectually identify and discuss problems and how to empathize with our opponents.

---

34. Francis Oakley, *Conciliarism: Constitutionalism in the Catholic Church, 1300-1870* (Oxford: Oxford University Press, 2003), 262.

PART I

Definitions of Catholic Enlightenment

2

What is Catholic Enlightenment? Some Characteristics

Over the last decades, our picture of the Enlightenment as a monolithic movement has been challenged by the acknowledgement, not only of a variety of Enlightenments,[1] but also of a religious side to this worldwide process.[2] This religious Enlightenment expressed an "alternative to two centuries of dogmatism and fanaticism, intolerance

---

1. J. G. A. Pocock, *Barbarism and Religion. The Enlightenments of Edward Gibbon* (Cambridge: Cambridge University Press, 1999), 13. Critical of this approach are, for example, John Robertson, "The Enlightenments of J. G. A Pocock," *Storia della storiografia—History of Historiography* 39 (2001): 140–51; John Robertson, *The Case for the Enlightenment. Scotland and Naples 1680-1760* (Cambridge: Cambridge University Press, 2005); Robert Darnton, "The Case for the Enlightenment: George Washington's False Teeth," in Robert Darnton, *George Washington's False Teeth: an Unconventional Guide to the Eighteenth Century* (New York/London: W. W. Norton, 2003), 3–24.
2. Hugh Trevor-Roper, *The Crisis of the Seventeenth Century: Religion, the Reformation and Social Change* (London: Harper & Row, 1967), ch. 4. Cf. Reinhart Koselleck, "Aufklärung und die Grenzen der Toleranz," in *Glaube und Toleranz. Das theologische Erbe der Aufklärung*, ed. Trutz Rendtorff (Gütersloh: Gütersloher Verlagshaus 1982), 256–71; Werner Schütz, "Die Kanzel als Katheder der Aufklärung," *Wolffenbütteler Studien zur Aufklärung* 1 (1974): 137–71. Samuel J. Miller, *Portugal and Rome. An Aspect of the Catholic Enlightenment* (Rome: Universita Gregoriana, 1978), 1–2. Christine Northeast, *The Parisian Jesuits and the Enlightenment, 1728-1762* (Oxford: Oxford University Press, 1991); James V. H. Melton, *The Rise of the Public in Enlightenment Europe* (Cambridge: Cambridge University Press, 2001), 48–49; cf. M. Printy, *Enlightenment and the Creation of German Catholicism* (Cambridge: Cambridge University Press, 2009).

and religious warfare."[3] Recently, a great interest in the Catholic Enlightenment has emerged. Nevertheless, for most historians, it is still unclear what the term "Catholic Enlightenment" means and what characteristics marked this movement—problems this chapter will address. Here, the term "Catholic Enlightenment" is used as a *heuristic* concept that describes the diverse phenomenon that took hold of Catholic intellectuals in the mid-eighteenth century and early nineteenth century, which combines many different strands of thought and a variety of projects that were implemented to reform Catholicism. Through the use of this concept, we will be able to find and examine the dynamics common to the Catholic Enlightenment throughout Europe, as well as connect this phenomenon to philosophical, political, and social changes—all of which would not be possible with a disintegrated view of the Catholic Enlightenment. This view, however, does not argue for a uniformity to this intellectual movement or process and fully acknowledges that the Catholic Enlightenment was expressed in different ways during distinctive time periods and contexts, and that there were also some radical individuals who did not fit into the category of ecclesiastical reformers. It is important to note that this concept excludes all those who did not engage in at least a somewhat positive way with the overall European Enlightenment process, e.g., *radical* Jansenists.

What is Catholic Enlightenment?[4]

As a an ecclesiastical reform movement, the Catholic Enlightenment was an apologetic endeavor designed to defend the essential dogmas of Catholic Christianity by explaining their rationality in modern terminology and by reconciling Catholicism with modern culture, e.g., by the acceptance of new theories of economy, science, but also of judicial thought.[5] The Catholic Enlightenment was in dialogue with contemporary culture—not only by developing new hermeneutical

3. D. Sorkin, *The Religious Enlightenment. Protestants, Jews and Catholics from London to Vienna* (Princeton: Princeton University Press, 2008), 6.
4. For an overview of the Catholic Enlightenment in Europe, see Ulrich L. Lehner and Michael Printy, eds., *Brill's Companion to the Catholic Enlightenment in Europe* (Leiden: Brill, 2010).

approaches to the Council of Trent or to Jansenist ideas, but also by implementing some of the core values of the overall European Enlightenment process that tried to "renew" and "reform" the whole of society, and thus truly deserves the label "Enlightenment."

Jonathan Israel's recent magisterial history of the Enlightenment portrays radical Enlighteners such as Spinoza, d'Alembert, or d'Holbach as the leading members of the Enlightenment, since they propagated relatively unrestricted tolerance, free speech, and equality. The Catholic Enlightenment, in this light, appears to be a defensive attempt at modernization, or perhaps, even a bulwark of the anti-Enlightenment. The latter, however, seems unsatisfactory, since much of the content of the Catholic Enlightenment—namely, its Tridentine spirit—actually predates the Enlightenment, and thus cannot be considered a reaction to it. Moreover, a close look at the primary sources tells us that Catholic publications from the eighteenth century were only to a negligible degree directed *against* the Enlightenment as a whole. What we nevertheless *can* detect is a resistance against certain *radical* Enlightenment ideals, indicating that many Catholics actually fought for what Israel calls a moderate or mainstream Enlightenment.[6]

Similarly, a great number of historians saw in the Protestant Enlightenment the measuring stick for the Catholic reform movement and gave too much credit to the eighteenth-century Protestant criticism of the Catholic Enlightenment. This has changed because Catholic erudition, with its different methodology, and Catholic culture, with its idiosyncratic dynamics, are now taken more seriously, and because the personal and often economic motives behind anti-Catholic propaganda, e.g., of Friedrich Nicolai,[7] are meanwhile known facts. Today, scholarship "historicizes" the Catholic Enlightenment and no longer judges it according to what extent it followed its Protestant

---

5. Mario Rosa, "Roman Catholicism," *Encyclopedia of the Enlightenment*, ed. Alan C. Kors (Oxford: Oxford University Press, 2002), 3:468–72.

6. Sylviane Albertan-Coppola, "Counter-Enlightenment" in *Encyclopedia of the Enlightenment*, ed. Alan Charles Kors (Oxford: Oxford University Press, 2002), 1:307–11.

7. Wilhelm Haefs, "Reformkatholizismus und Komödien der Religion, Katholische Aufklärung als Gegenstand literaturwissenschaftlicher Forschung," *Zwischen Aufklärung und Romantik. Neue Perspektiven der Forschung. Festschrift für Roger Paulin*, ed. K. Feilchenfeldt (Würzburg: Königshausen & Neumann, 2006), 255–88, at 257.

counterpart or contributed to a secular, national culture. All this makes it apparent that the Catholic Enlightenment does not easily fit into a neatly defined conceptual category. Moreover, these findings made clear that the "light" of the Catholic Enlightenment shone less brightly and less distinctly in different contexts, but was nevertheless projected, recalibrated, and refocused in others.

History of the Term

In 1908, the German church historian Sebastian Merkle introduced the term "Catholic Enlightenment." He intended to point his fellow Catholics to the fact that the Enlightenment was not per se anti-religious and anti-ecclesiastical, but had an important and positive impact on the life of the Church.[8] Merkle's critics, however, rejected his concept because it associated Catholicism with the alleged agnostic and atheist Enlightenment, but also with the Protestant churches and their enlightened theologies. Scholars of the next generation started to use the term *Reform Catholicism,* which, however, is more problematic, since it meant, for Liberals, progressive, and for Ultramontanists, restorative (and essentially, unchanged) Catholicism.[9] Furthermore, the term did not take into account that this movement was influenced by the European Enlightenment process.[10] In France, Louis J. Rogier and Bernard Plongeron have asserted in the 1960s and 1970s[11] that only the twentieth-century reforms of the Second Vatican Council (1962–65) made an unprejudiced investigation of eighteenth-century Catholicism

8. Sebastian Merkle, *Die katholische Beurteilung des Aufklärungszeitalters* (Berlin: Fredebeul, 1909); Bernhard Schneider, "Katholische Aufklärung. Zum Werden und Wert eines Forschunsgbegriffs," *Revue d'Histoire Ecclesiastique* 93 (1998): 354–97, at 359.
9. Schneider, "Katholische Aufklärung," 363; cf. Rudolph Schlögl, "Secularization: German Catholicism at the Eve of Modernity," *German Historical Institute/London Bulletin* 25/1 (2003), 5–21; Anton Schindling, "Theresianismus, Josephinismus, katholische Aufklärung," *Würzburger Diözesangeschichtsblätter* 50 (1988): 215–44, at 217; Rainer Bendel and Norbert Spannenberger, *Katholische Aufklärung und Josephinismus: Rezeptionsformen in Ostmittel- und Südosteuropa* (Cologne: Böhlau, 2015).
10. Cf. Schneider, "Katholische Aufklärung," 384–85. Horst Möller, *Vernunft und Kritik. Deutsche Aufklärung im 17. und 18. Jahrhundert* (Frankfurt: Suhrkamp, 1986), 16–18.
11. Louis Rogier, "L'Aufklärung catholique," in *Nouvelle Histoire de l'Église* (Paris: Éditions du Seuil, 1966), 4:137–61; Bernard Plongeron, "Wahre Gottesverehrung und das Problem des Unglaubens. Debatten um Inhalte und Wege von Religiosität und Seelsorge," *Geschichte des Christentums,* ed. Bernard Plongeron (Freiburg: Herder, 2000), 10:233–93.

possible. From then on, historians tended to view the Catholic Enlightenment even as an anticipation of Vatican II, since it tried—like the council—to bring the Church up-to-date while respecting its tradition.[12] The 1980s saw a further differentiation and acceptance of the term "Catholic Enlightenment," for which Harm Klueting was especially responsible.[13] A few years later, Bernhard Schneider argued convincingly that if we understand the term "Catholic Enlightenment" as the description of a process similar to other Enlightenments, but shaped by specific Catholic characteristics regarding content and structure, then a differentiation between Enlightenment reforms and the spirit of Trent was impossible.[14] Likewise, Dieter Breuer stated that Catholicism in the eighteenth century was essentially shaped by confessional impulses that had their roots in Trent or its aftermath. These peculiarities made it a uniquely *Catholic* Enlightenment. As a consequence, one is not merely dealing with a Catholic philosophy or theology of the Enlightenment, but with a Catholic Enlightenment *culture*, of which Peter Hersche has recently given a masterful overview.[15]

Some Enlightenment Influences on the Catholic Enlightenment

The natural sciences, the foundation of academic societies and new universities forced Catholics in the seventeenth and eighteenth centuries to reshape their view of education in order to keep up with scientific achievements. As a result, theology gradually underwent an inversion of teleology that favored a more mechanistic explanation of nature. Around the same time, the idea of a natural religion began to gain acceptance among theologians and even found its way into Catholic textbooks. Political philosophy ceased to see the sovereign

12. Plongeron, "Wahre Gottesverehrung," 253. Cf. also Franco Venturi, *Settecento riformatore*, 5 vols. (Torino: Einaudi, 1969–1990).
13. Harm Klueting, "Der Genius der Zeit hat sie unbrauchbar gemacht. Zum Thema Katholische Aufklärung–Oder: Aufklärung und Katholizismus im Deutschland des 18. Jahrhunderts. Eine Einführung," in *Katholische Aufklärung*, ed. Harm Klueting (Hamburg: Meiner, 1993), 1–35, at 8–9.
14. Schneider, "Katholische Aufklärung," 390.
15. Dieter Breuer, "Katholische Aufklärung und Theologie," *Rottenburger Jahrbuch für Kirchengeschichte* 23 (2004): 75–90; Peter Hersche, *Musse und Verschwendung: Europäische Gesellschaft und Kultur im Barockzeitalter*, 2 vols. (Freiburg: Herder, 2006).

as the guarantor of supernatural salvation for his people, and instead saw him as a caretaker of public welfare and earthly happiness, which led to rationalist territorialism that authorized the state to interfere in ecclesiastical decisions, or even to take possession of its property for the common good. Enlightened skepticism also had its impact on Catholic thinkers and motivated the Benedictines of St. Maur to defend the possibility of historical certainty.[16] Most Enlightenment concepts of reason and the limitations of the human mind, especially Kant's, were also compatible with Catholic optimism about epistemological access to reality, which affirmed that creation is intelligible because it was brought into existence by truth and wisdom personified, i.e., God.[17]

Around 1740–50, theological Wolffianism, which applied the so-called mathematical method to the Bible and tried to verify the harmony between reason and revelation, was introduced to Catholic institutions of higher education, primarily by Benedictines and Piarists. In the last two decades of the eighteenth century, the primary interest of Catholic theologians shifted from Christian Wolff to the critical work of Immanuel Kant (1724–1804), who was considered valuable in the fight against atheism.[18] However, only a minority embraced Kant's or Fichte's idealism and attempted to reform theology with it.

Despite the numerous differences between the European states and the development of the Enlightenment process in these countries, one can determine a number of common characteristics or *leitmotifs,* which serve as heuristic and pragmatic tools for further research. With the secular Enlighteners, the Catholic Enlightenment shared a number of common ideals, e.g., striving to shed light on dark conceptual language

---

16. Ulrich L. Lehner, "Ecumenism and Enlightenment Catholicism," in *Beda Mayr—Verteidigung der katholischen Religion,* ed. Ulrich L. Lehner (Leiden: Brill, 2009), I–LXXXIX.

17. An example for this rational outlook on creation is the Jesuit defense of certain Chinese traditions as a kind of pristine, natural theology. Another is their initial reluctance to accept Newton's theories, since the master of physics did not give a rational, ontological explanation of gravity. For Jesuits in early modern science, see Marcus Hellyer, *Catholic Physics* (Notre Dame: University of Notre Dame Press, 2005).

18. Ulrich L. Lehner, "Theologia Benedictina ac Kantiana. Zur Kant-Rezeption der Benediktiner Ildefons Schwarz und Ulrich Peutinger," *Kant und der Katholizismus,* ed. Norbert Fischer (Freiburg: Herder, 2005), 234–61.

and substituting confusing terms with distinct and clear ones.[19] Besides this, they also appealed to eclecticism, critical judgment, and intellectual maturity as positive goals of erudition.[20] Although few Catholic Enlighteners demanded absolute freedom of thought and speech in the Church, the doctrine of free will had officially been Catholic dogma since the sixth session of Trent (1547), and has always been a core feature of Catholic philosophy, which made it principally open to all philosophies that thought likewise. Moreover, the belief in the perfectibility of social structures and organizations, but also of the human mind and race, can be named as a common characteristic. Nevertheless, there were two streams of Catholic thought, which argued for two different anthropologies, and consequently for two different understandings of progress. While Catholic Enlighteners who were influenced by Jansenism had a rather pessimistic view of the post-lapsarian human being, Enlighteners who were influenced by Molinism (sometimes, they were neo-Pelagian) had a more optimistic view. Yet, the tension between these two groups makes it impossible to speak of one neatly defined idea of progress, since for the former, this meant the restoration of the church of antiquity, but for the latter it meant something new, e.g., the abolition of the belief that un-baptized children could never enter heaven. In many cases, the beliefs of both groups were mixed. Nevertheless, Catholic thinkers who had a more optimistic anthropology, even if other parts of their work were influenced by Jansenism, tended toward a more positive exchange with secular Enlightenment, which is why this group more adequately defines the ideals of Catholic Enlightenment.

Secular and Catholic Enlighteners also joined in battle *against* some

---

19. Norbert Hinske, "Die Grundideen der deutschen Aufklärung," in *Die Philosophie der deutschen Aufklärung. Texte und Darstellung*, ed. R. Ciafardone (Stuttgart: Reclam, 1990), 407–58, at 416; Werner Schneiders, *Die wahre Aufklärung. Zum Selbstverständnis der deutschen Aufklärung* (Freiburg: Alber, 1974).

20. Eclecticism was closely related to criticism: it meant the unbiased scrutiny of authors and arguments and presupposed faith in the capacity of reason as well as the courage to accept new conclusions. This is a biblical principle, cf. 1 Thess. 5:21. See Michael Albrecht, *Eklektik. Eine Begriffsgeschichte mit Hinweisen auf die Philosophie- und Wissenschaftsgeschichte* (Stuttgart-Bad Cannstatt: Fromann-Holzboog, 1994); Martin Mulsow, "Eclecticism or Skepticism? A Problem of the Early Enlightenment," *Journal of the History of Ideas* 58 (1997): 465–77.

ideas, especially against dogmatism,[21] "dark concepts," prejudice, superstition, and enthusiasm.[22] For the Catholic Enlighteners, however, this did not entail an attack on sacred doctrine or the hierarchy *per se*, but a constructive critique of outdated ecclesiastical structures and theologies as well as the ecclesiastical abuse of power. Instead of blind faith and obedience—concepts that allegedly could be found in the constitutions of the Jesuits—Catholic reformers propagated an enlightened and rational obedience and faith (*obsequium rationabile;* Rom. 12:1).

The Pre-Enlightenment Roots of the Catholic Enlightenment

At the end of the seventeenth century and the beginning of the eighteenth century, a few decades before explicit Enlightenment influences surfaced in the Church, the spirit of Trent was finally, after a long delay, in full force. Among the fruits of this *ripresa tridentina* were the establishment of seminaries for the better education of the clergy, the fostering of child education, and the strengthening of local parish life, but also attempts to improve theological and philosophical enterprises. The Catholic Enlightenment reformers rationalized and deepened these reform attempts.[23] Clearly in dialogue with the ideas of his time was Pope Benedict XIV (1740-58), who issued numerous reform decrees in order to increase the depth of pastoral care and rational theology.

The emphasis on a practical Christianity of good and charitable deeds was also no invention of the eighteenth century, but derived

---

21. When Catholic Enlighteners fought against dogmatism, this did not mean that they fought against dogmas of faith, but against a certain style of philosophizing and theologizing. *Dogmatism* can mean the method by which deductions are exercised and connected with each other, based on a few "certain" principles, or the uncritical presupposition that knowledge of things is possible and reliable etc. See Max Apel and Peter Ludz, ed., *Philosophisches Wörterbuch* (Berlin, New York: De Gruyter, 1976), 71.
22. Hinske, "Die Grundideen," 427-34.
23. Plongeron, "Wahre Gottesverehrung," 268. See also Peter Hersche, *Muße und Verschwendung. Europäische Gesellschaft und Kultur im Barockzeitalter* (Freiburg: Herder, 2006), 1:155-61; Owen Chadwick, *The Popes and European Revolution* (Oxford: Oxford University Press, 1981), 94-95. See especially Bernard Dompnier, "Die Fortdauer der katholischen Reform," in *Geschichte des Christentums*, ed. Bernard Plongeron (Freiburg: Herder, 1998), 9:211-300 as well as Hersche, *Muße und Verschwendung*, 1:152-211.

from the religious fervor of the new orders of the sixteenth- and seventeenth-century Catholic Reform, which took care of the sick and dying, were involved with organized education, and provided shelter for the abandoned and marginalized. The Benedictine reform congregations that, through the spirit of St. Maur, contributed so much to the Enlightenment of Catholicism, also originated in a monastic renewal, according to the spirit of Trent.[24] It must be pointed out, though, that despite the fact that Trent served as an inspiration for the Catholic Enlightenment, it did so *only* because of the Enlighteners' idiosyncratic and diverse readings of its decrees.

Jansenism, whose driving idea was a rigorist reform of the Church in the spirit of the early church fathers,[25] is sometimes thought to be the most important influence on Enlightenment Catholicism.[26] Rome's failure to engage wholeheartedly with reform contributed to its rise in the seventeenth and eighteenth century—first in France, then throughout Europe.[27] It aimed at a reorganization of church practices and fought for a decentralized church, an increase in monastic discipline, better education and pay for the clergy, practical education of the laity, and a certain liberality concerning individual religious practices (including the use of the vernacular in the liturgy).[28] Jansenist ideals were soon adopted by Enlightenment Catholics such as Muratori,[29] who had already called for a reduction of the cult of the saints and of pilgrimages and for the discouragement of superstitious religious practices. Even Pope Benedict XIV seemed to have been, to some degree, sympathetic to the Jansenist cause.[30] The Jansenist cry

24. Thomas Wallnig, *Gasthaus und Gelehrsamkeit* (Vienna: Oldenbourg, 2007), 89.
25. Karl O. von Aretin, "Katholische Aufklärung im Heiligen Römischen Reich," in Karl O. von Aretin, *Das Reich. Friedensgarantie und europäisches Gleichgewicht 1648-1806* (Stuttgart: Klett-Cotta, 1986), 403–33, at 403–5; 423.
26. Brian Strayer, *Suffering Saints: Jansensists and Convulsionnaires in France, 1640-1799* (Eastbourne [England]: Sussex Academic Press, 2008).
27. Chadwick, *The Popes and European Revolution,* 392–95.
28. Samuel J. Miller, "Portugal and Utrecht. A Phase of the Catholic Enlightenment," *The Catholic Historical Review* 43 (1977), 225–48. On the use of the vernacular within the Enlightenment, see also Albrecht Beutel, *Aufklärung in Deutschland* (Göttingen: Harrassowitz, 2006), 170–202.
29. Sergio Bertelli, *Erudizione e storia in Ludovico Antonio Muratori* (Naples: Istituto Italiano per gli Studi Storici, 1960).
30. Chadwick, *The Popes and European Revolution,* 396–99; Regis Bertrand, "Modelle und Entwürfe zum christlichen Leben. Die katholische Spiritualität und ihre Vermittler," in *Geschichte des*

for a more individualistic approach to spirituality was a religious phenomenon that was also sociologically influenced by the rise of "bourgeois self esteem."[31] Since the Jansenist movement emphasized the importance of national churches independent from Rome, it gradually became politicized, especially after the dissolution of its main religious enemy, the Jesuits. From that point on, it no longer restricted itself to moral rigorism and the critique of Baroque spirituality, but also engaged in purely political debates.[32] After all, Jansenism was influenced by Conciliarism and Gallicanism.[33]

Usually forgotten, however, is the influence of classical ascetic theology on Catholic Enlightenment and on Jansenism. After the theological battles of the seventeenth century, the eighteenth century saw the rise of a new mystical theology: the debates over Quietism in the last two decades of the seventeenth century led a majority of theologians to believe that contemplation is a gift for only a few chosen souls, but not for the community as a whole.[34] With Giovanni Scaramelli SJ (1687-1752) and his handbook, the differentiation between asceticism and mysticism was universally accepted—the former embodying the attempts of the ordinary faithful to achieve salvation; the latter, the contemplative way of a few. The trend in canonization processes toward an emphasis on heroic virtues

---

Christentums, ed. Bernard Plongeron (Freiburg: Herder, 1998), 9:823–65, at 847–48. For a detailed account of reforms of Catholic piety in the Holy Roman Empire, see Michael Müller, *Fürstbischof Heinrich von Bibra und die Katholische Aufklärung im Hochstift Fulda (1759-1788)* (Fulda: Pazeller, 2005).

31. Cf. Bernhard Groethuysen, *Die Entstehung der bürgerlichen Welt-und Lebensanschauung in Frankreich*, 2 vols., (Halle: 1927-1930; Frankfurt: Suhrkamp, 1978) [English title: *The Bourgeois. Catholicism vs. Capitalism in Eighteenth-Century France* (New York: Rinehart and Winston, 1968)].

32. This called for an austere conversion and contrition, and had predestinarian tendencies. Jesuits accorded greater efficacy to the will. On the public support for the Jansenists, see David Bell, *Lawyers and Citizens. The Making of a Political Elite in Old Regime France* (Oxford: Oxford Univeristy Press, 1994) Cf. Anton Schindling, "Theresianismus, Josephinismus, katholische Aufklärung," in *Würzburger Diözesangeschichtsblätter* 50 (1988): 215–44.

33. Conciliarism was a Catholic reform movement that attempted to curtail the power of pope and Curia, and instead place a universal council as authority over the supreme pontiff (see Oakley, *The Conciliarist Tradition*). Gallicanism was the state-sponsored belief that the pope had only spiritual authority over the Church of France while the French government—represented by the king—had true jurisdiction and full authority over ecclesiastical affairs (see Colman James Barry, *Readings in Church History* (Westminster, MD: Newman Press, 1960-1965), 2:241–45 (The Four Gallican Articles of 1682); Okaley, *The Conciliarist Tradition*, 141–81).

34. For an overview of Catholic spirituality in Early Modernity, see Bertrand, "Modelle und Entwürfe." Cf. M. Olphe-Galliard, *La théologie mystique en France au XVIIIe siècle. Le Père de Caussade* (Paris: Beauchesne, 1984).

accessible to all, instead of mystical union, visions, and extraordinary gifts, had begun with the case of St. Charles Borromeo in 1610.[35] This theological shift accelerated over the next 150 years until it became institutionalized in academic theology, when Prospero Lambertini's standard work on the canonization of saints, *De servorum Dei beatificatione et beatorum canonizatione* (1734), was published. When Lambertini became Pope Benedict XIV in 1740, this view began to shape the whole Catholic Church.[36]

Some Leitmotifs of the Catholic Enlightenment

When the Catholic Enlightenment suggested making the faith more useful and practical, it was able to improve already existing traditions and institutions, e.g., parishes. Bishops now increasingly took the lifestyle of their priests more seriously and even erected correctional facilities for problematic clergymen. The number of parish missions and reforms dramatically increased, as well as the number of local education facilities. This increased concern for the welfare of parishes was also a result of the secularization of the state. The latter was responsible for the pursuit of happiness and for proper worship, and the church for the spiritual welfare of the faithful. If the Church wanted to retain any influence on society at all, it had to prove the usefulness of religion by making a contribution to the moral welfare of the state. Pursuing such a contribution required educated and committed clergymen whose first concern was not for their own income, but for the needs of their parishioners. However, in order to strengthen the bishop's authority, parishioners were only allowed to practice their faith in the approved ways, so that the parish—and not

---

35. Bertrand, "Modelle und Entwürfe," 842–43; Dompnier, "Die Fortdauer der katholischen Reform," 240, 293–96; Christian Renoux, "Une source de l'histoire de la mystique moderne revisitée: les procès de canonisation," in *Mélanges de l'École française de Rome, Italie et Méditerranée* 105 (1993), 177–217.

36. Romeo de Maio, "L'ideale eroico nel processo di canonizzazione della Controriforma," in *Riforme e miti nella Chiesa del Cinquecento* (Naples: Guida, 1973), 257–58; Catrien Santing, "Tirami su: Pope Benedict XIV and the Beatification of the Flying Saint Guiseppe da Copertino," in *Medicine and Religion in Enlightenment Europe*, ed. Ole P. Grell and Andrew Cunningham (Aldershot: Ashgate, 2007), 79–99. See also Anne J. Schutte, *Aspiring Saints: Pretense of Holiness, Inquisition, and Gender in the Republic of Venice, 1618-1750* (Baltimore: John Hopkisn University Press, 2001).

the home—became the center of worship and of moral surveillance. Moreover, in the last quarter of the eighteenth century, the clergy were increasingly acting as educators and moral teachers on topics such as the importance of vaccinations, midwifery, and hygiene, but also on the disastrous consequences to the economy of taking too many religious holidays.[37] With the discovery of the transforming power of religion in the lifestyle of the faithful, the Catholic Enlightenment gave rise to a new awareness of social problems within Catholicism, which led in the nineteenth century to the creation of a new theological discipline—Catholic social ethics.[38]

The more the Enlighteners pushed for a practical Christianity, however, the closer their movement came to rationalism, because in order for doctrinal and moral teachings to be practical, they need to be *understandable*. Jesuit scholasticism, with its disregard for Lockean empiricism, was looked upon by more and more thinkers as a fruitless enterprise. The first attacks against it were already launched in the seventeenth and early eighteenth centuries, e.g., by the Oratorian Nicholas Malebranche (1638–1715) and the Benedictine Robert Desgabets (1610–78).[39] Soon, the Jesuits also started to integrate Locke and Malebranche into their curriculum, especially in France; but in many European countries, the resentment against their school remained.[40] In Italy, for example, Gianvicenzo Gravina (1664–1718) affirmed the liberation from *Aristotelian slavery* (1700)[41] and the Italian Benedictine Celestino Galiani (1681–1753) introduced his fellow monks to a more up-to-date approach to science—namely, the thought of Newton and Locke—as early as 1713.[42] Also, high-ranking cardinals, such as Domenico Passionei (1682–1761)[43] and Angelo Maria

---

37. For the charitable works of the French clergy see Bernard Plongeron, *La Vie quotidienne du clergé français au XVIIIe siècle*, (Paris: Hachette, 3rd ed. 1989), passim.
38. Scholder, "Grundzüge der theologischen Aufklärung," 307–8.
39. J.-R. Armogathe, *Theologia Cartesiana. L'Explication physique de l'Eucharistie chez Descartes et dom Desgabets* (The Hague: 1977).
40. Jeffrey D. Burson, *The Rise and Fall of Theological Enlightenment: Jean-Martin de Prades and Ideological Polarization in Eighteenth-Century France* (Notre Dame: University of Notre Dame Press, 2010).
41. Jonathan Israel, *Radical Enlightenment. Philosophy and the Making of Modernity 1650-1750* (Oxford: Oxford University Press, 2001), 113.
42. Israel, *Radical Enlightenment*, 113; Hanns Gross, *Rome in the Age of the Enlightenment. The Post-Tridentine Syndrome and the Ancien Regime* (Cambridge: Cambridge University Press, 1990), 252.

Quirini OSB (1680–1755)[44] were, to a certain degree, enchanted by the new philosophy, even with the French philosophes. However, even the greater appreciation of experiential knowledge among Catholics, especially of Locke and Newton, led only a few to pure empiricism. Most Catholic Enlighteners, nevertheless, tried to combine some of the new ideas with traditional ways of achieving rational knowledge, especially concerning the existence and the nature of God.[45]

Due to the quasi monopoly of the Jesuits in education and the order's overall unwillingness to reform its schools, the Jesuits attracted a lot of anger and disappointment.[46] In Spain, Diego Zapata (1701) and Benito Jeronimo Feijoo OSB (1676–1764) were the spokesmen of this antipathy.[47] Over the course of the eighteenth century, this critique of Jesuit scholasticism grew exponentially. Moreover, governments throughout the Catholic world became increasingly uncomfortable with the political and economic influence of the order, its strict defense of papal prerogatives, and its jurisdictional exemption. This was the best time for the other religious orders to challenge the Jesuit monopoly on education: the Oratorians in France and Portugal, the Piarists in the Habsburg territories and Poland, Augustinian Regular Canons and Benedictines in the Holy Roman Empire. However, only the suppression of the Jesuits (1759: Portugal; 1762 and 1764: France; 1767: Spain; 1773: Papal suppression) allowed for serious reforms.[48] Such reforms were brought about, for example, in the Habsburg countries (1782), by the Benedictine Franz Rautenstrauch (1734–85).

An important characteristic of the Catholic Enlightenment was that it was conscious of the history of the church, mainly the dogmatic development, and thus of the relativity of traditions. Such historical awareness was mostly brought about by the Benedictine congregation

43. See Alfredo Serrai, *Domenico Passionei e la sua Biblioteca* (Milano: Edizioni Sylvestre Bonnard, 2005).
44. Johannes Madey, "Quirini, Angelo Maria," *Bibliographisch-Biographisches Kirchenlexikon* (Nordhausen: Bautz, 1999), 16:1305–7.
45. See Hellyer, *Catholic Physics*.
46. Breuer, "Einleitung," 12; 14.
47. Richard Herr, *The Eighteenth-Century Revolution in Spain* (Princeton, NJ: Princeton University Press, 1958).
48. See also C. Vogel, *Der Untergang der Gesellschaft Jesu als europäisches Medienereignis (1758-1773). Publizistische Debatten im Spannungsfeld von Aufklärung und Gegenaufklärung* (Mainz: Zabern, 2006).

of St. Maur/France under the able guidance of Jean Mabillon (1632–1707). The Maurists had started an enormous research project, connecting dozens of monasteries and hundreds of scholars to bring about new editions of the church fathers, but also of monastic traditions and history. Moreover, the Maurist movement wanted to show that scholarship is an important part of monastic life, and also a service rendered to God—equivalent to prayer and worship. The research, however, also had an apologetic side: the Maurists attempted to answer Spinoza's remarks about the historicity of the Bible, as well as the historical Pyrrhonism of François de La Mothe Le Vayer. The monks developed highly sophisticated rules for judging old documents, which would guarantee historical certainty.[49] The Maurist awareness of historical developments soon spread throughout Europe, especially due to the monastic communication networks, and consequently also accelerated Catholic Bible scholarship. Benedictines, such as Bernard Lamy (1640–1715), together with the Oratorians, especially Richard Simon (1638–1712),[50] requested a replacement of scholastic theology with a more scripture-oriented, so-called positive theology.

Catholic Enlighteners also had a common problem: the status of the local church, and consequently, the status of the pope's authority. Many of them revived medieval Conciliarism and fought even for the independence of their dioceses and national communities from papal prerogatives. In France, such ideas were already well-established due to Gallicanism and its codification in the *Declaration of the Clergy of France* in 1682. In the course of the seventeenth and eighteenth centuries, the Jansenists used this Gallican tradition to gain parliamentary support against the papal persecutions of their movement. Gallicanism, combined with Jansenist ideas, spread throughout Europe, partly due to the monastic correspondences and exchanges of the Benedictines. Abbots and priors of different orders—often supported by the Curia—fought against the attempts of

---

49. The programmatic work of this school was Jean Mabillon's *De re diplomatica* (1681) and his *Traité des Etudes Monastiques* (1691), cf. Lehner, "Ecumenism and Enlightenment Catholicism."

50. Sascha Müller, *Kritik und Theologie. Christliche Glaubens- und Schrifthermeneutik nach Richard Simon (1638-1712)* (St. Ottilien: EOS, 2004).

the bishops and the state to restrain their monastic sovereignty.[51] The Gallican and Jansenist pamphlets that called for a separation from Rome, or at least, a considerable limitation of papal authority, articulated the widespread dissatisfaction with curial interferences in ecclesiastical affairs. In the second half of the eighteenth century, these anti-Roman sentiments were summarized in Johann Nikolaus von Hontheim's (1701–90) *Febronius*.[52] The book inspired a reform movement within the Church that sought to strengthen the position of the bishops and the secular sovereigns and almost eradicate papal influences.[53] This Episcopalism seemed necessary at the time due to the fact that since 1751, the year of the condemnation of Montesquieu's *Spirit of the Laws* and the second condemnation of freemasonry, the official dialogue between the papacy and the Enlightenment had almost entirely ceased, and finally faded away with the death of the relatively open-minded Pope Benedict XIV. The Enlighteners' hope for change lay entirely on the bishops and the sovereigns.

Crucial to all Catholic Enlighteners was also the desire to distinguish themselves from the religious fanaticism that had separated the Christian churches for centuries. Thus, they conceived networks, e.g., in Fulda, that provided peaceful interdenominational dialogues on the legitimacy of papal faculties and the position of bishops and Catholic princes, but also about sacramental union, the abolition of celibacy for priests,[54] and the subjugation of the church under the state (Gallicanism, Febronianism, Theresianism, Josephinism). Three hundred years after the Reformation, it was these Catholic individuals, rather than the Roman Curia, who began to see Luther's revolution for the first time in a more positive light. They did not even shy away from calling their demands a "reformation," not just a reform, of

---

51. Cf. Gustave Leclerc, *Zeger-Bernard van Espen (1646–1728) et l'autorité ecclésiastique* (Zurich: Pas, 1964); *Zeger-Bernard van Espen at the Crossroads of Canon law, History, Theology, and Church-State Relations*, ed. Guido Cooman et al. (Leuven: Leuven University Press, 2003).
52. See ch. 7 in this volume.
53. Miller, *Portugal and Rome*, 6–7.
54. Paul Picard, *Zölibatsdiskussion im katholischen Deutschland der Aufklärungszeit. Auseinandersetzung mit der kanonischen Vorschrift im Namen der Vernunft und der Menschenrechte* (Düsseldorf: Patmos, 1975), 187, reports that many canon law specialists regarded celibacy as the true stumbling rock for a reunification.

Catholicism.[55] It was in this context that Catholic ecumenical theology had its beginning. The groundbreaking reunification plan of Dom Beda Mayr (1742–94) might suffice to show that.

Conclusion

The Catholic Enlightenment had an ambivalent dynamic. On the one hand, it was a cosmopolitan force; on the other, it was national. It was also both radical and conservative. It was cosmopolitan in the sense that enlightened Catholic theologians throughout Europe started from the same *imperatives*—namely, the Judeo-Christian revelation in scripture and tradition. From this, they drew their conclusions, under the influence of some Enlightenment thinkers. Changes to this concept could be made, but the main premises were impossible to give up. It was national, since every Catholic country provided a different setting for the Church: in France, it was Gallicanism; in the Holy Roman Empire, it was the *Reichskirche*, and so on. The Catholic Enlightenment was radical: once certain traditions were identified as contrary to "true" belief or the pristine church and as impediments for the flourishing of society, they were abandoned. Nevertheless, Catholic Enlighteners understood themselves not as inventors, but as reformers, since their work had been an adaptation or a development of what the Church originally believed. There is, in this regard, as Plongeron observed, a gulf that separates the Radical Enlightenment from the Religious, and, in our case, the Catholic Enlightenment. Whereas the former was concerned with turning politics into a completely secular endeavor without reference to God as designer, judge, and sovereign over the universe, the latter adhered to the principle *that grace perfects nature.* In this context, it meant that religion was regarded as necessary to bring a civil society to perfection. Even if there were passionate discussions about the essence of ecclesiology, its basic principle—the hierarchy—was almost never denied. Therefore,

55. Aretin, "Katholische Aufklärung im Heiligen Römischen Reich," 410–11. Hersche, *Muße und Verschwendung,* 2:1025; Peter Hersche, "Lutherisch machen—Rekonfessionalisierung als paradoxe Folge aufgeklärter Religionspolitik," *Ambivalenzen der Aufklärung,* ed. Hans Haas et al. (Vienna et Munich: Verlag für Geschichte und Politik, 1997), 155–68.

the Catholic Enlighteners could not meet their secular colleagues on the same ground, and therein lays one of the reasons for the drama of this movement, which was crushed by the forces of Ultramontanism and the rise of theological conservatism in the nineteenth century.[56]

---

56. Bernard Plongeron, "Was ist katholische Aufklärung," in *Katholische Aufklärung und Josephinismus*, ed. Elisabeth Kovacz (Munich: Böhlau, 1979), 39–45, at 27.

3

The "Heresy-Hunting" of the Obscurantists and the "Martyrdom" of the Enlighteners: Forgotten Characteristics of Anti-Enlightenment and Catholic Enlightenment

The characteristics of the Counter-Enlightenment, and whether this term is at all useful for historians, are still hotly debated. Contemporary eighteenth-century sources preferred to speak of "Obscurantists" or "enemies of the Enlightenment."[1] In order to characterize such a group properly, one would have to establish not only its self-understanding and its reception history, but also how it was seen by opponents. This chapter seeks to contribute to the latter by presenting a feature of anti-Enlighteners, frequently referred to

---

1. Christoph Weiss and Wolfgang Albrecht, *Von "Obscuranten" und "Eudämonisten": gegenaufklärerische, konservative und antirevolutionäre Publizisten im späten 18. Jahrhundert* (St. Ingbert: Röhrig, 1997); Darrin M. McMahon, *Enemies of the Enlightenment: The French Counter-Enlightenment and the Making of Modernity* (Oxford: Oxford University Press, 2001).

by their contemporaries—namely, their compulsive desire to brand different theological views as "heretical." The anti-Enlighteners were, according to contemporaneous descriptions, addicted to spotting heresies and sought to out-believe believers; they were heresy-hunters. The German term that describes this behavior, "Verketzerungssucht," appears in countless brochures and articles of the time. Until now, however, nobody has researched where the Enlighteners saw the root of such hatred. This chapter tries to unravel how Catholic Enlighteners viewed their critics and how they understood their attacks and polemics. Consequently, this helps us to better comprehend the self-understanding of the Catholic reformers and the negative reception history of the Counter-Enlightenment (if we want to use that label).[2] It becomes clear that the reformers felt not only unjustly treated, but persecuted, and viewed themselves as the group "owning" the truth, although they charged their opponents with the same view. Perhaps a look back into this history will also help us understand better the often vitriolic theological discussions at the Second Vatican Council, but in particular the name-calling by different interpreters in its aftermath.[3]

Wilhelm Castello and Aloysius Sandbichler: On the Reasons for Theological Cantankerousness

The Trier diocesan priest Wilhelm Joseph Castello (1758–1811),[4] in his hitherto neglected dissertation, *On the Immoderate Lust to Charge Others with Heresy* (1791), protested vehemently against theological censorship.[5] Already in the first footnote, he compares the authorities

2. For a basic view of what Catholic Enlightenment is, see Ulrich L. Lehner, *The Catholic Enlightenment: The Forgotten History of a Global Movement* (Oxford: Oxford University Press, 2016).
3. Hans Küng's memoirs are full of examples in which theologians who disagree with him are labeled as "pre-conciliar," although they fully endorsed the council. See Hans Küng, *Disputed Truth: Memoirs* (New York: Continuum, 2008) and the still untranslated third volume *Erlebte Menschlichkeit* (Munich: Piper, 2013).
4. Regarding Castello, see Rudolf Reichert, "Das Trierer Priesterseminar zwischen Aufklärung und Revolution (1786–1810)," *Archiv für Mittelrheinische Kirchengeschichte* 38 (1986): 107–44; Eduard Lichter, "Johann Wilhelm Josef Castello und die Aufklärung im Erzstift Trier," *Archiv für Mittelrheinische Kirchengeschichte* 21 (1969): 179–228.
5. Wilhelm Joseph Castello, *Dissertatio de Immoderata Alios Haereseos Insimulandi Libidine . . .* (Trier: 1791).

of the Protestant and even Masonic Enlightenment—namely, Christoph Meiners (1747–1810) and Johann Adam Weishaupt (1748–1830)—to the Catholic Enlightener Ludovico Muratori (1672–1750).[6] It becomes clear that he believes that Muratori was doing groundbreaking work for Catholic thought, liberating it from the ballast of centuries and freeing it for a more "liberal" way of theologizing. Castello shows that the pathological desire to brand others as heretics does not come about as an outcry warranted by the decline of religion, but as "passionate embitterment."[7] The reformers, who like the apostle Peter, try to gain insight into their faith (*ut sciant reddere rationem Fidei*), must fear the persecution of the fanatic guardians (sometimes called "guards of Zion") of alleged orthodoxy. Books that offer a sane doctrine (*sana doctrina*), but use a different theological classification and terminology, are redacted and "mutilated" by the censors, while books that contain nothing more than theological chit-chat and lack, in their polemical tone, all Christian charity, are printed with glowing endorsements by these censors and other Obscurantists.[8] The Salzburg Augustinian Aloysius Sandbichler (1751–1820) agrees with Castello's judgment and considers the polemic against the Catholic Enlightenment as irrational and short-sighted:

> If the danger to faith and good morals was really as big and urgent as the cries, the pushes, and the urging from all sides would indicate . . . then it would indeed be irresponsible carelessness and betrayal of religion and state not to shout out, too, not to push and urge, too . . . in order to preserve and protect the highest good humanity has . . . namely the true faith and to join the . . . guards of Zion.
>
> Yet the opposite is the case and the whole uproar is merely the work of short-sighted and mean persons, who are enticed by ignorance or impure . . . passions. . . . Thus it is the duty of all good-thinking people not only to teach the ignorant about the inanity of the alleged danger in

---

6. He names Christoph Meiners, *Ueber den thierischen Magnetismus* (Lemgo: 1788) and Johann Adam Weishaupt, *Geschichte der Vervollkommung des menschlichen Geschlechts* (Frankfurt und Leipzig: 1788); and cites Muratori's *Antiquitates Italicae*, vol. 5 (Milan: 1738ff).
7. Aloysius Sandbichler, "Wahre Ursachen der vielfältigen und gräulichen Verketzerungen in unseren Zeiten," in *Revision der Augsburger Kritik über gewisse Kritiker*, ed. Aloysius Sandbichler (Salzburg: 1792), 2:281–325, at 284.
8. Castello, *Immoderata*, 4–5.

fraternal charity, but also to reveal the vicious roisterers in their . . . utter hideousness to the public.[9]

Innocent and well-meaning reformers would be persecuted only for doubting theological opinions, rather than dogmas.[10] Since such opinions do not contain defined truths of faith, they are, by the standards of theological classification, open for discussion. As examples of the persecution of Catholic theologians, Sandbichler names Jakob Danzer (1743–96), Stephan Wiest (1748–97), Anton Oehmbs (1735–1809), and Benedict Oberhauser (1719–86), but also cites cities where such name-calling occurs, including Graz,[11] Vienna, Bonn, and Würzburg. The persecutors, Sandbichler thinks, are usually only mediocre thinkers, who did not engage in much research, but rather enjoyed the world (*quiete hoc mundo frui*). Their victims, however, were never ignorant professors, but rather educated men who had left behind old prejudices and begun searching tirelessly for the truth:[12]

> These are men, who accept truth wherever they find it and defend it. They love truth in action and are not afraid to take a new path to finding truth instead of an old one, and to show others such a path, too. These are men, who put aside the old barbaric disputes over words, . . . avoid . . . useless speculations, and love only truth. In short, they are men who abandon the yoke of prejudice imposed on them by ignorant and perverted people, and destroy without fear the realm of [theological] opinions these others . . . have built.[13]

Castello also analyzes the method according to which the obscurantists, whom he also calls "guards of Zion" and "counterfeit zealots" (*Afterzeloten*), work. He identifies two roots for their compulsive hunting of heretics. The first is their intellectual ignorance

---

9. Sandbichler, "Wahre Ursachen," 284–85.
10. On the levels of theological certitude (theological notes), see Harold E. Ernst, "The Theological Notes and the Interpretation of Doctrine," *Theological Studies* 63 (2002): 813–25; Ludwig Ott, *Fundamentals of Catholic Dogma* (Rockford, IL: Tan, 1974), 1–10.
11. For Graz, see *Actenstücke zur Geschichte der Verfolgung einiger Zöglinge aus dem k. k. Seminarium zu Graz von dem fürstbisch. Konsistorium daselbst* (Frankfurt: 1790).
12. Castello, *Immoderata*, 12: "Nullibi autem reperies inertes, minus habentes, stupidos, qui usitate hucusque & ab illis praesignatae viae fideliter inhaeserunt, inhaerentque adhuc, diffamatos & adcusatos esse. . . ."
13. Sandbichler, "Wahre Ursachen," 286.

and a deep-seated prejudice for the traditional.[14] This preference for tradition,[15] however, is excessive, and thus best translated as "traditionalism." Such traditionalism is, in the eyes of Castello and Sandbichler, the greatest obstacle to liberating the mind to think for itself.[16]

The sensual impressions, which gradually form ideas, also form the human character insofar as they leave either a pleasant or unpleasant impression. If one's reason is only occupied with symbols and philosophical terms and formulas, one's human imagination turns to them. It begins to see the formulas as tantamount to the holy realities they refer to. It is extremely difficult to converse with such human beings; one needs "great wisdom and patience if one wants to guide them to better ways; and it is often not so much their fault as their teachers' if . . . one cannot prevail against their intellectual inflexibility, resentment, and stubbornness."[17] This inflexibility in thinking leads necessarily to becoming set on such formulas and theological opinions, which consumes all intellectual power that would be necessary to empathetically engage with new ideas, explains Castello, referencing the work of Heinrich Feder, *Investigations on the Human Will.* Consequently, such a traditionalist sees in every innovation a danger.[18] One root of such intolerance, as Castello calls it, is the persistent

---

14. Castello, *Immoderata,* 32.
15. Castello talks about a prejudice; it is a guiding principle. I decided to translate it rather as preference.
16. Cf. Traugott Thieme, *Ueber die Hindernisse des Selbstdenkens in Deutschland* (Gotha: 1791). Cf. Johann Michael Sailer, *Vernunftlehre für Menschen wie sie sind . . .*, 2nd ed. (Munich: 1795), 2:138: "Vorurtheil des Alten. Wenn ein Satz von Gründen gar nicht verlassen ist, sondern vielmehr das Gepräge des Wahren mit sich führt, zugleich aber das Unglück hat, dem Hörer oder Leser unbekannt zu seyn, und seiner bisherigen Überzeugung oder Übung zu widersprechen: so regt sich in ihm manchmal eine besondere Achtung für die alte Meynung, für die alte Übung, und der Verstand macht dem Willen ein Kompliment: indem er den Satz schlechtweg verwirft, ohne ihn zu prüfen, bloß weil er neu ist; und die alte Übung auf ein neues approbirt, bloß weil sie die alte ist. Diese Denkart, diese Handlungsart ist das Vorurtheil des Alten. Dies Vorurtheil ist tief gewurzelt. Man liebt das Alte, weil das Neue den längst vorgefassten Meynungen zu dürre widerspricht. . . ."
17. Sandbichler, "Wahre Ursachen," 291.
18. Johann Heinrich Feder, *Untersuchungen über den menschlichen Willen,* 2nd ed. (Göttingen: 1785), 1:75: "Vermöge aller dieser Ursache muss die Neigung zum Gewohnten um so viel stärker seyn je älter sie ist; je weniger Kraft man hat, in neue Vorstellungsarten sich hinein zu denken, neue Fertigkeiten sich zu erwerben, neue Einrichtungen zu machen; je wichtiger die Dinge sind, oder scheinen, die man ändern, in Ansehung derer man Unwissen gewesen zu seyn gestehen müsste, oder je mehr derselben sind; endlich je mehr gleichartige Beyspiele man auf seiner Seite hat."

clinging to old terminology, which he sees in the traditional method of catechizing youth. For the priest from Trier, the approaches used in the classroom are hopelessly outdated.[19] The second root is the "preference for authority." This means that instead of thinking rationally and independently, one rather praises blind faith in the opinions of theological authorities. It is, of course, always easier to follow in the footsteps of others than to undertake the hard work of thinking independently, but Castello also sees institutional problems in Catholicism that hinder independent thought. He speaks of an "insufficient culture of genius" (*non sufficientem ingenii culturam*) in Catholicism: censorship and hierarchical oversight do not let creative theologians and philosophers flourish.[20] Moreover, theologians are afraid to follow the insights of their research and escape to "lifeless" scholasticism, which has led to "useless" theological demonstrations and an almost rationalist theology (*perversa demonstrandi & procedendi ratione in Theologia*).[21]

Therefore, the biggest enemy of Obscurantism is the real desire to do research and search for truth. Instead of asking the "big questions," obscurantist theology is all about splitting hairs, "pygmy struggles"—"theological play with balloons."[22] In the newer and enlightened theology books, such things were omitted.[23] Both Sandbichler and Castello hope that such theological battles will die out and that a theology based on authorities, which is merely a "machine religion," will cease to exist.[24]

---

19. Castello, *Immoderata*, 40.
20. Ibid., 52.
21. Ibid.
22. Sandbichler, "Wahre Ursachen," 297. On the dispute concerning grace, see José Martin-Palma, *Gnadenlehre: von der Reformation bis zur Gegenwart. Handbuch Der Dogmengeschichte*, vol. 3 (Freiburg: Herder, 1980).
23. Sandbichler, "Wahre Ursachen," 298: "die bessern Köpfe sind von jenem ärgerlichen Kleingeiste, der jene Zänkereyen aushechte, so glücklich gesäubert worden, dass sich die noch übrigen Männer des alten Sauerteigs nun umsonst bemühen, ihren Armseligkeiten Respekt, und Ansehen zu verschaffen, und nur bey ihres gleichen durch Cabale und List noch einiges Glück, welches, wie ich hoffe, mit nächstfolgender Generation aufhören wird, machen können . . . Freylich scheinen diese Leute an, eine solche gänzliche Katastrophe noch nicht gläubig geworden zu seyn: sie führen einen Ton, der alle Zuversicht verräth, und thun mit ihren Distinktinuceln und hergebrachten Auktoritäten noch eben so groß, als vormahls irgend ein Professor der Kasuistik, oder gar der erlauchten Theologia speculativa sich damit breit gemacht haben möchte."
24. Ibid.

The third root of the addiction to anathematizing others is the ignorance and stupidity of the obscurantist theologians (*eorum stupiditate, ignorantia, negligentia*),[25] who know only a few authoritative writers, but do not pay attention to the scientific discourse of their day, and completely neglect the other sciences. Only such ignorance explains why students denounce their professors to authorities because they spoke about the "poetic style" of a scriptural text, and thought poetic to be equivalent to "poetic fiction."[26]

The fourth root is the hatred the Obscurantists have for their opponents. This hatred increases if reformers refute their excessively imprudent arguments (*nimia praecipitantia et imprudentia*) and forcefully "amputate" (*amputare*) their prejudices. It seems that Castello alludes here to the attempts to purge liturgical books and worship from old superstitions and Baroque exuberance.[27] Such new forms of worship, however, were not carefully introduced, wherefore the faithful disliked them and considered them artificial.[28] It is this elitism of the Enlighteners, conceded by Castello, of which the Vicar General of Münster, Franz von Fürstenberg (1729–1810), complained in 1790 (regarding the professors in Bonn):

> Unfortunately, it seems to be a characteristic of enlightened professors that they hinder the good cause more through pride and bad temper than they help it. To call people fools will certainly not make them listen better to the truth.[29]

---

25. Castello, *Immoderata*, 66.

26. Ibid. This is an allusion to the case of Johann Martin Jahn in Vienna, who understood the Book of Ruth as a poetic poem. Cf. Johann Martin Jahn, *Einleitung in die göttlichen Bücher des Alten Bundes*, 2 vols. (Vienna: 1793).

27. Cf. Felix Anton Blau, *Ueber die Bilderverehrung mit Rücksicht auf das angeblich neue Algesheimer Wunderbild* (Mainz: 1788); Blau and Anton Dorsch, *Beyträge zur Verbesserung des äussern Gottesdienstes in der katholischen Kirche* (Frankfurt: 1789). Cf. also Philipp Brunner, *Neues Gebethbuch für aufgeklärte Katholiken* (Heilbronn: 1801).

28. Rezension von Benedict Anton Cremeri, *Neueste Sammlung der auserlesenen Gebethe* (Linz: 1791), in *Oberdeutsche Allgemeine Litteraturzeitung* (1792), 5:vi, 93: "Man reißt dem Handwerker seinen geistlichen Seelenwecker, und der Betschwester ihren Himmelschlüssel aus der Hand, und dringt ihnen aus unkluger Aufklärungssucht mit Gewalt ein nagelneues Erbauungsbuch, wo sie lauter Betrachtungen, Lebensregeln, Lieder und Verse, aber keinen einzigen Hymnus, kein einziges Gebeth, keinen einzigen Stoßseufzer u.dgl. antreffen."

29. Eduard Hegel, *Geschichte der katholisch-theologischen Fakultät Münster* (Münster: Aschendorff, 1966), 1:44. About Fürstenberg, see Thomas Flammer, ed., *Franz von Fürstenberg (1792-1810): Aufklärer und Reformer im Fürstbistum Münster* (Münster: Aschendorff, 2012).

The last reason that Castello mentions is that Obscurantists fear the substance of the faith could be damaged by innovative theologies. Every Enlightenment thinker is, for them, a proponent of rationalism, naturalism, indifferentism, or anti-clericalism. Due to the fact that they do not know the new conceptual language, they suspect every reformer of heresy. This "seed of distrust" (*semen suspicionis*) is a sign of the fear of dealing with something new, and demonstrates their inability to search for the truth without prejudice.[30]

On the side of the human will, there are also reasons that lead to compulsive heresy-hunting. The main reason is a corrupted will, which is guided by egoism, avarice, jealousy, pride, and self-righteousness. Yet the fear of losing reputation and privilege contributes to the decay of the will, and ultimately to "theological hatred" (*facile vindicta seu odium vere Theologicum*). Some certainly also have a desire to dominate others (*libido dominandi*) or personal hatred (*odium personale*), and so indulge in calling others heretics.[31] It is remarkable that Castello refers here to Pope Clement XIV (1769–74) in his letter to an unknown cardinal on religious zeal and intolerance.[32] Noteworthy also is the last reason Castello gives: namely, that religion is treated like politics (*religionem politice tractant*). Then, one persecutes others only under the pretense of piety, but in reality it is because they do not fit into one's worldview (*sub forma pietatis . . . haereticos dicunt*).[33]

For Sandbichler, theology is plagued by the "monster of those who have to be right" (*Ungeheuer der Rechthaberey*), despite substantial progress over the last decades of the eighteenth century. Although now, more and more theologians differentiate between dogma and school opinion—as Berti, Stattler, Bertieri, Gazzaniga, Schwarzhueber, Wiest, and Klüpfel do—he thinks they do not go far enough, because even they tend to present themselves as authorities and their

---

30. Castello, *Immoderata*, 76 "quidquid agit, sinistre explicant, quidquid dicit, perversum in sensum detorquent."

31. Ibid., 78–84. On the *odium theologicum*, see Johann Lorenz Mosheim, *De odio theologico commentatio* (Göttingen: 1748).

32. Giovanni Battista Piccolomini, ed., *Merkwürdige Briefe des Pabstes Clemens des XIV (Ganganelli) nebst Reden, Lobreden und andern wichtigen Schriften* (Frankfurt: 1777), 3:225–42.

33. Castello, *Immoderata*, 89.

arguments as ultimate.[34] The reformers who are attacked by the ex-Jesuits, whom Sandbichler calls "spiritual despots," are guilty of one sin in particular:

> They are thinkers and not ... boot lickers ... they are not creating systems according to preconceived schemes—that is their great crime. They are thinkers and therefore become the reason that others begin to think, too. Yet is thinking really so corrupting to Catholic religion that everybody who tries it deserves to be branded as the church's enemy?[35]

Sandbichler makes clear that Catholic Enlightenment does not have to be rationalist, but can be orthodox and within the boundaries of established doctrine. Consequently, he rejects the thoughtless identification of Enlightenment with free-thinking or deism. If Catholicism does not respect the rights of reason, Sandbichler says, then it mutates into fideism or "Islamic superstition."[36] The use of reason makes the Catholic Enlighteners suspicious because the Obscurantists deny the rights of reason, and indeed subscribe to a sophisticated fideism, which accepts reason only insofar as it helps to "realize their secret goals: their advantage, their jealousy, their avarice, pride, etc."[37] Looking back at his own formation, he remembers:

> I have freed myself with the help of my dead teachers—the books—gradually from prejudices ... authors who tried to force their alien opinions upon their readers did nothing to convert me ... but it was those who taught patiently and subtly with reasons—to those voices I listened and reflected about what they said . . . Thus more and more delusions vanished, and I realized the inanity of the terminology in which my own philosophical and theological ideas had previously been so safely stored ... This healing I experienced could also be applicable to others.[38]

Jakob Salat on Obscurantism

Jakob Salat (1766–1851), who had already become a friend of

34. Sandbichler, "Wahre Ursachen," 312.
35. Ibid., 315.
36. Ibid.
37. Ibid., 316.
38. Ibid., 292.

Enlightenment philosophy as a university student, got into difficulties as pastor of Zusamzell in the diocese of Augsburg in Bavaria, because after the dismissal of the theology professors Joseph Weber (1753–1831), Johann Michael Sailer (1751–1832), and Benedict Zimmer (1752–1820), he offered theological discussions for the students of Dillingen College. He acquainted them with Enlightenment thinkers, and his parish soon became known as a "center of the Illuminates."[39] By 1798 he was suspected of heresy, being an Illuminate and mason, and had to answer to the local board of diocesan inquisitors. Ex-Jesuits from the Augsburg St. Salvator community had denounced him. He was cleared of all charges, but the request to punish his denouncers was rejected. This hurt the young and gifted Salat so deeply that from that point forward, he nourished a profound hatred for the enemies of the Enlightenment.[40]

Between 1795 and 1798, he published a series of essays for German journals in which he rejected the claim that the Enlightenment would lead necessarily—as in France—to a revolution. He was not alone in this fight; Gregor Zirkel (1762–1817) of Würzburg published similar thoughts.[41] Yet for our purpose, the last chapter of an article published in 1802 is of special importance, since the author deals here explicitly with heresy-hunting and Obscurantism.[42] Of equal importance is his 1797 essay, *Even Enlightenment has its Dangers!*, which was republished in 1801 as a little brochure. In this work, Salat shows that true Enlightenment does not harbor danger, but produces moral progress. Nevertheless, he acknowledges impediments to the Enlightenment process and for the Enlightener himself. Without zeal for truth, the virtue of intellectual temperance easily can be perverted into indecisiveness,[43] and insight into the necessity for change can be perverted into pride and pretentiousness.[44] Out of the inability to

39. Adam Seigfried, *Vernunft und Offenbarung bei dem Spätaufklärer Jakob Salat: Eine historisch-systematische Untersuchung* (Innsbruck: Tyrolia, 1983), 37.
40. Ibid., 39.
41. Franz Berg and Gregor Zirkel, *Predigten über die Pflichten der höhern und aufgeklärten Stände bey den bürgerlichen Unruhen unserer Zeit* (Würzburg: 1793).
42. Jakob Salat, *Auch ein paar Worte über die Frage: Führt die Aufklärung zur Revolution?* (München: 1802). On Salat, see Ulrich L. Lehner, "Jakob Salat," in *Dictionary of Eighteenth-Century German Philosophers*, ed. Manfred Kuehn and Heiner Klemme (Bristol: Thoemmes, 2010), 972–74.

eradicate injustice or error, discontentment can arise, and with it melancholy and lack of fortitude.[45] This shows that Enlightenment is, for Salat, not just a stance of the mind, but also of the heart; or rather, of the whole person. True Enlightenment fosters the development of moral integrity and vice versa.[46] He summarizes the intention of true Enlightenment thus:

> To be open for all that is true and good, wherever it may come from, and always move forward to the better, more perfect moral and intellectual goods: that should be our motto, or better the maxim of our intentions, the soul of our actions![47]

Whoever rejects such progress, and thus the eradication of error and prejudice, becomes, according to Salat, a "slave of the establishment" and gives up hope for societal progress and perfection. One becomes a "living machine" and loses the "dignity of the human person," which consists in the answer to the God-given call to perfection.[48] The opponents of such progress are, consequently, the proponents of darkness (*Dunkelmann, Finsterling, Verfinsterer*).[49] Salat differentiates two main roots of such Obscurantism—namely, that of an immorally formed heart and that of a prejudiced head. Moreover, he differentiates between two kinds of Obscurantists—"rough" and "refined." The former really intends to do good, but due to his unenlightened mind, sticks to the letter of theology. If his heart remains pure, he is a "rough Obscurantist," but if he becomes evil, then he becomes a "refined Obscurantist." The latter appears to be cultivated because he has a more sophisticated way of speaking, but

---

43. Salat's example of such misguided "Moderantismus" is Edmund Burke (1729–1797); see Salat, *Auch die Aufklärung hat ihre Gefahren* (Munich: 1801), 29.
44. Ibid., 23–24.
45. Ibid., 10.
46. Ibid., 40. Seigfried, *Vernunft*, 40.
47. Salat, *Auch die Aufklärung*, vi.
48. Ibid., 7: "Wer hingegen alles gut findet, wie es ist, nie den Gedanken einer Abänderung wagt, und das ganze Maas seines Verstandes nur dazu anwendet, dass er lerne und handhaben könne, was da ist: der mag für die gegenwärtigen verhältnisse so brauchbar werden, als man es nur immer von einer—belebten Maschine erwarten kann; allein er verliert an der Würde des Menschen, da er, eben als solcher, zur eignen und auf stete Vervollkommnung hinstrebenen Thätigkeit bestimmt war."
49. Salat, *Auch ein paar Worte*, 163.

this is only outward appearance. He might have given up some prejudices, and is theoretically free of error, but not practically, because in regard to morality, he is still held back by "sophistry."[50] His thinking is not from real Enlightenment, but fake Enlightenment (*Aufklärerey*), wherefore he is not an Enlightener, but only an "Enlightenling" (*Aufklärling*).[51] Where the error concerns the intellect and the will remains good, that is, with the "rough Obscurantist," there is good hope that one day, he will be hit by a "beam of higher light," which will encourage him to defend the right of having an independent mind.[52] Then, he will excel in "humility, temperance in judgment, and tolerance of people of different opinion, with one word: he will excel in humaneness."[53] Such an Obscurantist, however, then ceases to be a real Obscurantist. If the good will is not victorious over the error, the error becomes practical, and thus a maxim of the will. It gradually corrupts morality and creates passion, vanity, ambition, and the lust for domination; all this creates the "fanatic Obscurantist":[54]

> He thinks of a highest, infinite being, whom he worships and to whom he sacrifices everything. "God" comes out of his mouth but remains an idol. . . .[55]

Such an idolatrous view of God binds the conscience of the Obscurantist; however, his conscience remains silent, "when he falls into wild zeal, hatred, and the spirit of persecution . . . therefore he does not act against his conscience but without one."[56] Religion is, therefore, for him not love of the highest, but outwardly projected self-love.[57] Consequently, in the framework of Obscurantism, the virtuous are not rewarded, but rather those who pretend submission and who flatter are; Salat sees this buttressed by the papal policy of his day. As

---

50. Ibid., 165–67.
51. Ibid., 183.
52. Cf. Seigfried, *Vernunft*, 45.
53. Salat, *Auch ein paar Worte*, 169.
54. Ibid., 172.
55. Ibid., 174.
56. Ibid., 175.
57. Seigfried, *Vernunft*, 46.

an example, he refers to the censoring of Benedict Stattler (1728–97), who was punished more harshly because he was a virtuous man.[58]

In two societal groups—the nobility and the clergy—Obscurantism is especially common. If a nobleman sees the common good as the highest good, the right to property as a human right, and the moral dissonance between a worker and a lazy person, then he is on the best path to overcoming his Obscurantism. Yet, if he thinks only of his own privileges and gain, then he collaborates with the clergy (*Pfaffentum*) for the sake of a devilish plot.[59] Simultaneously, with Salat, the enlightened bishop of Constance, Ignaz Wessenberg (1774–1860), described his disgust at Obscurantism:

> To the noble and wise men of this nation the hypocritical clergyman must appear as a monster. . . . Hypocrisy makes one suspicious, impatient, hard, and cruel; and the hypocritical clergyman is therefore always a heresy hunter and persecutor. Love is alien to him as well as truth.[60]

Only a priest who is not a weathervane of what is currently en vogue, but who researches and ponders over every innovation well, and does not defend "stubborn superstitions" without using his brain, contributes to the progress of the age. He improves the old with the new instead of turning his faith into "a dead mummy, a bleak and rotten monument."[61]

Heresy-Hunting According to Philipp Brunner

Philipp Joseph Brunner (1759–1829), who, by virtue of his Jewish descent alone—his mother had converted to Catholicism—was viewed suspiciously, was a favorite target of many enemies of the Catholic

58. Salat, *Auch ein paar Worte*, 177. Benedict Stattler, *Authentische Aktenstücke wegen dem zu Rom theils betriebenen, theils abzuwenden getrachteten Verdammungsurtheil über das Stattlerische Buch: Demonstratio Catholica* (Frankfurt: 1796). On Stattler, see Ulrich L. Lehner, "Benedict Stattler—Renewal of Catholic Theology with the Help of Wolffian Metaphysics," in *Enlightenment in Catholic Europe. A Transnational History*, ed. Ulrich L. Lehner and Jeffrey Burson (Notre Dame: University of Notre Dame Press, 2014), 169–92.
59. Salat, *Auch ein paar Worte*, 195–207.
60. Ignaz von Wessenberg, *Der Geist des Zeitalters: Ein Denkmal des achtzehnten Jahrhunderts* (Zurich: 1801), 191.
61. Wessenberg, *Der Geist*, 192. See Manfred Weitlauff, "Ignaz Heinrich von Wessenberg (1774–1860)," *Jahrbuch des Vereins für Augsburger Bistumsgeschichte* 44 (2010): 1–335.

Enlightenment during the last third of the eighteenth century. The priest, who published in journals and newspapers and authored a number of books, had indeed been a member of the infamous Illuminati group since 1782, but never defended its flat rationalism or deism; instead, he propagated a Catholic theology that was adapted to the needs of the age by a new philosophy, and in which baroque exuberance was replaced by simpler, more biblical forms of worship.[62] His writings on the reform of the liturgy stand in the tradition of Ludovico Muratori, but his 1785 homily on the "true and false concept of prayer" enraged the Capuchins in Karlsruhe so much that they publicly denounced it as heretical.[63] In 1793, the Prince Bishop of Speyer, August von Limburg-Styrum (1721–97), even seized Brunner's papers because he was suspected of being a member of the forbidden Illuminati group. In his papers, a letter from his friend, the priest Adam Gärtler (1731–1818), was found, in which he ironically complained about his superiors.[64] Gärtler then became *persona non grata* and had to accept an official investigation into his orthodoxy. Brunner revealed this "inquisition" of Gärtler to the public in his book, *The Last Documented Account of Heresy-Hunting under the Government of the Prince-Bishop of Speyer* in 1802.[65] We do not want to reconstruct the case or look at the reasons Gärtler was accused, but rather at the motives Brunner identified as the roots of the hatred turned against his friend and himself.

The first reason for this hatred lies, according to Brunner, in the wrong-headed hermeneutics of the Obscurantists, who connect their scholastic terminology with terms of the Enlighteners that do not correspond to them. Thus, the meaning of the reformers is changed

62. Josef Bayer, "Dr. Philipp Brunner, Ministerialrat in Karlsruhe und Pfarrer in Hofweier," *Freiburger Diözesanarchiv* 92 (1972): 201–22; Norbert Jung, *Der Speyrer Weihbischof Andreas Seelmann (1732–1789) im Spannungsfeld von "nachgeholter" Aufklärung und "vorgezogener" Restauration* (Mainz: Gesellschaft für mittelrheinische Kirchengeschichte, 2002), 336–51; 374–83.
63. Philipp Brunner, *Christliche Reden, welche von katholischen Predigern in Deutschland seit dem Jahr 1770 bei verschiedenen Gelegenheiten vorgetragen worden sind* (Heidelberg: 1789), 4:149–82 (Ueber den falschen und wahren Begriff des christlichen Gebeths).
64. Anton Wetterer, "Johann Adam Gärtler: Prediger und Kanonikus an der Stiftskirche zu Bruchsal," *Der Katholik* IV-21 (1918): 245–59; 327–41.
65. Philipp Brunner, *Die letzte aktenmäßige Verketzerungsgeschichte unter der Regierung des Herrn Bischoffes von Speier August Grafen von Limburg-Stirum: Mit Beilagen* (Germanien: 1802).

or perverted. This happens, though, because the Obscurantist does not wish to engage thoroughly with the context of the new idea because he blindly trusts suspicion and prejudice.[66] Brunner refers to Muratori, who in 1714, had already argued, in his groundbreaking book *De ingeniorum moderatione,* that a panel of judges should not condemn a heretic, but must rather try to understand the author and the reasons for his propositions. These intentions are not at all taken into consideration in heresy trials, demonstrates Brunner.[67] The priest does not reject any possibility of condemning a heretic, but considers it the proper right of the authority to do so if the author really preached a heresy; however, he perceives in the contemporaneous context too many condemnations of non-heretical propositions because they do not touch upon established doctrine, and mourns a lack of human maturity in the censors.[68]

An impetuous condemnation of heretics also disregards the difficulties of discerning what really constitutes a heresy. After all, a heresy is only an error in matters of doctrine if it is publicly defended with a certain obstinacy. Thus, the admonition about the error has to precede the punishment—and it has to pertain to a defined dogma, and not to a theological opinion about which many different views are licit. Otherwise, the inquisition of heresy becomes a synonym for despotism within the Church.[69]

The "Martyrdom" of Catholic Enlighteners

All Catholic Enlighteners I brought together here agree in their bitter hostility toward Obscurantism, which, in their view, is either based on ignorance or moral decay. Only a few of these Enlighteners conceded mistakes in the dissemination and articulation of their ideas—for

66. Ibid., 14: "man muss also sorgfältig und streng forschen, welchen Sinn der gemeine Sprachgebrauch it diesen Worten verbinde, welchen Begriff die Provinz oder das Land, in dem diese Worte geschrieben wurden, denselben beilege; man muss auf den Ort und die Zeit der Erziehung, des Studiums, die persönliche Lage eines Verfassers, seine Absicht etc. genau Acht haben, und dann die etwa dunkeln Worte mit den übrigen des ganzen Kontextes vergleichen."
67. See Ludovico Muratori, *De ingeniorum moderatione in religionis negotio* [1714] (Augsburg: 1779), 19:182ff.
68. Brunner, *Verketzerungsgeschichte,* 18.
69. Ibid., 27; Wessenberg, *Der Geist,* 226.

example, the elitism in prescribing certain liturgical forms while ridiculing others. Nevertheless, they do not seem to think that their opponents might have uttered warranted criticism here and there. Instead, the reformers immunize themselves against such criticism and charge their opponents with the most heinous intellectual shallowness or moral degeneration. Consequently, they do not feel the obligation to take their words seriously. It cannot surprise us then that the tensions between reformers and traditionalists—if we want .to use these terms—accelerated over the next few decades and turned into an outright theological war. Both camps attacked each other with ferocity and without much respect or personal integrity. The Obscurantist side—or better, the enemies of Enlightenment theology, in the form of a narrow neo-Thomism as propagated by Joseph Kleutgen (1811-83)—won this war in the Modernist crisis under the pontificate of St. Pius X (1903-14).[70] Yet, the mutual anathematizing caused deep distrust and also convinced Catholic and non-Catholic bystanders that there was something inherently wrong with Catholic theological discussion and that it was intellectually flawed. As a consequence, it became more and more marginalized and lost the intellectual appeal it once had.

It is noteworthy, however, that the Enlighteners were the first to acknowledge a new, hitherto neglected form of thought—"refined Obscurantism." This refined anti-Enlightenment agenda was only acknowledged by historians over the last few years under the label, "enlightened conservatism." Meanwhile, it is established consensus that this enlightened conservatism produced original, creative, and relatively open-minded theories, and was unconsciously shaped by Enlightenment ideas.[71] However, research about its importance, variations, and reception history, as well as its place in the wider intellectual history of the nineteenth century, is still—more or less—a lacuna.

70. Manfred Weitlauff, *Kirche zwischen Aufbruch und Verweigerung: Ausgewählte Beiträge zur Kirchen-und Theologiegeschichte des 19. und frühen 20. Jahrhunderts* (Stuttgart: Kohlhammer, 2001).
71. The term "enlightened conservatism" was coined by Carolina Armenteros, *The French Idea of History: Joseph de Maistre and his Heirs, 1794-1854* (Ithaca: Cornell University Press, 2011).

It also becomes clear that the Catholic Enlighteners saw themselves as fighters for truth, who were persecuted by hateful Obscurantists. Their opponents are described according to the hagiographical tradition of martyrdom, so that the reformers suffer, like the martyrs, the "odium" of their enemies. This should not cast doubt about the veracity of the accounts, in particular of historical events such as the Inquisition trials of Gärtler and Salat, but should rather lead us to a forgotten aspect of the self-understanding of Catholic Enlighteners: they understood themselves, so it seems, as the flag-bearers of truth and wisdom, for which they suffered on behalf of the rest of humanity.[72] This hitherto unacknowledged characteristic of Catholic Enlightenment could be helpful for reconstructing the "inner life" of this movement.[73]

72. On the persecution paradigm, see Candida Moss, *The Myth of Persecution: How Early Christians Invented a Story of Martyrdom* (New York: HarperOne, 2013).
73. Cf. Emma Rothschild, *The Inner Life of Empires: An Eighteenth-Century History* (Princeton, NJ: Princeton University Press, 2011).

PART II

Ecumenism and Theological Pluralism as Main Tenets of the Catholic Enlightenment

4

——

Ghosts of Westphalia:
Fictions and Ideals of Ecclesial Unity in
Enlightenment Germany

One of the major tenets of Enlightenment theology was its interest in irenic, at times, even ecumenical, endeavors. Discussions about the nature of ecumenism developed naturally in a confessionally divided territory such as the Holy Roman Empire. Yet, it has been widely overlooked that the constitution of the Empire, the *Peace of Westphalia* (referred to as *Westphalia*), which ended the Thirty Years War, not only guaranteed and established a confessionally fragmented realm, but still upheld the vision of ecclesial unity. The instruments of the peace treaty, such as parity and nonsectarian jurisprudence, were intended to pave the way for an irenic approach to theological differences with an eye toward a reunion of faiths. At the same time, however, they also impeded any potential reunion because of their political consequences. In the eighteenth century, under the influence of the academy movement, the time seemed to have come for a new way of approaching a reunion. I will look at two different ways of how religious unity could be approached: the *Neuwied Academy* conceived it in a universalist manner that disregarded theological truth claims, while the *Fulda Academy* focused on improving mutual theological understanding as the way to overcome differences.

The Ghosts of Westphalia: Fictions of Religious Unity

The *Peace of Westphalia* of 1648, consisting of the peace treaties of Osnabrück and Munster, not only ended the Thirty Years War, but also brought about an armistice between Protestants and Catholics concerning the nature of the true Catholic Church. In order to reinstate order and unity in the realm, the opposing religious parties agreed to regard their confessional differences as unsettled doctrinal conflicts that would no longer fragment the political balance of the Empire. What the Empire had achieved in the treaties was therefore not a tri-confessional nation, but a legal, constitutional foundation for a reunion of the churches. Any other conclusion would have meant sacrificing the religious truth claim of one of the parties. It was only because the *Peace of Westphalia* was an instrument for a reunion of the churches that the severe restrictions on the power of the pope and bishops and the suspension of canon law (e.g., to wage holy war against heretics) were acceptable to Catholic princes.[1] This theological view of the treaty only disappeared in the eighteenth century, when Protestant scholars of jurisprudence began to see the *emergency* laws,[2] which gave Protestant sovereigns rights over the churches, as settled and perpetually established positive law. Catholics, however, continued to interpret the religious peace as an exterior armistice, which only suspended canon law until all Protestants were once more in full communion with the Roman Catholic Church.[3] Only at the end of the eighteenth century

---

1. Martin Heckel, "Die Wiedervereinigung der Konfessionen als Ziel und Auftrag der Reichsverfassung im Heiligen Römischen Reich Deutscher Nation," in *Die Reunionsgespräche im Niedersachsen des 17. Jahrhunderts. Rojas y Spinola—Molan—Leibniz*, ed. Hans Otte and Richard Schenk (Göttingen: Vandenhoeck & Ruprecht, 1999), 15–38, at 30. Mathias Fritsch, *Religiöse Toleranz im Zeitalter der Aufklärung: naturrechtliche Begründung-konfessionelle Differenzen* (Hamburg: Meiner, 2004), 5.
2. See the excellent book by Thomas Hahn, *Staat und Kirche im deutschen Naturrecht* (Tübingen: Mohr Siebeck, 2012).
3. Heckel, "Die Wiedervereinigung," 33–34; Fritsch, *Religiöse Toleranz*, 5–6. On the duty of holy war

did Catholic jurists seem to have given up this notion, especially under the influence of Christian Wolff (1679–1754) and the church reforms of Emperor Joseph II (1780–90).[4] The reason for the State's existence was now solely seen as relating to the welfare of the people, without any reference to religion. This new principle also served as legitimization for Catholic princes to absorb more powers over ecclesial property.[5] The more sovereigns controlled church possessions and policy (*jus circa sacra*), however, the less likely it became that they would reduce such precious influence for the sake of Christian unity. Thus, a crucial part of Westphalia—the command for a reunion of faiths—had become a fiction nobody paid much attention any more.

Another result of the peace treaties that initially appeared to settle religious dispute was that of religious parity.[6] The best example for the parity of religious groups was the *Imperial Diet*, the *Reichstag,* where majority votes on religious topics were suspended. Instead, the two confessional bodies of the *Imperial Diet,* Protestants (Lutherans and Calvinists in the *Corpus Evangelicorum*) and Catholics (*Corpus Catholicorum*), were expected to vote on religious issues separately (*itio in partes*) so that one body could not impose their majority vote upon the other.[7] These bodies, however, were not officially and

against heretics, see Bernd Mathias Kremer, *Der Westfälische Friede in der Deutung der Aufklärung. Zur Entwicklung des Verfassungsverständnisses im Hl. Röm. Reich Deutscher Nation vom konfessionellen Zeitalter bis ins späte 18. Jahrhundert* (Tübingen: Mohr Siebeck, 1989), 40–41; Konrad Repgen, "Der päpstliche Protest gegen den Westfälischen Frieden und die Friedenspolitik Urbans VIII," *Historisches Jahrbuch* 75 (1956): 94–122; Michael F. Feldkamp, "Das Breve 'Zelo domus Dei' vom 26. November 1648—Edition," *Archivum Historiae Pontificiae* 31 (1993): 293–353.

4. Kremer, *Der Westfälische Friede,* 29.
5. Fritsch, *Religiöse Toleranz,* 31–53.
6. Kremer, *Der Westfälische Friede,* 119–52; Fritsch, *Religiöse Toleranz,* 7–12; Winfried Schulze, "Pluralisierung als Bedrohung: Toleranz als Lösung," in *Der Westfälische Friede. Diplomatie—politische Zäsur—kulturelles Umfeld—Rezeptionsgeschichte,* ed. Heinz Duchhardt (Munich: Oldenbourg, 1998), 115–40. On parity in the Empire in general, however, with almost no material on the confessional corpora, see Lothar Weber, *Die Parität der Konfessionen in der Reichsverfassung von den Anfängen der Reformation bis zum Untergang des alten Reiches 1806* (Bonn: Fuchs, 1961).
7. Kremer, *Der Westfälische Friede,* 177; Fritsch, *Religiöse Toleranz,* 8; Martin Heckel, "Itio in partes. Zur Religionsverfassung des Heiligen Römischen Reiches Deutscher Nation," in Martin Heckel *Gesammelte Schriften* (Tübingen: Mohr Siebeck, 1989), 2:636–737. On majority decisions of the *Imperial Diet,* see Winfried Schulze, "Majority Decision in the Imperial Diets of the Sixteenth and Seventeenth Centuries," *Journal of Modern History* 58. Supplement (1986): S46–S63. For the development of the *itio in partes* see Klaus Schlaich, "Maioritas—protestation—itio in partes—Corpus Evangelicorum. Das Verfahren im Reichstag des Hl. Römischen Reichs Deutscher Nation nach der Reformation," in Klaus Schlaich, *Gesammelte Aufsätze. Kirche und Staat von der Reformation bis zum Grundgesetz. Ius Ecclesiasticum* 57 (Tübingen: Mohr Siebeck, 1997), 68–134.

constitutionally recognized as the corporate voices of Protestantism and Catholicism, but were somewhat semi-official. While centuries later, the *itio in partes* has been recognized as a means of keeping religious peace, contemporaries disliked it because it easily became an impediment to the regular activities of the *Imperial Diet,* and was, therefore, only invoked in extreme cases (only ten times between 1672 and 1806).[8]

The *Peace of Westphalia* also guaranteed equal rights to Reformed Churches in the Empire's ecclesial landscape for the first time. Consequently, institutions which were sworn to religious parity had to provide the Reformed Church with an equal number of offices, just like the Lutherans and Catholics. An interesting application of this newly conceived parity was the Imperial Cameral Court (*Reichskammergericht*), the highest court of the Empire (together with the *Imperial Aulic Council* in Vienna), where Reformed judges had sat on the bench since 1654.[9] A simple majority vote of the judges was sufficient to decide a case, and every judge was perfectly free in his decision and—at least officially—protected from external influences.[10] The statutes of the court also made clear that every judge or court member had to declare his religion unmistakably so that *absolute* parity could be exercised. Thus, the case of a Catholic judge, who was married

---

Indispensable for the legal background of the two corpora is still Fritz Wolff, *Corpus Evangelicorum und Corpus Catholicorum auf dem Westfälischen Friedenskongress. Die Einfügung der konfessionellen Städteverbindungen in die Reichsverfassung* (Münster: Aschendorff, 1966). While the concepts *Corpus Catholicorum* and *Corpus Evangelicorum* are not entailed in the Peace Treaties of Osnabrück and Münster, they are contained in the relevant protocols. However, judicially, the term *Corpus Evangelicorum* was not used until 1691, and *Corpus Catholicorum* not until 1714 (Peter Brachwitz, *Die Autorität des Sichtbaren. Religionsgravamina im Reich des 18. Jahrhunderts* (Berlin and New York: de Gruyter, 2011), 73; Wolff, *Corpus,* 124–28.

8. Härter, "Das Corpus Catholicorum," 76.
9. For the conflicts regarding the appointments to the Imperial Cameral Court, see the detailed description and analysis at Sigrid Jahns, *Das Reichskammergericht und seine Richter: Verfassung und Sozialstruktur eines höchsten Gerichts im Alten Reich* (Cologne et al.: Böhlau, 2011), 1:168–327. A good survey of the legislative landscape of Germany, and especially the importance of the *Imperial Aulic Council* (Reichshofrat) is given in Edgar Liebmann, "Reichs- und Territorialgerichtsbarkeit im Spiegel der Forschung," in *Gerichtslandschaft Altes Reich,* ed. Anja Amend et al. (Cologne et al.: Böhlau, 2007), 151–72; Volker Press, "Der Reichshofrat im System des frühneuzeitlichen Reiches," in *Geschichte der Zentraljustiz in Mitteleuropa. Festschrift für Bernhard Diestelkamp zum 65. Geburtstag,* ed. Friedrich Battenberg and Filippo Ranieri (Cologne and Vienna: Böhlau, 1994), 349–65.
10. Wolfgang Sellert, "Richterliche Unabhängigkeit am Reichskammergericht und am Reichshofrat," in *Gerechtigkeit und Geschichte. Beiträge eines Symposions zum 65. Geburtstag von Malte Dießelhorst,* ed. Okko Behrends (Göttingen: Wallstein, 1996), 118–32.

to a Reformed wife and who raised his daughters in the Reformed Church, looked suspicious as to his Catholicity as late as 1760, especially because a convert would lose his seat on the bench.[11] Despite much research on the *Reichskammergericht*, its religious dimension and its impact on religious history has been utterly neglected; nothing has been written about its role in religious matters in the eighteenth century, although it was arguably the best working tri-confessional institution of the realm and protected most efficiently the religious rights of the Emperor's subjects, while simultaneously keeping the idea of a united realm alive. The statutes of the court, which propagated a "non-sectarian jurisprudence,"[12] reminded the judges to be tolerant of each other's religious convictions:

> Judges of the [three] . . . religions as well as all persons of the Cameral Court must not despise others for their religion, nor scorn at each other, or give in to ill will, but must be always friendly to each other and of good will, and have to demonstrate in every way that they work peacefully and tranquilly together and will so in the future.[13]

Following this rule, the court did not reject religious truth claims, but only suspended its judgment on religious matters and solved cases pragmatically. Mutual disagreement and corruption brought the court to a lame-duck-position in the midst of the eighteenth century. Until its end in 1806, the court never fully recovered, and all plans for a

---

11. Dagmar Feist, "Der Fall von Albini–Rechtsstreitigkeiten um die väterliche Gewalt in konfessionell gemischten Ehen," in *In eigener Sache. Frauen vor den höchsten Gerichten des Alten Reiches*, ed. Siegrid Westphal (Cologne and Weimar: Böhlau, 2005), 245–70. For the Reichskammergericht in the Eighteenth Century, see Monika Neugebauer-Wölk, "Das Alte Reich und seine Institutionen im Zeichen der Aufklärung. Vergleichende Betrachtungen zum Reichskammergericht und zum Fränkischen Kreistag," *Jahrbuch für fränkische Landesforschung* 58 (1998): 299–326.

12. Benjamin Kaplan, *Divided by Faith. Religious Conflict and the Practice of Toleration in Early Modern Europe* (Cambridge, MA: 2009), 232.

13. Johann Wilhelm Ludolff, ed., *Concept Der neuen Kayserlichen und Reichs-Cammer-Gerichts-Ordnung* (Wetzlar: 1717): *Cammer-Gerichts-Ordnung of 1613*, title 4, §4, accessed November 24, 2015, http://virr.mpdl.mpg.de/virr/view/escidoc:414781/image/38. This valuable edition of the statutes of the Cameral Court, visitation protocols, commentaries on the statutes etc. contains over 1,300 pages, but is inconsistently paginated. For each part, the page number begins with 1, wherefore I decided to indicate also the image nu. of the scan of the digitized online-version to make it easier for the reader to check the respective page. For the 1654 decree of the Imperial Diet, see Arno Buschmann, ed., *Verfassungsgeschichte des Heiligen Römischen Reiches Deutscher Nation vom Beginn des 12. Jahrhunderts bis zum Jahre 1806 in Dokumenten, Teil 2* (Baden-Baden: Springer, 2nd ed. 1994), 180–273, *Recessus Imperii Novissimus* of May 17, 1654, §23 at 194.

reform were either blocked or never implemented.[14] The idea, however, that a court of non-sectarian jurisprudence, using law and reason alone, would resolve religious (and political) problems, remained a crucial ideal for the formation of the reunion academies.

A Union of All Religions: The Neuwied Academy

The *Free Society for the Renewal [Aufnahme] of Religion* was founded in 1754[15] by the Reformed theologian Johann Heinrich Oest (1727–77) on the Frisian Islands. For Oest, religion had become marginalized in society and divided people into two categories: those who were overzealous in religious matters and those who were disinterested in religion. Both groups were the target of society, since it explicitly desired to overcome fanaticism and indifferentism. In October 1756, the Count of Neuwied-Runkel was introduced to this project, and immediately, gave it his special protection. He even lifted any restrictions of censorship from the society. Oest was appointed head of the academy and received the title "professor of polemical theology." From then on, the society was called the *Academy of Neuwied for a Reunion of Faiths and for the Continuous Improvement of Religion* and was the first institutionalized attempt at ecumenism on German soil.[16] On January 1, 1757, the establishment of the academy was publicly announced in a 72-page brochure.[17] The academy's organization echoes the juridical context of *Westphalia*—namely, a sense for parity,

14. See, for example, Karl Otmar von Aretin, "Reichshofrat und Reichskammergericht in den Reichsplänen Kaiser Josephs II," in *Friedenssicherung und Rechtsgewährung. Sechs Beiträge zur Geschichte des Reichskammergerichts und der obersten Gerichtsbarkeit im alten Europa*, ed. Bernhard Diestelkamp and Ingrid Scheurmann (Bonn and Wetzlar: Arbeitskreise selbständige Kulturinstitute), 51–81. For an English description of the German juridical system see Joachim Whaley, *Germany and the Holy Roman Empire*, vol. 2 (Oxford: Oxford University Press, 2012).

15. *Schriften der Ostfriesischen freyen Gesellschaft zur Aufnahme der Religion* (n.p.: 1756). The only surviving copy is in the Dukal Archive in Neuwied. This archive also holds a number of archival files about the Neuwied Academy. The files are not accessible. See Johann Mathias Schroeckh, *Unpartheyische Kirchen-Historie. Alten und Neuen Testaments . . . Vierter Theil, in welchem die Geschichte vom Jahr nach Christi Geburt 1751 bis 1760 enthalten sind* (Jena: 1766), 698.

16. One of the few, accessible archival documents about the academy (especially about the quarrels in 1757) can be found in the *Haus-, Hof-, und Staatsarchiv Vienna*: Kleinere Reichstände 537-1-1, including a membership diploma.

17. *Nachricht, Einrichtung, Rechte und Gesetze der Hoch-Gräflich Neuwiedischen Akademie zur Vereinigung des Glaubens und weiterer Aufnahme der Religion* (Neuwied: n.p., 1757). Also published *in Acta historico-ecclesiastica* 120 (1758): 582–621, on which I rely here.

neutrality, and high regard for nonsectarian, mere "reasonable" judgment. Due to its name, one can also detect a strong influence of the European academy movement, which aimed at organizing scholarship and free discussion in academic societies.

The aim of the academy was to bring "enlightened" minds together in order to extract the truths from all "religions" and confute doubts about God's existence and revelation. This society was headed by a clerk (*Greffier*), who was supposed to collect the theological opinions from other members. These statements were then to be read by all society members in private. No meetings should ever occur, nor any discussions. Surprisingly, the *Neuwied Academy* did not discriminate against gender, religion, or nationality among its members. Also, the number of members was not limited. One could become a scholarly member, and only as such was one expected to participate in the theological discussion, if one had written a "good essay about one or more and especially disputed" theological propositions.[18]

The introduction to the statutes of the academy called religion the "Inbegriff," the core of the most important truths of humanity, which the society was founded to re-discover by resolving the differences between all (!) religions. The underlying belief was that the conflicting truth claims of religions demonstrate that God and his revelation must have been misunderstood by some—or even all—religions. In order to bring about one faith for all people and in order to silence agnostic as well as atheist doubt, one had to confute the wrong concepts and uncover the real truth about the divine. A necessary presupposition for this, however, was that members could speak their mind, wherefore freedom from censorship was considered essential.[19] Although the statutes speak frequently of differences between Christian theological systems, mostly they use "religions" and mention, at times, Judaism, Islam, and even Paganism, wherefore one can understand why this document can be read as a manifesto of syncretism, as most contemporaries did.

18. *Nachricht*, 612.
19. *Nachricht*, 585–86.

The *Neuwied Academy* renounced the conversational methods of earlier reunion attempts and understood itself as a community of unprejudiced academics. Unlike earlier reunion attempts that often ended in the heat of oral discussions, exclusively written communication was used in order to avoid ambiguity and emotional distress. This was supposed to be a more serious, undisturbed, and intelligible way of communicating.[20] The statutes read: "We write and read. . . . The community among us consists not in congregations or talks, but in written communication . . . of our thoughts."[21] Such written communication was not entirely new since other major literary or academic societies had begun using it a few decades earlier. However, to make it part of an ecumenical or universalist strategy was a major innovation.[22]

To ensure that the members would speak their minds, all members had to be kept unaware of the identities of the others, except for the main clerk and the secretary. Each person was asked to submit statements, which were then condensed and edited without indicating the identity of the author.[23] This policy also ensured that the discussion was about arguments and that the arguments were taken seriously, regardless of the reputation of the authors.[24]

Already by July 1757, a number of critics attacked the academy because they believed it was a successor to the *Neuwied Ducats-Society*, a lottery ponzi scheme.[25] The Giessen professor and Lutheran pastor

20. For the advantages of written "conversations," see, for example, the reflections of Dirk Baecker, "Hilfe ich bin ein Text!," in *Paratexte in Literatur, Film, Fernsehen*, ed. Klaus Kreimeier and Georg Stanitzek (Berlin: Oldenbourg, 2004), 43–52, at 45; on academic communication in Early Modernity, see Martin Gierl, "Res public litteraria—Kommunikation, Institution, Information, Organisation und Takt," in *Kommunikation in der frühen Neuzeit*, ed. Klaus-Dieter Herbst and Stefan Kratochwil (Frankfurt: Peter Lang, 2009), 241–52; Martin Gierl, "Kompilation und die Produktion von Wissen im 18. Jahrhundert," in *Die Praktiken der Gelehrsamkeit in der Frühen Neuzeit*, ed. Helmut Zedelmaier and Martin Mulsow (Tübingen: Niemeyer, 2001), 63–94. For an excellent overview of the Christian reunion attempts in the form of personal dialogues see Otto Scheib, *Die innerchristlichen Religionsgespräche im Abendland*, 3 vols. (Wiesbaden: Harrassowitz, 2010).
21. *Nachricht*, 588.
22. Cf. Rudolf Vierhaus, "Die Organisation wissenschaftlicher Arbeit. Gelehrte Sozietäten und Akademien im 18. Jahrhundert," in *Die Königlich Preussische Akademie der Wissenschaften zu Berlin im Kaiserreich*, ed. Jürgen Kocka (Berlin: Akademieverlag, 1999), 3–22.
23. *Nachricht*, 589.
24. *Nachricht*, 612.
25. Arwid Liersch, *Dukaten-Sozietät und Glaubens-Akademie. Zwei Wiedische Gesellschaften des 18. Jahrhunderts* (Neuwied: 1904), 47–48.

Johann Hermann Brenner (1699–1782) thought a reunion of all faiths and common worship were impossible. The new academy did not convey the necessary message of Christian irenicism, but rather of religious pluralism, because it also sought to bring non-Christian religions into dialogue with the churches.[26] Some German sovereigns also protested against the academy because they feared that by circumventing censorship, the academy could publish polemics against basic Christian convictions or against the established parity of confessions in the realm. Especially troublesome was the fact that the academy could consider one or perhaps all of the three officially acknowledged denominations as inferior and attempt to reform them without ecclesiastical or imperial mandate. Moreover, a successful reunion of the Christian denominations would have ended the sovereigns' say over church affairs. Theologically educated sovereigns feared that the Neuwied project could lead to a fourth religion in the realm—one of syncretism or indifferentism. In light of this, it became necessary for the count of Neuwied to respond to these charges. He claimed that such dangers did not exist and were based on a misinterpretation of the statutes of the academy. He also revoked the freedom from censorship the academy had enjoyed and ordered that the academy proceedings be regarded as a scholarly journal that was bound by Imperial censorship law.[27] Since the academy never attracted a sufficient number of members, and also because famous German theologians such as Johann David Michaelis (1717–91) protested against it, it soon fell into financial trouble.[28] In order to prevent a

---

26. Johann Hermann Brenner, *Prüfung der neuen Aufrichtung einer Hochgräflich-Neuwiedischen freyen Akademie zur Vereinigung des Glaubens und Aufnahme der Religion* (Giessen: 1758); Johann Hermann Brenner, *Zeugnis über die Neuwiedische Anstalten* (n. p.: 1758). On Brenner see *Das Neue gelehrte Europa* 17 (Wolfenbüttel: 1762), 941–53.

27. Liersch, *Dukaten-Sozietät,* 55.

28. Michaelis rejected the Neuwied academy also because he considered its democratic way of resolving theological issues, namely by majority vote, as inadequate. See Johann David Michaelis, "Briefe von der Schwierigkeit der Religions-Vereinigung, an Herrn Pastor Aurand, Secretaire der Neuwidischen (*sic!*) Unions-Academie," in Johann David Michaelis, *Syntagma commentationum* (Göttingen: 1759), 1:121–70. Johann Michael von Loen (1694–1776), Goethe's uncle, and Johann Daniel van Hoven (1705–93) were ardent supporters of the Neuwied project (see Joris van Eijnatten, *Liberty and Concord in the United Provinces. Religious Toleration and the Public in the Eighteenth-Century Netherlands* (Leiden and Boston: Brill, 2003), 135–36. For Loen, see his *Des Herrn von Loen kurzer Entwurf der allgemeinen Religion, zur Beförderung des Glaubens der Christenheit. Nebst*

pending lawsuit of the Protestant count of Hessen-Darmstadt, as well as the Catholic Electors of Cologne and the Palatinate, the count of Neuwied withdrew his protection of the academy and dissolved it in August 1758. Thus, the threat and insult for the established churches was eliminated.[29]

Mutual Theological Understanding:
The Re-Union Academy of Fulda

This reunion project began at a time when the Protestant willingness to actively tolerate Catholics had begun to decrease and slowly gave way to a vibrant anti-Catholicism that lasted well into the twentieth century.[30] Nevertheless, the intellectual climate was still friendly enough to motivate the Protestant Erfurt scholar Jakob Heinrich Gerstenberg (1712–76) to publish his thoughts about a possible reunion with the Catholic Church in 1773.[31] Surprisingly, he had been intrigued by Johann Friedrich Bahrdt's (1713–75) universalism insofar as it attempted to come to a purely rational Christian theology, which all denominations could share.[32] Such an attempt was, in Gerstenberg's eyes, necessary in order to protect Christianity against the forces of atheism and deism. Among his personal friends and supporters was the Catholic sovereign of Erfurt, the future archbishop of Mainz, and then vice-regent of Erfurt, Carl Theodor von Dalberg (1744–1817). Dalberg was also devoted to the unity of Christianity and publicly declared

einer näheren Erklärung an die Gesellschaft der Wissenschaften zu Göttingen von J. D. von Hoven (Lingen: 1754).

29. The dissolution decree mentions explicitly the threat of the academy for the established churches, at Liersch, *Dukaten-Sozietät*, 58: ". . . dennoch zum Theil einiger Orten als anstössig und wohl gar denen im Reich gebilligten Kirchen und Religionen zuwider angesehen werden will."

30. Olaf Blaschke, "Das 19. Jahrhundert. Ein zweites konfessionelles Zeitalter?," *Geschichte und Gesellschaft 26* (2000): 38–75. Manuel Borutta has argued that Protestant Enlighteners viewed the Catholic South of Germany very much like the Orient—a region that had to be cultivated, and speaks therefore of a Protestant "Orientalism" as basis for the renewed anti-Catholicism (Manuel Borutta, *Antikatholizismus: Deutschland und Italien im Zeitalter der europäischen Kulturkämpfe* [Göttingen: Vandenhoeck, 2010]).

31. See Christoph Spehr, *Aufklärung und Ökumene. Reunionsversuche zwischen Katholiken und Protestanten im deutschsprachigen Raum des späteren 18. Jahrhunderts* (Tübingen: Mohr Siebeck, 2005), 85–107.

32. Spehr, *Aufklärung und Ökumene.* 105–6. See Carl Friedrich Bahrdt, *Neueste Offenbarungen Gottes*, 4 vols. (Riga, 1773–74). One of Bahrdt's conversation partners was the Catholic convert and former Lutheran pastor Johann Justus Herwig (1742–1801).

in his *Reflections on the Universe (1778)*, very much to the dismay of his Jewish correspondence partner Moses Mendelssohn (1729–86), who believed that "religious pluralism, not uniformity was the design of Providence,"[33] that all societies, including religions, aim at unity in God.[34] This unity, he perceived, was best embodied in the Catholic Church, and therefore Dalberg expressed his hope that "the time will come when the light of religion will be preached to all humans of the earth without exception. . . . Be it that the desire of good hearts be fulfilled! Be it that the different Christian religious parties (*Religionspartheyen*) return to the motherly lap of the church!"[35] Two years later, he composed a *Plan for a Reunification of Religions*, which he sent to his friend Johann Gottfried Herder (1744–1803), whose text is, unfortunately, lost.[36] Also, other Catholics such as the Franciscan Jacob Berthold (1738–1817) in Bamberg argued that mutual denominational tolerance was insufficient, but that a real reunion of the churches was desirable.[37] However, only the plan of the Benedictine Beda Mayr (1742–94), who proposed in 1777–78 an academy for the reunification of the churches, caused a stir among his peers because he suggested a restriction of ecclesiastical infallibility.[38] In contradistinction to Mayr, five Benedictines of Fulda, under the leadership of the Reformed theologian Johann Rudolph Piderit (1720–91), began to work on a reunification academy the same year, which deserves more serious attention.[39] It was inspired by the works of Gerstenberg and Dalberg.

The project leaders among the Benedictines were Peter Böhm (1747–1822) and Karl von Piesport (1716–1800).[40] Piderit, however,

33. Alexander Altmann, *Die trostvolle Aufklärung. Studien zur Metaphysik und politischen Theorie Moses Mendelssohns* (Stuttgart-Bad Cannstatt: Frommann-Holzboog, 1982), 225; Karl Theodor von Dalberg, *Betrachtungen über das Universum*, 3rd ed. (Mannheim: 1787).
34. Dalberg, *Betrachtungen*, 6; 100; 105. ibid., 136: "Gesetz des Universums. Einheit is vollkommen in Gott. Die Schöpfung strebt sich der Einheit zu nähern. Religion ist Weg zu dieser Annäherung. Also Einheit ist Urquelle, Zweck und Grundgesetz des Universums."
35. Dalberg, *Betrachtungen*, 134.
36. Konrad Maria Färber, *Kaiser und Erzkanzler. Carl von Dalberg und Napoleon am Ende des Alten Reiches* (Regensburg: Mittelbayerische Verlagsgesellschaft, 1988), 24.
37. Jakob Berthold, *Cogitationes Pacis et Unionis inter Religiones Christianas* (Würzburg: 1778).
38. See Ulrich L. Lehner, ed., *Beda Mayr—Vertheidigung der katholischen Religion* (Boston and Leiden: Brill, 2009).
39. Jahns, *Das Reichskammergericht und seine Richter*, 1:297–342.
40. Spehr, *Aufklärung*, 153–61.

seems to have been the main author of the statutes of the *Reunion Academy* and its theological plans. The main idea of this group was similar to that of Neuwied: an academic society for the purpose of a reunification of the three main churches should be founded. Just like at the *Imperial Cameral Court*, one aimed at strict parity. Besides Piesport (Böhm was an extraordinary member), other members included the Lutheran theologians Wilhelm Franz Walch (1726–84) and Christian Wilhelm Schneider (1734–97), while the Reformed were represented by Heinrich Otto Duysing (1719–81), Piderit, and Petrus Abresch (1735–1812).[41] Members were sought out in private letters and conversations. For the Catholic side, one could find the support of Johann Gertz (1744–1824), one of the first exegetes who tried to implement historical criticism, but most Catholics were hesitant since the recent censoring and punishment of modernizing theologians deterred them. The statutes of the new society were finished by April 1779. Johannes Schmitt, a dogmatic theologian of Mainz, of whom nothing else is known, was also asked to join, since he had greatly sympathized with the plan. Even the Mainz Archbishop Friedrich von Erthal (1718–1802) seemed to sympathize with the newly created society or at least paid careful attention to the plan when he received Schmitt and Böhm in private audience in 1780. Erthal even ordered Schmitt to inform the Elector of the Palatinate, Karl Theodor (1742–99), of the society. The Elector's advisor, however, prelate Johann Kasimir Häffelin (1737–1827), vehemently rejected it, and finally motivated Schmitt to also withdraw his support. Häffelin, a seasoned diplomat, could not imagine that the project of a few theologians could really bring about change, let alone theo-political alterations. Other enlightened theologians declined a membership, mostly because one feared wasting time if the discourses were not supported by any ecclesial authorities.[42] Other concerned Catholic theologians complained to the papal nuncio about the new academy and feared

---

41. Spehr, *Aufklärung und Ökumene*, 162–63.
42. Spehr, *Aufklärung und Ökumene*, 184–95. On Häffelin see Rudolf Fendler, "Johann Kasimir von Häffelin, 1737–1827. Historiker, Kirchenpolitiker, Diplomat," *Quellen und Abhandlungen zur mittelrheinischen Kirchengeschichte* 35 (Mainz: 1980).

that the project gave up the essentials of Catholic teaching. Nuncio Giuseppe Garampi (1725–92) wondered what common basis the three denominations could have in case of a reunion, "a Catholic, a heretical one or newly invented devilish invention"?[43] He went so far as to protest at the Imperial Chancery in Vienna in 1780 against the Fulda plan. The chancery, however, decided to request reports about the activities of Böhm and Piderit, but not to intervene, not even when Garampi warned about potential "seditious" consequences of a reunion of the churches. The nuncio's fear was increased by the sympathy important Catholic Church leaders, especially the Archbishop-Electors of Trier and Mainz, but also the Prince Abbot of St. Blasien showed toward the reunion plan. The Curia now acted promptly. On June 10, 1780, Pope Pius VI issued a secret brief that admonished the monks to abstain from their plans since all previous ecumenical dialogues had been unsuccessful. Moreover, the pope warned about the dangers of receiving theological knowledge from Protestant theologians. It could destroy the faith of the Benedictine monks, he feared. At last, the pontiff insisted that the Benedictines had no proper authority for their ecumenical endeavor. The bishop of Fulda, simultaneously, abbot of the Fulda abbey, was ordered to stop the project immediately. Heinrich VIII of Bibra (1759–88) was a man of the Enlightenment, but he obeyed. Nevertheless, he did not punish his Cathedral Chapter, consisting only of Benedictine monks, which outright rejected the papal decree and wanted to go ahead with the academy plan. He was pleased with so much self-confidence and allowed the monks to appeal directly to Rome. The pope, of course, never responded to the appeal, which only confirmed Böhm's conviction that the brief had been written *not* by the bishop of Rome, but by the "archenemy" of Christianity.[44]

The last resort of the academy to gain support was to publish its

---

43. Spehr, *Aufklärung*, 167. On Garampi, see Dries Vanysacker, *Cardinal Giuseppe Garampi, 1725-1792: An Enlightened Ultramontane* (Bruxelles: Institut historique belge de Rome, 1995).
44. Spehr, *Aufklärung*, 178. On Bibra, see Michael Müller, *Fürstbischof Heinrich von Bibra und die katholische Aufklärung im Hochstift Fulda (1759-88). Wandel und Kontinuität des kirchlichen Lebens* (Fulda: Parzeller, 2005).

plan and to attract support. Piderit, as a Reformed Christian, was not bound by any papal proscription and went ahead with this plan. The publication in 1781 really stirred up broad interest.[45] Most readers, however, associated the new academy with the universalist project of Neuwied or the rationalism of Bahrdt.[46] Piderit responded that everybody who actually read the plan of the new academy would see that they were not at all interested in "uniting all religions by suppressing the name of Jesus."[47] Instead, the academy aimed at a reunion without giving up the essentials of Christianity and explicitly despised indifferentism. The mutual dialogues of the academy were not intended to dilute differences, but to educate the members. A tolerance that would sacrifice truth claims, a wrong-headed indifferentism, was not the aim of the academy members, Piderit insisted.[48] Tolerance through mutual education about the varying theological traditions would bring about a new, nobler tolerance, and finally harmony among faiths:

> Tolerance . . . [combined] with education [Belehrung] . . . is elevated to a noble level. . . . Tolerance leaves a human person . . . in uncertainty. . . . Education has the intention to eradicate gradually all prejudices and maxims that hold the heart . . . captive. If this is achieved, one has harmonious opinions [einerlei Gesinnungen].[49]

The plan of Piderit and the Benedictines made clear that the members understood the society as a loose congregation of private persons and the academy's work as private business until a plan was worked out that deserved to be shared with the public.[50] The plan invokes already,

---

45. Johann Piderit, *Entwurf zum Versuche einer zwischen den streitigen Theilen im Römischen Reiche vorzunehmenden Religions-Vereinigung* (Frankfurt and Leipzig: Bayrhoffer, 1781). The plan (*Entwurf*) was published initially without an introduction so that a few months after the original publication, a new edition was printed with a 141-page-long introduction by Piderit. Johann Piderit, *Einleitung und Entwurf zum Versuche einer zwischen den streitigen Theilen im Römischen Reiche vorzunehmenden Religions-Vereinigung von verschiedenen Katholischen und Evangelischen Personen, welche sich zu dieser Absicht in eine Gesellschaft verabredet haben* (Frankfurt and Leipzig: Bayrhoffer, 1781).
46. See, for example, Johann Jakob Moser, *Unterthänigstes Gutachten wegen der jezigen Religions-Bewegungen, besonders in der Evangelischen Kirche wie auch über das Kayserliche Commissionsdecret in der Bahrtschen Sache* (n.p.: 1780), 4–5; on the constitutional aspect ibid., 32–42.
47. Piderit, "Einleitung," in Johann Piderit, *Einleitung und Entwurf*, 9.
48. Ibid., 141.
49. Ibid., 36–37.

on its first page, the *Peace of Westphalia* that prescribed a reunion of the Christian faiths. All discussions among members were considered private and no suggestion should cause any church any disadvantages or advantages until a final decision was reached. The members would discuss whatever was best for a universal church and conducive for a restoration of universal peace between the confessions. If such proceedings would be published, they were not intended to bind any party to it or to force anybody to accept them. Instead, the theologians understood themselves as a think-tank for peaceful, inter-denominational theology, which declared explicitly its trust in divine providence and its conviction of human frailty.[51]

Only persons who could subscribe to the high ideals of mutual theological education and tolerance and to the uncertainty of the outcome of the project (e.g., that one tradition could be utterly wrong) could become members. Every member had to be willing to eradicate error and prejudice, and converse according to "the law of love ... and let go of any personal displeasure and to embrace ... ways of peace."[52] This brotherly love should become the key to solving confessional disputes, because it demonstrated a deeper commitment—namely, that of one's heart to the cause. This did not mean an indifferent embrace of diversity: "Error will remain error and will have to be called as such: it will be always free for a member to call ... what one perceives as error an error ... but without slander."[53] Unlike Neuwied, the Piderit-Fulda-Project did not seek to establish a universalist religion and did not threaten the interior or exterior constitution of any church.[54] Whatever was passed by the society members in majority vote could never be binding law or oblige any church unless it was officially accepted and implemented by the relevant church authority.[55] It is also

50. Ibid., 4.
51. Piderit, *Entwurf,* prologue and §1, 1–6.
52. Piderit, *Entwurf,* §3, 9.
53. Piderit, *Entwurf,* §4, 11.
54. Piderit, *Entwurf,* §6, 14: "Nach allem diesem, was bisher angeführt worden, verstehet es sich von selbsten, dass diese vorläufige brüderliche Vereinigung, in der inneren und äusseren Verfassung einer jeden Kirche, keine weitere Aenderung oder Irrung mache."
55. Piderit, *Entwurf,* §6, 14: "Alles dasjenige, was in dieser Vereinigungs-Gesellschaft genehmiget, und mit der wahren christlichen Religion genehmiget, und mit der wahren christlichen Religion

remarkable that the members of the society regarded their business as so important that they wanted to disconnect their work from their academic personas so that the "business"—working in mutual tolerance and education for a reunion of faiths—continued until its completion.[56]

Like the *Imperial Cameral Court,* the society had to consist of twelve ordinary members. The ratio of these members according to their confessions, however, was different from the court as six were supposed to be Catholic and six Protestant. Nevertheless, the idea of an *itio in partes* of two separate bodies is explicitly invoked when it is stated that doctrinal differences among Protestants should be handled solely among them. A reunion should only come about as the result of a search for truth.[57] Therefore, the members should regard themselves as "servants" in the vineyard of God and should be ready to suffer for the cause.[58] Although it was left up to the confessional groups how they wanted to name and appoint members, the statutes demonstrate great sensibility when they state that before a member is appointed, one should inform the other members and see if anybody had something against this person. Only if nobody objected could the appointment be made. Another paragraph speaks explicitly of the "good friendly harmony" [*gutes, freundliches Einverständnis*][59] between the members, which sounds very much like the constitutional principle of an *amicabilis compositio* (friendly compromise) of the *Imperial Diet* or the statutes of the *Cameral Court* about friendly interaction. Every new member had to sign an oath in which he professed to accept the suggestions of the academy and to be a "loving co-worker of the savior."[60] Once all slots of the society were filled, the oldest two

---

übereinstimmend, oder der gesammten Christlichen Kirche, nützlich und nothwendig erkannt wird, kann niemalen reichsgesetzmässig, niemalen ganzen Gemeinden und Kirchen verbindlich werden, als bis solches unter dem Ansehen derjenigen, welche hierin etwas vestzustellen [sic!], und zu verordnen das Recht haben, auf eine sich rechtfertigen lassende Weise, für ganze Kirchen und Gemeinden ist eingeführet worden."

56. Piderit, *Entwurf,* §8, 17.
57. Piderit, *Entwurf,* §10, 23.
58. Piderit, *Entwurf,* §10, 24.
59. Piderit, *Entwurf,* §13, 33.
60. Piderit, *Entwurf,* §12, 31.

members—a Protestant and a Catholic—should preside as presidents of the academy for one year. For the Protestant side, a member of the other confession could be appointed co-president, especially if important discussions pertained to the theological heritage of this group, e.g., if a Lutheran was president, a Reformed could be co-president and full president the following year, and so on. Since the presidents would not meet in person, the statutes prescribed one real presider among the presidents, whose office was to alternate between Catholics and Protestants.[61]

Most important, however, was that every member worked "in true fear of God, through prayer, holy obedience and sacrifice of one's heart to the faithful guidance of our Savior and the Spirit he has given us, so that everything a member does can be regarded a real fruit of the spirit of Christ."[62] While unanimity was required for the ultimate solution of doctrinal issues, for other questions, e.g., themes to work on, a simple majority of vote was considered sufficient. This majority was not just the majority of simple votes; there had to be a consensus between the two sides, even if the number of votes was smaller. It was measured according to the *grade* of consensus; only common votes [*vereinigte Stimmen*] counted! "According to this principle, four Catholics and four Protestants who vote for one solution count more than six Protestants and two Catholics, or six Catholics and two Protestants."[63] The doctrinal question that should be investigated was then handed over to a Catholic and a Protestant to write up how this issue was treated in their theological tradition. Their statements had to be checked by their churches and authorized. It was crucial that one used only approved theological sources and definitive theological judgments for such a statement and not theological school opinions. These documents were then read by two other appointed members of the society as to where they agree or disagree. The result was shared with the other members, and if nobody objected, the "real business" began.[64] Since the

61. Piderit, *Entwurf,* §15, 34–52.
62. Piderit, *Entwurf,* §18, 62.
63. Piderit, *Entwurf,* §19, 73. Spehr's description that a "majority vote" decided the themes of the discussion is insufficient, see Spehr , *Aufklärung und Ökumene,* 223.

differences between the confessions were now clearly stated, the statements could now go to the respective denominational camps for discussion as to how the doctrinal difference could be resolved. When the issue at question did not pertain to the basic beliefs of either confession, then one could reach a compromise [*Vergleich*] and should attempt to enlighten each other in friendship and love over time, but should not waste time in heated discussions or let such a minor issue, even if it was considered an error, impede a reunion.[65] It was, however, also possible that one side could consider an issue as minor while the other considered it as shaking the foundations of their church.[66]

As we saw above, the idea to use the power of corporate reason, an academy, for resolving theological differences was not new. However, Böhm and Piderit had learned from the temptation of indifferentism, which brought the academy of Neuwied down, as well as from the failures of the constitutional institutions to suspend judgment on theological truth, and instead resolve problems pragmatically. Like the judges of the Imperial Cameral Court, the theologians of the academy had to agree on a common constitution. While for the judges, it was predominantly the Peace of Westphalia, for the academy members, it was the Bible in its Hebrew and Greek original; but as a concession to Catholics, the Vulgate was also accepted. Piderit and Böhm thought that such a biblical approach would eliminate excessive doctrinal differences, "false mysticism, enthusiasm and fanaticism."[67] Like the

---

64. Piderit, *Entwurf*, §22, 84–87.
65. Piderit, *Entwurf*, §23, 92: "Wenn demnach der streitige Punkt so beschaffen ist, dass derselbe den Grund des Glaubens, wie er von den andern geleget ist, nicht zerüttet, vielmehr solchen wie er liegt unverändert liegen lässt, nur aber nicht nach aller Vollkommenheit darauf bauet, so ist zwar der [!] Gegentheil nicht schuldig, den Irrthum, aus allzugrosser, und in der That tadelhafter Gefälligkeit, Wahrheit zu nennen, und solchem als richtig nachzugeben: Gleichwohl kann doch dieser Irrthum, nach Beschaffenheit der Umstände, und wenn sonst nichts om Wege steheet, kein Hindernis machen, mit dem Gegentheile einen Vergleich zu errichten, und den Irrthum, auf seinen Einsichten und seinem Gewissen, bis dereinst etwa erfolgenden besseren Aufklärung, zumal, wenn man die ausdrückliche Absicht hat, für solche Aufklärung noch ferner zu sorgen, und sich dazu wechselweis die Hand zu bieten, ungerügt stehen zu lassen: und vergeblich, wenigstens unschicklich würde es seyn, durch itzt unzeitiges Disputiren, das ohnehin nach getroffenem Vergleiche, freundschaftlicher und mit mehr kaltem Blute, geschehen kann, die Vereinigung aufzuhalten."
66. Piderit, *Entwurf*, §23, 94–98; §25, 100–101.
67. Spehr, *Aufklärung*, 226; cf. 230. However, if the Vulgate deviated from the original, the Protestants were allowed to use the original text for a rebuttal. Other sources besides scripture should not be

judges, the theologians were supposed to be free in their judgment and should come from different German states so that no sovereign could overly influence or pressure the outcome of the discussions. Like the *Neuwied Academy*, the members of the *Fulda Academy* rejected personal meetings and preferred written correspondence.[68] Likewise, each theological tradition had to express its teachings in a creedal statement, which was supposed to be forwarded to the other members as a foundation for the dialogues. From such documents, the theological differences could be derived, themes identified, and difficulties resolved. Only the Catholic members sent their creedal statement—namely, the *Professio Tridentina* (1565)—in 1782. The monks, however, never received an answer or a similar document from their Protestant peers. It was this lack of cooperation and not papal interference that ultimately killed the project in 1783.

Conclusion

The Neuwied and Fulda projects testify to the fact that there were two fundamentally different ways of ecumenical dialogue in eighteenth-century Germany. While Neuwied aimed at a universalist union by means of the smallest common denominator, the Fulda project saw mutual understanding of creedal traditions as the key to theological harmony. By shedding light on such ecumenical projects of the past, I do not propose that contemporary ecumenical theologians can learn from the past how to shape the theological future, but rather that historical theology improves our sensibility due to the fact that we are standing in a cloud of witnesses, whose successes and failures we should remember in order to sharpen our self-reflection.

used or only to a minimum. To understand a biblical passage, explanations of the church fathers were admissible and even regarded as "witnesses of truth."

68. The Göttingen scholar Christoph Meiners (1747–1810), who was not involved in any ecumenical enterprises, regarded academic "Geselligkeit" and oral conversation as superior to written correspondence. See Marian Füssel, "Akademische Aufklärung. Die Universitäten im Spannungsfeld von funktionaler Differenzierung, Ökonomie und Habitus," *Geschichte und Gesellschaft. Sonderheft* 23 (2010): 47–73, at 69.

5

Enlightenment and Ecumenism: Beda Mayr (1742–94)

The contribution of monasticism to the framework of Christian theology in almost all periods is undisputed. However, the eighteenth century as a period of monastic theology is still, unjustly, overlooked. That was precisely the time when monks, mostly Benedictines, challenged the traditional ways of theologizing, and, along with a number of dedicated individuals, initiated what came to be called the Catholic Enlightenment.[1] This movement worked not only for a renewal of ecclesiastical practice and thought, but also for a peaceful dialogue between the Christian churches and even toward an

---

1. Cf. Ulrich L. Lehner and Michael Printy, eds., *Brill's Companion to the Catholic Enlightenment in Europe* (Leiden: Brill, 2010). On the importance of religious orders for the intellectual development of the West, cf. Derek Beales, *Prosperity and Plunder: European Catholic Monasteries in the Age of Revolution, 1650–1815* (New York: Cambridge University Press, 2003). The most recent study on German Benedictine Enlightenment is Ulrich L. Lehner, *Enlightened Monks* (Oxford: Oxford University Press, 2010). Despite the importance of the monks of St. Maur for the development of modern historical criticism, hardly any works of this school are translated. An exception is John Paul McDonald, ed., *Jean Mabillon—Treatise on Monastic Studies (1691). Translated with an introduction* (Lanham, MD: University Press of America, 2004). Cf. also Dom Aidan Bellinger, "Superstitious enemies of the flesh? The Variety of Benedictine Responses to the Enlightenment," in *Religious Change in Europe 1650–1914*, ed. by Nigel Aston (Oxford: Clarendon Press, 1997), 149–60.

ecumenical theology. One of the most intriguing figures of this enlightened theology is the Swabian Benedictine Beda Mayr (1742–94)—the forgotten "grandfather" of ecumenical theology.

Benedictine Enlightenment

There is no clear, monocausal explanation of why the Benedictines became the champions of the Catholic Enlightenment. However, a number of factors contributed to this phenomenon.

First, unlike the Jesuits or the mendicants, the prelate orders were organized in a decentralized way. The advantage of this decentralization was that each superior was free to open or close the doors of his monastery to Enlightenment thought. No abbot was bound, as other religious superiors were, to a specific theological school.[2]

Second, the houses of the prelate orders communicated with each other on a regular basis and maintained common colleges or novitiates for their monastic students. Only the Benedictines, however, who enjoyed a privileged status in the *Ancien Régime* Church, seem to have engaged thoroughly in international relations. The correspondence of German Benedictines with their fellows in France and Italy brought the ideas of Cornelius Jansen (1585–1638), Malebranche (1638–1715), and Muratori (1672–1750) to study cells in southern Germany.

Third, we can detect not only letter exchange, but another medium of communication—namely, the exchange of scholars and students—that contributed to the transfer of knowledge. For example: the monks of St. Emmeram in Regensburg or of St. Blasien in the Black Forest invited professors of the French Maurist abbeys to teach their young monks sacred and modern languages. In exchange, some German monks studied in St. Maur. Even a Parisian study house for Benedictine students from Germany was planned—although never established. The 1683 journey of the erudite French Benedictine Jean Mabillon (1632–1707) through German, Austrian, and Swiss abbeys

---

2. Heribert Raab, "Das Fürstbistum Fulda (1752–1802/03)," *Archiv für Mittelrheinische Kirchengeschichte* 41 (1989): 173–201, at 184.

increased the monks' enthusiasm for the spirit of St. Maur, i.e., for the integration of church history into the theological curriculum and for the careful, critical analysis of historical documents. Even when the monks of St. Maur tried to convert their German brothers to Jansenism or at least Philo-Jansenism, the German abbeys (e.g., St. Emmeram in Regensburg) initially rebutted such attempts.[3] Yet, over time, the publications of the Maurists spread the ideas of Jansenist church reform in Germany. This philo-Jansenism included a clear preference for the church of the first centuries over medieval theology, criticism of privileges for the clergy connected with an appeal for the renewal of church structure in the light of the holy scriptures, criticism of ecclesiastical and papal infallibility, and support for a stronger influence of local churches on dogmatic decisions or episcopal appointments. Separated from their origin in a dogmatic heresy about predestination and rigorism, these ideas soon became central to eighteenth-century Catholic Enlightenment.

Fourth, besides letters and scholars, a book exchange system was established. The Benedictine monks in Southern Germany not only sent free copies of their publications to other abbeys—including ones abroad—in order to receive their scholarly works in return, but they also had invented a highly sophisticated inter-library loan system that allowed Benedictine scholars to have access to the rarest books on the continent.

Fifth, Benedictines all over Europe tried to organize themselves into scholarly societies.[4] While the founding of a Benedictine academy in the Empire was not successful until the 1790s, the monks contributed heavily to the other scholarly societies, e.g., the Olmütz Academy of the Unknown or the Bavarian Academy of Sciences.

Sixth, these innovative ways of communication and transfer of knowledge steadily decreased the fear of contamination with

---

3. Joseph Anton Endres, *Die Korrespondenz der Mauriner mit den Emmeramern und die Beziehungen der letzteren zu den wissenschaftlichen Bewegungen des 18. Jahrhunderts* (Stuttgart: 1899).

4. Ludwig Hammermayer, "Die Benediktiner und die Akademiebewegung im katholischen Deutschland (1720–1770)," *Studien und Mitteilungen des Benediktinerordens und seiner Zweige* 70 (1959): 45–146.

Protestant thought and increased the readiness of the Benedictines to engage with the most pressing contemporary problems in theology, philosophy, science, and church politics. Many monks saw no problem in corresponding with Protestants. Just a few examples: when the Italian Benedictine Cardinal Quirini travelled to Swabia in 1748, he met a Lutheran theologian in order to discuss the works of Christian Wolff. Around the same time, Oliver Legipont wanted to start a Benedictine Academy of Sciences, for which he recommended a Protestant, Johann Christoph Gottsched, as honorary member.

Seventh, the influence of the Enlightenment on Catholics increased around 1740–50, when the philosophy of Christian Wolff (1679–1754) became acceptable to Catholic scholars, since it promised to be a positive improvement of philosophical theology and an apologetic weapon in the fight against free-thinking.[5] In his books, Wolff gave a rebuttal to skepticism and Spinozism, as well as an integration of all sciences to the end of an encyclopedia of knowledge. He principally acknowledged the rights of theology in his system, which was based upon rigorous application of the "mathematical method," and was intended to be understood as modern scholasticism.[6] However, for the Benedictines, Mabillon was not far off from Wolff, since the latter regarded the *cognitio historica* as foundation of philosophical knowledge and the application of historical scholarship—very much like Bossuet—as an important tool for teaching the virtues.[7] This might explain, to a certain extent, why Wolff's "mathematical method" gained ground, particularly in those Benedictine abbeys of Germany that had been influenced by Maurist historical-critical scholarship.[8]

5. Bruno Bianco, "Wolffianismus und katholische Aufklärung. Storchenaus' Lehre vom Menschen," in *Katholische Aufklärung—Aufklärung im katholischen Deutschland*, ed. by Harm Klueting (Hamburg: Meiner, 1991), 67–103. Wolff concedes that he is more influenced by Thomas Aquinas than by Leibniz—a fact mostly overlooked (Wolff, *Gesammelte Werke II. Abt.*, 9: xviii, 34).

6. Sonia Carboncini, *Transzendentale Wahrheit und Traum. Christian Wolffs Antwort auf die Herausforderung durch den Cartesianischen Zweifel* (Stuttgart–Bad Cannstatt: Frommann-Holzboog, 1991), passim. Jonathan Israel, *Radical Enlightenment: Philosophy and the Making of Modernity 1650–1750* (Oxford: Oxford University Press, 2001), 541–62; Gomez Tutor, *Die wissenschaftliche Methode bei Christian Wolff* (Stuttgart–Bad Canstatt: Frommann-Holzboog, 2005); cf. my review of the latter in *Theologie und Philosophie*, 81 (2006): 105–7.

7. Christian Wolff, *Discursus Praeliminaris* , ed. Günter Gawlick (Hildesheim: Olms, 1996), §11; Cf. Christian Wolff, *Vernünftige Gedanken Von Den Kräfften Des Menschlichen Verstandes (Deutsche Logik).* Reprint of the 1754, ed. By Hans Werner Arndt (Hildesheim: Olms, 1965), c. 10, §6, 220–21.

A Benedictine Wolffianism evolved, which was followed by a broad and positive reception of Immanuel Kant (1724–1804)[9] and Johann G. Fichte (1762–1814) until the nationwide dissolution of the monasteries in 1802-03 put an end to the experiment of Monastic Enlightenment, in which the Swabian Benedictine Abbey of the Holy Cross in Donauwörth, near Augsburg, had played a crucial part.

Life and Work of Beda Mayr OSB

Beda Mayr was born on January 17, 1742, in Taiting, close to the village Dasing (diocese of Augsburg) to an upper-middle-class family of farmers and was given the name Felix Nolanus.[10] After attending the abbey school at Scheyern and the high school in Augsburg, he studied philosophy in Munich for two years, and then mathematics in Freiburg, Breisgau. In 1761, he was received into the Abbey of the Holy Cross in Donauwörth, where he professed his solemn vows on September 29, 1762, and received the name "Beda." After three years of studying theology at the common Benedictine college in Benediktbeuern, he was ordained a priest on January 6, 1766. Just a year later, Mayr was appointed to serve as professor of philosophy and theology within the abbey—a duty which he fulfilled until 1785. Occasionally, he also taught natural sciences and mathematics, and even published in these fields.[11] However, it was his 57 other publications that made Beda Mayr a famous name within German theology. The Catholic universities of Ingolstadt, Dillingen, and Salzburg offered him professorships, all of which he declined.[12]

8. Cf. Ulrich L. Lehner, *Enlightened Monks.*

9. Ulrich L. Lehner, "Theologia Kantiana ac Benedictina?," in *Kant und der Katholizismus*, ed. Norbert Fischer (Freiburg: Herder, 2005), 234–61.

10. Gerhard J. Rauwolf, "P. Beda Mayr OSB (1742–1794): Versuch einer ökumenischen Annäherung," *Jahrbuch des Vereins für Augsburger Bistumsgeschichte* 33 (1999): 317–53.

11. Beda Mayr, "Brief über den neulich gesehenen Kometen," *Baierische Sammlungen und Auszüge* 17 (1766), 546–566; Beda Mayr, *De Copernicano mundi systemate dissertatio* (Dillingen: 1768). Gabriele Deibler, *Das Kloster Heilig Kreuz in Donauwörth von der Gegenreformation bis zur Säkularisation* (Weißenhorn: Konrad, 1989), 101–3. In der Fürstlich Wallersteinschen Bibliothek a manuscript exists of some lectures of Beda Mayr, written by Bronner "R. P. Bedae Mayr . . . Loci Theologici" (cf. Joseph Hörmann, "P. Beda Mayr von Donauwörth. Ein Ireniker der Aufklärungszeit," *Festgabe Alois Knöpfler zur Vollendung des 70. Lebensjahres*, ed. by Heinrich Gietl and Georg Pfeilschifter (Freiburg: Herder, 1917), 188–209, at 189).

12. Deibler, *Das Kloster Heilig Kreuz*, 96.

From 1772 until 1776, Mayr worked as a pastor in the village of Mündling, where he made contact with the Protestant superintendent Wasser and other Protestants.[13] He hoped for a reunion of the great Christian denominations and to solve the problem of its alleged biggest stumbling block—the papacy and ecclesiastical infallibility. During these years, Mayr also became acquainted with popular Enlightenment publications, which prompted him to publish a plea for the use of the vernacular in the Roman liturgy in 1777. In 1776–77, he became prior of his monastery.[14]

A year later, however, Beda was at the center of an enormous scandal when a personal letter to his friend, the school reformer and ex-Benedictine (Abbey of Tegernsee) Heinrich Braun (1732–92), was published without his knowledge or consent under the title *First Step towards the Future Reunification of the Catholic and Protestant Churches* (1778).[15] It was put on the *Index of Forbidden Books* on July 31, 1783. The uproar was so great that a number of theologians started to conspire against Mayr. Even some of his fellow monks denounced him as a "Lutheran heretic."[16] As a result, an official episcopal visit to the monastery of Donauwörth took place.[17] Its board members asked Mayr to give a written explanation of his letter. This explanation was officially approved, but never published because the abbey did not want to contribute to the ongoing theological controversy over one of its members.[18]

Even though Beda was acquitted, in 1779, the episcopal chancery

13. Rauwolf, "P. Beda Mayr," 322; Hörmann, "P. Beda Mayr," 190.
14. Beda Mayr, *Prüfung der bejahenden Gründe, welche die Gottesgelehrte anführen, über die Frage, soll man sich in der abendländischen Kirche bey dem Gottesdienst der lateinischen Sprache bedienen* (Frankfurt und Leipzig: 1777). Cf. Beda Mayr, *Vertheidigung der natürlichen, christlichen, und katholischen Religion nach den Bedürfnissen unsrer Zeiten* (Augsburg: 1789ff), 3:321; ibid., 424. Cf. also Manfred Probst, *Gottesdienst in Geist und Wahrheit. Die liturgischen Ansichten und Bestrebungen Johann Michael Sailers (1751–1832)* (Regensburg: Pustet, 1976).
15. Original title: *Der erste Schritt zur künftigen Vereinigung der katholischen und der evangelischen Kirche, gewaget von—Fast wird man es nicht glauben, gewaget von einem Mönche: P. F. K. in W. 1778.* Hörmann, "P. Beda Mayr," 200. Cf. Wilhelm Haefs, *Aufklärung in Bayern. Leben, Werk und Wirkung Lorenz von Westenrieders* (Neuried: Ars Una, 1998), 107–8.
16. Beda Mayr, *Apologie seiner Vertheidigung der katholischen Religion; eine Beylage zu seiner Vertheidigung der natürlichen, christlichen und katholischen Religion* (Augsburg: 1790), 168.
17. Hörmann, "P. Beda Mayr," 204.
18. Mayr, *Apologie*, 130–131. Hörmann, "P. Beda Mayr," 207.

of Augsburg pressed for Mayr's dismissal as professor of the monastic college.[19] The only person to disapprove of this step and to defend Mayr was Abbot Gallus Hammerl (1776–93),[20] under whose patronage the Abbey of the Holy Cross had become a center of enlightened thought and liberal arts. He was already used to encountering resentment to Enlightenment ideals in his own monastery[21] and in the diocese of Augsburg.[22] Mayr could continue to work, but he was required to send his lecture notes and theses to the abbot and the episcopal chancery for approval.[23] The censors were never able to find anything "revolutionary" in these writings, since the basis of his lectures were *auctores probati*. Mayr's new ideas were reserved for the academic circles outside the monastery.[24] He never taught his theology students the new philosophy, because, in his view, the Enlightenment seduced young monks all too easily to adopt a libertine lifestyle, which was essentially hostile to the monastic one.[25] If a monk were to find enlightenment on his own, then Mayr regarded this as a blessing, although he did not encourage him to pursue it. This was because Beda Mayr knew very well the dynamics of living in a community, and the clash of new and old ways of thinking could easily destroy a monastery. "Either all have to think—on the same level—in an enlightened manner, which is hard to hope for, or nobody."[26] Supporting a monk's ideas about the Enlightenment could also easily make him proud, so he would look down on his brothers and protest against monastic obedience.[27] Finally, he might regard his vows as null and void, but because of the state laws, he would be forced to stay for the rest of his life "unhappily" wed to his community.[28] This considerate kind

19. Hörmann, "P. Beda Mayr," 193.
20. Arnold Schromm, "Wissenschaft und Aufklärung im Benediktinerstift Heilig-Kreuz Donauwörth," in *Zeitschrift für Bayerische Landesgeschichte* 54 (1991), 287–98, at: 288.
21. Mayr, *Apologie,* 167.
22. Hörmann, "P. Beda Mayr", 191. The visitation minutes were destroyed in World War II. Therefore, I quote Hörman, who was able to work with the originals long before the war.
23. Hörmann, "P. Beda Mayr," 208.
24. Hörmann, "P. Beda Mayr," 192; Mayr, *Apologie*, 4.
25. Mayr, *Apologie,* 163.
26. Ibid.
27. Mayr defends the monastic lifestyle, cf. Mayr, *Vertheidigung*, 2/1:189–90; 2/2:131. Nevertheless, he does not regard monastic rules as infallible, cf. Mayr, *Vertheidigung*, 3:321–24.
28. Mayr, *Apologie,* 164.

of theologizing, which was not in the least directed against divine revelation, the sacraments, or the church, disappointed radical Enlighteners, who thought that Mayr would stand by their side.

Like Benedict Stattler SJ (1728-97),[29] Beda Mayr attempted to implement Enlightenment thought in his theology in order to reform Catholicism from within and to free it from the "burdens" of scholasticism.[30] Stattler, professor of systematic theology in Ingolstadt, was certainly the most prominent Catholic theologian of the German-speaking lands. His multi-volume Wolffian philosophy was initially praised as a renewal of the Catholic university curriculum, but when he applied Wolff's principles to theology, he increasingly caused unease among theologians, who feared that these ideas would result in semirationalism. The rise of Kant, his main opponent, brought an end to his reception in the academy; and Stattler's influence in the Church became limited when his greatest theological work was censored because of the weak position he assigned to the pope. However, unlike Stattler, Mayr built his own theological system without the help of Wolffianism. Mayr never questioned Christ's role as the only Savior or the legitimacy and authority of the Catholic Church[31] since he was convinced that Christianity was the source of all true Enlightenment and that only the neglect and abuse of doctrines had led to the eclipse of reason.[32] Furthermore, he was confident that, in the face of the massive critique of religion in the eighteenth century, the doctrines of (ecclesiastical and papal) infallibility and tradition needed to be redefined with the newest means of logic and Enlightenment insights into morality and praxis, lest they wither away altogether.[33]

One of Mayr's major theological writings was a trilogy called *Defense of Natural, Christian and Catholic Religion*[34] (1787–89), written to address in detail the work of late Enlightenment thinkers (especially Lessing)

29. For a good overview, see Ulrich L. Lehner, "Benedict Stattler—Renewal of Catholic Theology with the Help of Wolffian Metaphysics."
30. Mayr, *Vertheidigung*, 3:302–3.
31. Mayr, *Apologie*, 137.
32. Mayr, *Vertheidigung*, 2/2:421.
33. Mayr, *Vertheidigung*, 3:v–vi.
34. *Vertheidigung der natürlichen, christlichen, und katholischen Religion* (Augsburg: 1787–89).

and to propagate the moderate Catholic Enlightenment ideals of Ludovico Muratori and others. These volumes were considered a new *summa* of Catholic theology. Not only a brilliant academic, Mayr also supported reform: he thought that the powers of the papacy regarding jurisdiction and the declaration of magisterial teaching should be more restricted than did most of his contemporaries, but more than anything else, he became famous as a champion of ecumenism. Unfortunately, the late publication of this important work resulted in his never achieving the fame of his work's contemporaries: the second and third volume were printed when the French Revolution began. Soon afterwards, the Napoleonic wars put an end to the German ecclesiological system and contributed indirectly to Ultramontanism, to which Mayr's view of the papacy was unacceptable. Moreover, Mayr's most important works, his *The First Step Towards Future Reunion Between the Catholic and Protestant Church* (1778)[35] as well as his trilogy, had been placed on the *Roman Index of Forbidden Books*.

Despite the censoring or because of it, the *Defense of Natural, Christian and Catholic Religion* became a Catholic bestseller. However, a number of theologians felt uncomfortable about Mayr's sympathies toward certain Enlightenment ideas, e.g., criticism, and charged him with Enlightenment proselytizing, which he vehemently denied. Yet, critics, especially the intransigent ex-Jesuit Johann Evangelist Hochbichler (1740–1817), claimed he was an apostate. Responding to these accusations cost him considerable time and energy. Exhausted, he died at the abbey in Donauwörth on April 28, 1794.[36]

The Ecumenical Desire

The growth of radical Deism in Germany in the second half of the eighteenth century forced Protestant and Catholic scholars sincerely to consider reuniting their forces. Already, Johann Friedrich Wilhelm Jerusalem (1709–89), in his speech *On the Reunification of the Churches* (*Von der Kirchenvereinigung*), which was published without his consent

---

35. See n. 15 above.
36. Rauwolf, "P. Beda Mayr," 320.

in 1772, spoke of the necessity of ecumenical task forces. At the same time, however, he described Catholic traditions (e.g., the hierarchical structure of the Catholic Church) as illegitimate "additions."[37] The Catholic thinker Jakob Heinrich von Gerstenberg (1712–76) made this view more precise in his *Universal Thoughts about the Separation of Christians* (*Allgemeine Gedanken von der Trennung der Christen*, 1773). He stated that ecclesiastical infallibility is the centerpiece of Catholic theology and the biggest stumbling block for reunification.[38] Mayr read Jerusalem's *Reflections on the Truth of the Christian Religion* (*Betrachtungen über die Wahrheit der christlichen Religion*) and his short piece on the reunification,[39] and it is very likely that he also knew Gerstenberg since his book was available in the monastery library.[40] Mayr was, like Gerstenberg, inspired by the thought of a reunion of the Christian churches, even if he personally had doubts that such a step would be taken within his lifetime.[41] His twenty-two-page publication, *The First Step towards the Future Reunification of the Catholic and Protestant Churches* (1778),[42] which was put on the *Index* in 1783, expresses a decisive farewell to "classical," but fruitless polemic theology. It is an honest piece of theological reflection, mostly because it was never intended for publication, but was a private letter to a friend.

The pamphlet starts with an analysis of the current state of ecumenical dialogue. Mayr describes how both sides—Protestant and Catholic—cling to sectarian monologues instead of talking with each other. Mayr wanted to soften the petrified denominational borders, first of all by acknowledging Protestant erudition, goodwill, and good conscience, all of which were great achievements. Only a few decades before, the Catholic theologian Nikolaus Weislinger,[43] himself a

---

37. Christopher Spehr, *Aufklärung und Ökumene.* Reunionsversuche zwischen Katholiken und Protestanten im deutschsprachigen Raum des späteren 18. Jahrhunderts (Tübingen: Mohr Siebeck, 2005), 66. Mayr's knowledge Jerusalem's work is proved by two quotations, cf. Mayr, *Vertheidigung, Anhang*, 3:392 n; 415.
38. Spehr, *Aufklärung und Ökumene*, 97.
39. Ibid., 116.
40. Ibid.
41. Mayr, *Vertheidigung*, 3:xvii.
42. See n. 15 above.
43. Nikolaus Weislinger, *Vogel Friß oder Stirb*, 2nd ed. (Oberammergau: 1751). Mayr alludes to Weislinger's acrimonious diction cf. *Vertheidigung, Anhang*, 3:483. Cf. Gerhard Kaller "Weislinger,

convert, had severely damaged interdenominational rapport with his ferocious attacks on Luther. With this statement, Mayr tried to bring both camps of theology together to join in rigorous academic negotiations concerning a possible reunion.[44] An *Academy of Reunification* consisting of Protestant and Catholic theologians would be, in Mayr's mind, the institutional framework for this kind of challenge.[45] The theologians of the academy would review all different doctrines, and then work on possible solutions. The final drafts of the solutions were then supposed to be handed over to the church (most likely Catholic) for a decision.[46] As a formal secretary of the academy, the professor for reunification would have to guide the committed theologians to be tolerant, irenic, highly argumentative, and constructive.[47] In the revised edition of the *First Step,* published in the third volume of the *Defense* (1789), Mayr himself seems to play the role of the reunification professor when he collects all different doctrines and gives suggestions for ecumenical agreements.[48] It was not extraordinary for a Benedictine to put so much trust in a society of academics. Some decades earlier, it was the Benedictine Order which helped to start the distinguished *Bavarian Academy of Sciences* (1759). Simply put, the monks trusted in the corporate power of reason.[49]

Like the Protestant thinkers who inspired him, Mayr considered ecclesiastical and papal infallibility to be the central problem of ecumenism. Therefore, he focused on a critical examination of the concept of infallibility in regard to its legitimacy and extension. He hoped that a compromise on this subject could bring about—or at least start—the reunification process.[50] Other *divisive* doctrines, e.g.,

Nikolaus", in *Biographisch-Bibliographisches Kirchenlexikon* (Nordhausen: Bautz, 1998), 13:639–40. Weislinger (1691-1755) belonged to the most influential Catholic polemical thinkers of the eighteenth century, not because of his theological insights, but because of his offensive writing style.
44. Mayr, *Der erste Schritt,* 14.
45. Mayr, *Der erste Schritt,* 12–14.
46. Spehr, *Aufklärung und Ökumene,* 121.
47. Mayr, *Der erste Schritt,* 18–19.
48. Spehr, *Aufklärung und Ökumene,* 134.
49. Ludwig Hammermayer, *Geschichte der Bayerischen Akademie der Wissenschaften 1759-1807,* 2 vols (München: C. H. Beck, 1983), passim; Ludwig Hammermayer, "Die Benediktiner und die Akademiebewegung im katholischen Deutschland (1720-1770)," *Studien und Mitteilungen des Benediktinerordens und seiner Zweige* 70 (1959): 45–146.

sacramental confession, confirmation, purgatory, and so on, were reduced by Mayr to the level of school disputes, which must not impede the reunification.[51]

Reception and Resistance

Benedikt Werkmeister (1745-1823), the radical ex-monk, considered Mayr's *First Step* one of the groundbreaking events of Enlightenment Catholicism[52] because it was considered by contemporaries the first public commitment of a Catholic professor to ecumenism. The attempts at reunification by the Benedictines of Fulda (c. 1776-83), initiated by the reformed theologian Johann Rudolf Anton Piderit (1720-91), were influenced by Mayr's work, even if their leaders, Peter Böhm OSB (1747-1822) and Karl von Piesport OSB (1716-1800), a philo-Jansenist,[53] criticized the *First Step* severely.[54] Böhm considered Mayr's pamphlet—like the Cathedral preacher of Augsburg, Aloys Merz (1727-92)[55]—as being outside the boundaries of Catholic theology. Since Böhm was still unaware of Mayr's authorship, he doubted the Catholicity of the writer: "In my opinion, this is a *Step* which cannot come from a Catholic; if he really is Catholic, this was his '*First Step*' towards becoming Protestant."[56] Despite this harsh critique, Mayr was asked to join the ecumenical circle around Piderit[57] and Böhm, but it is highly unlikely that he accepted the invitation. Prince-Abbot Martin II Gerbert OSB (1720-93) of St. Blasien also refused to participate in the ecumenical Fulda plan by pointing to the failure of the *First Step* and its

---

50. Mayr, *Der erste Schritt*, 11.
51. Ibid., 9–10.
52. Benedikt Werkmeister, *Thomas Freykirch: oder freymüthige Untersuchungen über die Unfehlbarkeit der katholischen Kirche* (Frankfurt and Leipzig [i.e., Göttingen]: 1792), xv.
53. Piesport, who was also quite critical of papal infallibility, had good contacts with the Jansenist Maurist monks in France. Cf. Spehr, *Aufklärung und Ökumene*, 155n40.
54. Cf. Spehr, *Aufklärung und Ökumene*, 127–245.
55. Aloys Merz, Frag, *Ob die der Schritt, den ein namenloser Projectant, aus Hoffnung die Protestanten mit den Katholiken zu vereinigen, gewagt hat, ein erlaubter und zu seinen Absichten dienlicher Schritt sey. In den heiligen Pfingstfeyertagen beantwortet* (Augsburg: 1778), 3. About his life, see Horst Fredmann, *Aloys Merz, Dom- und Kontroversprediger von Augsburg, als Opponent der Aufklärung* (Frankfurt et al.: P. Lang, 1997).
56. Letter of Peter Böhm to Johann Gertz (1744-1824); quoted in Spehr, *Aufklärung und Ökumene*, 161.
57. Piderit's main critique focused on Mayr's proposal to advertise a "reunification award" for the best submitted essay. Cf. Spehr, *Aufklärung und Ökumene*, 218; 240.

inappropriate critique of infallibility.[58] The Protestant Johann Salomo Semler (1757–91) criticized the Piderit-Böhm plan as well in his *Outspoken Letters* (*Freimütige Briefe*, 1783) because the reunification project sacrificed, in his opinion, the positive side of personal religious subjectivism for the sake of institutional ecclesiastical belief and unity.[59]

Some critics of the *First Step* even spread the rumor of Beda Mayr's apostasy, a rumor which was unfortunately only too plausible, as he would not have been the first Benedictine to have broken with the Church.[60] Alois Merz said in 1778 that even the slightest disagreement with parts of the doctrine on infallibility would lead to doubts about the incorruptibility of the Church and its doctrines, or at least, indifferentism about them.[61] Matthias von Schönberg (1734–92) thought almost the same thing[62] because he posited that ecclesiastical infallibility ensured the truth of the Christian faith. Furthermore, leading Protestant scholars, e.g., Justus Möser (1720–94),[63] also commented on Mayr's pamphlet in his *Letter to P. J. K. in W. about the First Step toward A Future Reunification of the Evangelical and Catholic Church* (*Schreiben an den P. J. K. in W. den ersten Schritt zur künftigen Vereinigung der Evangelischen und Catholischen Kirche betreffend*, 1780), with the main difference being that Möser regarded the primacy of the Pope as a political, rather than a theological, stumbling block.[64]

Germany's leading Catholic theologian, the ex-Jesuit Benedikt Stattler, a moderate Wolffian,[65] praised Mayr's work in the appendix to his treatise on the sacraments in the *Theologia Christiana Theoretica*,

---

58. Spehr, *Aufklärung und Ökumene,* 194.
59. Ibid., 360.
60. Cf. Gregor Rothfischer from St. Emmeram in Regensburg. Cf. Lehner, *Enlightened Monks*, passim. Hochbichler compared Mayr *expressis verbis* with Rothfischer, cf. Mayr, *Apologie*, 149–51.
61. Merz, *Frag*, 7–8; 32.
62. Matthias von Schönberg, *Die Wahrheitsgründe des katholischen Hauptgrundsatzes für die Unfehlbarkeit der Kirche wider den sogenannten ersten Schritt* (Munich: 1779).
63. Cf. Franz von Wegele, "Möser, Justus," in *Allgemeine Deutsche Biographie*, 22:385–90. Cf. Karl Welker, *Rechtsgeschichte als Rechtspolitik. Justus Möser als Jurist und Staatsmann*, 2 vols. (Osnabrück: Verein für die Geschichte und Landeskunde von Osnabrück, 1996).
64. Cf. Mayr, *Vertheidigung*, Anhang, 3:428.
65. The Enlightenment tendencies of the Jesuits in Southern Germany before the dissolution in 1773 are described by Winfried Müller, "Aufklärungstendenzen bei den süddeutschen Jesuiten zur Zeit der Ordensaufhebung," *Zeitschrift für Bayerische Landesgeschichte* 54 (1991): 203–17.

even if it went too far for his taste. Instead, he put forward his own thoughts about a possible reunification. But unlike Mayr, Stattler did not see the magisterial definitions of doctrines as a "burden" for ecumenical discussions, and he regarded the idea of the common, most fundamental belief that Protestants and Catholics could draw directly from the Bible[66] (in the spirit of John Locke) as a bad compromise. Stattler gave a detailed critique of the *First Step* and the ecumenical thoughts of the *Defense* in his pro-reunification book, *Plan for the alone Possible Reunification in Faith of Protestants with the Catholic Church and the Limits of this Possibility* (*Plan zu der alleinmöglichen Vereinigung im Glauben der Protestanten mit der katholischen Kirche und den Grenzen der Möglichkeiten,* 1790).[67] However, recent scholarship has overlooked the fact that Mayr was indebted to the achievements of Stattler. As an analysis of the third volume of Mayr's *Defense* demonstrates, he was especially influenced by Stattler's grand new system of Catholic theology.[68] Unlike some other of Stattler's concepts, however, Mayr considered Stattler's plan for a reunion with Protestants to be futile, because it did not make any concessions regarding the stumbling block of ecumenism—infallibility.[69]

Mayr's harshest and most malevolent critic, though, was the ex-Jesuit, Johann Evangelist Hochbichler from Augsburg. He rightly recognized tradition and infallibility as the focal points of Mayr's third volume of the *Defense*, but he himself lacked a coherent concept of tradition. Also, his polemical tone is a sad example of the viciousness that Beda Mayr had to endure. Hochbichler even alluded to Mayr's hair color and his limp in order to compare him with Judas Iscariot.[70] Such personal attacks, which also declared Mayr a godless atheist or

---

66. Benedict Stattler, "Anacaephaleosis ad DD. Protestantes in Germania et Proposition Conditionum sub quibus solis Unio Religionis Exoptata possibilis est," in Benedict Stattler, *Theologia Christiana Theoretica, De Sacramentis* (Eichstätt: 1780), 6:ii–iv.
67. Benedikt Stattler, *Plan zu der alleinmöglichen Vereinigung im Glauben der Protestanten mit der katholischen Kirche und den Grenzen der Möglichkeiten* (Munich: 1791), 159–279.
68. Stattler is quoted numerous times with praise or at least appreciation, especially his *Demonstratio Catholica* and his *De Locis Theologicis,* both of which later ended up on the *Index of Forbidden Books.*
69. Mayr, *Vertheidigung,* 3:284, cf. Stattler, "Anacaephaleosis".
70. Johann Hochbichler, *P. Beda Mayrs Vertheidigung der katholischen Religion theologisch untersuchet,* (Augsburg: 1790), 11; 25. Cf. Rauwolf, "P. Beda Mayr," 343. Mayr, *Apologie,* 133.

heretic without ever addressing his ideas, were especially harmful to the monk's soul.[71] Other critics were appalled by Mayr's statement that his work was deliberately on the cutting-edge of Catholic doctrine.[72]

Content of the *Defense of Catholic Religion*

The third volume of Mayr's *Defense* is not a mere apology of the Catholic faith. It is an ecumenical attempt to find a common denominator with Protestant theology in terms of divisive doctrines. For this reason, Mayr regards it as necessary to alter even traditional school opinions, i.e., non-defined doctrines.[73] He begins by making a number of suggestions and awaits a thorough examination by the Magisterium and his fellow academic theologians. However, he is eager to emphasize that such "suggestions" are not his own "standpoints," but merely points worthy of further consideration:

> I will not be afraid . . . to present my thoughts to the academic public. Should they be misjudged by some and disapproved by others without thorough examination because they are new, or because they appear to be new, there are others among Catholics and Protestants who make it their obligation to examine everything and to keep the good things. They judge an opinion not according to ordinary prejudices . . . like: No theologian ever went so far before. That is new, therefore condemnable. That is old, therefore good. Did he receive heavenly inspiration, so that he now claims to have insight into what nobody saw before? The old theologians were no fools, and they did not know of such things, etc. I hope that I find one or two theologians who are not against me before they have actually examined what I wrote. I even hope to find some Protestants who will say of me That man deserves to be heard. What he says is not completely worthless.[74]

The new idea that Mayr alludes to is his concept of limited infallibility, which he had already proposed in the *First Step*. He does not give up

71. Mayr, *Antwort*, 34. Cf. the works of the Benedictine Meinrad Widmann (Abbey of Elchingen), *Freymüthige Anmerkungen zu der Frage: Wer sind die Aufklärer?*, 4 vols. (Augsburg: 1789–90); Meinrad Widmann, *Wer sind die Aufklärer? beantwortet nach dem ganzen Alphabet*, 2 vols. (Augsburg: 1786; 2nd ed. 1787).
72. Mayr, *Antwort*, 14–16.
73. Mayr, *Vertheidigung*, 3:iv–vii.
74. Ibid., 3:vi–vii; xx.

infallibility as a whole, but he carefully attempts to find its essential and original core.[75] Then, he goes on to show how the Catholic Church can enable a reunion with the Protestant churches by compromising on this doctrine, without giving up its *depositum fidei*. In this respect, Mayr regarded the distinction between *immediate* or *direct*, and *mediate* or *indirect revelation* as especially helpful (see below).[76]

An essential component of his proposal is an *ecumenical methodology*. To achieve an interdenominational agreement, the Catholic side cannot follow the majority of its scholastic authorities in a discussion about a doctrinal difference *if* this majority opinion would be an impediment to a reunion. Rather, it must follow the minority opinion as long as that would not compromise magisterially defined doctrines, and as long as it would be truly beneficial for ecumenism.[77] This shows Mayr's staunchly held belief that the scandal of a separated Christianity must be overcome. However, this revolutionary principle of ecumenical theology not only demonstrates the self-confidence of this Benedictine, but it also indicates a considerable disagreement on the merit of "theological school opinions" in the late eighteenth century,[78] and suggests that Mayr was ready to stretch Catholic doctrine to its very limits.[79] He was prepared to leave the majority of Catholic theologians behind for the sake of ecumenism.

The Limits of Infallibility

Mayr's discussion about the concept of infallibility has its background in early modern Catholic ecclesiology, which was written, in reaction to the Reformation, almost entirely in the form of an apologetic treatise. It was not the doctrine of the church as God's people that was the focal point in scholasticism, but the Church's hierarchical structure and its Magisterium. Therefore, Cardinal Yves Congar (1904–95)

75. Ibid., 3:xviii–xix.
76. Ibid., 3:xv.
77. Ibid., 3:xi.
78. Mayr, *Vertheidigung*, 3:xiv: "Schulmeynungen dürfen doch das Vereinigungsgeschäft nicht aufhalten."
79. Ibid., 3:xi.

described the classical treatise on ecclesiology as "hierarchology," and Ulrich Valeske defined it more subtly as "apologetic ecclesiology."[80] Infallibility, in this instance, meant the *infallibilitas in docendo*, which, according to such authorities as Gazzaniga, Engelbert Klüpfel OESA (1733–1811),[81] Simpert Schwarzhueber OSB (1727–95), Stephan Wiest OCist (1748–97), Aloys Merz, and Johann Evangelist Hochbichler, is extended to the universal episcopacy alone.[82] In their view, only the worldwide episcopacy is the highest and infallible judge in questions of faith and morals. With this definition, the above German theologians distanced themselves polemically from Protestantism, rationalism, any kind of private revelation theory, and an exaggerated Ultramontanism. The theories about ecclesiastical and papal infallibility were not yet dogmatically defined, and, thus, were disputable school opinions.

Therefore, the sixth part of the *Defense*, in which the Benedictine argues for a new understanding of infallibility, is the most theologically challenging part of his book. For, if the aim of infallibility is the certainty of salvation for the faithful, infallibility cannot extend beyond the *necessary* elements of faith and morals.[83] Mayr thought it was a crucial mistake of polemical theology to remain silent about the limits of infallibility. With his new ecumenical theology, he wanted to encourage the Protestants to "accept all doctrines of the Catholic Church as revealed by God."[84] This new and limited concept of infallibility had, for Mayr, the potential to remove the last big stumbling block for a denominational reunion:

> I call *infallibility* the privilege which Christ gave to his church: to teach everything without the danger of falling into error and to teach what is necessary or useful for the faithful to achieve eternal blessedness. This also includes that she cannot teach anything that leads the faithful away from the order of salvation.[85]

80. Bei Franz Xaver Bantle, *Unfehlbarkeit der Kirche in Aufklärung und Romantik: eine dogmengeschichtliche Untersuchung für die Zeit der Wende vom 18. zum 19. Jahrhundert* (Freiburg: Herder, 1976), 41.
81. In Klüpfel's view, not only the bishops, but also the priest participates in ecclesiastical infallibility. Cf. Engelbert Klüpfel, *Institutiones theologicae dogmaticae in usum auditorum,* 2 vols., (Vienna: 1789), at 1:150–51.
82. Bantle, *Unfehlbarkeit der Kirche,* 45.
83. Cf. Mayr, *Apologie,* 210–11.
84. Mayr, *Vertheidigung,* 3:264.

He viewed the Church as being not only fallible in the realm of the dogmatic facts (*facta dogmatica*), but possibly also in the realm of truths about the faith. Certainly, such an error could not be material, but only formal, e.g., if the Church were to declare an unrevealed doctrine to be revealed (such as purgatory). Such a virtual and formal error would not affect the holy order of salvation, even if the doctrine in question was useful for the advancement of saving one's soul.[86] If somebody did not believe a doctrine that the Church teaches to be revealed, he certainly would not lose salvation, but only lose a good and helpful means that could have helped him achieve his final end. Therefore, even an "erroneous" teaching, that is, a wrong proposition about the revelation status of a doctrine, would not be completely wrong, because the Church can never err in teaching something helpful for achieving eternal bliss. Interestingly, Mayr saves the infallibility of the Church by pointing to the primacy of ethics and praxis:

> The doctrine, which we presuppose, is good and leads us into the order of salvation. In this the Church does not err, since she recommends a certain doctrine as useful. But the faithful do not necessarily need to know whether the doctrine is of *direct divine origin*, because the doctrine aims at the improvement of the heart, and such a proposition does not have any necessary influence on doctrines of faith or morals. Therefore such declarations cannot be part of ecclesiastical infallibility. Consequently, the Church does not lose trustworthiness if she errs in things that are beyond the sphere of infallibility.[87]

In Mayr's view, such a limited account of infallibility would be appealing to Protestants.[88] Again, he denied the claim, made by some of his fellow Catholics, that his project would undermine the authority of the Church by explaining once more, and in detail, his differentiated concept of revelation: even if a doctrine is not directly revealed through Jesus Christ and the apostles, there remains the possibility, which becomes an obligation in the light of the Church's authority, to regard such a doctrine as indirectly revealed. However, such a mediate

---

85. Ibid., 3:269.
86. Mayr, *Vertheidigung,* 3:270–71.
87. Ibid., 3:27.
88. Ibid., 3:277–79.

revelation has to possess a biblical foundation, even if its main point is derived from reason. With such a distinction, Mayr distanced himself from most of his contemporaries (e.g., Eusebius Amort),[89] who regarded mediate revelation as a necessary deduction or consequence from directly revealed truths.[90] Nevertheless, doctrines of such a mediate character must not be mistaken for "school opinions" (*sententiae*), which never have the weight of the whole Church's witness on their side. When, for example, the Council of Trent declared the Seven Sacraments to be directly instituted by Christ,[91] whereas most Protestants accept only Baptism and Eucharist as sacraments because of their biblical foundation, Catholicism could regard the latter two as directly revealed, and the other five as indirectly revealed through Christ in the church (*viam ecclesiam*):

> Nobody can really deny the Church the power of instituting new sacraments, because of the ordinary promise of Christ to bind his grace to external signs, which the Church finds necessary to remind the faithful of important truths and to strengthen their inner holiness.[92]

Even a hint from Christ (and Mayr viewed it as much more than that) would have given the Church enough authority to institute the other sacraments.[93] It is also worth noting that Mayr tried to reinforce his "project" by using the decrees of Trent, which, in his eyes, left the direct or indirect revelation of the sacraments open for discussion—a bold and idiosyncratic way of reading Trent![94] Some of Mayr's authorities for the differentiation of the concept of revelation were well-known theologians; however, a detailed recent study could show that that there is an unbridgeable gap between these theologians and Mayr:[95]

---

89. Eusebius Amort, *Theologia eclectia, moralis et scholastica*, (Augsburg and Würzburg: 1752), 1 tract. 4, pars 2 de fide, disp. 1, q. 6, Notandum 5, 55.
90. Mayr, *Vertheidigung*, 3:280.
91. Council of Trent, 7th session (1547) DH 1600–1630, at Can. 1 (1601).
92. Mayr, *Anhang*, 3:368.
93. Ibid., 3:369.
94. Mayr, *Vertheidigung*, 3:282–83. Ibid., Mayr also shows that in his view the diaconate as well as the indissolubility of marriage are only "indirectly" revealed, cf., *Vertheidigung*, 3:365–71.
95. Mayr, *Anhang*, 3:371.

> What the theologians of the past and of more recent times understand by
> *mediate* or *indirect revelation* would fall in Mayr's system in the category
> *immediate* or *direct revelation*. Is it possible that Mayr did not realize this?
> In my opinion he realized it very well! It appears to me that Mayr wants to
> minimize or even hide the "new" and "outrageous" aspect of his project.[96]

In sum, Mayr opposed the totality of Catholic theologians with his
reading of Trent, but most importantly he opposed the self-
understanding of the Council inasmuch as he refused to understand
the defined doctrinal differences as part of the Christian revelation
(*de fide divina*). Furthermore, the question is justified as to whether
Mayr's concept of ecclesiastical fallibility would harm the reputation
of the Church, since it would mean that the Church had taught in
error for over 200 years that certain propositions were *dogmata fide
divina credenda*.[97] However, such criticism leaves out Mayr's main
point—namely, that the different, dividing doctrines are necessary to
achieve salvation.[98] Even if the reputation of the Church were
damaged, its doctrines and practices would not have to change, Mayr
insisted.[99]

If one does not take the theological concept of revelation into
account, Beda Mayr's theses seem insipid. In the context of a *classicist
canon of revelation*, though, which saw the Church only as witness, an
infallible definition of the Magisterium entails that this definition is
implied in the *depositum fidei*.[100]

The Dilemma of Historical Criticism

Despite the enormous influence of Protestant theology on Beda Mayr,
it would be an exaggeration to reduce his sensitivity for the historical
development of dogma solely to Protestant impact since the
Benedictine was, first and foremost, a champion of Enlightened
Catholicism.[101] As recent scholarship has shown, this line of thought

96. Bantle, *Unfehlbarkeit und Kirche*, 403.
97. Ibid., 405.
98. Mayr, *Apologie*, 190.
99. Ibid., 191; 235.
100. Bantle, *Unfehlbarkeit in der Kirche*, 84.
101. Cf. Franz-Josef Niemann, *Jesus als Glaubensgrund in der Fundamentaltheologie der Neuzeit* (Innsbruck:

was less influenced by non-Catholic sources than previously had been thought. Rather, it was the late implementation of the reform spirit of Trent, combined with Enlightenment ideas. One of the most direct influences on the development of the Catholic Enlightenment was the scholarship of the Benedictine congregation of St. Maur in France.[102] The monks there pioneered historical-critical erudition and initiated a new interest for serious historiography throughout Catholic Europe.[103] However, with the new interest in history, there also arose a new sensitivity for the historical growth of theological and monastic traditions.[104] That Beda Mayr was fully aware of the wide-ranging consequences which historical criticism had for theology is shown by his preoccupation with Gotthold Ephraim Lessing (1729–81).[105] Despite his sincere attempt to refute some of Lessing's ideas, the Benedictine did not hit the real point of Lessing's argument: whether absolute certainties (e.g., God's existence) can be built on hypothetical certainties (miracles, etc.), "by simply turning the problem around: in his work [Mayr's] the truths of reason guarantee the truths of history."[106] So, Beda's meritorious treatment of Lessing, possibly the first Catholic one, misunderstood the Wolfenbüttel librarian. Mayr's view of Lessing conforms to the overall view of the system of Mayr's theology that we have gained so far: although he accepted ideas from Protestant historical criticism, he could not work with them fruitfully because he was unable to free himself completely from the ahistorical concept of revelation in Catholic scholasticism:[107] At the bottom of Mayr's theology, the faith of Jesus and the apostles was identical with his own in the eighteenth century.[108] Thus, one can detect two

Tyrolia, 1983), 289. For an overview of the Catholic Enlightenment, see Ulrich L. Lehner, *The Catholic Enlightenment* (New York et al.: Oxford University Press, 2016).
102. On Maurism, see Lehner, *Enlightened Monks*, ch. 1.
103. Cf. Rene Prosper Tassin's (1697–1777) *Histoire litteraire de la Congregation de Saint–Maur* (1770), which was translated into German as *Gelehrtengeschichte der Congregation von St–Maur, Benedictiner Ordens* (Frankfurt and Leipzig: 1773–1774).
104. For a first orientation, see David Knowles, "The Maurists," in David Knowles, *Great Historical Enterpises* (London: Nelson, 1963), 33–62.
105. Niemann, *Jesus*, 275.
106. Ibid., 280.
107. Cf. Niemann, *Jesus*, 289; Bantle, *Unfehlbarkeit der Kirche*, 406–10.
108. Niemann, *Jesus*, 290. Similarily Ildefons Schwarz, "Rezension von Felix Blaus *Kritische Geschichte der kirchlichen Unfehlbarkeit* (1791)," *Fortgesetzte auserlesene Litteratur des katholischen Deutschland*, 1: 4th

contradictory principles in Mayr's thought: historical awareness and ahistorical scholasticism. This foreshadows the dilemma of Neo-Scholasticism in the nineteenth and twentieth centuries.

But what could have been the reason for Mayr's dilemma? Beda Mayr read the historical achievements of Protestant scholarship through the lenses of Maurist erudition, which explains why he viewed the ideas of Semler, Walch, Less, and Döderlein critically. His colleagues Matthias Dannenmayer (1744–1805) and Kaspar Ruef (1748–1825) at the University of Freiburg, Breisgau, did the same regarding the doctrine of infallibility. They, too, emphasized the primacy of historical scholarship, which alone could bring about the identity of ecclesiastical dogma and Christian revelation, even if this meant that the tradition of the Church has to be "corrected."[109] Felix Anton Blau's (1754-98)[110] De regula fidei catholicae, also stuck to historical-critical thinking and asked for a clear proof of infallibility in the scriptures or the oldest traditions.[111] The absence of such a "clear" proof even led him to deny this doctrine completely. The Benedictine (until 1791) Benedikt Maria Werkmeister (1745–1823) did the same in his infamous book, Thomas Freykirch.[112] As distinct from Gazzaniga, Wiest and the authorities of Catholic school theology, Dannenmayer, Ruef, and Blau, did not identify the content of Catholic faith with the one the apostles held.[113] However, their historical-critical thinking, like Mayr's, stopped halfway through, since they merged the historical awareness of Maurist and Protestant historiography with the ahistorical concept of a revelation that does not develop over time. Mayr proved himself to be a captive of this line of thought; he realized that ahistorical apologetics were the theological means of the past; yet, at the same time, he could

---

extract (1792), 480–521. According to Bantle, *Unfehlbarkeit der Kirche*, 468–71 Engelbert Klüpfel as well as Simpert Schwarzhueber followed Schwarz's critique.

109. Bantle, *Unfehlbarkeit der Kirche*, 343.
110. Ibid., 418–72; Jörg Schweigard, *Felix Anton Blau: Frühdemokrat, Theologe, Menschenfreund* (Obernburg: Logo, 2007).
111. Felix Anton Blau, *De regula fidei catholicae* (Mainz: 1780), 10–18.
112. Benedikt Werkmeister, *Thomas Freykirch: oder freymüthige Untersuchungen über die Unfehlbarkeit der katholischen Kirche [. . .]*, (Frankfurt und Leipzig [pseud., i.e., Göttingen]: 1792). Cf. Bantle, *Unfehlbarkeit der Kirche*, 473–526.
113. Bantle, *Unfehlbarkeit der Kirche*, 363.

not find a way to reconcile historical-critical achievements with the Catholic creed.[114]

Mayr's most up-to-date idea was his differentiation between direct and indirect revelation since it led to an ecumenical concept of a hierarchy of truths that was "reanimated" in the Church during Vatican II.[115] During that council, Mayr's ideas were discussed—even if his name was not mentioned and even if it is doubtful that the council fathers knew of him—and through council fathers such as Archbishop Andrea Pangrazio (1909–2005), Mayr's concept received acceptability. Pangrazio differentiated between dogmatic truths which derive from God's final aim (i.e., redemption) and those derived from the means of the order of salvation (*Heilsmittel*). Only the first (e.g., the Incarnation, etc.) can claim to be necessary for salvation, not the latter (e.g., seven sacraments, etc.). Interestingly, Pangrazio put the different dividing doctrines, like Mayr, into the second category.[116] Taken together, recent Catholic theology in the twentieth and twenty-first centuries has much more in common with the work of Beda Mayr than he had with his contemporary critics.[117]

Enlightenment Ecclesiology?

Much more radical than his critique of the Curia, which owed its due share to Jansenist influences, is Mayr's ecclesiology. In his theological system, the church could no longer hold claim to the title mediator of salvation, except as a teacher whose dogmas are helpful, but *not* essential or necessary for achieving eternal beatitude. This reductionism is probably derived from radical Enlightenment theology, which had lost sight of the sacramental character of the church, and instead regarded it only as a moral teacher. Furthermore,

114. Ibid., 333.
115. Richard Boeckler, "Grenzen der Lehraussagen im römisch-katholischen Ökumenismus," *Kerygma und Dogma* 15 (1969): 340–53, at: 346 (342–45 references to B. Mayr) reference to the Vatican II decree on ecumenism, *Unitatis redintegratio*, c. 11, art. 1.
116. Cf. Boeckler, "Grenzen der Lehraussagen," 347.
117. Ulrich Valeske, *Hierarchia Veritatum—Theologiegeschichtliche Hintergründe und mögliche Konsequenzen eines Hinweises im Ökumenismusdekret des II. Vatikanischen Konzils zum zwischenkirchlichen Gespräch,* (Munich: Claudius, 1968).

Mayr claimed that the church had to remain absolutely silent about the revelation status of all doctrines.[118] Only then could the divided Christian brethren accept a doctrine as an "ecclesiastical teaching" and not as a "truth of faith." Whoever did not want to accept such doctrines as "ecclesiastical teachings" would not be committing heresy, but rather acts of disobedience. In the case of speculative doctrines (e.g., the transubstantiation of the Eucharist), such disobedience must not be made public, according to Mayr. However, in his *Apologie,* Mayr corrected this terminology, since it could allow for a Protestant to doubt the infallibility of the Church: "Since the church herself does not regard speculative teachings as revealed, it must be up to the Protestant to hold them as a necessary part of the faith or not, as long as he is not doubting the truth of the teaching itself."[119] This means that, in Mayr's reunited church, a Protestant could believe that transubstantiation is not a necessary part of the Christian faith as long as he did not doubt the doctrine as such.

We can see a twofold change in Mayr's work: a change in the understanding of what the church is and in the meaning of membership in the church. The church is no longer the mediator of Christ's salvation, but a mere pedagogical advisor.[120] With regard to individual members, the consequence is that the church loses the authority to ask for obedience of will and intellect; church teachings are surrendered to individual judgment. Additionally, the faithful are absolved in advance from private disobedience, which harms the unity of the church, since disobedience is an indispensable part even of Mayr's ecclesiology and his plan for reunification. However, the result would be a dogmatically divided, yet indifferent community, yet one indifferent to the quest, for it seeks not unity and truth—and here, Benedikt Stattler's criticism hits the nail on the head.[121] The community would only be concerned with finding the most utilitarian

118. On the discussion about the authority of the Magisterium in eighteenth-century Catholic theology, see Philipp Schäfer, *Kirche und Vernunft,* (Munich: Hueber, 1974).
119. Mayr, *Apologie,* 250–51.
120. Mayr, *Anhang,* 3:363.
121. Stattler, *Plan zu der allein möglichen Vereinigung im Glauben,* 159–279. Spehr, *Aufklärung und Ökumene,* 138.

way to Heaven. The agenda for this "new church" is summarized by Mayr in six points:

I. All teachings about faith and morals that have been accepted at all times, everywhere, and by everyone as teachings of Christ and his apostles, are teachings which are necessary parts of the order of salvation [Heilsordnung]. These are shared with the Protestants anyway.

II. All teachings that have been accepted only by Catholics are such teachings as do not necessarily belong to the order of salvation. It remains in doubt as to whether they have been regarded at all times, everywhere, and by everyone as directly revealed teachings.

III. The church does not force these teachings on Protestants as being directly revealed. And the church should leave it open as to whether they are directly revealed or not, because at issue is only whether these teachings do not contradict revelation and whether they advance the final goal [of revelation]; and not whether they are directly revealed.

IV. Catholics will acknowledge that *all* divisive doctrines [Differenzlehren] do not contradict revelation, but indeed advance its final aim, and Protestants will accept them [the divisive doctrines, i.e., Differenzlehren] as such.

V. If the teachings are only of speculative character, Protestants should have a free choice to believe them in their hearts or not, but publicly must remain silent about their disbelief or restrain from criticizing the doctrine in question. But if a speculative doctrine is at the same time of practical importance, the obligation will depend upon whether the exercises of the doctrine in question are prescribed by the church only as useful, or as being necessary. Protestants should not have to embrace the former, but should embrace the latter.

VI. Even if Protestants do not accept these doctrines and do not exercise the actions which are connected with them, they cannot be called heretics; but the church nevertheless will be authorized to exclude them from its visible community, since they disobey its administration.[122]

For Mayr, the church would not lose its authority as a teacher if it admitted to having made mistakes in calling certain doctrines "revealed," since the infallibility promised to the church prevents it from leading anyone astray. Even incorrectly labeled doctrines can advance the attainment of Heaven.[123] Yet, because of Christ's continuous assistance to the Magisterium through the guidance of the Holy Spirit, Protestants must accept the Church's teaching as such, even if they do not consider it to be directly revealed teaching.[124]

Despite Stattler's justified critique, one has to defend Mayr against the harsh criticism of Johann Evangelist Hochbichler and a number of ex-Jesuits, since Mayr never denied the importance of infallibility for the system of Catholic theology. Nor did he deny its reality.[125] For him, finding the limits of infallibility was nothing new; rather, such a search entailed a more generous reading of traditional doctrine with ecumenical principles in mind.[126] A more generous hermeneutic could furthermore state that Beda's project was the attempt to give a rational as well as an ecumenical explanation of papal and ecclesiastical infallibility as ministry of service, which receives its authority and legitimization directly from God.[127]

A Faithful Theologian

Beda Mayr died at the abbey in Donauwörth on April 28, 1794.[128] His

---

122. Mayr, *Vertheidigung*, 3:288–89.
123. For a more recent exposition of how the Catholic Church understands the infallibility of its Magisterium cf. Giovanni Sala, "Fallible Teaching and the Assistance of the Holy Spirit: Reflections on the Ordinary Magisterium in Connection with the Instruction on the Ecclesial Vocation of the Theologian," *Nova et Vetera (English Edition)* 4 (2006): 29–54.
124. The Magisterium, which is—according to Catholic doctrine—guided by the Holy Spirit, clarifies revelation by defining *dogmata ecclesiastica*. Mayr, *Apologie*, 236; Mayr, *Vertheidigung*, 3:293–94.
125. Mayr, *Apologie*, 209: "Die Unfehlbarkeit der Kirche können wir unmöglich aufgeben. Sie ist und bleibt der Grundstein des katholischen Lehrgebäudes."
126. Mayr, *Vertheidigung*, 3:304–5.
127. On Friedrich Nicolai's attacks on the doctrine of infallibility, cf. Bantle, *Unfehlbarkeit der Kirche*, 131–201.

critics called him a "Judas," an "apostate," and worse. However, he always stated that he affirmed "before God and the world that I do not regard these [opinions stated in the third volume of the *Defense*] as certain conclusions, but rather as suggestions presented for examination so that I may learn whether they are true or false."[129] Unfortunately, hardly anyone gave him credit for this.

Beda Mayr's theology certainly has its limitations; however, it is noteworthy that his way of theologizing never led to a divisive dissent, as was the case with many radical Enlighteners, but remained ever loyal to church authority and committed to the unity of Christianity.

128. Rauwolf, "P. Beda Mayr," 320.
129. Mayr, *Apologie*, 131. Cf. Mayr, *Apologie*, 160–62.

6

A Tolerant Theology?
Catholic Irenicism, Pluralism, and Indifferentism

Eighteenth-century theology witnessed a number of changes; among them, a growing understanding by Catholics of Protestant culture and thought. This new understanding was, first of all, non-polemical, but not shared by a majority of Catholics—only a small group of Catholic Enlighteners subscribed to it. It was based on the idea of toleration as the lawful acceptance of dissident groups, and tolerance as the value of maintaining civil relations in disagreement. However, irenicism was not always ecumenical in the modern sense: both Benedict Stattler (1728–97) and Maximilian Prechtl (1757–1832) envisioned a reunion of the churches by a reversion of Protestant communities to the fold of Catholicism. Nevertheless, their attempts at empathy with Protestant traditions are noteworthy and deserve to be rediscovered, because as hesitant as these attempts might seem, they nevertheless prepared the way for a peaceful multiconfessional society, which targeted indifferentism as a common enemy.[1] More radical than Stattler and

Prechtl were writers at the Eastern periphery of the Holy Roman Empire, who lived in multiconfessional and multireligious societies: their works developed a Catholic vision of pluralist, and even indifferent, theology. The theological discussions of the Catholic Enlightenment somewhat mirror contemporary debates about the nature of the church, the value of ecumenism, and the controversies over religious pluralism.

Toleration as the Key Characteristic of the Century

One cannot paint a picture of the religious and theological landscape of the time with a broad brush—toleration and intolerance coexisted simultaneously. Two examples might suffice: when the first Evangelical Lutheran Church in Vienna opened in December 1784, Catholics also attended the ceremony, very much to the joy of their Protestant brethren; while in more rural areas (e.g., Upper Carinthia), intransigent clergy still resisted such peaceful coexistence. At the Catholic University of Freiburg, in Habsburg territory, the only Protestant professor, Johann Georg Jacobi (1740–1814), was elected rector in 1790, which was seen by the Protestant world as a sign of tolerance and respect.[2] In the Archbishopric of Mainz, Protestants could even gain high office, regardless of their religion, and could receive doctoral degrees in all departments except theology—both exceptions at the time.[3] In 1788, a traveler described the city as such:

> Mainz shines like a guiding star for all German provinces regarding toleration. Every Protestant, if he has a head and a heart, will find protection and support there. Many Protestant provinces should blush when looking at this example of toleration and should be ashamed that they let starve some righteous Catholics. . . .[4]

1. Christoph Schäfer, *Staat, Kirche, Individuum: Studie zur süddeutschen Publizistik über religiöse Toleranz von 1648 bis 1819* (Frankfurt: Peter Lang, 1992), 51; Ursula Stephan-Kopitzsch, *Die Toleranzdiskussion im Spiegel überregionaler Aufklärungszeitschriften* (Frankfurt: Peter Lang, 1999), 57.
2. Stephan-Kopitzsch, *Die Toleranzdiskussion*, 73–76; 82.
3. Helmut Mathy, "Toleranz im Kur-und Erzstift Mainz," in *Toleranz am Mittelrhein*, ed. Isnard Frank (Mainz: Verein f. MRh. Kirchengeschichte, 1984), 45–77.
4. Stephan-Kopitzsch, *Die Toleranzdiskussion*, 83; on the possibility for Protestants to receive academic degrees in philosophy and law in the Habsburg territories since 1778, see Karniel, *Die Toleranzpolitik Joseph II* (Gerlingen: Bleicher, 1985), 208.

In 1788, the enlightened Archbishop Karl Theodor von Dalberg (1744–1817) even buried his Protestant friend and secretary, Redeker, in the Cathedral of Mainz, although such practice contradicted canon law.[5] Dalberg's thought was saturated with Enlightenment ideas.[6] An incident in 1784 is a good example of how much religious toleration, but also tolerance, had developed in Mainz—in comparison to Cologne, where it was still impossible for Protestants to worship in public, mostly due to strong resistance by the citizens themselves. At the commencement ceremony of the theology department, Professor Johann Kaspar Müller (1749–1810) spoke about the issue of whether the present times support a reunion of Catholicism with "dissident" Christians (as he called Protestants). His speech was so full of hatred and intolerance that the entire audience, which also included Protestant ministers, was shocked. Moreover, as a consequence, several professors apologized to their Protestant friends and colleagues for Müller's action. Even the Archbishop expressed that he was not at all amused and wondered how Müller's even more bitter pamphlet on the same issue could have been approved by his censors.[7] In 1787, Mainz's Secret Chamber even suggested to the elector that he transform a recently dissolved charterhouse into an industrial park for Dutch immigrants of Protestant faith, in order to give Mainz's economy a substantial boost.[8] A last example of toleration in Mainz is Niklas Vogt (1756–1836), arguably the most important Catholic German historian of the century. For him, tolerance was *the* characteristic of his time.[9] In his *System der Allgemeinen Weltgeschichte* of 1785, a systematic outline of world history, he showed that the rise of toleration and tolerance was a key element in the world's development since 1500. He saw the strongest evidence of toleration in Prussia, the Habsburg lands, and Russia; and the weakest in Spain and Portugal. For him, humanity

---

5. Stephan-Kopitzsch, *Die Toleranzdiskussion*, 82.
6. Antje Freyh, "Dalbergs schriftstellerische Tätigkeit in Erfurt," in *Aufklärung in der Dalbergzeit*, ed. Michael Ludscheidt (Erfurt: Ullenspiegel, 2006), 21–44, at 33.
7. Helmut Mathy, "Toleranz im Kur- und Erzstift Mainz," at 61. Johann Kaspar Müller, *Dissertatio de ortu, vero religionis systemate, progressu, statu hodierno sectae unitarie seu Socinianae ac de prono e secta protestantium ad illam transitu* (Mainz: 1784).
8. Mathy, "Toleranz im Kur- und Erzstift Mainz," 73–76.
9. Schäfer, *Staat, Kirche, Individuum*, 135.

found its way to tolerance in the period between 1492 and 1650, while between 1650 and 1785, the value of tolerance was established.[10] Consequently, Spinoza and Machiavelli were, despite being "moral atheists" due to their dedication to the eternal laws of nature and reason, preachers of the divine.[11]

In the Electorate of Trier, Auxiliary Bishop Nicolaus of Hontheim usually is presented as an example of religious toleration due to his groundbreaking book, *Febronius*, which attempted a reunification of the Christian churches. However, Elector and Archbishop Clemens Wenzeslaus (1768–94), who openly supported Joseph II's toleration policy, was much more tolerant than Hontheim. His highest-ranking lay official, Chancellor Georg Laroche (1720–88), who had penned sharp attacks on monasticism, also defended the idea of salvation outside the Catholic Church, and even of Christianity, when he stated in 1773: "I do not believe that whoever loves God and his neighbor, and who is a righteous man, will be eternally damned."[12] In 1783, the elector also passed a law by which Protestants were now legally tolerated and welcome in the principality, which had been "purged" of "heretics" only fifty years earlier. Certainly, it was predominantly the bad economic situation that motivated Clemens Wenzeslaus to take this step, but he also always insisted that an equal motive was his intention to free Catholicism from the old spirit of persecution and intolerance, and thus make it more attractive to the modern world.[13]

10. Hermann Weber, "Niklas Vogt: Ein aufgeklärter Historiker der alten Mainzer Universität," in *Aufklärung in Mainz*, ed. Hermann Weber (Wiesbaden: Steiner, 1984), 31–46; Niklas Vogt, *System der allgemeinen Weltgeschichte* (Mainz: 1785), 38–40.The other three key characteristics are a new political balance of powers, a new culture that penetrates eceonomic and intellectual life, and globalization, which he described as the increasing connection of the entire world. On Vogt's philosophy of history and political philosophy, see the detailed study of Ursula Berg, *Niklas Vogt (1756-1836): Weltsicht und politische Ordnungsvorstellungen zwischen Aufklärung und Romantik* (Stuttgart: Steiner, 1992).
11. Niklas Vogt, *Gedanken über das Allerheiligste im Menschengeschlechte* (Bamberg: 1812), 20. Nevertheless, Vogt did not regard the Reformation as progress, but instead saw in it the beginning of the end of the European Christian community and the Lutheran Reformation as a "merely negative religion" (ibid., 106–8). Only a direct divine action could eliminate religious lethargy and reunite the faiths. He even advocated that the Bible should be amended with a third testament (Steven A. Stargardter, *Niklas Vogt, 1756-1836: A Personality of the Late German Enlightenment and Early Romantic Movement* (New York: Taylor and Francis, 1991), 115).
12. Georg Laroche, *Briefe über das Mönchswesen* (s.l.: 1772), 80 at Stevens, *Toleranzbestrebungen*, 20.
13. Stevens, *Toleranzbestrebungen*, 18–36; Heribert Raab, "Toleranz im Kur- und Erzstift Trier," in *Toleranz am Mittelrhein*, ed. Isnard Frank (Mainz: 1984), 21–43.

An even more progressive idea of toleration was propagated by Catholic Enlighteners in Bonn, which belonged to the archdiocese of Cologne. The Franciscan Eulogius Schneider, who later became a strong supporter of the French Revolution and died on the scaffold in Paris in 1794, summarized what an enlightened theologian should look like: "The theologian, who teaches toleration and turns dry dogmas into morals is enlightened."[14] His former colleague, the Carmelite exegete Thaddäus Dereser (1757–1827), articulated a similar vision on December 19, 1790, in the court chapel in Bonn. His homily was entitled "Jewish and Christian Phariseeism."[15] For Dereser, Jews in the time of Jesus were on a *"Gängelband"* (toddler harness) of religion—he uses Kant's term, which was characterized by human rules and presupposed the wrath of God that had to be mollified. These human inventions and ceremonies had made the Jewish people unsusceptible to the radical teachings of Jesus—for example, of God as a loving father, or of faith and love for one's neighbor as more meritorious than ceremonies. This "Phariseeism" is also the reason why the gospels do not change the world, Dereser thought. It is still at work in Christianity and hinders the acceptance of the "light" of Christ. He identifies the enemies of the Enlightenment as such hypocritical "Pharisees":

> They . . . sigh in general terms about the Godlessness of our times, about the decay of morals, about the demise of faith and the increase of freethinking, about the evils that philosophy and Enlightenment cause, without knowing that Enlightenment is nothing else than replacing erroneous, dark, confused, and incomplete concepts with correct, clear, distinct, and complete concepts. They complain without knowing that Enlightenment is utterly useful for religion and state and that the most enlightened prince, priest, and citizen will be because of his state of mind the best prince, the best priest, and the best citizen. . . . These are no friends of religion . . . but a pest on humanity, a stain on the fabric of Christianity . . . children of hell.[16]

14. Eulogius Schneider, *Gedichte* (Frankfurt: 1790), 267.
15. Anton Dereser, "Der jüdische und christliche Pharisäismus," in *Allgemeines Magazin für Prediger, Seelsorger und Katecheten* 2 (1793): 329–59. Historical research has shown that the Christian perception of Phariseeism as it was commonly held until the midst of the twentieth century is highly distorted.
16. Anton Dereser, "Der jüdische und christliche Pharisäismus," 349–50.

If it was the "children of hell" who espoused intolerance in hypocritical ceremonial laws, then it was the "children of Heaven" who supported Enlightenment and toleration.

Benedict Stattler's Ecumenism of Reversion

Yet, how were toleration and tolerance, which were obviously lived and preached by Catholic Enlighteners, applied theologically? While some pushed toleration toward indifferentism, others used it to articulate an irenic theology, which tried to bring Protestants back to the Catholic fold. The most important German theologian of this group was Benedict Stattler.[17] For him, it was impossible for Catholics to give up the "fundamental doctrine" of the divine authority of their church. As long as Protestants denied such divine authority, a reunion would be impossible.[18]

Stattler's work on the reunion of the churches is, in fact, a criticism of modern liberties, especially Protestantism's emphasis on freedom of conscience. He detects a contradiction in the Protestant praxis: the withholding of toleration for the Socinians and other anti-Trinitarians. Moreover, he points to the conundrum that if everybody has the freedom to interpret holy scripture according to one's own judgment, then one is consequently also allowed to decide for oneself about the divine or only human authority of scripture. This way, Protestants indeed violate their own principles if they remove pastors who claim just this right and teach materialism or naturalism.[19] Stattler also foretold that the philosophy of liberty would soon undermine the dogmatic body of Protestantism:

> Soon no Protestant teachers will be found any longer for Protestant communities, because all will follow the new churches of the Socinians or the Deists or the Naturalists. And then—good night Luther and Calvin![20]

17. Ulrich L. Lehner, "Benedict Stattler," in *Catholicism and Enlightenment*, ed. Ulrich L. Lehner and Jeffrey Burson *(Notre Dame, IN: University of Notre Dame Press, 2014), 169–92.*
18. Benedict Stattler, *Wahres Jerusalem* (Augsburg: 1787), 415.
19. Benedict Stattler, *Plan zu der allein möglichen Vereinigung im Glauben der Protestanten mit der kath. Kirche, und den Gränzen dieser Möglichkeit* (Augsburg: 1791), V-VI.
20. Ibid., VII.

Thus, "true" Protestantism as a form of orthodox Christianity could only be saved if it gave up its ideology of freedom of conscience and embraced Catholicism. Stattler's starting point is the personal rights of each individual. Every person is entitled to freely pursue happiness, and possesses the moral authority for this search as long as it does not violate the rights of others, or force them to be used as a means for this purpose, or hinder them in their own pursuit of happiness. Internally, one has all rights to do whatever is necessary for one's own happiness, and to judge and decide for oneself. Consequently, duties of self-love and love for others cannot be enforced on persons, since everybody has the right to decide for himself what is best. However, no person has an absolute liberty to do evil, but only to do good in achieving the ultimate goal of happiness, and only a relative right to do good *and* evil.[21]

He distinguishes further between innate rights, which derive from the free and active use of reason; acquired rights, which derive from moral action; and essential rights, which are innate rights that can never be surrendered. Full personal liberty from any servitude is an innate right; it is an essential right that persons have the moral authority to abstain from evil and do good, because no human authority can force them to be moral. The relative rights of liberty of will and reason to do good and evil are also essential, and thus only under God's authority. In regard to God, however, nobody has freedom of reason and will, since God requires that humans decide with the help of natural law and by the use of reason, and that if they are unable to do so, to follow a person for whose moral integrity and insight one has sufficient respect.[22] Since most people do not make full use of reason and follow natural law, God has revealed himself and erected the church as the interpreter of this revelation. To justify the surrender of a faithful individual to this church, Stattler reasons that someone can only surrender to a person if such person has full insight into the duties required of him, is proven to be prudent over a long period of time, has benevolent love for persons and justice, and

21. Ibid., 3–8.
22. Ibid., 9–11.

can bring about the common good. Such a person's authority consists, therefore, in the fact that he proscribes, as the wisest and most prudent person, the rules and means of how to achieve the common good and happiness. Thus, if persons *can* surrender certain innate rights to a sovereign, then it seems likely that one's duties of self-love and love of others could also be surrendered to an authority. In this regard, Stattler contradicts most law theorists, who insist that one can only surrender the rights for external—not internal—happiness.[23] It is clear to him that such rights can be surrendered, since not only ignorance of the duties of orderly self-love, charity, and justice, but also the existence of evil inclinations that hinder charity, show that for these fields of human action, much greater wisdom and prudence are necessary than for achieving a temporal common good.[24] Thus, the Protestant notion that the Catholic insistence on authority over scriptural interpretation and conscience is incomprehensible, is rejected.

While true Enlightenment has, according to Stattler, the right to express itself, false Enlightenment, which only leads to destruction and sedition, does not. The criterion for such true Enlightenment in the field of religion is proper legitimization from God. While the apostles were legitimized by their sanctity of life, miracles, and the universal acceptance of the church, Stattler points to the missing legitimization of the Reformers. If Luther and Calvin requested permission to teach their doctrines and had no legitimization other than the knowledge of some ancient languages, "then all of our contemporary Enlighteners, deists, naturalists, and even atheists have the same right."[25] The apostles were also given the gift of ecclesiastical infallibility, which is, for Stattler, the centerpiece of his book. It is the fundamental law of the church instituted by Christ and the ultimate criterion of which teacher to believe.[26] Such infallibility is a revealed truth about the teachings and laws of Christ, as well as the institution of the sacraments, but it

23. Ibid., 24–25.
24. Ibid., 26–36.
25. Ibid., 53.
26. Ibid., 67; see also Benedict Stattler, *Demonstratio Evangelica* (Eichstätt: 1770), §278–87.

contains human additions—for example, when a conclusion is drawn from a revealed doctrine. Such conclusions are certain and justified, even if not formally revealed.[27] Human additions that are, for Stattler, not part of the gift of infallibility pertain to natural law and the moral teachings that Christ never mentioned.[28] Thus, the church "teaches at all times with the assistance of the Holy Spirit (and thus infallibly) what belongs to the teachings of Christ or what was revealed by him, be it a doctrine of faith . . . or of morals."[29] However, if this is true, then it was not wise to persecute so-called heretics if they taught different doctrines not covered by infallibility. They did not really sin against the faith, but rather against the unity of the church, violating its authority and causing scandal. Their persecution by the Inquisition was therefore inappropriate, Stattler claims.[30] The last statement is especially remarkable, as many contemporaries of Stattler still defended the Holy Inquisition and the persecution of heretics; Stattler, however, shows that such persecution has its moral limits when no dogmas are questioned.

What concessions could the Catholic Church make to Protestants? First, it can never give up proclaiming defined truths of faith, but it can abstain from asking converts to recite explicit creeds that mention such teachings and leave them to the conscience of every new Catholic, as long as they are not *revealed* teachings. However, Beda Mayr's idea, as we show in a different chapter, of proving infallibility by demonstrating that even falsified revealed teachings would always be useful, is, for Stattler, the wrong way of going forward. It rests on the presupposition that Jesus' main mission was redemption from sin and the opening of a way to eternal bliss. This, however, leaves out that Jesus, also and equally importantly, pointed to the *best* means of how to achieve salvation and what was necessary for salvation. Consequently, ecclesiastical infallibility must pertain to those teachings, so that Mayr's ecclesiological thesis that the church only teaches *how* one is

27. Stattler, *Plan*, 153, 195.
28. Ibid., 143, 153.
29. Ibid., 192.
30. Ibid., 198.

saved (through Christ) is only a half-truth—which eclipses the fact that she also infallibly teaches *what* is necessary for salvation. A church that erred in such questions would cause "an infinite loss" of certainty for the faithful, and thus create "infinite" harm to humanity, argues Stattler.[31]

Moreover, Stattler believed that Beda Mayr's (1742–94) view of a reunited church (see "Enlightenment and Ecumenism," in this volume) in which Protestants would only be required to believe and embrace what was believed by *everyone at all places at all times*, as Vincent of Lerins taught, would lead to a minimization of the deposit of faith. Such homogeneity of faith did not even exist for the most important doctrines, such as the Trinity, Stattler stated. Moreover, it makes human witness alone the criterion for true faith and eclipses the divine, supernatural assistance God promised his church, so that it is questionable whether a reunion of churches at such cost would be according to his will.[32] Most clearly, this problem surfaces for Stattler in the question of the Eucharist: obviously, both Catholic and Protestant churches believe that its reception is necessary; however, this presupposes that only the *true Eucharist* is necessary for salvation. Thus, the Catholic sacrament, the true sacrament, is necessary for salvation, according to Stattler. This renders Beda Mayr's thesis wrong—the different divisive doctrines do, in fact, pertain to salvation. The same applies to other divisive doctrines that Catholics believe are formally revealed; for example, the priestly authority to forgive sins. Also, since explicitly revealed, they cannot be given up because they belong to the deposit of faith and are necessary for salvation. For Stattler, therefore, Protestants "only" have to accept these divisive doctrines, which Catholics believe to be formally revealed and necessary for salvation; however, there is then no need for a reunion plan, as Stattler concedes, because then they become formally Catholic. A reunion of the churches is, therefore, only possible if Protestants fully embrace the Magisterium of the Catholic Church.[33]

31. Ibid., 199–212.
32. Ibid., 226.
33. Ibid., 227–28, 233, 269.

This does not mean, however, that Stattler proposed a triumphalist or maximalist view of papal authority; quite the opposite. For him, the pope as the head of the college of bishops has to find support for his fundamental decisions among his peers. If the entirety of the episcopate disagrees with the pope, the latter cannot possess moral authority to legislate. If he passes illicit laws that limit the rights of the bishops, they are not required to follow them. Instead, they are required to admonish the pope regarding his error:[34]

> In questions which are not immediately connected to salvation or damnation the head of the Church can err. Therefore he should not rely in these issues too much on his own prudence and should not legislate against the will of the bishops . . . especially if these consider the laws not useful or even harmful.[35]

Stattler appears as a Catholic Enlightener, who says a decisive farewell to Aristotelian scholasticism by embracing the philosophy of Christian Wolff, but nevertheless is hesitant in his requests for toleration and quite traditional in his view of how a reunion of churches could be brought about. Still, the non-polemical tone of his book and the sincere attempt to make his position intelligible have to be emphasized.

Maximilian Prechtl's Irenicism

Of equal importance are the irenic writings of the last abbot of Michelfeld in the Upper Palatinate, Maximilian Prechtl.[36] From 1786 until 1792, he was professor of canon law, and later dogmatic and moral theology in his abbey. Due to the acceptance of the Bavarian schooling system by the Benedictines, in 1794, he became professor of dogmatic theology and canon law at the lyceum in Amberg; in 1798, he was appointed its rector. In January 1800, he was elected abbot—one of the last in the Holy Roman Empire, since, on March 13, 1803, the monastery

---

34. Benedict Stattler, *Demonstratio Catholica* (Pappenheim: 1775), Nr. 164 VI.
35. Ibid., Nr. 164 III.
36. Gerhard Philipp Wolf, "Maximilian Prechtl (1757–1832)—Letzter Abt des Benediktinerklosters Michelfeld in der Oberpfalz," *Zeitschrift für Bayerische Kirchengeschichte* 68 (1999), 77–124.

was officially dissolved. In the next two decades, Prechtl tried in vain to restore his abbey, and died on July 2, 1832 in Amberg.[37]

Like many other theologians who became involved in the irenic or ecumenical movement, Prechtl began as a historian of his own monastery, relying heavily on archival studies. Michelfeld was located in a Protestant state—a fact that motivated Prechtl to dig deeper to find out why the area around his monastery had become Lutheran during the Reformation. In his history of Michelfeld, he described the devastation of his monastery: "Where the praise of God was daily sung, was now sad silence; where daily God was present and where his word was preached to the faithful, there was now desecrated silence."[38] Only in 1669 was monastic life restored. In his *Friedensworte an die katholische und protestantische Kirche für ihre Wiedervereinigung,* he argues that the confessional disunity within the Holy Roman Empire was one of the main reasons for its fall in 1806.[39] He admonishes both churches to look back dispassionately at the origins of their separation.[40] Such an endeavor was heavily criticized by Gottlieb Jacob Planck (1751–1833), who, in Prechtl's view, only maintained the separation of the churches out of fear.[41] The best means for a reunion, however, would be mutual understanding and Enlightenment, not the lowest common denominator.[42]

Prechtl analyzes whether a reunion would be at all desirable. Considering religious fragmentation, it would be wrong to use force to bring about religious unity, but he is convinced that such a move would be useful for the state: "I mean here the unity of religion in essential things: difference in form and vocabulary does not mean a difference in religion."[43] A reunion would increase toleration and

37. Ibid., 77–84; cf. Erwin Herrmann, "De reconciliatione Christianorum: Gedanken eines Abtes zur Wiedervereinigung der Konfessionen," in *Glaube und Gesellschaft: FS Wilhelm F. Klasch,* ed. Klaus D. Wolff (Bayreuth: Fehr, 1981), 177–87.
38. Stadtarchiv Regensburg: Bestand MSO/897/I—Maximilian Prechtl, *Succinta historia Monasterii Michaelfeldensis (1793),* §60, 49 at Wolf, "Maximilian Prechtl," 91.
39. Herrmann, "De reconciliatione Christianorum," 180.
40. Ibid., 182.
41. Wolf, "Maximilian Prechtl," 101; Prechtl, *Friedensworte an die katholische und protestantische Kirche für ihre Wiedervereinigung,* 2nd ed. (Sulzbach: 1820), I–VII.
42. Prechtl, *Friedensworte,* XII; Wolf, "Maximilian Prechtl," 101.
43. Prechtl, *Friedensworte,* 3.

eliminate confessional polemics. Nevertheless, he sees Protestantism as especially in need of such a reunion, which would save it from drifting into "mere rationalism." The "positive religion of Christ," which, according to Prechtl, entails the essentials of the confessions, did not gain much from Protestantism:

> It made the Bible into a mere collection of documents, whose divine authority is explained away by reason. History is turned into Myth. Even Christian doctrines are treated as Jewish theological opinions, which Christ and his disciples only used out of convenience, but . . . could be purged away . . . instead of these doctrines one erects dogmas of a rational religion and calls such a thing "authentic Christianity."[44]

Despite such harsh polemics, Prechtl desired a "true Enlightenment," which would enable Catholics and Protestants to discern the essential from the marginal. "True Enlightenment alerts us to the prerogatives and powers of human reason, but it also shows us its weakness and limits when it comes to religious truths. It demonstrates the desirability, impact and assistance of Supreme Reason."[45] Such a stance, Prechtl argues, should also lead to a rediscovery of the reformers. While true Christianity means the taming of passions, clemency, love of neighbor and enemy, he could not perceive such traits in Luther and Calvin.[46] Instead, he sees in the Reformation the triumph of subjectivism and freethinking, and a marginalization of free will. If the Reformation had not happened, the reforms of Erasmus and his fight for a reasonable and intelligible Catholicism would have been disseminated; yet, the outbreak of the Reformation brought such reform to a halt.[47]

For a reunion, three things are central—namely, the teachings on scripture, infallibility, and papal primacy. Like Stattler and Mayr, Prechtl thinks it would be unreasonable to suggest that Christ would not have secured a faithful interpretation of his words and teachings, so that infallibility and papal primacy are inherently intertwined.[48] He

44. Ibid., 17.
45. Ibid., 121.
46. Ibid., 137.
47. Ibid., 166.

suggests that in the case of a reunion, one should give up the word "papacy," which is so detested in the Protestant tradition, as long as the church's infallibility is maintained.[49] Only an ecumenical council could bring such a reunion about.[50] It would be the most poignant defense against the rising armies of deism and indifferentism, because such a council would reassert the centrality of Christ and mutual charity.[51] Apart from a common faith, common forms of liturgical expressions also should be found, although different liturgies could be maintained.[52] While mutual learning about each other's tradition is necessary, Prechtl sees in Luther's writings only impediments to a reunion, because they are entrenched with "prejudices and the acid of sectarian hatred."[53]

Despite some progress toward a better understanding of the "other," Prechtl's writings proved useless for the ecumenical dialogue, especially because they did not abstain from polemics—in particular, against the fathers of the Reformation.[54]

Pluralistic Theology

Karl Theodor von Dalberg's most important published work was his 1778 *Reflections about the Universe*.[55] His main idea was that one can detect an inherent similarity in all creation, which aims at a reunification of all things in the unity of the Trinity. Creation flows back to God.[56] Consequently, people do not found societies and develop languages in order to avoid conflict or out of bare necessity, but to become more alike, to assimilate their souls.[57] This assimilation, however, is love, and since Christianity is the religion of love, it is

48. Ibid., 208.
49. Ibid., 234.
50. Ibid., 301.
51. Ibid., 304–5.
52. Ibid., 314.
53. Maximilian Prechtl, *Seitenstück zur Weisheit Martin Luthers* (n.p.: 1817), 419.
54. Wolf, "Maximilian Prechtl," 122.
55. Karl Theodor von Dalberg, *Betrachtungen über das Universum*, 3rd ed. (Mannheim: 1787).
56. Dalberg, *Betrachtungen*, 6; 100; 105; ibid., 136: "Gesetz des Universums. Einheit ist vollkommen in Gott. Die Schöpfung strebt sich der Einheit zu nähern. Religion ist Weg zu dieser Annäherung. Also Einheit ist Urquelle, Zweck und Grundgesetz des Universums."
57. Dalberg, *Betrachtungen*, 55.

the key to bringing about the main purpose of creation.[58] Christian revelation educates and forms the will and the heart, and complements the natural relationship of creature and creator, but it also illuminates the mind to recognize in Christ the ultimate role model for a bond between creation and God.[59] This religion is "universal" in space and time, and "the time will come when the light of religion will be preached to all humans of the earth without exception. . . . Be it that the desire of good hearts be fulfilled! Be it that the different Christian religious parties return to the motherly lap of the Church!"[60] Such a vision of human unity or uniformity was misplaced in the eyes of Dalberg's friend, the Jewish philosopher Moses Mendelssohn (1729–86). He, instead, saw God's providence at work in the plurality of faiths and rejected uniformity. Mendelssohn criticized the idea that the

> . . . universal law governing the coexistence of things was to be found in their tendency to assimilate with each other. . . . He distinguished between sameness and unity. Sameness cancels the manifold, unity connects it. The degree of unity depends on the variety it combines. The more the manifold is connected, the greater the ensuing unity. The forces of nature seem to aim not so much at the obliteration of differences as at the connection of the manifold. . . . Religious pluralism, not uniformity was the design of Providence.[61]

Similar to Mendelssohn, some Catholic theologians followed a more pluralist concept of theology. Franz Rudolph Grossing (1752–c. 1790), an ex-Jesuit, and Joseph Alxinger (1755–97) both argued for such. While Alxinger considered himself no longer a Catholic, but a deist and mason, as his *Common Creed of All Religions* proves, Grossing still considered himself Catholic, albeit a Catholic freethinker.[62] The ex-

58. Ibid., 106, 110.
59. Ibid., 110–18.
60. Ibid., 134.
61. Altmann, *Die trostvolle Aufklärung*, 225.
62. Wangermann, *Die Waffen der Publizität* (Vienna: Verlag für Geschichte und Politik, 2004), 112. Alxinger's *Creed* originally passed the censor but was then forbidden in April 1784 (Wangermann, *Die Waffen der Publizität*, 114; Sashegyi, *Zensur und Geistesfreiheit*, 191–92). In a reply to Friedrich Nicolai, who regarded German Protestantism as the one and only role model for Austrian Catholics, Alxinger replied in 1785 with sarcasm: "If a blind man wants . . . to see, he should wish for a proper eye and not a lazy one." For Alxinger, even liberal Protestant theology made too many compromises with reason (Sigrid Habersaat, *Verteidigung der Aufklärung: Friedrich Nicolai in religiösen und politischen Debatten* (Würzburg: Königshausen & Neumann, 2001), 65).

Jesuit Aloysius Blumauer (1755–98) of Vienna had also become a pluralist and mason. Due to the fact that he was a member of the censorship commission, the printing of many liberal-minded skeptical books was permitted. In many of his poems, he manifests—often by means of rhetorical questions—his deism, and the conviction that the revelation of God in nature is equivalent to or even clearer than the historical revelation of God in holy scripture. Patrizius Faust, a cathedral canon in Vienna, contradicted Blumauer, and instead reminded his readers of Catholic exclusivism:

> All [religions] are pleasing to God, one more than the other . . . but if the worship of a Brahman and heathen is as good as that of a Christian then the cross of Christ is powerless: his death in vain; then we do not need a redeemer; the heathen gets to heaven as does the Christian.[63]

Franz Rudolph Grossing, whose real name was Franz Matthäus Grossinger, was certainly one of the most illustrious pluralists of the time. Born in Hungary in 1752, he was probably a Jesuit for about five years before he became a private tutor in Vienna, and then, in 1777, a state employee. In 1782, he lost his position and was sentenced to prison for publishing improper material, and soon afterwards was forcibly exiled. He then began a career as a writer on religious and political issues, was harried from city to city, until he was again imprisoned in Vienna in 1788 and died therein around 1790.[64] His theological work is completely forgotten, because Grossing became a synonym for the infamous Rosicrucian order—although Schiller immortalized this scoundrel in his poem "the famous Lady."[65] His

63. At Wangermann, *Die Waffen der Publizität*, 116; on the censorship commission, see Oskar Sashegyi, *Zensur und Geistesfreiheit unter Joseph II* (Budapest: Akademie Verlag, 1958), 37–52; Thomas Olechowski, "Zur Zensur am Ende des 18. Jahrhunderts: Dichter als Zensoren," in *Jahrbuch der Österreichischen Gesellschaft zur Erforschung des 18. Jahrhunderts* (Bochum: Winkler, 2007), 21:135–43.
64. Derek Beales, *Enlightenment and Reform in the 18th Century* (London: Tauris, 2005), 135–39; cf. Karniel, *Toleranzpolitik*, 356–57.
65. See Friedrich Franz Daniel Wadzeck, *Leben und Schicksale des berüchtigten Franz Rudolph von Grossing, eigentlich Franz Matthäus Grossinger genannt: nebst, der Geschichte und Bekanntmachung der Geheimnisse des Rosen-Ordens* (Frankfurt: 1789), 6; Heinrich Düntzer, "Zu Schiller," *Archiv für Literaturgeschichte* 4 (1875): 79–88; Anonymous, "Eine gefälschte Briefsammlung Joseph II," *Historisch-Politische Blätter für das katholische Deutschland* 133 (1904): 786–94 states that Franz G. was for five years a member of the Jesuits.

thoughts on toleration are summarized in his *Universal Tolerance and System of Religion for all States and Peoples of the World* (1784).[66]

In the foreword, he mentions that this book is the seventh he has published since 1779, but that it is only the second one to which he signed his name.[67] In it, he argues that humans could only be convinced to give up their freedom in religious matters by the founders of religions and states, who claimed to have spoken with God directly. Therefore, the first state laws always consisted of laws about religion. Ceremonies and creeds were prescribed in order to keep "the deceived human mind ignorant."[68] This ignorance led to superstition, and also supported the poverty of the masses, and, consequently, the privileges of a few. "The stupidity of the people was also the reason for the stupidity of the superiors. Where the people are stupid, there cannot exist a reasonable monarch."[69] Jesus restored the main rules of moral order, which were eclipsed due to pagan and Jewish priestcraft.[70] Therefore, Grossing is convinced that Christian belief would produce—if taught according to the original intention of its founder—the "happiest form of government . . . since the religion which Jesus of Nazareth taught was nothing but a religion of reason."[71] However, for him, this religion died with its founder. He writes: "By birth I am a Roman Catholic Christian, but out of conviction a Christian without adjective. . . . The Church I live next to is my parish."[72]

In an explanation of Joseph II's toleration edicts, he states that whatever is useful and good for the State is obligatory, and monarchs

---

66. Franz Rudolph von Grossing [Franz Grossinger], *Allgemeines Toleranz und Religions System für alle Staaten und Völker der Welt* (Leipzig: 1784).

67. The other book was *Der Souverain, oder die ersten Haupt- und Grundsätze einer monarchischen Regierung* (Vienna: 1780). He also admits to writing under the name of Peter von Osterwald, *De religiosis ordinibus et eorum reformatione liber singularis quem e Germanico in Latinum traduxit, suisque auxit animadversionibus* (1781).

68. Grossing, *Allgemeines Toleranz und Religions System*, 6.

69. Ibid., 7.

70. Ibid., 13.

71. Ibid., 14.

72. Ibid., 16. Grossing also mentions that in order to understand other religions better, he forced himself to accept one religion after the other and to remain in it for some time: "I was pagan, Christian, Jewish, Muslim, and all sects called me . . . their brother in faith. . . . I am totally convinced . . . that all humans without exception have . . . one and the same religion. Wherein they differ is only childish . . . games."

must act without fear, according to the welfare of their State.[73] Moreover, all questions of religion pertain to conscience, and are therefore outside the sphere of any earthly power:

> By nature every human being has the most perfect right to believe what he wants. This liberty he cannot forsake when he enters civil society ... since it can never be part of a civil contract. .... I furthermore state that every human being is allowed, due to the fact that he lives in a civic society, to believe what he wants.[74]

The creed is a man's possession, like his shirt. To take this right away is a crucial violation of a basic right. "A human being is regarding religion still in a state of nature, that is: in the state of perfect liberty, and the person who disturbs me in my religion, robs me as if he would take away the shirt I wear on my body."[75] This view is a radicalization of the thoughts of William Penn (1644–1718), John Locke (1632–1704), and Mendelssohn, but also of German law theorists such as Justus Henning Boehmer (1674–1749), who claimed that at the foundation of the State, citizens reserved the right to religious matters to their consciences, but had a very limited understanding of toleration.[76] Humans have no way of judging somebody else's conscience.

For Grossing, every person who sins is, in that moment, a formal atheist, because he acts against the divine commandments. Likewise, there is no person who is completely ignorant of God. For Grossing, even the expression "I want to be an atheist" is only possible if one already knows something about God.[77] So-called atheism is, then, ignorance of God that derives from an ignorance of one's own existence as a human being. Paganism is a misunderstanding. The differences between religions can be reduced to varying concepts and differences in education. "This is truly toleration of reason, by which every reasonable person is obliged to leave his neighbor human being

73. Ibid., 48.
74. Ibid., 49.
75. Ibid.
76. On religious liberty as birthright and property, see Forst, *Toleranz im Konflikt* (Frankfurt: Suhrkamp, 2003), 223; 231; 273–307. On Boehmer see Matthias Fritsch, *Religöse Toleranz im Zeitalter der Aufklärung* (Hamburg: Meiner, 2004), 204–5.
77. Grossing, *Allgemeines Toleranz und Religions System*, 54.

in the free exercise of his religion undisturbed. . . ."[78] Christian toleration pertains to all religions without exception—heathens, Jews, Turks, and other Christians—because a core feature of Christian faith is that it is a free gift from God.[79] Joseph II's concession to Catholicism for the maintenance of its status as the privileged public religion (*exercitium publicum*) is, for Grossing, "the source or consequence of intolerance."[80] Despite the fact that he insists on complete liberty in religious matters, Grossing believes that the clergy of all religions should be employed by the State. Grossing thinks such an egalitarian state employment would be necessary due to the different endowments of the churches; nevertheless, no more priests have to be tolerated than are necessary—for example, if there are more Protestants than Catholics in a village and if the means of the State are insufficient to pay priests for both confessions, the Protestant pastor should be employed.[81] Moreover, it is inconceivable as to why only a restricted public exercise of religion is allowed: if a religious service is not dangerous, it must be allowed in the same way as the established religion.[82]

Even the enlightened Benedictine Beda Mayr confirmed in a homily that "no Jew, no Turk, no heathen" will enter purgatory, and ultimately heaven; "they go directly after their death to hell."[83] The primary example of Catholic pluralism in the German lands, however, is the anonymous book, supposedly written in 1791 by a Catholic priest in Silesia, with the interesting title *Neither the Christian Religion nor the Roman Catholic Church Are the Only Ways to Salvation*. The author seems to agree with the position of the Spinozist and free-thinker Johann Christian Edelmann (1698–1767) and his motto of an "equality of all religions," which entails that God can make anybody in any religion a Christian through good works.[84] He agrees with the Protestant

78. Ibid., 56.
79. Ibid., 59–60.
80. Ibid., 105.
81. Ibid., 129–31.
82. Ibid., 101.
83. Beda Mayr, *Festpredigten und Redem von dem guten Tode für das Landvolk* (Augsburg: 1778), 2:261.
84. A good summary of Edelmann's concept of religion is found in Ernst Feil, *Religio* (Göttingen: Vandenhoeck & Rupprecht, 2007), 4:143–63.

dogmatic theologian Johann Jakob Griesbach (1745–1812) that no church can claim itself to be exclusively in possession of the truth, and that no Christian church fully preserved the faith of the apostles, but mixed it with a varying number of errors. The aim of his enterprise is to "demolish the fortress of intolerance" and renew theology by purifying the concept of God with reason.[85] He anticipates opposition, since the subtitle of his book suggests the rigorous application of reason to revelation. When theologians argue that reason cannot judge revelation this might be true, but the author claims that theologians thus protect their own theological works and not God's word. Moreover, most problems arise from unreasonable interpretations of scripture and not the application of reason.

According to our author, no proscription of Jesus was more ignored by theologians and priests than his command not to judge.[86] He especially questions Cyprian's (c. 200–258) dictum that outside the church, there is no salvation, and wonders why the fathers of the church followed a man who was known to be a zealot. Moreover, he laments the authority Catholics give to the fathers of the church: "If it was only said by a church father! Then his word counts more than a thousand lucid arguments."[87]

He lays out that after each schism and the Reformation, each new church claimed to be the exclusive way to salvation. What happened to the commonsense belief that every righteous person could please God? In the author's eyes, it is blasphemy for theologians to claim that only the members of their church would get to heaven.[88] In the first

85. Anonymous, *Weder die christliche Religion noch die römisch-katholische Kirche ist die Alleinseligmachende: Aus entscheidenden Vernunftgründen erwiesen von einem römisch-katholischen Pfarrer in Schlesien* (Frankfurt: 1791), preface 2–3; cf. Johann Jacob Griesbach, *Anleitung zum Studium der populären Dogmatik* (Jena: 1789), 211: "obgleich keine [Kirche] im ausschliesslichen Besitze der Wahrheit und untrüglich ist, noch sich für die alleinseligmachende ausgeben darf, so wie es auch keine christliche Kirche giebt, die nicht sehr viele wichtige und nützliche Wahrheiten, wenn schon mit mehr oder weniger Irrthum vermischt, bekennete." The attempted refutation of the anonymous work by the Braunau Benedictine Bonaventura Müller, *Widerlegung einer Schrift, worinn ein seyn sollender römisch-katholischer Pfarrer in Schlessien unternommen hat zu erweisen, dass weder die christliche Religion (. . .)* (Prague: 1790) remains on a polemical level. A positive review of the anonymous book was published in *Allgemeine deutsche Bibliothek* 107 (1792): 112–19, 350–53.
86. Anonymous, *Weder die christliche Religion*, 1.
87. Ibid., 4.
88. Ibid., 7.

part of his book, he introduces and rejects the claim of Christians that Christianity is the one and only true religion; in the second part, he deals with the exclusive claims of the churches. Mark 16:16, which indicates the necessity of Baptism, is thrown out as inauthentic, as proven by Johann David Michaelis (1717–91). But even if the verse was authentic, one has to understand it in the context of the Lord's command to missionize: "Go and teach." Then, however, being taught the faith is the necessary precondition to having faith; therefore, nobody who has not had the faith preached to them can be condemned.[89] John 6:47 is to be understood in the context of verse 41, which says that one has to see Jesus to believe. It would be completely contrary to reason to suppose that only those who saw Jesus in his earthly life would then be saved.[90] Peter's word "there is no other name," he interprets as a speech in front of Jews, who indeed had no other name than Jesus. Faith can only be the divinely ordered means to salvation if this faith was really preached to somebody. According to John 9:41, people who do not see and hear, and, consequently, have never heard of the faith, cannot be blamed for not being Christians, and are thus not damned:[91]

> A Christian has the . . . duty to think, believe and act as Christian—to live and die as a Christian since God has put him out of gratuitous grace in circumstances in which he can have a better knowledge of God and his nature, . . . in order to become worthy of a higher happiness. . . . From this, however, it does not follow that non-Christians will be damned, only that it is also their duty to become Christians once they have gained a sufficiently convincing knowledge of Christianity.[92]

The fulfillment of such duty can be seen in the life of Cornelius, who is called a pious and righteous man as a heathen, before he received Baptism (Acts 10). For the author, this means that God wants to remind the Jewish Christians that they are not better than the heathens and that there is no exclusivity in salvation. Therefore, anybody who

89. Ibid., 10–11.
90. Ibid., 12–13.
91. Ibid., 17.
92. Ibid., 22–23.

receives from God the interior desire for Christianity has to become a Christian in order to be saved. Thus far, one could think the author would defend an inclusivist position—but he rejects the opinion that heathens who live a righteous life will not be damned, but will enter heaven, albeit ultimately as Christians, since God will give them at the end of their lives the light of faith. This opinion, which goes back to Augustine and Aquinas, remains an opinion if one only considers scriptural data. He claims that reason, however, gives us the certainty that an all-wise God will not let myriads of people perish, so that heathens qua heathens will be saved. Moreover, he detects in this theological opinion a grain of truth, because the theologians obviously think the actions of a heathen count more than his faith. Also, in the Bible, one could find numerous places where good actions without faith are remunerated.

Can there be the shadow of a doubt that God will save the non-Christian, especially in circumstances in which he would have to perform a miracle so that he would accept the Christian faith? Or, is it really more in conformance with the nature of God to believe that he must perform a miracle for each righteous heathen before he can enter heaven?[93] What does faith mean regarding eternal life? Does it mean simple assent without critical thinking or any doubt? Or, should my faith influence the actions in my life and transform me into a person pleasing to God? Since the latter is obviously the case, the author concludes that faith cannot lead to salvation, but only action can. But is there a qualitative difference between the works of a Christian, which he does in faith, and those of a non-Christian, who does them out of the knowledge of natural law? Can there be such a difference, "that God only finds the works of the Christian worthwhile, but rejects the works of the non-Christian, and moreover has to condemn him eternally?—What blasphemy!"[94] For the Silesian priest, an omnibenevolent God cannot reject such works and has to remunerate them, according to his wisdom.

93. Ibid., 29.
94. Ibid., 38. For clarification: the works of heathens were not considered sinful, but merely not meritorious.

If exclusivism were true, then God has predestined "several hundred millions of people to be damned to hell"—namely, those from whom he will withhold the gift of faith.[95] If it is true that God wants to save all, then it cannot be true that he requires explicit Christian faith as the entrance ticket to eternity, since hundreds of millions died before this faith was even possible—namely, before the arrival of Christ. Otherwise, God would desire something, and at the same time not provide the conditions for its acceptance:

> If . . . the Christian faith was . . . the only means of salvation for all people, one would have to draw the conclusion that it is irreconcilable with the nature of God: God would have decreed . . . non-Christians . . . to hell. . . . Whether the theologian concedes that not all human beings are saved through Christian faith, but myriads of people in other ways, or he must concede that God has decreed all nations, where the Gospel has never been preached . . . to eternal damnation.[96]

If the first proposition is true, then exclusivism is not possible. Nevertheless, our author shies away from a pure pluralism, and instead suggests that non-Christians are saved through Christ—however, not through intellectual faith, but by doing "what he did." As a scriptural basis, he refers to Matthew 12:50, that whoever does the will of the Father is to Jesus like a brother and sister. For the author, this means that all virtuous people will be saved. He summarizes his statement that one is not saved through *faith* in Jesus Christ, but still, *through* Jesus Christ. Moreover, he argues that the Catholic Church never stated in its teaching documents that only Christians can gain salvation. And he also rejects the opinion that nothing certain can be said about the fate of non-Christians.[97] He harmonizes this with the creed of the Council of Trent by stating that the text is merely an inclusion and not really part of the creed, otherwise it would have had to sound something like "I believe that nobody else will be . . ." If this article was a necessary part of the Catholic faith, it would have had to be in the earlier forms of the creed. Here, he quotes the great Catholic

95. Ibid., 39.
96. Ibid., 42–43.
97. Ibid., 55–57.

133

Enlightener Ludovico Muratori (1672–1750), from his book *On the Limits of Our Cleverness in Religious Matters*,[98] chapter 13, according to whom, many sayings of councils or church fathers should not automatically be considered confirmation of church teachings; for example, when the fathers do not really teach a certain doctrine, but just mention it in a relative clause. Since this is, in his eyes, the case, there is no doctrinal support for exclusivism.

Moreover, the Silesian priest also claims that the category of heresy—especially of so-called voluntary heresy—is a mere phantom. If somebody questions his faith, he can come to one of three conclusions: he can find the truths of his faith confirmed, continue to doubt, or find errors in it. In the second case, he suspends his judgment until he has found better proofs, and thus one cannot call such a person guilty of an error or having the will of a pertinacious heretic. This is also the case in the third example, since the person has come to the conclusion that errors exist in his belief system. It only depends on whether he wants to make his beliefs about errors public or not, and the public statement itself can be pertinacity. Nevertheless, this shows in the author's view that one cannot speak of an error of the mind in heretics, since the mind knows or comes to the conclusion that x is an error, and simultaneously, no longer considers x as an error of the mind. He is convinced of the truth of his proposition, like somebody who tells an obvious lie, but is convinced of its truth. Is such a person now a voluntary and pertinacious liar?

> If according to the definition of our theologians a heretic is only the person who voluntarily and obstinately errs in his mind about the true faith, then it is metaphysically impossible that there is a single heretic at all.[99]

Surprisingly, the author refers to Benedict Stattler, whom he calls "enlightened," who said the same in his major work on toleration, *True Jerusalem* (1787).[100] Also, according to Stattler, modern-day Protestants

98. Ludovico Muratori, *De ingeniorum Moderatione* (Paris: 1714).
99. Anonymous, *Weder die christliche Religion*, 74.
100. Stattler, *Wahres Jerusalem*, 385–87.

cannot be considered heretics or excommunicated, since their connection to the Catholic Church continues. Thus, they are members of the Catholic Church.[101] Consequently, one cannot interpret *extra ecclesiam nulla salus* in an exclusivist way.

However, does not the Bible admonish unity and did the heretics, who might share the spirit and faith of St. Paul, not destroy that unity by denouncing the true earthly head of the Church—the pope? And are they, consequently, not excluded from the one true Church? The anonymous author denies this by referring to Ephesians 4:12 and 16, according to which, one is a member of the body of Christ if one lives in the spirit and in faith. "Is not Jesus all in all—and does virtue cease to be virtue as soon as it is outside the borders of a certain system?"[102] Consequently, he criticizes the standard explanation of ecclesiastical infallibility because he does not see that the church has received the promise to teach and decide infallibly, but only Jesus' promise of perpetual assistance.[103] With reference to Andre Duval (1564-1638), he also asserts that it is not *de fide* that the Pope is infallible, but only certain.[104] The disobedience of the first Protestants is interpreted as a complaint:

> Is this really punishable disobedience? Was it really opposed to any article of this religion? . . . I wish one would have given in to the claims of Luther and his adherents . . . then the term Protestant would be *unknown* today.[105]

Luther is appreciated as a true Christian reformer, who carefully preserved the teachings of the fathers, and the Reformation is seen as a necessary purging of the Church. He explicitly rejects the definition of the church by Cardinal Bellarmine ("The one and true church is the assembly of men, bound together by the profession of the same Christian faith, and by the communion of the same sacraments, under the rule of legitimate pastors, and in particular of the one Vicar of

---

101. Ibid., 390; Anonymous, *Weder die christliche Religion*, 74–75.
102. Anonymous, *Weder die christliche Religion*, 77.
103. Ibid., 78.
104. Andre Duval, *De suprema Romani Pontificis in Ecclesiam potestate disputatio quadripartita* (Paris: D. Langlaeus, 1614); cf. Anonymous, *Weder die christliche Religion*, 86–87.
105. Anonymous, *Weder die christliche Religion*, 89–91.

Christ on earth, the Roman Pontiff"),[106] since it disregards the common belief of the fathers that *Christ is the center of the church*. He concludes that Bellarmine invented a definition that was alien to tradition. Moreover, it does not mention the most important feature, namely, that of "religion . . . or with other words, the right worship and cult of God in spirit and in truth. . . ."[107] Bellarmine's definition sounds too judicial for him, so he words his definition thus: "The true Christian Church is a society of human beings, who under the guidance of commissioned pastors and teachers confess the religion of Jesus Christ in their hearts and deeds."[108]

He claims that the unity of all Christians is impossible due to the law of diversity inherent in nature, but also, because the Bible teaches differing articles of faith (unfortunately, he does not give an example). The most important thing to him seems to be that all Christians agree on the most necessary and basic beliefs—namely, on the divinity of Jesus Christ and the words of his apostles. All differences between Christian denominations are only about exterior, marginal things.[109] The promise of the incorruptibility of the church pertains only to the Christian religion as a whole, and not to what persons added to this religion—that is, doctrinal Catholicism.[110] Consequently, the church does not have the right to define faith with authority, but it is the right of every Christian to investigate and judge in religious matters as he pleases.[111] This conceptualization of ecclesiology is intellectually close to that of Mendelssohn in his *Jerusalem* of 1783, in which he developed the idea of a liberal, authority-free church.[112]

If official Catholic doctrine were true, claimed the author, then one

---

106. Robert Bellarmine, "Disputationes de controversiis christianiae fidei adversus huius temporis haereticos [1581–1592]", in *Opera Omnia* (Paris: 1870), 2:317 (controversia de conciliis, lib. III, cap. II): "Ecclesiam . . . esse coetum hominum ejusdem Christianae fidei professione, et eorumdem Sacramentorum communione colligatum, sub regimine legitimorum pastorum, ac praecipue unius Christi in terris Vicarii Romani Pontificis." Cf. Thomas Dietrich, *Die Theologie der Kirche bei Robert Bellarmin (1542-1621): Systematische Voraussetzungen des Kontroverstheologen* (Paderborn: Bonifatius, 1999).
107. Anonymous, *Weder die christliche Religion*, 99.
108. Ibid., 101.
109. Ibid., 107.
110. Ibid., 117–18.
111. Ibid., 118.
112. Moses Mendelssohn, *Jerusalem oder über die religiöse Macht und Judentum* (Berlin: 1783).

had to imagine a merciful God excluding millions and millions from heaven only because they did not share certain doctrines, even though they lived according to his word. Likewise, Protestants have to retract their exclusivist claims. That Jesus descended into hell and preached salvation to those spirits who did not obey or believe (1 Peter 3:18–20) is proof enough that those are also saved, and that the so-called unanimous consensus of the fathers that one has to be a member of the church to be saved is not a proper exegesis of holy scripture.[113] He even provides the reader with a calculation of how brutal an exclusivist God might be. He estimates the number of human beings in his time at 800 million. Within thirty-five years, these 800 million will be dead. The population of Europe, he estimates at 150 million people, 10 million of whom are Muslim. In America, he estimates 80 million, so that there are probably around 300 million Christians worldwide:

> If one deducts the millions of Lutherans, Reformed, Disunited Christians, Copts, Armenians, Episcopalians, Presbyterians, Zwinglians, Hussites, Mennonites, Herrnhut Brethren, Arians, Nestorians, Socinians, etc., one can arrive at the sum of not more than . . . 200 million Catholics. And these people . . . would be the only legitimate and certain candidates for Heaven? . . . Here again one has to make an estimate. Many theologians interpret the words of Christ: Many are called, but only few elected, and explain that also in this Church only the smallest number will be saved. For the sake of the argument we want to assume that at least one third will be saved, so 50 million.[114]

Since only the children of these Catholics go directly to heaven, though, for all thirty-five years, Satan can celebrate gaining 100 million Catholic and 75 million Christian souls, plus 375 million non-Christians, for a total of 550 million souls. He even calculates how much this means for different units of time:

---

113. Anonymous, *Weder die christliche Religion*, 127–29.
114. Ibid., 133–34.

Each year	15,714,285
Each month	1,309,523
Each day	43,650
Each hour	1,818
Each 15 minutes	454
Each minute	30

For forty generations, this means that 22 billion people were damned to everlasting hell, while only 5 billion were saved.[115] He deplores everybody who can—facing such horror—still believe in the exclusivity of the Catholic Church or Christianity:

> O you miserable man, you who can still hold this proposition true. . . . You defile all noble gifts of God. . . . You desecrate the holy utterances of scripture . . . by giving them a meaning, which irrationality has produced and ignorance has cherished. You make God according to your attitudes a despotic tyrant, who does not reign according to the eternal laws of justice and equity, but according to passion, favor, stubbornness and arbitrariness—who only makes a fraction of his creatures, his favorites, happy and . . . plunges the rest into deepest misery. You can never look at him with a joyful heart, never pray: Father of all humans! and if you do it, you do it mechanically, and you do not know what you are really doing. Like a knight in armor the thought should throw you down to earth: God, God! Only such a fraction of humanity you have elected for eternal bliss, and three or four times as many you have condemned to eternal unhappiness?[116]

Considering such odds it is, in his eyes, highly unlikely for a grown-up Catholic to be saved.[117] Most interestingly, however, is his mining of the works of Catholic theologians to at least buttress some of his claims. He reminds the reader that most dogmatic theologians teach that material heretics also are saved, as long as they live and die good Christians. If this, however, is true, then there cannot be a Catholic exclusivism:

115. Ibid.
116. Ibid., 135–36.
117. Ibid., 140.

If the first proposition is true, namely that the Roman Catholic Church is indeed the only church that saves, then it is impossible that a formal or material heretic can be saved. He might err innocently . . . but according to the principles of my theological brothers he is not a Roman Catholic Christian . . . not a believer . . . of this Chuch but a heretic or schismatic . . . and consequently, the opinion that a material heretic can be saved is wrong. However, none of our theologians concedes the consequence of the presupposition; but it is an ordinary teaching that material heretics can be saved. Can anybody reason more illogically?[118]

Simpert Schwarzhueber (1727–95), the Austrian Benedictine theologian, tried to resolve the contradiction by saying that material heretics are saved by God's victorious grace, which justifies them "by their inner desire" to be part of God's church. Through this desire, and thus through Christ's sanctifying grace and sanctifying love, they are part of the invisible church even if they are not part of the visible church.[119] However, if the first presupposition is correct, how can a person's faith in Christ be correct if true belief is found in the Catholic

---

118. Ibid., 143.

119. Simpert Schwarzhueber, *Praktisch-katholisches Religionshandbuch zum Gebrauche des gemeinern Stadt-und Landvolkes, wie auch zum Behufe der Christenlehrer* (Salzburg: 1784), 1:140, §52; Schwarzhueber, *Praktisch-katholisches Religionshandbuch*, 2nd ed. (Salzburg: 1790), 1:129–30 §49, accepts a differentiation of civil and theologial toleration. Theological toleration is humane and peaceful treatment of people who believe in a different religion because one is convinced that everybody should follow his own insights. While most restrict such toleration to Christians, some want to extend it to materialists, Muslims, Jews, and pagans. Civil toleration allows different religious groups certain civil rights. Theological tolerance is impossible if one holds that it is every human's duty to find God and his word, and to obey him in order to achieve salvation. It is only "frosty religious indifferentism" (132). For Schwarzhueber, there cannot exist several Christian truths. Jesus' message cannot be divided. "The true Church of Christ cannot be different than his unmistakably true doctrine; she has to condemn . . . those who do not agree with her, otherwise she would cease to be the true Church of Christ" (133–34). The idea that fundamental articles of the faith, as Le Clerc and Locke develop them, would help is for him pretentious. "One pretends that God obliges all humans capable of using reason to know, believe (or at least not to reject) certain, ordinary basic truths of the Christian religion . . . but that he obliges only those who have special insight into his revealed word . . . to the rest for the sake of their greater perfection" (134). For him, this entails that somebody can investigate and judge for himself what is fundamental, and that is for Schwarzhueber unbiblical. Is not the church there to fill in the gap for those truths one alone cannot grasp? Moreover, why was there at all the idea of fundamental articles? Because, he claims, of the Arminian controversies. Such ideas only lead to indifferentism and the articles should keep revealed religion somewhat alive. Since all theologians disagree about these articles, one can see that they are chosen arbitrarily. "Fundamental Articles are weak fences; one changes and turns them, just like scripture, according to one's own whim" (139). "Although our Catholic faith proscribes us all theological toleration, Christian charity obliges us to treat also those, who stand outside the Catholic and Christian community, with appropriate . . . respect" (145). Such charity also urges Catholics to accept those who err in matters of faith as neighbors, made in the image of God, saved by the blood of Christ (146).

Church? Heretics are banned from the Church because they gave up just this faith. Considering such conundrums, the Silesian priest comes to the conclusion that indifferentism is the "most noble, most biblical and most reasonable heresy."[120]

Conclusion

As usual, history is more complicated than grand narratives suggest. Too many accounts of Catholic history have overlooked the contributions of thinkers such as the ones introduced here, and have thus contributed to the impression that premodern Catholicism was not interested in its Protestant brethren, or the ideas of irenicism, ecumenism, or pluralism. Instead, one can demonstrate that Catholic thinkers contributed to such contemporaneous debates creatively and positively. Some will, of course, wonder whether one can view Grossing as a Catholic or should regard him as a Rosicrucian, and whether one can be sure that the Silesian priest was Catholic. These are legitimate methodological questions, and while the first question could be answered to the effect that Grossing was at least a Catholic freethinker, the second one remains unanswerable. Be that as it may—this chapter demonstrated that there existed a debate within Catholic circles about theological inclusivism, pluralism, and universalism two hundred years before Vatican II, which has hitherto been overlooked. The question of how one could be saved in other religions did not just come up in the twentieth century, but was already earlier on creatively wrestled with. Many other Catholic Enlighteners could also be mentioned who thought along such progressive lines, such as Andrew Michael Ramsey (1686–1743),[121] who—taken together—undermine the simplistic narrative still existent today that premodern Catholic theology was a narrow-minded scholastic enterprise.

---

120. Anonymous, *Weder die christliche Religion,* 127.
121. See Gabriel Glickmann, "Andrew Michael Ramsey: Catholic Freethinking and Mysticism," in *Enlightenment & Catholicism in Europe. A Transnational History,* ed. by Ulrich L. Lehner and Jeffrey Burson (Notre Dame, IN: University of Notre Dame Press, 2014), 391–410.

PART III

Church Reform

7

___

Johann Nikolaus von Hontheim's *Febronius*:
A Censored Bishop and His Ecclesiology

In the second half of the eighteenth century, the greatest enemy of
the Roman Curia was no longer French Gallicanism, but German
Febronianism, since it challenged papal primacy. It gained its name
from the pseudonymous author of the book, *De Statu Ecclesiae* (1763).
The author, auxiliary bishop Johann Nikolaus von Hontheim, was
immediately censored, and later forced to sign a retraction. This
chapter provides a synthesis and overview of the publishing history
of this important work and its ecclesiology, as well as shows how the
Curia dealt with this dissident theologian.[1] Many of Hontheim's
requests, especially those for a more collegial governing structure of
the Church and an increase of the authority of local bishops, were
fufilled at the Second Vatican Council. Yet, the influence of his ideas,
heavily shaped by conciliarism, have remained unacknowledged.

In 1763, the auxiliary bishop of Trier, Johann Nikolaus von

___

1. For Cardinal Garampi's role in the Hontheim affair, see now Dires Vanysacker, "The Role of
Giuseppe Garampi in the Hontheim Case," *Ephemerides Theologicae Lovanienses* 91 (2015): 281–93.

143

Hontheim, stirred up a hornet's nest when he dared to publish—under the pseudonym Justinus Febronius—his book *On the State of the Church and the Legitimate Power of the Roman Pope: Written for the Reunification of Dissident Christians* (*Justini Febronii JCti. de statu Ecclesiae et legitima potestate Romani Pontificis liber singularis: ad reuniendos dissidentes in religione christianos compositus*). Intransigent Roman theologians from different European countries immediately attacked the new publication and denounced it as highly biased, even heretical, and dozens of refutations were printed. Others regarded it as a sound piece of scholarship that united the tradition of conciliarism with the so-called Catholic Enlightenment.[2] However, *De Statu Ecclesiae* did not become a bestseller due to its originality or academic quality, but because it successfully articulated the dissatisfaction with the Holy See, with vigorous conviction, and summarized concisely the theses of Gerson, Cusanus, Bossuet, Natalis Alexandre, Claude Fleury, Van Espen, Johannes Schilter, Barthel, and others.[3] The early papal censoring (1764) increased the book's audience. This also explains why the work remained a *poltergeist* for Catholic authorities well into the twentienth century. This chapter will explore the publishing history of this groundbreaking work as well as the often-overlooked retraction Hontheim was forced to sign in 1778.

From Medieval conciliarism to Early Modern Gallicanism

Since the Council of Constance (1414–18), which helped to heal the Occidental Schism by displacing three popes, had issued the decrees "Haec Sancta" and "Frequens," the authority of the council over the

---

2. Cf. Harm Klueting, "Wiedervereinigung der getrennten Konfessionen oder episkopalistische Nationalkirche? Nikolaus von Hontheim (1701–90), der *Febronius* und die Rückkehr der Protestanten zur katholischen Kirche," in *Irenik und Antikonfessionalismus im 17. und 18. Jahrhundert*, ed. by Harm Klueting (Hildesheim: Olms, 2003) 258–77. Recently, Hontheim's main work was reprinted: Johann Nikolaus von Hontheim, *Justinus Febronius Abbreviatus et Emendatus* (1777), ed. by Ulrich L. Lehner (Nordhausen: Bautz, 2008).

3. Otto Mejer, *Febronius. Weihbischof Johann Nikolaus von Hontheim und sein Widerruf* (Tübingen: 1880), 43; Georg May, *Die Auseinandersetzungen zwischen den Mainzer Erzbischöfen und dem Heiligen Stuhl um die Dispensbefugnis im 18. Jahrhundert* (Frankfurt: P. Lang, 2007) 41–42; cf. Hermann Josef Sieben, *Traktate und Theorien zum Konzil. Vom Beginn des Grossen Schismas bis zum Vorabend der Reformation (1378-1521)* (Frankfurt: Knecht, 1983).

JOHANN NIKOLAUS VON HONTHEIM'S FEBRONIUS

pope had become a common theological issue. Nevertheless, it was unresolved how the relevant texts should be interpreted:[4] Should the superiority of a council over the pope be reserved to emergencies or should it be regarded as a truth of faith? At the Council of Basel (1431–39), it became clear that there was no peace in sight between conciliarists and curialists. This council viewed the decrees of Constance as a doctrine of faith against the resistance of Pope Eugene IV (in "Etsi non dubitemus", 1441). Soon, the conciliarist bishops lost the support of the secular princes and enabled the papacy to gain an enormously important political victory. Despite the lost battle, the war still went on. Conciliarism was still taught at a number of leading universities, e.g., in Paris, Erfurt, Cologne, Krakow, and Vienna. German-speaking Catholic scholars, in particular, remembered the deeds of Constance with reverence, but also with vehemence.[5]

The Reformation and the Catholic Reform after Trent transformed this movement, but they did not extinguish it. In France, it took the shape of Gallicanism. With its masterthinkers, Edmond Richer and Jacques Bossuet, the French ecclesiastics frightened and challenged the Roman Curia throughout the seventeenth and eighteenth centuries, since the oldest daughter of the Church considered herself officially in the *Declaratio Cleri Gallicani* (1682) as an *independent* national church. The *Declaratio* restricted the influence of the pope to the spiritual realm and declared the secular princes exempt from ecclesiastical power. Moreover, the French clergy also claimed that the pope could only teach infallibly if his teachings were received universally.[6] In the Holy Roman Empire, especially, Bossuet's defense of Gallicanism was widely read, and had an enduring influence on the author of the *Febronius*.[7]

---

4. Walter Brandmüller, *Das Konzil von Konstanz 1414-1418*, 2 vols. (Paderborn: Schöningh, 1991–97). Cf. Remigius Bäumer, "Interpretation und Verbindlichkeit der Konstanzer Dekrete," *Theologisch-Praktische Quartalschrift* 116 (1968) 44–53; Remigius Bäumer, "Die Bedeutung des Konstanzer Konzils für die Geschichte der Kirche," *Annuarium Historiae Conciliorum* 4 (1972), 26–45.
5. The decrees of Constance were published as early as 1550, cf. *Acta Scitu dignissima docteque concinnata Constantiensis concilii celebratissimi* (Hagenau, 1550). Cf. *Acta Concilii Constanciensis*, ed. Heinrich Finke, (Münster, 1896–1928) vols. 1–4; Hans Schneider, *Der Konziliarismus als Problem der neueren katholischen Theologie* (Berlin: De Gruyter, 1976), 44.
6. Schneider, *Der Konziliarismus*.
7. Robert Duchon, "De Bossuet a Febronius," *Revue d'histoire ecclésiastique* 65 (1970): 375–422; Schneider, *Der Konziliarismus* 57–61. Bossuet's *Defensio* is quoted 41 times. For an analysis of the

In the Empire, the tradition of conciliarism also continued. A point of culmination in the seventeenth century is certainly the *Gravamina* of the three Rhenish prince bishop electors (Cologne, Mainz, Trier) in 1673, in which they asked the emperor to continue to adhere to the concordat of Vienna of 1448 regarding the freedom of episcopal elections, tithes, and of other ecclesiastical appointments.[8] Whereas in the seventeenth and the first half of the eighteenth centuries, French theologians dominated the conciliarist and episcopalist "scene" (including Jansenism),[9] the focus of scholarly attention had since shifted to the Holy Roman Empire ever since canon lawyers there had adopted Zeger-Bernhard van Espen's (1646–1728) *Jus ecclesiasticum* (1700) as their main textbook, and thus started to buttress German episcopalism theologically.[10] *De Statu Ecclesiae* (1763) made its anonymous author, known to the public as Justinus Febronius Jurisconsultus, instantaneously famous.[11]

Justinus Febronius—*De Statu Ecclesiae*

At the time of the publication of *De Statu ecclesiae* (1763),[12] it was unresolved what authority the Holy See possessed in diocesan

connection between politics and religion in the work of Bossuet, see Kurt Kluxen, "Politik und Heilsgeschehen bei Bossuet. Ein Beitrag zur Geschichte des Konservativismus," *Historische Zeitschrift* 179 (1955): 449–69.

8. Heribert Raab, "Der reichskirchliche Episkopalismus von der Mitte des 17. bis zum Ende des 18. Jahrhunderts," in *Handbuch der Kirchengeschichte*, eds. Hubert Jedin et al., (Freiburg: Herder, 1970) 6:477–507, at 481–87.

9. Cf. Monique Cottret, "Der Jansenistenstreit," in *Geschichte des Christentums*, ed. Bernard Plongeron (Freiburg: Herder, 1998) 9:348–408; Jean-Pierre Chantin, *Le jansénisme* (Paris: Cerf, 1996).

10. *Zeger-Bernard van and Church-State Relations*, ed. Guido Cooman et al. (Leuven: Leuven University Press, 2003). On the reception of van Espen by Kaspar Barthel, see Heribert Raab, "Johann Kaspar Barthels Stellung in der Diskussion um die Concordata Nationis Germanicae," *Herbipolis Jubilans* (Würzburg: Echter, 1953), 599–616; cf. Matthias Fritsch, *Religiöse Toleranz im Zeitalter der Aufklärung. Naturrechtliche Begründung—konfessionelle Differenzen* (Hamburg: Meiner 2004), 269–80; Hermann Josef Sieben, *Die katholischen Konzilsidee von der Reformation bis zur Aufklärung* (Paderborn: Schöningh: 1988), 404–5; Francis Oakley, *The Conciliarist Tradition* (New York: Oxford University Press, 2003), 186.

11. The pseudonym stems from Hontheim's sister, who under the name *Febronia* was a nun in Juvigny, or from his niece *Febronia*, who had chosen the religious name *Justina*. Ludwig Rechenmacher, *Der Episkopalismus im 18. Jahrhundert in Deutschland und seine Lehren über das Verhältnis zwischen Kirche und Staat* (Regensburg: 1908), 2n1. Leo Just, "Zur Enstehungsgeschichte des Febronius," *Jahrbuch für das Bistum Mainz* 5 (1950), 369–82, at: 370.

12. Oakley, *The Conciliarist Tradition*, 184–95. Oakley believes that Hontheim's work is truly ecumenical (ibid., 187).

territories and affairs, e.g., regarding dispensations. The German prince bishops had to defend their autonomy against the papal nuncios in Vienna, Luzern, Cologne, and Dresden, who tried to intervene with papal jurisdiction within their diocesan lands. Therefore, the ecclesiastical princes fostered the publication of episcopalist canon law books, e.g., by Adam František Kollár (Adam Franz Kollar) (1718–83), and the edition of conciliarist, medieval documents, e.g., the Mainz instrument of acception of 1439.[13]

The tensions between Rome and the Empire reached a point of culmination when, in Lüttich, two bishops were elected on April 20, 1763—one with the approval of the Holy See and one without.[14] Therefore, support for Hontheim's *Febronius* was very much in the interest of German bishops, and indeed their *Monitum Palatinum* (1764) as well as the Koblenz Gravamina of 1769 made *De Statu Ecclesiae* a somewhat "canonized" book of the German Reichskirche.[15] When Pope Clement XIII put the work on the *Index of Forbidden Books* on February 27, 1764, many liberal-minded thinkers across Europe regarded this as a sign of literary quality.[16] Therefore, it is not surprising that within a short time, Hontheim's book was translated into several languages and reprinted again.[17] However, only ten of

13. Heinz Hürten, "Die Mainzer Akzeptation von 1439," *Archiv für Mittelrheinische Kirchengeschichte* 11 (1959), 42–75.
14. Cf. Heribert Raab, *Clemens Wenzeslaus von Sachsen und seine Zeit, 1739-1812* (Freiburg: Herder, 1962), 215–40.
15. Heribert Raab, *Die Concordata Nationis Germanicae in der kanonistischen Diskussion des 17. bis 19. Jahrhunderts. Ein Beitrag zur Geschichte der episkopalistischen Theorie in Deutschland* (Wiesbaden: Steiner, 1956), 132; Raab, "Johann Nikolaus Hontheim," 39. Raab informs us that Hontheim—after the death of Prince Elector Franz Georg von Schönborn (d. 1756)—applied for a Dutch bishopric in order to finish writing his *Febronius* under the protection of the government in Brussels. Cf. Leo Just, "Hontheims Bemühungen um einen Bischofssitz in den österreichischen Niederlanden (1756-62)," *Quellen und Forschungen aus italienischen Archiven und Bibliotheken* 21 (1929/30), 256–90.
16. On censorship in the Holy Roman Empire, cf. Martin Papenheim, "Die katholische Zensur im Reich im 18. Jahrhundert," in *Zensur im Jahrhundert der Aufklärung*, ed. Wilhelm Haefs and York-Gothart Mix (Göttingen: Wallstein, 2007), 79–98; Dominik Burkard, "Die kirchliche Bücherzensur in Deutschland," in *Inquisition, Index, Zensur. Wissenskulturen der Neuzeit im Widerstreit*, ed. Hubert Wolf (Paderborn: Schöningh, 2001), 305–27.
17. Even the nuncio in Cologne, Caprara-Montecuculi, thought that the enormous success was due to the hastened censoring of Hontheim's book by the Curia. Mejer, *Febronius*, 74-75; cf. Christopher Spehr, *Aufklärung und Ökumene. Reunionsversuche zwischen Katholiken und Protestanten im deutschsprachigen Raum des späteren 18. Jahrhunderts* (Tübingen: Mohr Siebeck, 2005), 34. Translations appeared in French, Italian, Spanish, Portuguese (listed in Volker Pitzer, *Justinus Febronius. Das Ringen eines katholischen Irenikers um die Einheit der Kirche im Zeitalter der Aufklärung*

twenty-six German clerical princes publicly announced that the book had been censored.[18] Pope Clement XIII even regarded it as necessary to call on the German bishops in three briefs to stop the "infamous" work with its attack on papal authority since it called for an ecclesiastical revolution that would leave the Church considerably weakened.[19]

The pope was right in a certain sense: with *De Statu Ecclesiae,* or, as it was more commonly called, *Febronius,* a "Catholic intellectual revolution" began,[20] which united not only Catholic intellectuals and Protestants in their antipathy to the Roman Curia, but also the otherwise competitive German bishops: Already on March 19, 1764, the three Rhenish prince bishop electors asked the newly elected Roman king (emperor since 1765) Joseph II (1764–90) to forbid all appeals to the nuncios and the Roman Curia.[21] A few months later, Hontheim, still in disguise, but aware of the turmoil he had started, offered his resignation as auxiliary bishop to the elector and prince-bishop of Trier, which was, nonetheless, not accepted.[22] He refused to retract, however, as such a step would be incompatible with his being a "man of honor."[23]

Due to the controversies, Hontheim still concealed his authorship. As a result, a number of episcopalist canonists—in particular, Benedikt Oberhauser OSB, Johann Baptist Horix, Christoph Neller, and Ludwig Philipp Behlen—were, instead, suspected as instigators. However, in spring 1764, the papal nuncio, Niccolo Oddi, learned from the Frankfurt canon, Damian Friedrich Dumeiz (1728–1802) that Hontheim was the

(Göttingen: Vandenhoeck & Rupprecht, 1976), 191–92). On the free "PR" the forbidden books received, see Peter Godman, *Weltliteratur auf dem Index* (Berlin: Propyläen, 2001).

18. Manfred Weitlauff, "Von der Reichskirche zur 'Papstkirche'" Revolution, Säkularisation, kirchliche Neuorganisation und Durchsetzung der papalistischen Doktrin," *Zeitschrift für Kirchengeschichte* 113 (2002), 355–402, at: 378.
19. Mejer, *Febronius,* 58–60; May, *Die Auseinandersetzungen,* 48.
20. Heribert Raab, "Die katholische Ideenrevolution des 18. Jahrhunderts. Der Einbruch der Geschichte in die Kanonistik und die Auswirkungen in Kirche und Reich bis zum Emser Kongress," in *Katholische Aufklärung—Aufklärung im katholischen Deutschland,* ed. Harm Klueting (Hamburg: Meiner, 1993), 104–18.
21. Raab, *Die Concordata,* 133; Mejer, *Febronius,* 61–62.
22. Mejer, *Febronius,* 61.
23. Ibid., 75.

creator of the *Febronius*.[24] Nevertheless, the Trier auxiliary bishop publicly denied his authorship until 1776–77.[25]

In 1769, after the death of Pope Clement XIII, the ecclesiastical climate changed. His successor, Clement XIV (Lorenzo Ganganelli), was less fervent when it came to objecting to the interference of the state in church affairs. Also, Trier received a new bishop in February 1968, Clemens Wenzeslaus, Prince of Saxony (1768–1802). Like his predecessor, Johann Philipp von Walderdorf (1756–68), the new shepherd of Trier protected his auxiliary: Wenzeslaus did not answer the protest notes that two different popes wrote to him, asking for strict measures against the second edition of *De Statu Ecclesiae*. He asked Hontheim, the author of the incriminated book, to answer to Rome. Not surprisingly, the latter denied that it contained any "dangerous" content.[26]

The life of Johann Nikolaus von Hontheim (1701–91)[27]

Johann Nikolaus Hontheim was born January 27, 1701, in Trier, where his family had made a career as administrators for the archdiocese. A gifted lad, he attended the Jesuit *Gymnasium* in his hometown, then studied law, theology, and classics at the University of Trier. He continued his studies in Louvain and Leiden. However, despite his stay at a Protestant university, he never gained a profound knowledge of Protestant theology. His time in Louvain seems to have shaped him more deeply. There, he encountered a lively Jansenist culture and the Gallicanist works of Zeger van Espen.[28] After he received his doctorate in civil and canon law from the University of Trier in 1724, he began a

---

24. Cf. Heribert Raab, "Damian Friedrich Dumeiz und Kardinal Oddi. Zur Entdeckung des Febronius und zur Aufklärung im Erzstift Mainz und in der Reichsstadt Frankfurt," *Archiv für mittelrheinische Kirchengeschichte* 10 (1958), 217–40. Dumeiz was an interesting character: Hontheim delegated him to supervise the printing of *De Statu Ecclesiae*. Even after his betrayal, he continued to take care of the printing of the supplement volumes to Hontheim's controversial work. Heribert Raab calls him a man with "two souls in his chest." (Raab, ibid., 217) Cf. Schneider, *Der Konziliarismus,* 77.
25. Christopher Spehr, *Aufklärung und Ökumene,* 35; Raab, "Georg Christoph Neller und Febronius," 202.
26. Mejer, *Febronius,* 67–69; 79. Wolfgang Seibrich, *Die Weihbischöfe des Bistums Trier* (Trier: Paulinus, 1998), 148.
27. Seibrich, *Die Weihbischöfe,* 140–150 (incl. list of archival files and bibliography).
28. Pitzer, *Justinus Febronius,* 13; Schneider, *Der Konziliarismus,* 70; Mejer, *Febronius,* 22.

three-year journey through Europe, during which he stayed for almost a year (1726–27) in Rome, where he handled judicial affairs at the Roman Curia for his bishop. After his ordination to the priesthood (May 22, 1728) in the Cathedral of Trier,[29] he began his career as a canon lawyer for the consistory there, and received a canonry at St. Simeon in the same city. Between 1733 and 1738, he also lectured there as a professor of Roman law and published a number of articles in the fields of diocesan history and canon law.[30] Following a promotion within the consistory, Hontheim was appointed auxiliary bishop and general vicar in 1748. In the same year, the canons of St. Simeon also elected him dean. As auxiliary bishop, he was also vice-chancellor of the University of Trier, where he tried to implement a reform of the educational system against the ferocious resistance of the Jesuits.[31] In 1753, he even suggested replacing the intransigent Jesuits with Benedictine monks, who, on the whole, were very open to the ideas of a moderate Enlightenment. However, this could not be realized until 1764.[32] Hontheim was also in charge of the French-speaking parts of the diocese, where he encountered the practice of highly developed Gallicanism.[33]

It is not surprising that Clemens Wenzeslaus, who was doctrinally an orthodox Catholic, protected Hontheim and disappointed the Roman Curia, which had hoped for a political change when the old archbishop died in 1768. Clemens Wenzeslaus was a grandson of Emperor Joseph I, and as such had good relations with the court in Vienna. Maria Theresia, however, urged him to continue to support Hontheim.[34] The archbishop changed his mind only because he was eager to obtain the rich abbey of Mettlach, which the Curia promised him in exchange for censoring the loathed author of the *Febronius*. Nevertheless, it was also Hontheim himself who contributed to his fall, when he backed the

29. Raab, "Johann Nikolaus von Hontheim," 26; Seibrich, *Die Weihbischöfe*, 142.
30. Mejer, *Febronius* 23; Seibrich, *Die Weihbischöfe*, 142.
31. Seibrich, *Die Weihbischöfe*, 146.
32. Mejer, *Febronius* 34–35; 63. For the role of the Benedictines within the Catholic Enlightenment, see Ulrich L. Lehner, *Enlightened Monks* (Oxford: Oxford University Press, 2011).
33. Just, "Zur Entstehungsgeschichte des Febronius," 371; cf. Schneider, *Der Konziliarismus* 70.
34. Mejer, *Febronius*, 65–67; 69–72.

Enlightenment theologian Isenbiehl. However, it was not until spring 1779, one year after his famous retraction (see below), that the old auxiliary bishop's resignation was accepted. Hontheim retired to his castle Montquintin in Luxemburg, where he died on September 2, 1790.[35]

The Background of *De Statu Ecclesiae*

The main theses of *De Statu Ecclesiae* probably go back to 1742, when the electors and their delegates disputed article 14 of the election treaty that they had requested from the designated Emperor Charles VII. Since Charles V, 1519, this article had been binding the emperors to the Vienna Concordat of 1448, in which the head of state promised the bishops his protection against papal punishments as well as interference in their dioceses by the nuncios. Hontheim and his friend Jakob Georg von Spangenberg (1695–1779), a convert from Protestantism, being delegates for the elector of Trier, even suggested at this event denial of all papal jurisdiction for dioceses in the Holy Roman Empire.[36] Already at this point, Hontheim rejected the defense of a monarchical power of the papacy, such as that provided by St. Robert Bellarmine (1542–1621), Guiseppe Agostino Orsi (1692–1761), Prospero Fagnani (1588–1678), and Benedict XIV (1740–58). Furthermore, the election treaty gave him the opportunity to study the history of conciliarism and the so-called "liberties of the German church" in more detail.[37] Nevertheless, one must not underestimate the personal influence on Hontheim's episcopalist system of Spangenberg and the elector himself, Franz Georg von Schönborn (1729–1756).[38]

Among the literary influences upon Hontheim, the most important

---

35. Spehr, *Aufklärung und Ökumen,e* 33; cf. Mejer, *Febronius,* 6–7.
36. Hontheim and Spangenberg were also election delegates when in 1745 Franz I was elected Roman King. Cf. Mejer, *Febroniu,s* 29.
37. Pitzer, *Justinus Febronius,* 103–7; Peter Frowein and Edmund Janson, "Johann Nikolaus von Hontheim—Justinus Febronius. Zum Werk und seinen Gegnern," *Archiv für mittelrheinische Kirchengeschichte* 28 (1976), 129–53, there 129. However, Hontheim never gained a profound knowledge of the different streams of conciliarism. He seems to be have been familiar mainly with Gerson, Cesarini and Andreas Escobar. Cf. Sieben, *Die katholische Konzilsidee,* 433–34.
38. Just, "Zur Enstehungsgeschichte des Febronius," 372.

one was certainly Bossuet's *Defensio declarationis cleri Gallicani* (1745),[39] which he quoted regularly and at length. However, he also used the works of Protestant scholars, e.g., historians such as Marquard Freher (1565–1614), Hermann von der Hardts (1660–1746), Johann Georg Schelhorn (1694–1773), Hermann Conring (1606–81), the philosophers Gottfried Wilhelm Leibniz (1646–1716), Samuel Pufendorf (1632–94), and Christian Thomasius (1655–1728). Among the few German Catholics whom Hontheim regarded as important thinkers were the Augustinian canon Eusebius Amort (1692–1775), arguably one of the most prominent proponents of the Catholic Enlightenment, Prince Abbot Martin Gerbert (1720–93), the German Mabillon, and last but not least, the Wolffian Jesuit Benedikt Stattler (1728–97). Hontheim also quoted frequently two of the main advocates of the Austrian school reforms, the enlightened Abbot Stephan Rautenstrauch (1734–85) and the canon lawyer Paul Joseph von Riegger (1705–75).[40]

The main idea of *De Statu Ecclesiae*

Like so many other works of the time, *De statu Ecclesiae* was influenced by a number of what Jonathan Israel calls conservative Enlightenment ideals, e.g., peaceful ecumenical dialogue, decentralized Church government, and relative freedom of expression. Nevertheless, Hontheim's book also stood in the tradition of Tridentine Reform Catholicism, which aimed at better pastoral care, simpler and less ostentatious piety, clear theological doctrines, and so on. This could also be a description of the phenomenon of the *Catholic Enlightenment*.[41] However, the book also paid its tribute to the conciliarist tradition of the Middle Ages. Thus, one can truly call Hontheim's work a "marriage" between "conservative." Enlightenment thought (heavily influenced by Jansenism) and conciliarism.

Febronius idealized the first eight centuries of the church (*ecclesia primitiva*)—very much as Jansenism[42] did—as the true and normative

39. Schneider, *Der Konziliarismus,* 71; Spehr, *Aufklärung und Ökumene,* 38. Cf. Duchon, "A Bossuet;" Sieben, *Die katholische Konzilsidee,* 433.
40. Pitzer, *Justinus Febronius,* 97–110.
41. Raab, *Die Concordata,* 125.

Christendom, and the later development, especially of the papacy, as a decline and perversion. Such a rigid view of history, which excludes from the beginning any doctrinal or organizational development, was not only a common feature of eighteenth-century scholastic theology, but also of the Catholic Enlightenment.[43] The Josephinist university reform, in particular, favored the expansion of church history as a discipline, not because of a sudden interest in history, but because it could legitimize the ecclesiastical policy that was exercised by the state. The reforms of Joseph II pretended to restore the true, pope-free Catholicism of the early patristic era.[44]

The content of *De Statu Ecclesiae*—an overview

Hontheim was not a clever innovator. Despite the fame his book received, it did not really say anything new and did not propose a new thesis. However, it brought the centuries-old critique of the papacy into a "coherent and pragmatic system."[45] Moreover, it did not start out with a philosophical foundation, but by stating a fact: the influence of secular princes on ecclesiastical affairs. For the author of *De Statu Ecclesiae,* the state was the primary guardian of the church's constitution, since it was—like the church[46]—institutionalized by God himself.[47] Therefore, Hontheim tried to convince the secular princes to use their influence to win back lost liberties that were usurped by the Curia.[48] In the same manner, the French,[49] and later the Austrian

---

42. Cf. Leo Just, "Weihbischof Hontheim und der Ausklang des Jansenismus in Orval, 1758–1788," *Vierteljahresblätter der Trierer Gesellschaft für nützliche Forschungen* 5 (1959), 33–40.
43. See Ulrich L. Lehner, "Enlightened Monasticism. Introduction," in *Beda Mayr-Vertheidigung der katholischen Religion,* ed. Ulrich L. Lehner (Leiden and Boston: Brill, 2009).
44. Cf. Emil Clemens Scherer, *Geschichte und Kirchengeschichte an den deutschen Universitaten. Ihre Anfänge im Zeitalter des Humanismus und ihre Ausbildung zu selbständigen Disziplinen* (Freiburg: Herder, 1927). Schneider, *Der Konziliarismus,* 79.
45. Edmund Janson, *Das Kirchenverständnis des Febronius* (Rome: Gregoriana, 1978), 62.
46. Hontheim gives a clear definiton of what he means by church in *De Statu Ecclesiae* (Frankfurt/ Leipzig: 1773), 4/1:23: "Ecclesia est societas hominum per Baptismum in Christo eum in finem unitorum, ut secundum normam in Evangelio praescriptam verum Deum colant, et aternam salutem consequantur. Est societas inaequalis, in qua sunt, qui imperium sacrum exercent; alii, quorum omnis sita est in obediendo gloria, attamen simul cum illis corpus unum mysticum seu morale constituens."
47. Seibrich, *Die Weihbischöfe,* 147.
48. Wolfgang Seibrich, "Aufgeklärtes Kirchenrecht als restaurative Reform. Die deutschen Episkopalisten um Johann Nikolaus von Hontheim und ihre Beziehung zu Zeger-Bernard van

Jansenists also sought the support of the civil authorities, but finally handed over the church to a limitless governmental influence.[50]

Febronius's concern is nevertheless a theological one: In the four prefaces (to Pope Clement XIII, the Christian kings and noblemen, the bishops, and the theologians/canonists), Hontheim elucidates that the office of bishop was of divine law, and therefore unrestrictable by a human institution such as the Curia. "The bishops are the true limits of the primacy."[51] To restore the ancient church order, the episcopal authority had to be reinstituted and the Curia had to be confronted with the reports about their abuse of power as well as with the fact that its legitimization was based on forgeries.[52] The papacy could only keep what it entailed in the first centuries of Christianity. Everything else had to be regarded as redundant or harmful historical ballast.[53] Hontheim even went so far as to claim that a "reformed" Catholicism has to avoid the "extremes" of Protestantism, which includes the complete abandonment of a papal office, and Ultramontanism, an exaggeration of papal authority. Such a proposition was a declaration of war: the auxiliary bishop had charged the defenders of curialism as extremists and had dared to compare them with Protestant heretics. Consequently, canonists who were loyal to Rome declared the ecclesiology of *De Statu Ecclesiae* as no longer within the boundaries of legitimate dissent. It was labeled heretical.[54] Hontheim, however, did not understand himself as an "innovator," but as a "restorer" or "reformer." The first edition with its nine chapters[55] was soon

Espen," in *Zeger-Bernard van Espen at the Crossroads of Canon Law, History, Theology and Church-State Relations*, eds. Guido Cooman et al., 229–65, at: 256.

49. Dale van Kley, *The Religious Origins of the French Revolution* (New Haven: Yale University Press, 1996) passim.
50. Pitzer, *Justinus Febronius*, 111; May, *Die Auseinandersetzungen*, 44; Rechenmacher, *Der Episkopalismus*, 16; cf. Johann Nikolaus von Hontheim, *Justini Febronii JCti. de statu Ecclesiae et legitima potestate Romani Pontificis liber singularis: ad reuniendos dissidentes in religione christianos compositus* (Frankfurt, 1763) [cited as: Febronius] ch. 9, §10; Engelbert Plassmann, *Staatskirchenrechtliche Grundgedanken der deutschen Kanonisten an der Wende vom 18. zum 19. Jahrhundert* (Freiburg: Herder, 1968) passim.
51. Schneider, *Der Konziliarismus*, 72.
52. Pitzer, *Justinus Febronius*, 87.
53. Rechenmacher, *Der Episkopalismus*, 3.
54. Pitzer, *Justinus Febronius* 33; 149n30.
55. *De Statu Ecclesiae* (Frankfurt, 1763) ch. 1: De exteriore forma regiminis, quam in sua Ecclesia Christus Dominus instituit (1–68); ch. 2: De Primatu in Ecclesia, et genuinis ejus juribus (69–127); ch. 3: De incrementis jurium Primatus Romani, illorumque ansis, tum fortuitis et innocuis, tum

expanded to four volumes and only in 1777 was an abridged version, the *Febronius abbreviatus,* published.[56]

The first part of *De Statu Ecclesiae* (chapters 1–2) lays out Hontheim's considerations about the external way of governing the church and its foundation in scripture and tradition. Christ is, thus, the true head of the church (*caput et perpetuus rector*)[57] and the pope is subordinate to the council of bishops. Furthermore, the papal office is not preserved from error (infallibility); only the teaching of the universal church is so preserved.[58] The legitimization of the papal office lies in the unifying function of the papacy. Therefore, the papacy is entitled only to the rights and privileges it needs to fulfill its purpose—all other liberties are not essential and can be abandoned.[59] To be *centrum unitatis,*[60] the pope has the right to get informed by all local churches (*jus*

sontibus (128–84); ch. 4: De causis, quae vulgo majores vocantur (185–220); ch. 5: De Legibus Ecclesiasticis, earum pro Universali Ecclesia ferendi jure; et de Appellationibus ad Romanum Pontificem (221–80); ch. 6: De Conciliis Generalibus (281–440); ch. 7: De authoritate Episcoporum ex Jure divino (441–514); ch. 8: De libertate Ecclesiae, eijusque restaurandae jure et causis; ch. 9: De mediis recuperandae Libertatis Ecclesiasticae (559–623). See also *Febronius abbreviatus* (Frankfurt, 1777): Epistula ad Thomam Mamachium (cf. Leo Just, "Iustini Febronii Epistola ad Thomam Mamachium," *Quellen und Forschungen aus italienischen Archiven und Bibliotheken* 22 (1930/31), 256–88); Discursus praevius: De subsidiis & methodo in tractandis Ecclesiasticis Disciplinis (1–6) ch. 1: De Ecclesia & ejus Statu (7–34); ch. 2: De Conciliis generalibus (35–100); ch. 3: De Primatus in Ecclesia (101–48); ch. 4: De Episcopatu (149–80); ch. 5: De Praebendis & Dignitatibus (181–209); ch. 6: De Legibus & Judiciis Ecclesiasticis (210–50); ch. 7: De Libertate Ecclesiae (251–95). Cf. Pitzer, *Justinus Febronius,* 31

56. Mejer, *Febronius,* 101; *Allgemeine deutsche Bibliothek,* 1780, Anh. 25–36. Bd., 1. Abt. 333–35.
57. *Febronius,* ch. 1, §8 ("Capitalis haec quaestio de forma Ecclesiae Monarchia in Concilio Tridentino agitata, nec tamen favore Romanis Pontificis decisa fuit") 40–41; ibid., §9: "Ecclesia hodieque regitur exteriore Christi institutoris assistentia." *Febronius abbreviatus,* ch. 1, §2.
58. *Febronius,* ch. 1, §9, 46–64; cf. ibid., §10, 64: "Ultramontanorum doctrina de Romani Pontificis infallibilitate neque ab aliis Catholicis Ecclesiis agnoscetur [. . .] Neque practicam habet utilitatem." Infallibility is for Hontheim the church's participation in the Divine, cf. Janson, *Das Kirchenverständnis,* 168.
59. *Febronius,* ch. 2, §4 ("In quo consistat natura Primatus, & quae sint genuina eijus jura?"), 83–88; cf. ibid., ch. 2, §2, 74–76: "Fundamentum huius Primatus est bonum Unitatis in Ecclesia.")
60. Already in the first sentence of the dedication to Pope Clement XIII the term *centrum unitatis* is used: "Junctus Cathedrae Petri, tanquam Centro Catholicae unionis, a quo separari nunquam permissum est [. . .] plenus sincera veneratione erga eum, quem divina Providentia locavit in Apostolico throne [. . .] qui Primatum in universa Ecclesia divinitus institutum, legitime tenet: de huius Primatus jure tractare praesumens, ejusdem veros terminos delineare agredior [. . .]" Neller seems to have the term from the *Febronius.* In 1786, we can also find it in the files of "Punctuation of Ems" and the Synod of Pistoia. Although the words were used in Gallicanism since around 1681 they were not restricted to it; even Thomassin and Duperron use *centrum unitatis.* However, at the end of the 18th Century, the term becomes somewhat identified with Febronianism. Theologians of the 19th avoid it, while the Second Vatican Council used it again. Cf. Frowein, "Primat und Episkopat," 227–29; Stümper, *Die kirchenrechtlichen Ideen des Febronius* (Aschaffenburg, 1908), 38–42.

relationis)—at least, regarding more general issues. If he decided to answer an informing letter, however, the pope's lines must not be understood as commands, but as advice. A second right of the pope consists in sending legates. Originally, Hontheim points out, legates were without jurisdiction and only during the course of the Middle Ages did they illegitimately acquire this authority.[61] This view of the nuncios as troublemakers is only a consequence of Hontheim's view of the episcopal office: every bishop has immediate jurisdiction over his local church, which is not derived from the Holy See, but from his apostolic succession.[62] Although the preservation of ecclesiastical unity is the central task of the papacy, Hontheim's coice of words is very reserved. He tries to avoid a causal connection between the church's unity and the necessity of the papal office, since for him, the unity of the church is the foundation of the primacy and not its consequence: "The Primacy [of the pope] has functional but not constitutive importance for the church."[63] Another papal responsibility is to be *vindex canonum*, securer of the deposit of faith.[64] However, this task also has to be considered subsidiary (*jus supplendi*). The pope also has the authority to decree provisional law, since it is impossible to convene a council often enough. Such law acquires universal validity only if all bishops, or at least a majority, agree with it.[65]

Hontheim's emphasis on conceding to the papacy, more than an honorary primacy, is irreconcilable with his assertion that the pope is

---

61. *Febronius*, ch. 2, §10: "Romanus Pontifex habet jus mittendi Legatus ad opus officii sui Primatialis," 113–16; *Febronius,* ch. 2, §5/6, 88–91 ("Ecclesia, cui Primatus annectitur, per hoc sit Centrum Unitatis;" §6: "Ea, quae ad Ecclesiae statum attinent, ubivis gerantur, ad Romanum Pontificem, tanquam Primatem, referenda sunt."). *Febronius abbreviatus*, ch. 3, §2; ibid. ch. 4, §3, 165: "Facultates Legatorum Sedis Apostolicae & immoderata eorum auctoritas [. . .]" Cf. Stümper, *Die kirchenrechtlichen Ideen des Febronius,* 39.

62. *Febronius*, ch. 2, §11, 120: "Graviter sane peccant, qui sensu Romanum Pontificem *Catholicae Ecclesiae Episcopum* dici existimant, quasi Catholica Ecclesia ejus dioecesis sit, in qu ipse proprio jure Episcopum agat, reliqui Epicopi, prater nomen, vicariam illius unius praefecturam tantum administrent." Cf. *Febronius abbreviatus*, ch. 4, §1–4. Even the title "bishop of Rome" was nothing extraordinary in the eyes of Hontheim: "Episcopus Urbis Romae contentus est, nihil aliud extraordinaria illa inscriptione designat, quam Catholicae communis Episcopus [. . .]" (*Febronius*, ch. 2, §11, 122).

63. Pitzer, *Justinus Febronius* 32. Cf. *Febronius abbreviatus*, ch. 1, §1–6.

64. *Febronius,* ch. 2, §7, 98–103: "Romanus Pontifex est tutor et vindex Canonum per universam Ecclesiam." Cf. *Febronius abbreviatus*, ch. 3, §5: "Custos & Executor Canonum."

65. *Febronius,* ch. 2, §9, 112. Neller taught the same, cf. Raab, "Georg Christoph Neller und Febronius," 195.

not *summus episcopus*, but only *episcopus primae sedis*. Thus, the bishops as successors of the apostles have an authority equal to that of the bishop of Rome (*omnes episcopi in episcopatu pares sunt*).[66] In the college of bishops, all are *coimperantes, coregnantes ac conjudices*.[67]

This is, however, not enough for the reformer of Trier: for him, the succession of St. Peter is divine law, instituted by Christ; however, the content and mode (location and rights) of this succession are human law.[68] Consequently, papal primacy is bound only by human law to the See of Rome and could be transferred to any other diocese.[69] This is the application of the Gallican axiom that the keys to the kingdom of God were not given to St. Peter, but to the whole church (Matt. 16, 18).[70]

The lengthy second part (chapters 3–7) analyzes the historical development of papal rights and privileges. In Hontheim's view, the early medieval *Pseudoisidorian Decretals* established a new ecclesiology that saw the pope as the bishop of the Catholic Church and the diocesan bishops as his subordinated chaplains. This "perverted" system is, in the eyes of the Trier auxiliary bishop, one of the main reasons for the church division created by the Reformation.[71] Consequently, *Febronius* distinguishes between the *Apostolic See* as the bearer of the primacy and the Roman Curia as the institution that

---

66. *Febronius*, ch. 2, §11, 119.

67. Frowein, "Primat und Episkopat," 219. *Febronius*, ch. 7, §1 ff; *Febronius abbreviatus*, ch. 1, §4.

68. Stümper, *Die kirchenrechtlichen Ideen des Febronius*, 22. *Febronius*, ch. 2, §3, 76–77: "Personas, quae post futurum Petri decessum primarium hoc in Ecclesia munus gesturae essent, salvator non designavit: Fecit id vel Petrus ipse, & solus; vel cum eo Ecclesia. Perinde est, qua ratione & quo tempore, id factum fuerit; sufficit Primatum a Christo institutm esse; provisione eatenus a Deo non facta. [. . .] Cum itaque firmum maneat, quoad personam & locum successoris in Primatu, a Deo nihil provisum statutumque [*sic*!] esse, reliquum est, ut penes Ecclesiam (cui, uti dictum, potestas clavium, & omnis Ecclesiastica authoritas tradita fuit) steterit, & etiamnun perduret jus determinandi, per quem unam alteramve partem clavium administrari, adeoque, per quem primum in Ecclesia officium, per quem inferiora munia, conformiterad institutionem Christi, geri velit. Hinc, sicut per rationes convenientiae *humana auctoritate* Romanae urbis Antistiti sacer Primatus creditus fuit; sic & ex rationabilibus motivis *auctoritate Ecclesiae* eundem ad alium Epicopum, eg. Mediolanensem, Parisiensen & ch. Transferri posse, recte statuunt." Hontheim refers on this page mostly to Scotus and Cusanus.

69. *Febronius*, ch. 2, §3, 76–77. *Febronius abbreviatus*, ch. 3, §1, 105: "*Successio ipsa & Ratio successionis*: illa est ex ordinatione Christi, haec ex instituto hominum." Cf. Rechenmacher, *Der Episkopalismus*, 5; Stümper, *Die kirchenrechtlichen Ideen*, 24–25.

70. *Febronius*, ch. 1, §2–3; *Febronius abbreviatus*, ch. 1, §3; Stümper, *Die kirchenrechtlichen Ideen*, 29; Janson, *Das Kirchenverständnis*, 114–35 (cf. ibid., 139–40 makes clear that the governance of the church cannot be executed by the faithful alone).

71. Cf. *Febronius*, ch. 3; *Febronius abbreviatus*, ch. 3.

had usurped the liberties of the local churches.[72] This also marks the difference between Hontheim's view and Gallicanism as well as episcopalism. He did not propose a diminution of papal rights, but a restoration of a primordial ecclesiology. Moreover, this explains why he never participated in the discussion regarding the German concordates (*Concordata Germaniae*). For Hontheim, every treaty would have been a compromise and an implicit acceptance of wrongful Roman claims.[73]

Especially important is chapter 6, in which the author again explains his concept of the papal office as service for the union of the church. Furthermore, he gives practical reasons along with historical ones as to why the college of bishops, when it is convened in a council, bears supreme jurisdiction over the church.[74] The main rationale for such a necessity is that the Curia has proved itself as remarkably resistant to all attempted reforms for the good of the Church.[75] A good example is that the decrees of Trent were not implemented until the seventeenth and eighteenth centuries, for which, not the bishops, but the popes, are to be blamed.[76] Moreover, in order to retrieve the liberties of the local church, it is not enough that the bishops claim their rights, but that the laity be educated, and that they ask, together with their shepherds, for a universal council to resolve the problem.[77] Only councils and regular synods of all bishops could stop the abuses of the Curia and prevent scandals.[78] Moreover, Hontheim goes so far as to say that whoever

---

72. May, *Die Auseinandersetzungen,* 43. "Primatus authoritatis et potestatis: primatus curae ac sollicitudinis, primatus quoque in ferendis una cum Corpore Episcoporum legibus et dijudicandis causis." *Febronius* (Frankfurt and Leipzig: 1770) 2:321 quoted from Seibrich, "Aufgeklärtes Kirchenrecht," 249. Cf. *Febronius abbreviatus,* ch. 3, §5, 125.

73. *Febronius abbreviatu,* xxx; Seibrich, "Aufgeklärtes Kirchenrecht," 249–50.

74. *Febronius,* Dedication to Papst Clement XIII; ch. 6, §2, 296–98: "Nulla lege divina aut humana convocatio Universalium Conciliorum summo Pontifico reservatur." Cf. ibid. ch. 6, §3, 299–301; ch. 6, §11, 216 and 219; ch. 1, §5, 18. *Febronius abbreviatus,* ch. 2, §7; ch. 3, §2–3; Pitzer, *Justinus Febronius,* 33. For Hontheim the writings of the Council of Constance (1414–18), of Jean Gerson, and of a number of Gallican authors were especially important. Nevertheless, he distances himself from Edmond Richer. Cf. Schneider, *Der Konziliarismus,* 75; cf. *Febronius abbreviatus,* ch. 2, §7.

75. Cf. *Febronius,* ch. 9, §11, 623.

76. Schneider, *Der Konziliarismus,* 77; Febronius, ch. 16. May, *Die Auseinandersetzungen* 43: "Das Konzil sei berechtigt, Appellationen gegen päpstliche Entscheidungen entgegenzunehmen, und der Papst könne sie nicht hindern … Mit derartigen Forderungen rannte Hontheim in Mainz offene Türen ein. Denn die Appellation gegen den Papst an ein künftiges Konzil hatte in Mainz Tradition."

77. Schneider, *Der Konziliarismus,* 77; Febronius, ch. 9; *Febronius abbreviatus,* ch. 7.

defends the grievances brought about by Roman ultramontanists departs from the real will of Christ, and therefore risks losing his eternal salvation![79]

Part 3 (chapters 7–9) can be regarded as a conclusion. It focuses on the liberty of the church (*libertas ecclesiae*). To regain it and to achieve a reunion between Catholics and Protestants, the papal primacy has to be reduced to its Christ-given size.[80] Unfortunately, Hontheim does not explain how the reunion should come about. He seems to imply that Protestant Christians should revert to a reformed Catholic Church that is purged of the primacy ballast. Nevertheless, they would have to leave behind their theological axioms (*sola gratia, sola fides, sola scriptura,* etc.). This oversimplification of ecumenism shows—according to Harm Klueting—that Hontheim did not really think of a reunion.[81] On the contrary, he used the disguise of ecumenism for his own episcopalist agenda. How else could one explain the complete absence of any discussion of justification or sacramental theology?[82]

Reaction and Retraction (1778)

The mass of pamphlets and books directed against *De Statu Ecclesiae* challenged the author to respond. Already, the second edition (Frankfurt: 1765) contained four appendixes.[83] Four volumes followed until 1774 (volumes 2–4).[84] However, not until 1778 did the influence of the nuncios Caprara, Bellisomi, Garampi, and the confessor Franz Beck bring Hontheim to "recant" his *Febronius.*[85] However, it was Giuseppe

78. Pitzer, *Justinus Febronius,* 36; Sieben, *Die katholische Konzilsidee,* 426–36. Cf. *Febronius,* ch. 6, §7, 329; §8, 331; §10, 359–61; §15, 398: "Adversus modernos abusus Ecclesia semper in Generalibus Conciliis reclamavit, & eorum reformationem studiose quaesivit. Sed per Romanam Curiam ab optimo proposito nunquam non impedimenta fuit." *Febronius abbreviatus,* ch. 2, §2.
79. Pitzer, *Justinus Febronius,* 37; *Febronius,* ch. 6, §14: "Illos quisquis sponte tolerat, summa injuria in Ecclesiam agit, nec potest salvare animam suam."
80. *Febronius,* ch. 8, §7; *Febronius abbreviatus,* ch. 7.
81. Cf. Klueting, "Wiedervereinigung der getrennten Konfessionen oder episkopalistische Nationalkirche?"
82. Spehr, *Aufklärung und Ökumene,* 42–43.
83. Printed separately as *Vindiciae Febronianae seu refutationes nonullorum opusculorum quae adversus Justini Febronii Jcti tractatum de statu Ecclesiae et potestate Romani Pontificis nuper prodierunt* (Zurich: 1765).
84. *Justinus Febronius—De Statu ecclesia . . . ,* 4 vols. (Frankfurt: 1770–74).
85. Raab, "Johann Nikolaus Hontheim," 40–41; Dries Vanysacker, "Der Widerruf des 'Febronius' und

Garampi (1725–91) who became the key figure of an anti-Febronian network between 1764 and 1776.[86]

Since 1771, it had become more and more problematic for the aging auxiliary bishop to deny his authorship. When Franz Heinrich Beck was called as confessor to the court of prince-bishop Clemens Wenzeslaus (1768–97), he immediately started to conspire against Hontheim.[87] He was successful in alienating the two bishops from each other. Nevertheless, Clemens Wenzeslaus still maintained a certain appreciation for the old man. Also, the suppression of the Jesuits (1773) delayed actions against the author of the *Febronius*.

The newly elected Pope Pius VI (1775), however, was not willing to continue the more lenient policy of his predecessor. At the ordination ceremony of the new nuncio for Cologne on September 24, 1775, the pope was hard on German episcopalism. He complained about the "self-indulgent" innovators who want to overthrow the apostolic foundation of the Church, the papacy. He called this school of thought a contagious disease (*contagio*), which originated in Germany.[88] However, it was not only a case of the pope and the archbishop of Trier increasing the pressure on Hontheim. A worldly motive also contributed to the fall of Hontheim: the Curia promised Clemens Wenzeslaus the abbey of Mettlach if he would silence Hontheim by appointing a coadjutor for him. On March 2, 1777, Johann Maria Herbain was, in fact, made coadjutor auxiliary bishop with the right to succeed Hontheim.[89]

Any remaining sympathy for the old man was lost when Hontheim recommended on November 6, 1777, the contested book *Neuer Versuch über die Weissagung von Emmanuel* by Johann Lorenz Isenbiehl (1744–1818), a professor of exegesis and Oriental languages.[90] Isenbiehl explained Isaiah 7:14 not as a foretelling of Christ's virginal conception,

---

Kardinal Guiseppe Garampi in Rom. Eine aufklärerische ultramontane Bekämpfung des Febronianismus, 1764–1792," *Kurtrierisches Jahrbuch* 43 (2003), 125–41, at 131–33.

86. Vanysacker, "Der Widerruf."

87. Franz Josef Heyen, *Das Erzbistum Trier. Das Stift St. Paulin vor Trier—Germania Sacra Neue Folge*, 6/1 (New York: DeGruyter, 1966), 766; Just, *Der Widerruf des Febronius*.

88. Zitiert nach Mejer, *Febronius*, 97–98.

89. Mejer, *Febronius*, 105–9; on Herbain see Seibrich, *Die Weihbischöfe des Bistums Trier*, 150–57.

90. Partially reprinted in Mejer, *Febronius*, 112–13; cf. Vanysacker, "Der Widerruf," 132.

but as a verse connected historically to Isaiah's time.[91] Since the exegete was already under suspicion (and was later on censored),[92] Hontheim's support—let us not forget, he was a bishop—caused a scandal: Wenzeslaus urged him to make a clarification. He acceded in a document dated from April 9, 1778. In it, Hontheim declares that he embraces and supports every ecclesiastical judgment over Isenbiehl. However, he still charged the Curia with abuse of power and distinguished it from the "true" Apostolic See.[93] This was a fatal diplomatic mistake. Now, the auxiliary bishop was even more vulnerable. The Trier elector Clemens Wenzeslaus requested in a lengthy letter dated April 21, 1778 that Hontheim not only embrace all possible outcomes of the Isenbiehl trial, but also retract his *De Statu Ecclesiae*. The archbishop suggested that he should follow the example of bishop Fenelon, who had recanted. Surprisingly, Hontheim immediately obeyed. Clemens now sent him a list of sixteen curialist sentences, which a French theologian (perhaps Nicolas Bergier) had collected. These should be the basis for the retraction.

Had Hontheim really changed his mind? Not at all; he only obeyed his superior. If one reads the manuscript Hontheim was working on during this year, this becomes obvious: he planned a refutation of Thomas Maria Mamachi's (1713–92) *Letter to Justinus Febronius* (*Epistula Justinum Febronium Ictum de ratione regendae Christianae Reipublicae deque legitima Romani Pontificis potestate*; Rome: 1776). Only the proscription of the prince-elector stopped the project.[94]

During the summer of 1778, the retraction was sent to Rome. Yet, in a letter dated August 22, 1778, the papal court criticized some passages of Hontheim's text. He was asked to change them according to the

---

91. On Isenbiehl see Norbert Jung, *Der Speyerer Weihbischof Andreas Seelmann (1732-1789) im Spannungsfeld von 'nachgeholter' Aufklärung und 'vorgezogener' Restauration* (Mainz: Gesellschaft für Mittelrheinische Kirchengeschichte, 2002), 624–62 as well as ch. 10 in this volume.
92. On the process of censoring Catholic theologians in the 18th Century, see Hans Paarhammer, "Sollicita ac provida. Neuordnung von Lehrbeanstandung und Bücherzensur in der katholischen Kirche im 18. Jahrhundert," in *Ministerium Iustitiae. Festschrift für H. Heinemann*, ed. Andre Gabriels and Heinrich J. F. Reinhardt (Essen: Ludgerus, 1985), 349–61.
93. Partially reprinted in Mejer, *Febronius* 113–14. Cf. Febronius, ch. 9, §7, 588: "Verum ab hac Prima Sede apprime distinguenda Curialistarum cohors [. . .]"
94. The manuscript was probably given to Pope Pius VI as a personal "trophy" when he met the Archbishop of Trier in 1782. Just, "Iustini Febronii Epistola ad Thomam Mamachium," 256–59.

attached annotations.[95] Moreover, he had to weave these changes into the text in such a way that every reader would assume that they were written by Hontheim himself. "It was the perfect instruction for play-acting. If the auxiliary would not accept everything from Rome and perhaps even more corrections he would not receive forgiveness."[96] The old auxiliary bishop refused to implement only the sentence that the papal government was rightly called monarchical (*ut proinde merito monarchium Ecclesiae regimen a catholicis Doctoribus appelletur*).[97] At least in one point, he remained truthful.[98] The affair took the whole summer: first, the prince-elector was not content with the text, then the Curia, and so on. In November 1778, Hontheim's text was finally endorsed both by the Archbishop of Trier and the Curia. The final draft was in the form of a letter to the pope, dated November 15, 1778.[99] In it, Hontheim admitted and repented his mistakes as well as surrendered himself to the Holy See.[100] However, the penitent had severe misgivings about a publication of his letter. Pius VI answered on December 19, already delighted.

The author of the *Febronius* seemed surprised when journals and newspapers all over Europe reported that Pope Pius VI had presented his letter to the college of cardinals at their Christmas meeting in 1778. The Curia now "invited" the German bishops to congratulate the pope on his victory, and thus indirectly to accept his jurisdictional claims. Hontheim's retraction was also considered politically valuable since the Curia thought it could be used against Josephinist canonists (e.g., Valentin Eybel, Paul Joseph von Riegger, Stephan Rautenstrauch).[101]

On January 15, 1779, Clemens Wenzeslaus required of Hontheim to

---

95. Mejer, *Febronius,* 116–25; cf. ibid., 135–36.
96. Mejer, *Febronius,* 127; cf. ibid., 131.
97. Ibid., 128.
98. Rechenmacher, *Der Episkopalismus,* 4. Hontheim rejected this term not because he denied an "imperium" within the Church, but because for him "monarchia" was connected to the dangers of arbitrariness and despotism, cf. Janson, *Das Kirchenverständnis,* 200.
99. Manfred Brandl, "Bemühungen der Wiener Nuntiatur um die Verbreitung von Hontheims (Febronius') Widerruf (1779)," *Römische Historische Mitteilungen* 20 (1978), 77–108.
100. Mejer, *Febronius* 130: "Monumentum revocationis omnium, quae adversum ea et si quae fortasse alia verae doctrinae capita seu universalis Ecclesiae jura, licet praeter intentionem, a me quavis via aut modo dicta scriptaque fuere vel scripta videri possent."
101. Brandl, "Bemühungen der Wiener Nuntiatur," 79.

prepare the publication of the Roman files about his retraction as well as the text of his letter. Hontheim was shocked, since he believed that his submission would remain private; much later, he told his biographer that he had made strict privacy a condition of his retraction. Hontheim's archbishop even pretended that he had not imagined that the pope would publicly announce the retraction letter. One cannot but feel sympathy for the old auxiliary bishop who tried to appease his superiors and was, as it seems, betrayed.[102] He played his part in the publication of the files and of his letter on February 4, 1779, probably too exhausted to fight his immediate superior in Trier and the Curia at the same time.[103] Nevertheless, Rome insisted that the deceived one stay in his office in order to keep the appearance of a completely settled strife.[104]

For all supporters of the Josephinist ecclesiastical policy, e.g., Ignaz de Luca, the retraction was one of the most dangerous writings, "against the worldly regents."[105] The papal victory, however, was a small one, first of all, because a number of German bishops and secular governments refused to allow the printing of the book (Austria, Spain, Milan, Venice),[106] and second, because Hontheim's friends publicized the truth about the retraction, which the "penitent" had only signed and not—as the Curia claimed—authored.[107]

The Commentary on Hontheim's Retraction (1781)[108]

In 1780, a choir of papers spread the news that the text of Hontheim's retraction had been forced. Hontheim was fully aware of this and encouraged it. Archbishop Clemens Wenzeslaus, however, requested a

---

102. Mejer, *Febronius,* 143–44.
103. Ibid., 148–51.
104. Brandl, "Bemühungen der Wiener Nuntiatur," 92–94.
105. Ibid., 86.
106. Mejer, *Febronius,* 159–61; Brandl, "Bemühungen der Wiener Nuntiatur," 89–90. On the editions of the *acta* consult Brandl, ibid., 100–5. In the Holy Roman Empire, there was no universal censoring of books like in France, cf. Papenheim, "Die katholische kirchliche Zensur im Reich," 91–92; Ulrich Eisenhardt, *Die kaiserliche Aufsicht über Buchdruck, Buchhandel und Presse im Heiligen Römischen Reich Deutscher Nation (1496-1806),* (Karlsruhe: Müller, 1970) passim.
107. Mejer, *Febronius,* 163–66.
108. The only detailed study is still Mejer, *Febronius,* 177–201.

public statement in which Hontheim should tell the public the "truth." On April 2, 1780, he indeed published a letter that asserted the voluntariness of his retraction. Yet, in his private correspondence, he admitted that he was moved by the immense pressure put on him to take this step. Even his close friend Krufft was disappointed—he thought the brave author of *De Statu Ecclesiae* had become a frail geriatric.[109]

At this point, Hontheim decided to comment on his retraction. The idea for this goes back to the year 1778, when he had to implement the sixteen curialist theses in his letter to the pope.[110] At that time, he did not have the energy for resistance. The legitimization for Hontheim's new work was the pope's reaction himself: he had asked the ailing auxiliary bishop to write an academic work that would defend the rights of the Holy See. That Hontheim's book, *Commentary on His Retractions* (*Commentarius in Suam Retractationem*), which was published under the pseudonym "Febronius" in Frankfurt 1781, was quite the opposite, is surprising. Finally, it seems, he had the courage to say what he thought.

In sentence seven, Hontheim explained how the papal office unified the Church. However, he also remarked on the illegal papal "interferences" with diocesan jurisdiction, since he described the bishops not only as successors of the Apostles, but also as vicars of Christ—the latter being a title reserved for the papacy alone! Even if Hontheim refused to acknowledge it, what jurisdiction he leaves to the pope gave him only the power of an honorary Primacy, which, again, was restricted by a general council.[111]

The state is given great influence (thirty-seventh proposition): first, it can justly revoke all ecclesiastical privileges; second, every church authority needs the approval of the state to make proclamations regarding faith, sacraments, or discipline that could have an effect on public life; third, the state *placeat* implies the publication of dogmatic decisions and censorships.[112] What Hontheim embraces here is *pure*

109. Mejer, *Febronius,* 180–85.
110. Reprint of Hontheim's "Promemoria" in Mejer, *Febronius,* 303–16.
111. Mejer, *Febronius,* 188.

Gallicanism, thereby showing that he had never changed his mind. Febronius was still Febronius![113] What then did he retract, according to his "commentary"? Only the public call for resistance against Rome and the acrimony of his critique, not the basic ideas of his work. Simultaneously however, Hontheim assured the pope that his commentary was a defense of papal rights and that he never engaged in spreading rumors about the nature of his retraction. This was certainly the culminating point of dishonesty.[114]

Thus, another book by Hontheim caused a scandal. Clemens Wenzeslaus tried to stop the delivery of it, but failed. The Curia was outraged—especially because Hontheim had not submitted his manuscript to the censors. Cardinal Hyacinth Gerdil (1718–1802), the prefect of the Congregation of the Index, received the order to analyze the new disturbing book from Germany: to what extent was it really a defense of papal rights? Gerdil did not need much time to realize that the commentary practically revoked the retraction. The pope, however, hesitated to publish Gerdil's findings so as to prevent an escalation of trouble with Austrian Emperor Joseph II, who since 1780, had instigated Febronian policies.[115] Only after Joseph's (February 20, 1790) and Hontheim's deaths (September 2, 1790) was Gerdil's book published (1792).[116]

A Milestone of Ecumenical and Ecclesiological Theology?

It is an established consensus that Georg Christoph Neller (1709–83),[117] professor of canon law in Trier and a student of Johann Caspar Barthel

---

112. Ibid., 189–90; Rechenmacher, *Der Episkopalismus,* 40.
113. Cf. Brandl, "Bemühungen der Wiener Nuntiatur," 82; Mejer, *Febronius,* 153–54.
114. Mejer, *Febronius,* 190–92.
115. Pope Pius VI travelled to Vienna in 1782 in order to convince Joseph II to stop his ecclesiastical politics.
116. Hyacinth Gerdil, *In commentarium a J. Febronio in suam retractationem editum animadversiones* (Rome: 1792); Mejer, *Febronius,* 194–99; 216.
117. Raab, "Georg Christoph Neller und Febronius." Raab thinks it possible that Hontheim arranged Neller's move to the university of Trier (ibid. 193). He also observes that whole sections of *De Statu Ecclesiae* are in fact borrowed from Neller's works (ibid., 201). Cf. Raab, *Die Concordata,* 96–115; Peter Frowein, "Analogia Ecclesiae cum Imperio Germanico. Zum Kirchenbild des Trierer Kanonisten Georg Christian Neller (d. 1783)," *Annalen des Historischen Vereins für den Niederrhein insbesondere das alte Erzbistum Köln* 177 (1975), 103–16.

(1697–1771),[118] as well as the convert and state minister Jakob Georg Freiherr von Spangenberg (1695–1779) contributed to the text of *De Statu Ecclesiae*. Spangenberg seems to have been responsible for the ecumenical tendencies of the book.[119] *De Statu Ecclesiae* shows a remarkable stance toward Protestantism, is free of polemics, but is shaped by irenicism. This was still unusual—one only has to read the works of Johann Nikolaus Weislinger (1691–1755) to encounter one of the most strident polemicists of the time.[120] Moreover, Hontheim even agrees with the Protestant critique of religious orders and monasticism, since they diminish (and often ridicule) episcopal jurisdiction.[121]

When the Jesuits initiated the *Antifebronio* by Francesco Zaccaria (1767),[122] sixteen refutations had already been printed. Among them is also one by St. Alphonsus of Liguori.[123] Nevertheless, Zaccarias's book gained wide appreciation and was reprinted until 1859.[124] Even the

---

118. Barthel was a student of Prospero Lambertini, the future Pope Benedict XIV (1740–58), and created through his transformation of Gallican principles the theoretical foundation of German episcopalism. Raab, *Die Concordata Nationis Germanicae*, 79–96.

119. Gunther Franz, "Neller-Hontheim und der Episkopalismus-Febronianismus," in *Aufklärung und Tradition. Kurfürstentum und Stadt Trier im 18. Jahrhundert: Ausstellungskatalog und Dokumentation*, ed. Gunther Franz, (Trier: Spee, 1988), 101–27; Spehr, *Aufklärung und Ökumene* 37. Raab, "Johann Nikolaus Hontheim," 32; Raab, *Die Concordata*, 116–22. It is possible that Gregor Zallwein OSB (1712–1766) also helped Hontheim with the text of the *Febronius*. On Zallwein, one of the most important canonists of the eighteenth century, see Stephan Haering, "Der Salzburger Kirchenrechtler Gregor Zallwein OSB (1712–66). Ein Beitrag zur Gelehrtengeschichte des kanonischen Rechts im Zeitalter der Aufklärung," *Studien und Mitteilungen zur Geschichte des Benediktinerordens und seiner Zweige* 103 (1992), 269–312.

120. Not mentioned in Manfred Brandl, *Die katholischen Theologen der Neuzeit: Aufklärung* (Salzburg: Neugebauer, 1978) but in Hugo Hurter, *Nomenclator Literarius Recentioris Theologiae Catholicae* (Innsbruck: Libraria Academia Wagneriana, 1881), 2/2:1271–72. Cf. Pitzer, *Justinus Febronius*, 112–13.

121. *Febronius*, ch. 7, §8, 498.

122. Mejer, *Febronius*, 87. Franciscus Antonius Zaccaria, *Antifebronio o sia apologia polemico-storica del primato del Papa . . .* (Pisauri, 1767; 2nd ed., 4 vols., Cesena, 1768–70). Latin Translation under the title *Antifebronius*, 5 vols. (Augsburg, 1783–85). Franciscus Antonius Zaccaria, *In tertium Justini Febronii tomum animadversiones Romano-catholicæ* (Rome, 1774); *Antifebronius vindicatus seu suprema romani pontificis potestas adversus J. Febronium eijusque vindicem Theolodorum a Palude iterum asserta et confirmata* (4 vols., Cesena, 1771–72; 2 vols., Frankfurt, 1771). Cf. Hugo Hurter, *Nomenclator Literarius Recentioris Theologiae Catholicae*(Innsbruck, 1883), 3/1:432.

123. St. Alphonsus of Liguori, "Vindiciae pro suprema Rom. Pontificis auctoritate contra Iustinum Febronium," in *Opere di S. Alfonso Maria de Liguori* (Torino: 1880), 7:991–1066.

124. Frowein/Janson, "Johann Nikolaus von Hontheim," 139–43. Sieben shows that Zaccaria was not only more innovative than Hontheim when it came to arguing, but also that his Latin was by far superior (Sieben, *Die katholische Konzilsidee*, 434–49). May, *Die Auseinandersetzungen* 49: "Es erging den Widerlegern [des Febronius, U.L.] wie allen Bemühungen, die eine herrschende Ideologie zu bekämpfen unternehmen: Ihre Wirksamkeit blieb eng begrenzt, der Strom des Zeitgeistes war

main propagator of the Catholic Enlightenment in Germany, the Augustinian Canon Eusebius Amort, criticized Hontheim's *Febronius* in his *Letter to Justinus Febronius . . . on the Legitimate Power of the Supreme Pontiff* (*Epistola Justiniani Frobenii ad Cl. V. Justinum . . . de legitima potestate summi pontificis*).[125] Most contemporary reviewers thought that Hontheim's proposal for a reunion of the churches, which used ideas of Johann Gerhard and Georg Calixt, but asked for a *conversio abberrantium*, and a conversion of the Protestants to a Catholic Church purified from all medieval exaggerations of papal primacy,[126] was ridiculously naïve:[127] to the extent to which Febronianism reduced papal powers, it increased the power of the bishops, which was no less problematic for Protestants.[128] A reunion was only possible, stated Hontheim's opponents, Zaccaria as well as the Heidelberg professor Georg Sigismund Kleiner (1725–86),[129] if the Protestant churches surrendered fully to the papal See. One can indeed speak of a "war of ecclesiologies": For Hontheim, all authority derives from service, which, in itself, is shaped by humility, exemplary charitableness, pastoral care, and great tolerance. For Zaccaria and Kleiner, the Church was a hierarchical society, built on the absolute, unquestionable power and authority of the pope. Unfortunately, nobody really engaged Hontheim's idea. The reaction was rather polemic and defamatory: the author of the *Febronius* could only be an apostate since his proposed reforms would cause the downfall of the Catholic Church.[130]

Among Protestant academics, *De Statu Ecclesiae* was reviewed positively, especially at the leading reform university in Göttingen, Germany. Friedrich Nicolai (1733–1811)[131] called the book a monument of "freedom of the mind" and as a Catholic approximation to the

stärker als jedes Argument. Fast alle katholischen Zeitschriften befanden sich in den Händen der Episkopalisten."
125. (Augsburg, 1764); (Bullonii [i.e., Ulm], 1764).
126. Klueting, "Wiedervereinigung der Konfessionen," 271–72.
127. Seibrich, "Aufgeklärtes Kirchenrecht," 250.
128. *Allgemeine deutsche Bibliothek* (1780), 333–35.
129. On Kleiner's critique of *Febronius*, cf. Pitzer, *Justinus Febronius*, 68–71.
130. Pitzer, *Justinus Febronius*, 63–65.
131. Spehr, *Aufklärung und Ökumene*, 44–47; Pitzer, *Justinus Febronius* 72–74; Just, "Zur Enstehungsgeschichte des Febronius," 376.

Reformation. The potential for ecumenical talks offered by Febronius, however, was viewed rather negatively: Carl Friedrich Bahrdt (1740–92)[132] renounced it since Hontheim had neither taken the *sola scriptura* principle into consideration nor freedom of conscience. Christian Wilhelm Franz Walch (1726–84)[133] and Johann Friedrich Wilhelm Jerusalem (1709–89) thought similarly. Gotthold Ephraim Lessing (1729–81) went so far as to call it a "sassy flattery" of secular princes.[134] None of them had the impression that Hontheim understood the essentials of Protestant theology. In their eyes, he downplayed the doctrinal differences and assessed them too much from the standpoint of governmental church politics.[135]

Nevertheless, *De Statu Ecclesiae* suggested a national church reform, recognized the necessity of ecumenism, rediscovered the sovereignty and liberty of the church as the people of God, and thus paved the way to the modern ecclesiologies of the twentieth century.[136]

How *Febronius* Affected the German Church

The immediate effect of *De Statu Ecclesiae* was an increase in the self-confidence of bishops. This led the Rhenish archbishops to the decrees of Koblenz (1769), and later to the decrees of the Congress at Ems (1786) as well as to the Synod of Pistoia (1786). Simultaneously, Hontheim's ideas influenced the reforms of Joseph II in Austria. However, *Febronius* did not accomplish its goals—mainly because the book asked for a politically strong position for the emperor, which would equal that of the French king. After the Seven Years War (1763), however, the position of the Habsburg emperors was so weak that one could not

---

132. Carl Friedrich Bahrdt, *De eo, an fieri possit, ut sublato pontificis imperio reconcilientur dissidentes in religione Christiani contra Justinum Febronianum dissertatio* (Leipzig: 1763).
133. Cf. Pitzer, *Justinus Febronius,* 72–74; cf. ibid., 78–80.
134. Rechenmacher, *Der Episkopalismus,* 10.
135. Pitzer, *Justinus Febronius,* 74.
136. Cf. Spehr, *Aufklärung und Ökumene,* 47. *Febronius abbreviatus,* ch. 7, §1: "Ecclesia usque ad Constantinum M. gemebat sub gravi servituti ethnicorum principum. Eadem post aliquot saeculorum decursum novam servitutem subiit ab iis, a quibus omne praesidium ex quo circa saeculum X. obstetricante ignorantia parta fuit, tantum non in dies incrementa cepit usque ad Constantiensem et Basiliensem synodum, a quibus aliquot lenimen accipere visa est." Harm Klueting also thinks that the main goal of *De Statu Ecclesiae* was not ecumenism but the strengthening of episcopalism, cf. Klueting, "Wiedervereinigung der Konfessionen?", 276–77.

expect from them the reconstruction of a German national church. Moreover, when Joseph II adopted Febronian ideas, he did this not to strengthen the position of the diocesan bishops, but only to contribute to the centralization of the State. Strong and independent bishops were not part of his agenda.[137]

It has not yet been investigated in depth what immediate influence the book had on the European movement of Febronianism, which taught the basic theses of Hontheim in combination with Jansenist or Enlightenment ideas and produced a radical episcopalism.[138] Pope Clement XIII (1758-69), of course, called the book a danger for all Catholics since it would make them insecure about the foundation of the church.[139]

In the German church, one can detect up to the eve of Vatican I (1870), a reserved stance toward papal claims of jurisdiction. Episcopalism and Josephinsm were also still very much alive at the Frankfurt Conferences of 1818.[140] Nevertheless, the basis for the movement of *Febronianism* disappeared gradually in the nineteenth century since the papacy knew how to make use of the sufferings it had endured during Napoleon's reign. After the end of the *Reichskirche*, the popes became the unchallenged moral leaders of Catholicism. From here, it was only a small step to the uniform common identity within Catholicism (1846-1958), which hardly ever challenged the infallibility of the popes.[141]

Critical Resume

The eminent German canon law historian Georg May has recently

---

137. Schneider, *Der Konziliarismus*, 78.
138. Pitzer, *Justinus Febronius*, 114.
139. *Briefwechsel zwischen weiland Ihrer Durchlaucht Dem Herrn Kurfürsten von Trier Clemens Wenzeslaus und dem Herrn Weihbischof Nikolaus von Hontheim über das Buch: Justini Febronii de statu ecclesiae et Legitima Romani Pontificis Potestate* (Frankfurt, 1813), 7, quoted in May, *Die Auseinandersetzungen*, 47.
140. May, *Die Auseinandersetzungen* 266; Georg May, *Mit Katholiken zu besetzende Professuren von 1817 bis 1945. Ein Beitrag zur Ausbildung der Studierenden katholischer Theologie, zur Verwirklichung der Parität an der württembergischen Landesuniversität und zur katholischen Bewegung* (Amsterdam: Gruner, 1975), 143–46; Georg May, *Das Recht des Gottesdienstes in der Diözese Mainz zur Zeit von Bischof Joseph Ludwig Colmar (1802-1818)* (Amsterdam: Gruner, 1987), 1:478–80.
141. Cf. Peter Hersche, *Muße und Verschwendung* (Freiburg, 2006), vol. 2 passim.

pointed out the weaknesses of *De Statu Ecclesiae*: it is a work ignorant of historical developments which sees the papal monarchy solely based on the Pseudoisidorian Decretals, a ninth-century forgery. However, these originated not in Rome, but in France. May rightly argues that the Decretals do not directly strengthen the primacy of the pope, but are rather ambiguous. They can be used either for an episcopalist or a papalist argument. "The idea of an ecclesiastical constitution, which adjudged the Roman Church a normative position, came into existence independent from the Pseudoisidorian Decretals."[142] The Decretals were, thus, not the basis for the primacy, but a symptom for its increase in authority. Even though, as May correctly remarks, Hontheim never combined the democratic and the aristocratic part of his ecclesiology, and also committed other sins of inconsistency,[143] one cannot but admit that *De Statu Ecclesiae* brought up an important question, which found its answer for Catholics exactly 200 years later, during the Second Vatican Council.

142. May, *Die Auseinandersetzungen,* 45–46.
143. Ibid., 46.

8

———

On the Way to *Sacrosanctum Concilium*: The Liturgical Renewal of the Eighteenth Century

It has been rightly observed that the Constitution on the Sacred Liturgy, *Sacrosanctum Concilium* (1963), is a key to understanding the Second Vatican Council. It attempted the promotion and reform of the liturgy, so that the importance of the paschal mystery and the church as the sacrament of universal salvation would be more visible to the world.[1] In the words of the council: "The liturgy is the summit toward which the activity of the church is directed; at the same time it is the font from which all her power flows. For the aim and object of apostolic works is that all who are made sons of God by faith and baptism should come together to praise God in the midst of his church, to take part

---

1. Reiner Kaczynski, "Kommentar zu Sacrosanctum Concilium," in *Herders Theologischer Kommentar zum Zweiten Vatikanischen Konzil* (Freiburg: Herder, 2012), 2:1–227; idem, "Liturgie in der Weite der Catholica? Fortschreitende Mißachtung und endgültige Aufhebung eines Konzilsbeschlusses," in *Was ist heute noch katholisch? Zum Streit um die innere Einheit und Vielfalt der Kirche (QD 192)*, ed. Albert Franz (Freiburg: Herder, 2001), 160–88; Gerald O'Collins, *The Second Vatican Council: Message and Meaning* (Collegeville, MN: Michael Glazier, 2014), 57–88.

in the sacrifice, and to eat the Lord's supper" (SC 10). Among the principles of reform were the promotion of liturgical instruction and active participation (SC 14–20). The council also articulated norms for adapting the liturgy to different cultures in order to avoid "rigid uniformity in matters which do not implicate the faith or the good of the whole community" (SC 37). Instead, the council fathers wanted to make clear that the Church "respect[s] and foster[s] the genius and talents of the various races and peoples" (SC 37).[2]

While it is well-known that the conciliar document would be unthinkable without the so-called "liturgical movement" of the first half of the twentieth century, spearheaded by scholars such as Joseph Andreas Jungmann (1889–1975) and Romano Guardini (1885–1968), it has been forgotten that the roots of this movement lay in the eighteenth century and that its achievements would have been impossible without the foundational work of these scholars' earlier peers.[3] It is the aim of this chapter to highlight the contributions of Catholic Enlighteners to liturgical theology in order to demonstrate the importance of this forgotten genealogy.[4]

Simplification and Adaptation of the Liturgy

The eighteenth century was perceived by contemporaries as an epoch in which customs and morals were refined in comparison to previous, more coarse centuries. This process made theologians realize that despite such changes, the liturgy had remained the same, and that a growing number of the faithful stopped participating in it, but nevertheless, still practiced superstitious rituals. The liturgy, as German Enlighteners realized, Protestant and Catholic alike, had

---

2. "SC" refers to the English translation of *Sacrosanctum Concilium* on the Vatican's website, accessed July 16, 2015, http://www.vatican.va/archive/hist_councils/ii_vatican_council/documents/vat-ii_const_19631204_sacrosanctum-concilium_en.html.

3. Andre Haquin, "The Liturgical Movement and Catholic Ritual Revision," in *Oxford History of Christian Worship*, ed. Geoffrey Wainwright and Karen W. Tucker (Oxford: Oxford University Press, 2006), 696–720. See also Konrad Klek, *Erlebnis Gottesdienst. Die liturgischen Reformbestrebungen um die Jahrhundertwende unter Führung von Friedrich Spitta und Julius Smend* (Göttingen: Vandenhoeck & Ruprecht, 1996); Ferdinand Kolbe, *Die liturgische Bewegung* (Aschaffenburg: Pattloch, 1964).

4. One of the few Anglo-American scholars who acknowledged and researched this genealogy is Leonard Swidler, *Aufklärung Catholism 1780-1850* (Missoula, MT: Scholars Press, 1978).

become isolated from the reality of life. In order to reinvigorate the faith, one therefore had to reform the liturgy by reconciling it to the contemporary culture.[5] Moreover, a renewal of the liturgy in the spirit of the first centuries, so it was believed, could also help bring the separated churches back together. Overall, one can identify three main threads among eighteenth-century reformers of the liturgy: they argue for a simplification of worship, an emphasis on the community of the faithful, and an increase in the intelligibility of the devotional character of the liturgy.[6] Wherever the liturgy could not meet the standards of reason and utility, it was made subject to the plans of the reformers.[7] Part of the last contention is that the liturgy is not only an expression of worship, but is also in the service of moral education.[8]

For Anton Joseph Dorsch (1758–1819), Felix Anton Blau (1754–98), and Benedict Werkmeister (1745–1823), the liturgy should lead to a virtuous life and the fulfillment of all our duties.[9] Vitus Anton Winter (1754–1814) defined every service humans exercise for God, including charitable works, as liturgy.[10] He even goes so far as to say that God is not venerated in the liturgy as the Lord of creation, but rather as moral regent of the world.[11]

Liturgical actions were no longer considered by reformers only as praise of God's sovereignty, but also the worship of a participatory community that should affect the spiritual life of the faithful, and consequently their daily life.[12] For most of the reformers, the papacy and the clergy were responsible for the decay of the liturgy—its decline into mechanistic prayer and anthropomorphism since the Middle Ages.

5. Alfred Ehrensperger, *Die Theorie des Gottesdienstes in der späten deutschen Aufklärung (1770–1815)* (Zürich: Theologischer Verlag, 1971), 86; cf. 84.
6. Waldemar Trapp, *Vorgeschichte und Ursprung der liturgischen Bewegung vorwiegend in Hinsicht auf das deutsche Sprachgebiet* (Würzburg: 1939), 22.
7. Klaus-Peter Burkarth, *"Raisonable" Katholiken: Volksaufklärung im katholischen Deutschland um 1800* (PhD dissertation; Essen: 1994), 164–65.
8. Ibid., 184–86. On the Enlightenment iconoclasm of sacred images, see 190–206.
9. Felix Anton Blau and Anton J. Dorsch, *Beyträge zur Verbesserung des äußeren Gottesdienstes in der katholischen Kirche* (Frankfurt: 1789), 100; Benedict Werkmeister, *Beyträge zur Verbeserung der katholischen Liturgie in Deutschland* (Ulm: 1789), 12.
10. Vitus Anton Winter, *Erstes deutsches kritisches Messbuch* (Munich: 1810), 24.
11. Ibid., 1.
12. Rainer Bendel, *Der Seelsorger im Dienst der Volkserziehung. Seelsorge im Bistum Breslau im Zeichen der Aufklärung* (Cologne: Böhlau, 1996), 393.

The way to reverse this decay consisted in restoring the simpler and purer liturgy of the first centuries, since it was perceived to be in tune with modern aesthetics and much more able to bring about spiritual edification than the liturgy of the time.[13]

The main impetus for the liturgical reforms of the eighteenth century, however, came from Ludovico Muratori (1672–1750), who had uncovered forgotten treasures of liturgical history and had written a manifesto of liturgical reform, entitled *The Science of Rational Devotion* (*Della regolata divozione*, 1747). According to him, Catholic liturgists had to go back to the sources and concentrate on the liturgy's essential core, Jesus Christ. Through academic societies—for example, the "Olmütz Academy of the Unknown" and the Salzburg Muratori reading group—his ideas began to penetrate the Habsburg lands as well as the empire,[14] until even a considerable number of bishops considered themselves disciples of the great Italian theologian. Between 1751 and 1791, more than twenty editions of this book were printed in the German-speaking lands alone. In this work, Muratori distinguishes between essential and non-essential aspects of the liturgy. The essential ones, in particular, foster and support the growth of true devotion as a virtue of piety. A litmus test for true devotion is good works, which are only possible through divine grace, for which one has to pray through Jesus Christ to the Father. Prayer is, for Muratori, always an act that involves the whole human being, and in the psalms especially he finds the most adequate expressions of human suffering and longing for God. The Mass is the pinnacle of prayer and devotion, since it is not only a meal but also the sacrifice of God's only son.[15] He especially points to the fact that the priest does not act singularly, that

13. Probst, *Der Ritus*, 84–87; Anton Mayer, "Liturgie, Aufklärung und Klassizismus," *Archiv für Liturgiewissenschaft* 9 (1929): 67–127.
14. Cf. Ulrich L. Lehner, *Enlightened Monks: The German Benedictines, 1740-1803* (Oxford: Oxford University Press, 2011).
15. Hans Hollerweger, *Die Reform des Gottesdienstes zur Zeit des Josephinismus in Österreich* (Regensburg: Pustet, 1976), 40–44; Ludovico Muratori, *Die wahre Andacht des Christen* (Aschaffenburg: 1751), c. 14–19, 195–289 [Italian: *Della regolata divozione* (Venice: 1747); Latin: *De recta hominis devotione* (Venice: 1760)]. On Muratori, see Paola Vismara, "Ludovico Muratori: Enlightenment in a Tridentine Mode," in *Enlightenment and Catholicism in Europe*, ed. Ulrich L. Lehner and Jeffrey Burson (Notre Dame, IN: University of Notre Dame Press, 2014), 251–70.

he does not offer God the Eucharistic sacrifice alone, but in communion with all the faithful present. As a consequence, Muratori insisted that the laity need to become informed about this important fact and to know the ordinary of the Mass.[16] In his commentary on the commandment of neighborly love, Muratori showed that his theology centers around love as the proper imitation of Christ.[17]

Inspired by Muratori, but also by Jansenism, in 1786, the Synod of Pistoia requested that the laity should more fully participate in the Mass. Although large parts of the synod's decisions were branded by Pius VI as heretical, its request remained uncensored that "all Christians are in a certain sense priests, because all can and should offer spiritual sacrifices . . . and . . . all who take part in [the Eucharist] offer the spotless lamb."[18] However, its desire to reform the liturgy "as an action common to priest and people . . . by bringing back the Liturgy to a greater simplicity of rites, by expounding the vernacular, and by pronouncing it in a clear voice" was censored. Conservatives feared that acknowledging the needs for reform and greater simplicity would validate Protestant criticism.[19] Thus, liturgical theologians had to be careful in the wording of their ideas if they desired to remain within the realm of established Catholic theology.

Active Participation and Vernacular Liturgy

A request that could be expressed without fear of censorship was for more active participation by the laity at Mass. Johann Josef von Pehem (1740–99) wrote that "one cannot want that the faithful stand around like wooden statues."[20] Therefore, he and others argued that the rosary

---

16. Muratori, *Die wahre Andacht*, c. 16, 225; Muratori, *De devotione*, c. 16, 177: "ceterique omnes, qui circumstant, peracta Consecratione, Deo Patri Divinum ejus Filium, Sacramento velamine abditum, quasi mysticam victimam, pergunt offere." Cf. Luca Brandolini, "La Pastorale dell'eucaristica di Ludovico A. Muratori," *Ephemerides Liturgicae* 81 (1967): 333–75; 82 (1968): 81–118.
17. Ludovico Muratori, *Des hochwürdigen Ludwig Muratori gründliche Auslegung des grossen Geboths von der Liebe des Nächsten*, 2nd ed. (Augsburg: 1768).
18. Charles Bolton, *Church Reform in 18th Century Italy* (The Hague: Nijhoff, 1970), 79.
19. Ibid., 82; cf. Albert Gerhards, "Von der Synode von Pistoia (1786) zum Zweiten Vatikanischen Konzil? Zur Morphologie der Liturgiereform im 20. Jahrhundert," *Liturgisches Jahrbuch* 36 (1986): 28–45.

during Mass should be abolished because it hinders such participation, just as private Masses do.[21] For Winter, one means of ensuring participation was to reverse the altar so that the priest would face the congregation, as in some Roman churches.[22] The Enlightenment-friendly Habsburg administration of Emperor Joseph II (1780–90), who was himself an ardent reader of Muratori, decreed on February 25, 1783 that only one Mass could be celebrated in a church at one time, thereby forbidding simultaneously celebrated Masses. Another law of 1785 even prescribed that newly built churches could only have one altar.[23] For Benedict Werkmeister (1745–1823), active participation could be improved by offering communion under both species and by admonishing the laity—relying on Protestant theologian Johann Salomo Semler's (1725–91) idea—that attendance at a private Mass would not fulfill the Sunday obligation; only if one worshiped with one's community, so Semler and Werkmeister argued, was such obligation fulfilled. Winter and others also insisted that the priest and the laity should receive communion at the same time to strengthen the community bond.[24] This emphasis on the community can also be seen in the idea that baptisms should be done during the Sunday Mass, and that confession of venial sins should be done publicly.[25]

The biggest obstacle to good participation by the laity was, in the eyes of the reformers, the liturgical language of Latin. Already the *Punctuation of Ems*, a document drafted by the German archbishops in opposition to the jurisdictional authority of the Holy See in 1784, had requested German songs for Mass and vespers.[26] Johannes Anton Theiner (1799–1860), in his *State of the Church in Silesia*, summarized the reasons for and against Latin as the liturgical language. First, the vernacular does not destroy unity with the Holy See, because unity

20. Johann Josef von Pehem, *Abhandlung von der Einführung der Volkssprache in den öffentlichen Gottesdienst* (Vienna: 1785), 105.
21. Trapp, *Vorgeschichte*, 25.
22. Winter, *Erstes deutsches kritisches Messbuch*, 321.
23. Trapp, *Vorgeschichte*, 25–26.
24. Winter, *Messbuch*, 151–55; Trapp, *Vorgeschichte*, 27.
25. Trapp, *Vorgeschichte*, 27–28.
26. Mayer, "Liturgie, Aufklärung und Klassizismus," 102–3. Mayer quotes at length from a draft of the Archbishop of Trier regarding a simplification of the liturgy.

in the church is about faith, not language. Second, Latin is preferable since it is a dead language, and thus not subject to change. If that were the case, the Apostles should have written in Sanskrit, Theiner argues. Moreover, catechesis is always taught in a vernacular language. If language changes, then "it is the holy duty of the bishops . . . to change the ritual books accordingly."[27] Another reason against use of the vernacular could be that local bishops have no authority to introduce a new rite. "Of this void reason the Ancient church knew nothing. . . . Only when Rome chained the whole world . . . the maxim was introduced that the Roman Bishop alone had the right to prescribe a liturgy."[28] Even Trent, said Theiner, had not forbidden the use of the vernacular, but only the idiosyncratic use of liturgical books by pastors. One could not find a single word about the proscription of the use of the vernacular in the council's documents or about the bishops' inability to introduce a new rite. The council's statement that the Mass should "not be celebrated everywhere in the vernacular" (sess. XXII, c. 8, 1562) should not be interpreted as a proscription, but rather as a statement that the vernacular liturgy seemed inopportune at that particular time, especially because it could have been interpreted as a surrender to Protestant demands.[29] For Theiner, if one maintains Latin as the liturgical language, then the council's emphasis on catechesis in the vernacular is obviously a bad joke: "In order to make the liturgy not totally useless . . . the faithful should be instructed in German about the liturgy, but it cannot be celebrated in German! How ridiculous is that. . . ."[30] He also rejects the argument that once people got used to the vernacular, they would become indifferent toward it and again produce a mechanistic attitude. "From this it follows that one should have no language at all in the liturgy . . . and that the Lord's Prayer should not be prayed by the faithful."[31] Even if a vernacular language

27. Augustin Theiner, *Die katholische Kirche Schlesiens dargestellt von einem katholischen Geistlichen* (Altenburg: 1826), 198.
28. Theiner, *Die katholische Kirche*, 198.
29. Theiner, *Die katholische Kirche*, 201; Benedict Werkmeister, *Ueber die deutschen Mess- und Abendmahlsanstalten in der katholischen Hofkapelle zu Stuttgart* (Stuttgart: 1787), 41–46.
30. Theiner, *Die katholische Kirche*, 203.
31. Ibid., 206.

sounds childish, this can never be a reason not to translate the liturgy into it. If the language is good enough for catechesis, it must be good enough for the official prayer. Likewise, the Latin rite is not simply more festive because a foreign language has an aura of majesty and leads to an encounter with the mystery. For Theiner, this is bad theology, since it seems to avoid intelligibility and reason (John 23:20–21):

> In religious affairs nothing can remain unintelligible, but everything must give us bright insight since only that leads us to virtue. A human being must know what he sees, what is spoken . . . a reverence that is based on uncertain emotions is despicable and leads to ignorance and to moral decay. Everything that is hidden and mysterious is of no value for humans. Christ did not die on the cross for a clerical mystery but for the truth which he preached to all people. . . .[32]

The most interesting counter argument conceived by Theiner is that one cannot change the language, because otherwise, the faithful would ask how the clergy could deprive them for so long of the goods of the liturgy. For Theiner, it would be a sign of magnanimity if the church could admit her mistakes; after all "only stupid, vain and egotistical people cannot admit their own mistakes."[33]

A vernacular liturgy was also intended to bring separated Christians back together, especially at a time when the Christian faith came under sharp attacks from deists, anti-clerical writers, and atheists. It is, therefore, of great importance that Benedict Werkmeister dedicated his 1789 book, *Contributions to an Improvement of the Catholic Liturgy in Germany* (1789) to Christian Gotthilf Salzmann (1744–1811), Gottlob Nathanael Fischer (1748–1800), and Johann August Hermes (1736–1822), the three most prominent German Protestant liturgists.[34] In fact, quite a few Catholic liturgists were ecumenically minded, such

---

32. Ibid., 210.

33. Ibid., 221. For the vernacular in the baptismal liturgy (and its critics), see Manfred Probst, *Der Ritus der Kindertaufe: die Reformversuche der katholischen Aufklärung des deutschen Sprachbereiches: mit einer Bibliographie der gedruckten Ritualien des deutschen Sprachbereiches von 1700 bis 1960* (Trier: Paulinus-Verlag, 1981), 90–92.

34. Ehrensperger, *Theorie*, 94; Waldemar Trapp, *Vorgeschichte und Ursprung der liturgischen Bewegung: vorwiegend in Hinsicht auf das deutsche Sprachgebiet* (Würzburg: 1939), 17.

as Anton Selmar (1757–1821),[35] Beda Pracher (1750–1819), and of course Werkmeister, Dorsch, and Blau. Selmar wrote:

> The many millions of non-Catholic Christians . . . deserve our attention. . . . One should make . . . their conversion to Catholicism easier by changing our many useless or even harmful practices. They and we need *one* God and father, who enlightens them and us, warms us and strengthens the religion of the *one* redeemer, who embraces them and us in one band of love. Should our liturgical practices, which were once different and could again be changed, separate us forever?[36]

Consequently, Catholic liturgists conceived a vernacular liturgy that focused on the common practices and beliefs of all Christians, and emphasized Christian charity and morality. For the Benedictine Beda Pracher, nothing more uplifting could be thought of than a religious service "in which all are equally spiritually uplifted, regardless of their confession . . . and in which every stranger or guest can participate without being in the least offended in his religious beliefs. . . . On the other side, nothing is more horrible than a public religious service which infuses a legion of doubts . . . so that one has to fight in horror . . . to calm the offended mind."[37] An example of such a non-offensive, rational, and uplifting liturgy is Pracher's creation of a prayer the priest was supposed to say before communion, which shows, at least, doubts about the real presence of Christ in the sacrament, if not unbelief:

> Brothers, we are today blessed to be able to eat from this bread and drink from this chalice. Not the physical consumption of the bread and wine . . . but what our mind thinks when we receive them and what our heart feels, enlivens our mind and is food for our eternal life.[38]

Liturgists agreed that whatever was not understood could not be

---

35. Anton Selmar, *Die öffentlichen Gottesverehrungen der katholischen Christen waren anfangs anders beschaffen als jetzt, und sollten wieder anders werden: Aus der Geschichte, Religion und Vernunft dargestellt von einem alten, katholischen Pfarrer in Baiern und königl. Bezirksinspektor der Volkschulen* (Landshut: 1810).
36. Ibid., 656.
37. Beda Pracher, *Neue Liturgie des Pfarres M. in K. im Departement L.* (Tübingen: 1802), 22; cf. Ehrensperger, *Theorie*, 153.
38. Pracher, *Neue Liturgie des Pfarres M. in K.*, 48.

helpful for the laity; wherefore the concept of mysteries and traditional scholastic explanations of the sacraments were rejected. Only if Catholics purged theology from the scholastic "nonsense" could the liturgy become as uplifting as the worship in Protestant churches:

> Protestants have less *opus operatum* than Catholics. This forces them to make their exterior ecclesiastical services as appealing and moving to the heart as possible. The edification of the faithful among them depends much more on useful means which stir up the sensual interest . . . than on immediate and secret effects of grace.[39]

For Werkmeister, the "exterior pomp" during Mass was a dangerous distraction for real prayer.[40] For Ignaz Heinrich Wessenberg (1774–1860), the Latin Mass was not necessarily an impediment for "conscious" participation as long as the priest prepared his flock accordingly. However, he actively promoted vernacular rituals, and by 1812, two-thirds of the priests in his diocese of Constance supported the liturgical reforms.[41]

It is almost forgotten that despite the lack of any approval, one liturgist even celebrated the Mass in the vernacular as early as 1786. Benedict Werkmeister celebrated this Mass on July 23, 1786, in the little court chapel of Stuttgart, where he served as chaplain to the Duke of Würtemberg. The Eucharistic Prayer was the only part that was still said in Latin.[42] He applied the ideas of Enlightenment rationality and practicality to the liturgy, and thus began an attack on the traditional Roman liturgy. He had not just produced a simple translation of the missal, but changed it to the taste and mores of the time. Later, he advocated such a change for the entire German church. Merely putting a translation in the hands of the laity, as produced by Anselm Schott in the 1880s, was, in his eyes, insufficient as long as the liturgy was still in Latin:

---

39. Werkmeister, *Beyträge*, 67; cf. Ehrensperger, *Theorie*, 167.
40. Werkmeister, *Beyträge*, 67–70.
41. Ehrensperger, *Tradition*, 175.
42. Rudolf Günther, "Die erste deutsche Liturgie der katholischen Kirche der Aufklärung," *Monatschrift für Gottesdienst und kirchliche Kunst* 6 (1901): 333–40; 368–73; Benedict Werkmeister, *Ueber die deutschen Mess- und Abendmahlsanstalten in der katholischen Hofkapelle zu Stuttgart* (Stuttgart: 1787).

It is a characteristic of every good liturgy that she connects the faithful, who are present with each other and the priest with everybody. In the Church all . . . Christians must constitute one moral person, must have one . . . mouth and heart. The prayer of one must be the prayer of all. This is public and community worship. All events that do not bring about this unification of the people with the priest lack an essential characteristic of devotional . . . worship. As long as the priest prays in Latin, that is in a non-understandable language, the faithful cannot join him. The German Missal shows the reader what happens at Mass but the people still cannot understand the priest himself, and thus they do not receive any spiritual support from him. . . . A German Missal brings about, if I may say so, a pre-stabilized harmony among the faithful but no true union, and consequently no community, no edification or devotion that touches the heart.[43]

Yet not all went as far as Werkmeister, who was a radical in many ways. His contemporary Johann Michael Sailer (1751–1832) argued in his lectures on liturgical theology, as early as 1785, that every liturgy has to correspond to the total expression of religion in the lives of humans, wherefore liturgical renewal did not necessarily mean the vernacular as liturgical language, but rather the "reexamination of the inner religion which expresses itself in a religious service."[44]

Joseph II disliked the idea of the Mass in German. He preferred the Latin books, because in his view, they contained fewer abuses than the diocesan rituals of the time. Thus, a Moravian pastor who had changed the rite of the Mass and the breviary, and who had read the readings of the Mass in the vernacular, was punished by the emperor's administration. Individuals were not authorized to invent reforms, Joseph II made clear. He even promulgated a law in 1781 that it was absolutely unacceptable for individual priests to offer idiosyncratic vernacular versions of the canon of the Mass, the sacraments, councils, or other sacred writers since this would lead to religious confusion and harm for the state.[45] Only the dioceses of St. Pölten and Seckau received approbation from Joseph II for their vernacular rituals, while under

43. Werkmeister, *Beyträge*, 346–47; cf. Ehrensperger, *Theorie*, 169–70.
44. Johann Michael Sailer, *Sämmtliche Werke* (Sulzbach: 1835), 18:552. Ehrensperger, *Theorie*, 174.
45. Hans Hollerweger, "Das Rituale im Bereich des Josephinismus," in *Aufklärungskatholizismus und Liturgie. Reformentwürfe für die Feier von Taufe, Firmung, Busse, Trauung und Krankensalbung*, ed. Franz Kohlschein (St. Ottilien: EOS, 1989), 181–99; Hollerweger, *Die Reform*, 102.

the reign of his brother Leopold II (1790–92), broader permissions were granted. As early as 1790, Joseph Anton Gall (1748–1807; from 1788 until his death, bishop of Linz), unsuccessfully requested permission from the new emperor to use German for benedictions. Despite the fact that he had not received official permission, starting in about 1805, he used vernacular formulas for the baptismal rite and the anointing of the sick, which he had composed himself, inspired by biblical language.[46]

The Fight Against Superstition

The Archbishop Elector of Trier, Clemens Wenzeslaus of Saxony (1739–1812), who contributed most of the liturgical suggestions at Ems, was also concerned with the marginalization of Christ in popular devotion. For him, this was equivalent to superstition. In his view, the veneration of the saints had replaced Christocentric prayer; therefore, he wrote in his 1780 circular to the faithful of his diocese:

> If you hardly bow your knee in our churches or even turn your back to the altar and show more reverence to the Saints than God . . . then Religion itself disapproves of your veneration and will reject it as superstition. She will charge you with transgressing the First Commandment and resent you for irritating our erring brethren.[47]

Such strongly worded pastoral letters or circulars were not rare in eighteenth-century Catholicism, and show the decisiveness of the bishops to reform their dioceses.[48] Even Immanuel Kant's (1724–1804) ideas about prayer and liturgy were positively received by Catholic reformers such as Winter or Wessenberg; for example, Kant's claim that all worship was the recognition of all our *duties as divine commands* and that mechanical prayer was useless.[49] Like their Protestant counterparts, Catholic liturgists also found then that the moral

46. Hollerweger, "Das Rituale im Bereich des Josephinismus," 190–99.
47. Mayer, "Liturgie, Aufklärung und Klassizismus," 108.
48. Ibid., 111–14.
49. Immanuel Kant, *Religion innerhalb der Grenzen der blossen Vernunft (1793)*, AA (Akademieausgabe) 6:153 (cf. 6:443); see also Vitus Anton Winter, *Erstes deutsches kritisches katholisches Ritual* (Landshut: 1811), 1; cf. Ehrensperger, *Theorie*, 70–72.

obligation of duties and work was more valuable than prayer.[50] The more an enlightened liturgy resembles the true inner and moral service to God, the fewer confessional elements it contains and the more appealing it is for Christians of all faith traditions—or so, they believed.[51] Even a rural pastoral conference in Saulgau in the diocese of Constance followed such ideas; in 1809, they defined that

> Prayer can never be an end in itself. One prays because one wants something else—namely to express one's highest reverence for God and to ennoble oneself . . . Thus it must be a means to increase the moral goodness of a person— and . . . that is its true purpose, namely to make a person better, wiser, more virtuous and happier. One does not influence God with one's prayer but only oneself. . . .[52]

The conference followed the ideas of Kant to a remarkable extent, but it did not share his conclusion that as moral purity progresses, prayer becomes redundant. The reformers attempted to replace the traditional repetitive prayers with short, newly written prayers. This, of course, created problems: the faithful had to be trained in a new way of reading and receiving prayers, not only formally, but also materially, since many new prayers were more abstract and rational or presupposed a subtle sense of aesthetics, which was absent in rural areas. Most counterproductive, however, was that the faithful (the priests said) recited their prayers in the conviction of influencing the supernatural and not for their own education or moral uplift.[53] Enlightened prayer was supposed to invigorate trust in God and bring freedom from fear and insecurity. God, the priests continued, was not the sovereign whose rights had been violated by sin, but the loving and merciful father who guarantees the reliability of reality. If one meditated on the omnipotence of God, the reformers were convinced, one would realize the miraculous nexus of all things and gain trust in the divine plans. This stoic trust in divine providence becomes obvious in the many quotations from the works of Jean-Jacques Rousseau with

---

50. Ehrensperger, *Theorie*, 73.
51. Ibid., 78–79.
52. Burkarth, *Raisonable Katholiken,* 93.
53. Ibid., 108–13.

which Werkmeister decorated his homilies and other devotional writings. Providence was no longer seen as a personal divine action, but a byproduct of the laws of nature. Thus, it cannot surprise us when he wrote about the Lisbon earthquake of 1755: "You see divine punishment, where I see the necessary achievements of natural laws."[54] Consequently, prayers for material well-being could never be prayers that tried to influence God to change his plans, but only to submit one's own mind to the eternal divine decrees. Also, Thaddäus Dereser (1757–1827) taught in his prayer book that one should not ask God for anything, "since he knows our needs before we utter them."[55] Prayer becomes therefore a moral exercise and is no longer a dialogue with God.[56]

Catholic Enlighteners saw one of the strongest superstitions in contemporary beliefs about the devil. Consequently, exorcisms in the liturgy became the target of reformers, who ridiculed them as remnants of the Middle Ages. Beda Pracher wrote:

> How can we call the blissful creation and all the beneficial creatures, which evoke us to be grateful, a nest of demons . . . ? I tremble if . . . one of our farmers would one day ask of us a literal explanation of all the prayers and benedictions we use on their behalf . . . Would he not yell at us: You hypocrites! You preach against superstition and yet you practice it in the church! You tell us that the devil's power is bound by Christ and yet you invoke him.[57]

Vitus A. Winter argued therefore for the elimination of the exorcism from the rite of baptism.[58] Dorsch and Blau agreed, and thought that the exorcism of a newborn baby was an insult to his human dignity and an abuse of religious power. Any imprecatory prayers, in which the devil was addressed, should also be eliminated and only prayers

---

54. Ibid., 114–18; 715. On the earthquake of Lisbon, see Benedict Werkmeister, *Predigten in den Jahren 1784–1791* (Ulm: 1812), 3:275.
55. Burkarth, *Raisonable Katholiken,* 119.
56. Ibid., 125–27.
57. Beda Pracher, *Sendschreiben an den Verfasser der Schrift: Ueber den Entwurf eines neuen katholischen Rituals* (Ulm: 1807), 8–9.
58. Vitus Anton Winter, *Deutsches, katholisches, ausübendes Ritual* (Frankfurt: 1813), 116–19; Josef Steiner, *Liturgiereform in der Aufklärungszeit: Eine Darstellung am Beispiel Vitus Anton Winters* (Freiburg: Herder, 1974), 218.

for relief from evil should be allowed to remain in the ritual, because they are, after all, able to arouse hope and faith in God.[59] Bishop Joseph Anton von Gall of Linz (1748–1807) also avoided addressing the devil in his formulary for the baptismal exorcism. Instead, he suggested this prayer, which is quite close to the post-Vatican II prayer:

> May the Seducer not overpower you like our forbears [*Stammeltern*] in paradise. The inherited inclination to evil . . . may not be victorious in you . . . but the Holy Spirit may reign over you, and his grace may guide your spirit and heart.[60]

Pracher felt the urge to come up with a new baptismal rite himself, for he could no longer in good conscience perform baptisms in the traditional way, mainly because of the prescribed exorcism.[61] In 1804, Winter suggested ways to rearrange the rite—one without any exorcisms at all; two years later, he signaled his willingness to compromise on this issue.[62] Other enlightened theologians, such as Carl Schwarzel (1746–1809) of Innsbruck/Freiburg, defended the exorcism as such, but warned of the frequent abuse of the rite.[63] Much later, in 1830, Philipp Lichter (1796–1870) of Trier analyzed the baptismal rite with great diligence and insight. He conceived a biblically-based interpretation of the exorcism, in which he argued that the church did in this act what Jesus did when he received people into the kingdom of God. She commands with divine authority that the devil will leave. Thus, the exorcism is the demonstration of the power of Jesus over sin and death, over hell and Satan.[64] An anonymous essay from 1804

59. Felix Anton Blau, *Ueber die Wirksamkeit der gottesdienstlichen Gebräuche in der katholischen Kirche* (Frankfurt: 1792), 49–51; 194.
60. Manfred Probst, *Ritus*, 171. The second exorcism of baptism is missing in 80 rituals of the Catholic Enlightenment in Germany, from which Probst concluded that a definite trend existed to eliminate it altogether (ibid., 184).
61. Ibid., 94.
62. Ibid., 95; see also 169–73.
63. Josef Müller, *Der Freiburger Pastoraltheologe Carl Schwarzel (1746–1809) unter besonderer Berücksichtigung seiner Stellung zu Jansenismus und Aufklärung* (dissertation, University of Freiburg, 1959, 2007), 51, accessed July 10, 2015, http://www.freidok.uni-freiburg.de/volltexte/2883/pdf/mueller_schwarzel.pdf.
64. Eduard Lichter, "Volksfrömmigket und Wissenschaft unter dem Einfluss von Bischof Josef von Hommer im Spiegel der Arbeiten des Trierer Klerus," *Archiv für Mittelrheinische Kirchengeschichte* 30 (1978): 161–90; Probst, *Der Ritus,* 96–97.

offered a compromise. It made clear that the church never believed that the baptized child was possessed by the devil or that he had power over its body, but only that the child was supernaturally in sin—namely, in original sin—and thus connected with the evil spirit. According to the author, every person in the state of original sin was metaphorically a slave of the devil, but only insofar as there was evil concupiscence in the person. The baptized person leaves this attachment to the realm of evil behind and enters the kingdom of God. Thus, the exorcism has no literal meaning, but only a metaphorical one. Consequently, all words that would confuse the faithful should be purged from the ritual books; moreover, he suggested that the priest should explain to the parents and godparents of the child with great diligence the meaning of the prayer for the liberation from evil.[65]

Prayers for Enlightened Catholics

One of Werkmeister's closest friends was Philipp Joseph Brunner (1758-1829),[66] who shared the conviction that "Catholicism . . . was utterly corrupted by fanatic and ignorant people"[67] and that especially the liturgy had to be reformed. Therefore, in 1801, Brunner published a remarkable book that became a bestseller and went through twenty editions by the 1840s, entitled a *Prayerbook for Enlightened Catholics.*[68] As the title suggests, this book was intended to propagate the ideals of the Catholic Enlightenment, especially religious tolerance toward Protestants, but also more understanding toward Jews. Moreover, it tried to teach Christians a more personal way of praying, especially by invoking biblical texts.

65. Anonymous, "Von den Exorzismen bei der heiligen Taufe," *Linzer Monatsschrift* 3/2 (1804): 233–51; Probst, *Der Ritus,* 97–99.
66. Josef Bayer, "Dr. Philipp Joseph Brunner: Ministerialrat in Karlsruhe und Pfarrer in Hofweier," *Freiburger Diözesanarchiv* 92 (1972): 201–22; Norbert Jung, *Der Speyerer Weihbischof Andreas Seelmann (1732-1789) im Spannungsfeld von "nachgeholter" Aufklärung und "vorgezogener" Restauration* (Mainz: Verlag für Mittelrheinische Kirchengeschichte, 2001), passim; Burchard Thiel, *Die Liturgik der Aufklärungszeit* (Breslau: 1926).
67. Benedict Werkmeister, *Vertheidigung des von Herrn Pfarrer Brunner herausgegebenen neuen Gebetbuches, für aufgeklärte katholische Christen: Gegen die Obscurenten zu Augsubrg, und ihre Brüder im übrigen katholischen Deutschland* (1802), III.
68. Originally published in 1797 as a prayerbook for all Christians, then specifically for Catholics. *Gebethbuch für aufgeklärte katholischen Christen* (Ulm: 1801).

Fidel Deubl, an ex-Jesuit, considered it a work of heterodoxy and indifferentism.[69] Even worse, Muratori's theology, whose ideas Brunner tries to implement, is, for Deubl, "stinking cabbage," which does not deserve to be "warmed up again."[70] In an act of friendship, Werkmeister took up his pen to defend Brunner in a little book. He even criticized the idea that every prayer was directed toward God.[71] While Brunner states that prayer helps to develop tolerance and charity toward men of all religion, Deubl thinks that human nature motivates us to show benevolence, first and foremost, to those of our own belief, namely Christians. Werkmeister comments: "Are Jews, Turks and Heathens not of our species—not also humans? From our human nature flows the duty to love humans. Deubl . . . claims that it is psychologically impossible to show benevolence, faithfulness and trust and love to people of" a different religion.[72]

The charge of indifferentism was an ad hominem argument, and completely unfounded. Deubl, however, thinks he found proof in Brunner's prayer for dissenting Christians:

> Let us pray for all Christians, who think differently in religious matters, that we can, even if we do not agree with their religious opinions, live together with them a good life in universal brotherhood. . . . With all differences in doctrine, people who hold a different belief can also be righteous and virtuous, and how could you, o holy God, punish virtue and righteousness, even if they are connected with error![73]

There is not a hint of indifferentism here. Brunner is far from equating religions or churches, even calling non-Catholics "erroneous."[74] Yet, for Deubl, the admission that there are good people in other confessions and religions was tantamount to heresy:

---

69. Werkmeister, *Vertheidigung*, 183–214.
70. Ibid., 10.
71. Ibid., 184.
72. Ibid., 186.
73. Ibid., 34–35.
74. A more indifferent view is offered by Carl Prugger von Pruggheim (formerly a Benedictine) (1763–1841), *Tugendhafte Gesinnungen und Thaten von Heiden, Juden und Türken, in Erzählungen für Leser aus allen Ständen,* 2 vols. (Munich: 1802).

> When I say: in all confessions there are good people, do I really want to say that the doctrines of these confessions are equally good? When I say that even among the uncultivated people and among Heathens one can find virtuous people, do I say that Paganism or Fetishism is as good or as true as the Catholic Religion?[75]

For Brunner and Werkmeister, one can find in every false and true religion a variety of concepts that can help humans to achieve virtue. Therefore, Socrates would much more deserve a place in the litany of saints than St. Benedict Labre, he reasons.[76] Their differing worldviews become apparent when one compares their views of Judaism. While Deubl considered it heterodox that Brunner asks in prayer that the Jews would become good and virtuous people, Werkmeister defends it. Brunner did not give up the belief that Jews should receive baptism, but his prayer asks in a reasonable manner for their conversion. How could Jesus not want a tolerant handling of his own people, a subtle and gentle handling of a people that suffered so much throughout history, he asks:

> How should these Jews start to like a religion, whose followers behave as enemies of their religion and even worse as persecutors? How could they believe that this religion is good and of divine origin if so many bad fruits, hatred and persecution of dissenters are connected with her . . . ?[77]

This stance toward Judaism is far from Vatican II's *Nostra Aetate* (1965), but it should be obvious that men such as Werkmeister and Brunner—the latter coming from a Jewish family—prepared the ground for Catholic theologians to begin thinking differently about their Jewish brethren.

Conclusion

The liturgists of the Catholic Enlightenment, as well as the proponents of the Synod of Pistoia, of whom some were Enlighteners and others

75. Werkmeister, *Vertheidigung*, 36.
76. Ibid., 42.
77. Ibid., 64.

Jansenists, helped articulate the theological idea of reforming the liturgy and the insight that even the sacred rituals of Christianity had possibly undergone change and decay. They reminded Catholic bishops of the need to constantly revise and update their approach to catechesis. Despite the fact that the reform ideas were discussed in a number of journals, their dissemination among the faithful failed due to pastoral insensitivity. The liturgists usually wanted sweeping reforms and despised the simple prayer life of the rural population, so that a common denominator could only rarely be found; the reformist agenda of Bishop Wessenberg was an exception to the rule.

Yet, the most important contribution of the Catholic Enlightenment liturgists is the founding of a new theological discipline—namely, that of liturgical studies. Before the eighteenth century, the liturgy was, at best, a dogmatic *locus* or only interesting to historians; now, a liturgical methodology was developed and the ritual life of the Church gained the attention it deserved. Without the groundbreaking work of liturgists such as Werkmeister, Winter, Pracher, and others, the discipline would not have developed as quickly as it did. After all, by the midst of the nineteenth century, most seminaries had professorships for liturgical studies, which in due time, became seedbeds for the liturgical renewal of the twentieth century. *Sacrosanctum Concilium*, as different as it is from the moralistic Enlightenment theology of the time, would have been unthinkable without the support of a well-established academic community of liturgical theologians, who stand in succession to the Catholic Enlighteners.

PART IV

Catholic Exegesis and the Challenge of Enlightenment Criticism

9

The Bible among Catholic Enlighteners

The history of early-modern Catholic exegesis is probably one of the worst-researched fields in literary history. The eighteenth century is no exception. It is worth reading treatises from this time because they encouraged—very much contrary to traditional belief—the laity to read holy scripture, wrestled with historical-critical scholarship, and tried to make the Bible theologically fruitful. The main focus of this chapter is on the German-speaking lands, where an especially lively debate existed. However, this does not mean that we should think of the Holy Roman Empire as an exception, but rather as a puzzle piece in the bigger, transnationally connected panorama of not-yet-researched Catholic exegesis. A good example of how the German-speaking lands were embedded in the big picture of Catholic Enlightenment is the steady stream of translations German theologians made of French or English Catholic scholars. Already in 1787, there existed a Latin translation of Alexander Geddes's (1737–1802) *Prospectus of a New Translation of the Holy Bible (1786).*[1]

---

1. Alexander Geddes and Ildephonsus Schwarz, *De vulgarium Sacrae Scripturae versionum vitiis eorumque remediis libellus* (Bamberg: 1787).

Figurative and Allegorical Hermeneutics

Eighteenth-century exegesis was torn between the classic application of allegorical, typological, and figurative interpretations on the one hand, and a historical-critical reading of the ancient texts, which stressed the literal meaning as the only licit one, on the other. A good example of the first are the rules of scriptural interpretation that the French oratorian and philo-Jansenist Jacques Joseph Duguet (1649–1733) published in 1716, and which were translated into German in 1735. At the height of the conflict between traditional and critical exegesis in the last quarter of the century, this translation was reprinted in 1777.[2]

Duguet makes clear at the beginning of his rulebook that Christ was prefigured in the entire Old Testament and was alone the object of all the prophets.[3] The *first* rule, however, is that one has to see Christ wherever the apostles have seen him.[4] When St. Paul uses an allegorical interpretation to confirm that Jesus is the prophesied end of the law (Rom. 10:4), it would be inappropriate to state that St. Paul did not understand the true meaning of the text. It would be absurd to state that St. Paul taught against the Holy Spirit, that he saw Christ where he was not, or that he leads his readers into error:

> He ceases to be a human being inspired by God and a person taught by Jesus Christ himself . . . because there is no middle ground between these two propositions: St. Paul knows the true meaning of a verse . . . and: St. Paul does not know it. . . .[5]

Thus, in order to understand the prophets, one has to follow the interpretation of the apostles, and not human learning, even if, for example, some of Paul's comments are not easily compatible with the Hebrew text of the Bible. Those who argue that the text does not warrant Paul's interpretation are not entrusted with the "key to

2. Jacques Joseph Duguet, *Regles Pour L'Intelligence Des Stes. Ecritures* (Paris: 1716); Duguet, *Regeln zum Verstande der heiligen Schrift* (Vienna: 1777).
3. Duguet, *Regeln,* 9; 21; Duguet, *Regles,* preface.
4. Duguet, *Regeln,* 67–68; Duguet, *Regles,* 33–34.
5. Duguet, *Regeln,* 39–40; Duguet, *Regles,* 3–4.

wisdom" and the guidance given by the Holy Spirit to the faithful.[6] A theologian should be careful even in the reading of verses that seem to have only a literal or historical meaning, since St. Paul sees in some of them a deeper meaning.[7]

This does not mean that according to Duguet, one should disregard the literal meaning or accept just any reading of a verse, as long as one sees Jesus in it. Duguet argues, instead, that the literal meaning of the text is the basis for any interpretation, but believes that it can contain two meanings. It is illicit for a theologian to seek his own opinions in the text. In the historical books of the Bible, the historical meaning always has to be the foundational one, and in the prophetic ones, it is the temporal prophecy.[8] The *second* rule is that one has to make Christ visible in the text if certain indicators or titles that can only pertain to him appear in the text—for example, that somebody is called a prince of peace, councilor, and so on (as in the prophet Isaiah).[9] If the concepts and words scripture uses for an object are too subtle and too exalted, one should take it according to the *third* rule—as a sign that a more profound message is intended.[10] As a *fourth* rule, Duguet states that in some instances only the prophetic meaning is the immediate and literal meaning of the text. If one reflected on this rule, then one would see immediately that Solomon and his earthly love could not be the object of the *Song of Songs*.[11] All promises of scripture for material goods have to be understood as promises of spiritual goods, says the *fifth* rule. This is because the whole of scripture commands nothing but true love, and condemns covetousness, which is all about earthly goods.[12] The *sixth* rule states that if a narrative is incompatible with our reasonable or established concepts of things, a mystery is entailed. Duguet gives the example of Abraham sending Hagar and Ismael into the desert without help, consolation, guidance,

6. Duguet, *Regeln*, 41–44; Duguet, *Regles*, 6–8.
7. Duguet, *Regeln*, 44; Duguet, *Regles*, 9. For example, Heb. 7:3ff.
8. Duguet, *Regeln*, 49–55; Duguet, *Regles*, 11–15.
9. Duguet, *Regeln*, 69–82; Duguet, *Regles*, 35–49.
10. Duguet, *Regeln*, 82–105; Duguet, *Regles*, 49–72.
11. Duguet, *Regeln*, 105–11; Duguet, *Regles*, 73–79.
12. Duguet, *Regeln*, 112–25; Duguet, *Regles*, 80–93.

or protection.[13] The *seventh* rule reminds the reader that there are mysteries that are inexplicable by reason alone. According to the *eighth* rule, there are some circumstances in scripture which have an "obvious" connection to Jesus and point to him, although they are contained in the Hebrew Bible. The *ninth* rule maintains that law, temple, and Jewish ceremonies have to be read as precursors of Christ, while the *tenth* declares that it is a clear sign of prophecy if it makes a number of other texts understandable. The *eleventh* rule states that texts about the Jewish law demonstrate the impossibility of justification outside of the Gospels. The *twelfth* and final rule makes clear that prophecies can contain several different meanings.[14] These rules summarize nicely how a Catholic exegete would approach scripture if he was not versed in the newest philological findings, or not acquainted with historical-critical scholarship.

Criticism of "Mystical Interpretations"

Especially in the second half of the eighteenth century, hermeneutics began to change. Reading their Protestant colleagues and the works of the great Oratorian Richard Simon (1638–1712) motivated many Catholic exegetes to publish their own approaches to scripture. A stream of hermeneutical texts was published in the latter half of the eighteenth century. In 1777, Adam Vizer of Tyrnau (d. 1803) published a hermeneutic,[15] while the Carmelite Alexius a Aquilino (1732–85) in Heidelberg added remarkable hermeneutical comments to his book on the Samaritan Pentateuch.[16] The Kremsmünster Benedictine Hieronymus Besange (1726–81) also published a three-volume critical hermeneutical introduction to the Old Testament.[17] While these books were erudite and wrestled with the newest literature in their fields,

---

13. Duguet, *Regeln*, 125–37; Duguet, *Regles*, 93–106.
14. Duguet, *Regeln*, 33.
15. Adam Vizer, *Praenotiones hermeneuticae Novi Testamenti* (Tyrnau: 1777).
16. Alexius a Aquilino, *Pentateuchi Hebraeo-Samaritani praestantia in illustrando et emendando textu masorethico ostensa, una cum aliis subsidiis hermeneutico-critici, ad totum textrum Hebraeum rite intelligendum servientibus* (Heidelberg: 1783).
17. Hieronymus Besange, *Introductio in Vetus Testamentum critico-hermeneutico historica,* 3 vols. (Styra: 1765ff).

they remained, in most issues, relatively traditional. In 1777, Lorenz Isenbiehl had questioned whether Isaiah 7:14 was a prophecy about the birth of Christ, and had caused a firestorm in the Church (see the chapter on Isenbiehl in this volume). Nevertheless, the chorus of critics who felt uneasy with the traditional reading of scripture grew steadily. In 1789, the Benedictine Johann Babor (1762–1846) argued that Genesis 49:10 could not be read as a foreshadowing of the Messiah.[18] He carefully demonstrated that the Council of Trent had not declared that the Vulgate should be preferred to the Hebrew text of the Bible, but that the Latin translation contained no errors in regard to faith or morals; it did not mean that the Vulgate could not contain errors that should be corrected, though.[19] He saw such an error in the traditional interpretation of Genesis 49:10. Babor believed, like most of his Protestant contemporaries schooled in historical criticism, that a text contained one literal meaning that was the dominant—and in most cases, only—licit meaning of a text.

Yet the fight against "mystical" interpretations of Scripture was far from over. Exegetes still had to fear censorship if they questioned traditional readings of a verse, especially those of the church fathers. Thus it is not surprising that in 1809, Benedict Werkmeister (1745–1823), who had nothing to lose as he was already the *enfant terrible* of the German Catholic Enlightenment and employed by the state of Würtemberg, publicly articulated a sharp attack on the biblical works of his contemporaries, but defended such exegesis if it operated within certain boundaries.[20]

For the ex-Benedictine, every deeper meaning of a Bible verse had to be founded on its literal meaning, as this is the one the Holy Spirit had intended in the act of inspiration.[21] With Aquinas, Werkmeister stresses that only on the basis of literal meaning can a theological proof

18. The verse reads: "The scepter shall never depart from Judah, or the mace from between his feet, until tribute comes to him, and he receives the people's obedience."
19. Johann Babor, *Kritische Untersuchung, ob die sogenannte Weissagung Jakobs 1. Mos. 49, 10 vom Messias handle* (n.p.: 1789), 9; see also Babor, *Allgemeine Einleitung in die Schriften des alten Testaments* (Vienna: 1794).
20. Benedikt Werkmeister, "Über den mystischen Sinn," *Jahrschrift für Theologie und Kirchenrecht der Katholiken* 2/2 (1809): 259–376.
21. Cf. Benedict Stattler, *De Locis Theologicis* (Weissenburg: 1775), 110: "Sensus mysticus nunquam sine

be made. The proper way of understanding the literal meaning of a text requires that one read it according to the usual use of the language. A mystical sense, however, can only be present if a sentence is about an object that figuratively signifies a future object. The mystical sense is, therefore, a "concept that is given to us by the object of a literally understood sentence, in so far as it signifies something in the future."[22] If the object aims at a moral message, the mystical sense is called tropological; if it is about truths of faith, it is allegorical; if it is about things Christians hope for, anagogical. A *metaphor,* however, must not be taken for a mystical meaning. When Christ is depicted as the Lion of Judah, the sentence entails a metaphor, "consequently its meaning is metaphorical-literal, but in no way mystical."[23]

If the mystical sense of scripture is based on the literal sense, then, according to Werkmeister, a number of conundrums arise—for example, how one should interpret Psalm 41:10: "Even my trusted friend, who ate my bread, has raised his heel against me." For Werkmeister, it is obvious that the sentence would have to be about a man who fulfills the meaning of the sentence literally. Since he had a fate similar to the one the Messiah would have, he could be a role model for the promised one, and to this extent the passage could have a mystical meaning:

> The mystical meaning is not the meaning that derives from the words of the text, not the literal . . . meaning, but it presupposes it. The mystical meaning is . . . the meaning of the message about which the words speak.[24]

Consequently, every Bible passage must have a literal meaning, and not

literali, bene tamen literalis sine mystic esse potest. . . . Sensus mysticus in literali fundari debet, id est, inesse rebus sensu." Cf. Alfonso Salmerón, *Prolegomena Biblica* (Madrid: 1598).
22. Werkmeister, "Über den mystischen Sinn," 262.
23. Ibid. This differentiation was common to school theology, cf. Stattler, *De Locis,* 108: "Recte itaque Catholici Doctores & interpretes SS. Scripturarum communi sententi duos sensus in istis distinguunt; primum literalem, quem verba, in toto contextu posita, propria virtute significativa exprimunt . . . alterum mysticum, qui est illi conceptus, quem res ipsae literali sensu conceptae & expressae, ceu figurae significativae, exprimunt."
24. Werkmeister, "Über den mystischen Sinn," 264: "Der mystische Sinn ist nicht der Sinn, welcher sich aus den Worten des Textes ergibt, nicht der wörtliche oder buchstäbliche Sinn des Textes, er setzt diesen schon voraus. Der mystische Sinn ist vielmehr der Sinn der Sache, von welcher die Worte handeln."

every text can have a mystical meaning. The questions that derive from these axioms are: (a) can the Holy Spirit intend a mystical meaning besides the literal meaning, which pertains to a future event (and if so how); and (b) how can one prove that the Spirit intended this or that mystical meaning? For Werkmeister, it is problematic to assume (a), since the mystical meaning of the text was not understandable to the people in whose time the text was written. Why would the Spirit intend a meaning that was not understandable to the first readers, asks Werkmeister? He concludes that the only proper reason for the Spirit to do so would be to make the harmony between Old and New Testament more obvious. Such a mystical meaning could, for most verses, only be discovered after the birth of Christ:

> Therefore, if one wants to find somewhere in the Old Covenant a mystical meaning . . . then one has to name the passage in the New Covenant, which narrates literally that it was fulfilled in the life of the Messiah, what one has found as prefiguration in the Old Testament.[25]

Thus, if somebody asserts the mystical meaning of a text, he has to find the literal sense of two passages—of the old one on which the mystical meaning rests, and of the new one that verifies the prediction. Thus, the fathers of the church are, in Werkmeister's eyes, unqualified exegetes in most cases, since they usually are unable to do so. Moreover, one has to prove clearly and strictly that the Holy Spirit intended a certain mystical meaning.[26] If a sentence does not have a literal meaning that can be found through the use of grammar and vocabulary, but is only about the future Messiah, it does not contain a mystical meaning, but is a true prophecy.[27] There are a number of negative principles that, according to Werkmeister, allow the investigation of the mystical meaning. Such a proof of a mystical meaning is *only* possible if the meaning does not contradict reason. Thus, Jacob's lie cannot be a prefiguration of the Messiah because his deception (Genesis 27) was truly sinful, and thus contrary to the Holy

25. Ibid., 268.
26. Ibid., 270.
27. Ibid., 276.

Spirit, even if St. Augustine tries to argue the opposite. Moreover, obscene passages cannot contain mystical meaning—for example, one could never see in the adultery of David and Bathsheba a prefiguration of Christ's marriage with the church. Third, everything that does not pertain to the Messiah cannot have a mystical meaning, since he is the culmination of God's revelation. Fourth, it is unlikely that the Holy Spirit wanted to prefigure unimportant circumstances of the Lord's life in prophecies.[28] More positively, it is justified to assume that the mystical meaning of an Old Testament passage is indeed intended by the Holy Spirit *if* the New Testament text explicitly refers to it; likewise, if the Church decreed in an ecumenical council that the meaning of a text is to be understood in such a way. These two principles are, for Werkmeister, the only ones with whose help, certainty about the truth value of a mystical meaning can be found.[29]

One could conclude from such principles that Werkmeister believed Isaiah 7:14 to be a prefiguration of the virgin birth. However, he denied this. For him, Matthew 1:23 does not say that Isaiah 7:14 is a clear prefiguration of Christ, and it also does not say that something happened then, which would also be true of the Messiah. Werkmeister thinks it more likely that Matthew wrote as a knowledgeable Jew, who happened to interpret the whole Bible in view of the Messiah. Matthew 1:23 and 2:15–22 are only his exegesis of a scripture passage (*sensus accomodationis*). The verse is, accordingly, the personal opinion of Matthew; since one cannot say with certainty, however, that such an opinion was assisted by the Holy Spirit, it should not be used as a dogmatic proof. Moreover, in the case of Isaiah 7:14, "all Catholic exegetes," as Werkmeister insists, agree that the literal meaning pertains to a historical person in Isaiah's time, which was a clear overstatement (see the chapter on Isenbiehl in this volume).[30] Equally, Paul's exegesis in the Letter to the Galatians, in which he uses an allegorical explanation of Genesis 16 and 21, cannot be regarded as proof for the mystical meaning of these Old Testament passages. It

28. Ibid., 270–72.
29. Ibid., 272–74.
30. Ibid., 282.

is Paul's exemplification of Christian freedom, and an *ad hominem* argument for his Jewish listeners.[31]

Is there any other way to prove that the Holy Spirit intended a certain mystical meaning for a text? Werkmeister denies that the liturgy can provide such authority.[32] In his view, the Church does not decide on doctrine when it allows certain prayers and liturgies, or explains magisterially a Bible passage. Also, the Church does not authentically decide that a text has a mystical meaning intended by the Holy Spirit. If a council uses such a text as dogmatic proof, a Catholic has only to accept its decision, but *not* the reasons for such a decision. One cannot prove a mystical meaning from theological authorities, either, as these are, for Werkmeister, always private theological opinions, even if a council referenced them. An example would be the Council of Trent, session 13, c.1 (DH 1636–1637) on the Eucharist. For Werkmeister, the Church only decided in this canon on the Real Presence, but not whether the quoted passage from 1 Timothy 3:15 really proves the infallibility of the Church and has this specific mystical meaning.[33] A text could be proven to have a mystical meaning if all fathers from the first five or six centuries agreed explicitly that the opposite of this mystical meaning was not the true apostolic faith. Moreover, one is permitted to leave the exegetical way of the fathers if good and new reasons can be presented. However, in matters of faith, one always has to cling to the fathers until a final decision of the Church is made.[34] Nevertheless, no explanation of scripture can be regarded as a dogma unless defined by a council.[35] Thus, even if the pope and some bishops decided that Isaiah 7:14 was about Jesus, it would still be "not a final decision, not a decision one has to accept necessarily, if one wants to be and remain Catholic."[36] The Benedictine knows, of course, that no council has ever defined the mystical

---

31. Ibid., 283.
32. Ibid., 289.
33. Ibid., 293–94.
34. Ibid., 296–97, with reference to Ludovico Muratori, *De moderatione ingeniorum* (Paris: 1714), bk. 1, c. 23.
35. Werkmeister, "Über den mystischen Sinn," 304.
36. Ibid., 311.

meaning of a scriptural passage. This is, in his eyes, no loss for the Church, since she is not in need of mystical explanations. The growing "Enlightenment" of humanity will decrease the need for them even further, he thinks, because religion will become less superstitious and more rational. Academic clarity is much more helpful than mystical interpretation for convincing atheists or agnostics, Werkmeister argues. But did Jesus and the apostles not also use the mystical interpretation of scripture? This, Werkmeister explains with historical conditions: Jesus and the apostles could only preach within the framework of late Judaism, and thus had to use the means of his time (*accommodation theory*).[37] In fact, a wrongheaded mystical reading of scripture can be highly dangerous, and Werkmeister refers to the cases of Popes Boniface VIII and Gregory the Great, because their exegesis "does not shed better light on the true grounds and natural connection of Christian duties. . . . Morality becomes undefined and uncertain if one can extract with the help of mystical exegesis everything one wants . . . and thus the teachers and students lose the urge to study the duties from the true sources. . . . Reason becomes dumb."[38]

After reading Werkmeister's explanations, it seems pretty obvious that not many allegorical or typological explanations of the traditional set of verses remain, perhaps not even a handful. This move, which a number of Catholics argued for, worried some Catholic Enlighteners so much that they feared a rationalist takeover of the Bible and began improving the traditional hermeneutic with the help of new ideas.

What is "Orthodox" Exegesis?

While many criticized attempts to modernize exegesis as Werkmeister envisioned it, and attacked what they perceived as rationalist, deist, or freethinking ideas, hardly any methodological expositions of what correct "orthodox" exegesis could and should look like were produced. A noteworthy exception is the work of the Bamberg Franciscan Jakob Berthold (1738–1817).[39] He appreciated the Bible as the source of

37. Ibid., 314–37.
38. Ibid., 357–58.

Christian life and his work centered around the thought that hearing and reading the word of holy scripture transforms the human will, since God desires the sanctification of his people (1 Thess. 4).[40] Since prayer is necessary for our perfection, Berthold also discusses how it should be done. Holiness is also the guiding principle here: the final aim for what we ask God, the use of means, everything has to be holy and has to improve our souls and contribute to the greater glory of God.[41] The highest principle of exegesis, however, is that everything God reveals through himself as first cause or through his authors in scripture must be true. The second one is that all scripture is divinely inspired and useful.[42] From 2 Peter 1:20, Berthold deduces the third exegetical principle that the scriptures should never be explained according to one's own whim but in accordance with the teaching tradition of the Church.[43] Berthold also takes pains to explain the accommodation of scripture, which is why the Bible sometimes uses human images or expressions to convey a deeper meaning, especially since passages that contain such terms often lead to confusion. More pressing for him, however, was the question of whether the authors of scripture intended a uniform doctrine. According to Salomo Semler, Christ did not intend unity of doctrine, but just a unity in spirit of love.[44] Referring to Matthew 28, Berthold refutes such a claim: "In this regard the faithful were never given the freedom to dissolve the unity of doctrine, even if it happened under the pretense of discerning the core from its cover or to improve harmless mistakes."[45] Christ entrusted the whole of faith to the apostles and to his church, and this pertains to all doctrines. When St. Paul uses accommodation, he does not give up any doctrine, he just tries to persuade his audience.

---

39. Jakob Berthold, *Orthodoxe Bibelexegese mit den nothwendigen Vorkenntnissen und Hülfswissenschaften, Schrift- und Moral-Principien sammt einem allgemeinen Schriftkriterium* (Bamberg: 1807).
40. Ibid., 81.
41. Ibid., 87.
42. Ibid., 184–85.
43. Ibid., 187: "Bey unseren Zeiten . . . hat Christus . . . dieses dringende Geschäft seiner Kirche . . . übertragen. Im Gegensatze wären wir Irrende, jedem Winde des Strauchelns ausgesetzte Schaafe, welches von Christo, dem Stifter der christlichen Kirche, der mit allen nothwendigen Heilsmitteln derselben immer beystehet, nicht zu denken ist."
44. Ibid., 215.
45. Ibid., 219.

Only in disciplinary questions—for example, the eating of non-kosher food—could changes occur, since these commands were given by humans and not by God, states Berthold.[46] This leads the Franciscan to the classic principle that there must be an ultimate judge in religious and scriptural questions, the Magisterium of the Church. Following the Catholic apologetic treatises of his time, Berthold argues that a knowledge of the Oriental languages, together with freedom of conscience, is not enough. No academic knowledge will bring certainty about a scriptural passage; therefore, Catholics believe in the teaching authority of their Church also in questions of scriptural interpretation.[47]

Berthold's book aims at a refutation of what he calls a mere "philosophical exegesis," one that only uses reason and explains scripture with the help of natural "psychology." Equally wrong, however, are, in Berthold's view, some romantic theologians who use the Bible as a basis, but develop upon its foundations a poetic or mythological religion that views celestial beings as symbols. With self-confidence, he states in the preface to his book: "I do not fear the bayonets of criticism: I am well versed in dealing with old and new literary weapons; I know old and new literary maneuvers."[48] Indeed, Berthold was acquainted with the literature of his time; he had already championed ecumenical and irenic thought in his youth, and now in old age he was one of the first to wrestle with the religious repercussions of the philosophy of Immanuel Kant (1724–1804).[49]

The next principle of exegesis is, for Berthold, the acknowledgement of the necessity of *knowing* the scriptures, since they are God's word, which every human being needs to achieve salvation, to fulfill his duties toward God, his fellow neighbors, and himself. Reason alone cannot realize that God is the true and last goal of man's search for happiness or provide the necessary vivid images and motives offered

---

46. Ibid., 221.
47. Ibid., 244.
48. Ibid., preface.
49. Jakob Berthold, *Nova litteratura de religione Kantii aliorumque in sacram scripturam neo-exegetarum refutata* (Augsburg: 1800).

by scripture. Without proper methodology, however, such knowledge can easily be corrupted. Every attempt to change the message of the Bible into something it does not intend has to be resisted, since it is God's own "event" (*Veranstaltung*). It has to remain unchanged.[50] However, does one have to renounce philosophy and reason altogether if one reads the scriptures? Not at all, states Berthold. As the first apologists used reason to defend the faith against critics such as Celsus, such philosophical "weapons" are necessary to battle with Socinians, deists, materialists, and naturalists:

> Where the Bible or commonly valid rules for its exegesis are rejected, reason must not be used in isolation but needs the support of . . . credibility and motives to silence the enemy.[51]

One has to show the critic the insufficiency of reason alone and make him acquainted with the credibility of revelation—a standard argument in school theology. The good use of reason, therefore, can be the door to all true sciences and also to theology, but as with every door, one must not remain on the threshold, but enter the room; that is, to embrace something beyond reason—namely, revelation. Good training in logic is therefore highly recommended, especially the art of making correct syllogisms, which includes finding and analyzing arguments. Equally important are physics and natural sciences to refute claims that miracles are impossible, or that the teleological argument would not work.[52] Berthold also argues with the help of the moral argument that there must be a God who judges good and evil, if morality is not to be an illusion. The counter argument, that humans could not have a clear enough concept of God, Berthold does not accept. He argues that there exist plenty of other aspects in everyone's life of which we do not have a clear concept, whose existence we do not doubt—for example, the influence of the soul on the body. Referring to Francis Bacon, Berthold states that when supreme reason teaches, inferior reason has to be obediently tacit.[53]

50. Berthold, *Orthodoxe Bibelexegese*, 1–7.
51. Ibid., 9.
52. Ibid., 9–12.

Reason is necessary for a human being to overcome naïveté and credulity, but also to defeat radical skepticism:

> It is one's duty to investigate why one believes something. . . . However, we also must know when it is licit to doubt something, and we have to know what sufficient reasons there are to state something with certitude.[54]

If reason is the ultimate judge, revealed religion has already lost, since its content is beyond reason—that is, supernatural. Thus, it is equally wrong not to use reason or to use it alone in religious matters. Healthy reason gives grounds and motives for the credibility of the faith. Once faith is accepted, reason has to accept a subsidiary role—namely, to bow to the almighty God and acknowledge its own weakness:

> Catholics who confide in these principles are consistent: their previous rational operations and the faith based upon them are in order; therefore, their faith is not passive, as Locke thinks. . . .[55]

Once no reasonable doubt remains about the divinity of the messenger (i.e., Jesus), faith in him is the only rational response. However, the former Barnabite monk and then Protestant philosopher Karl L. Reinhold (1757–1823) stated that such faith would be passive.[56] Reason, however, is abused if one mistakes one's own thoughts for the truth and one's own reading of scripture as the only correct one, as Kant, Fichte, and Heinrich Eberhard Gottlob Paulus (1761–1851) have taught:

> The new philosophers, who build a Babylonic Tower, and who do not understand each other, who throw humanity in the deepest darkness of a labyrinth, nevertheless proudly believe that they were disseminators of light and happiness for the world . . . and desire to bring their fight about words into every academic discipline. What will be the result? Confusion—since one will be unable to understand the sources any longer. . . .[57]

---

53. Ibid., 18–19.
54. Ibid., 20.
55. Ibid., 23.
56. Ibid., 23.
57. Ibid., 27.

Men of good will acknowledge the weakness of reason and trust the eternal rules of exegesis the church has developed with the assistance of the Holy Spirit (mainly the rule of faith), but they also understand that scripture should never be explained against the consensus of the fathers.[58] He even quotes, with approval, the Anglican theologian Brian Walton (1600–61), namely, his *Prolegomena*, chapter VI. According to him, a reading of scripture must always be preferred to another if it fits better with the analogy of faith or the witness of the fathers:[59]

> Not one philosophical system is real reason itself. . . . If they were . . . they would not share the fate of death. . . . Truth is always, and remains truth . . . and must always be truth.[60]

Where reason has, after scrutiny, acknowledged the supernatural, it has no longer the right to judge the other. Thus, he acknowledges, with Muratori, the right of reason in religious things, and also of doubt, but in moderation. Wherever doubt is subjective, it has to be stopped; wherever it is objective and comes from common sense, it has to be overcome to find ground for action.[61] Proud reason, however, does not acknowledge this and also does not acknowledge the unwritten tradition of the apostles. However, he who only uses psychology and metaphysics to explain the Bible will put "harmful mortar on the walls of his house . . . which the next wind will bring down."[62]

Berthold's insistence on the rule of faith and the role of faith for exegesis does not mean that he rejected the achievements of modern criticism or history. In fact, modern criticism was, for Berthold, of the utmost necessity, since he was convinced that many of his colleagues made out of the word of God something human, following their own whims in interpretation. How then is proper Biblical criticism done? It is in need of certain criteria. The inner criteria include that it does not entail contradictions; also, that the doctrines found are not relative,

---

58. Ibid., 99–115.
59. Ibid., 244; Brian Walton, *Biblia Polyglotta Prolegomena* (Leipzig: 1777). The latter is a separate printing of Walton's methodological thoughts from the edition of his Polyglot Bible.
60. Berthold, *Orthodoxe Bibelexegese*, 29.
61. Ibid., 52–54.
62. Ibid., 32.

but objective; that is, inherently good, true, holy, and so on. These criteria are confirmed by exterior ones—namely, through signs and miracles—but also by historical data, and historical proofs from other sources. The moral certitude one gains through the scrutiny of a source is called pragmatic criticism. Contrary to that is hypothetical criticism: it only assumes that the opposite might be true. Such hypothetical criticism is, for Berthold, without any merit and cannot really enlighten the reader or lead to truth. Equally unimportant are etymological and philological criticism, since the main aim of the interpreter is the intention of the author, who is God.[63]

Where does Berthold see the sources for the modern "addiction to doubt?" The first source lies, for him, in ignorance and misconceptions about religion, especially a widespread anthropomorphism. The second one consists in the fact that many people do not recognize the final aim of their existence; thus, they believe they are not in need of scriptural advice. The third is a one-sided Enlightenment of their mind, which neglects an improvement of their will, and thus of the human heart. The only means against such shortcomings is the clear and intelligible explanation of the purpose of God's revelation by theologians.[64] Of course, another reason to doubt God's existence and word is moral evil. Berthold, therefore, offers a classic Augustinian free-will defense and points to the fact that God's goodness has to be seen in connection with his holiness and justice, and cannot be viewed separately from them. Consequently, the punishments for the condemned in hell are just. The counter argument that every punishment should intend the improvement of the sinner, Berthold rejects. For him, not all punishments aim at that goal: the punishment of hell does not change the hearts of the demons. Once one has died, the time of probation is over. An improvement cannot take place: "Evil will remain evil and will—in this miserable state—not have any hope for eternal bliss."[65]

In the second part of the book, Berthold deals with more specific

63. Ibid., 40–42.
64. Ibid., 58–61.
65. Ibid., 78.

questions, the first of which is the authenticity of the Bible. Despite the fact that the original writings of the Old and New Testaments are lost, one can reasonably trust them due to the diligent witness of Judaism and Christianity. Even the discovery of many different variants and editions of the text only testifies to the need to scrutinize them through the rule of faith.[66] The books of the Bible are divinely inspired, not only because they contain the teachings of God, but also because God co-authored them. Moreover, Berthold makes clear that the Catholic Church does not teach new doctrines, but only illuminates what is contained in scripture, and thus answers a common charge of Protestant critics.[67]

Among the senses of scripture, the most important for exegesis are the literal, the mystical, and the moral. The mystical or spiritual sense of scripture is not too problematic for Berthold. While the literal sense always necessarily precedes a mystical one, not every literal sense also has a mystical one. A mystical sense is only acceptable if holy scripture mentions it explicitly, and it can only then be considered to be of divine origin. With such a statement, Berthold stands up to the over-allegorization of uncritical exegetes, but also refutes the critics who declare that every mystical meaning is invented by human readers.[68] Nevertheless, can there be several literal meanings of one passage? For Berthold, every passage can have only one meaning—the one intended by the author who was inspired by the Holy Spirit. If one assumed several literal meanings, one would destroy historical certainty—in the field of ancient writers, for example, this would call into question all ancient chronology and history.[69] The moral sense of scripture intends to improve our ethical behavior. The moral meaning is always secondary to the literal and historical meaning of scripture, otherwise morality loses its connection to dogma. If this meaning is not contained in the scriptural passage, but read into it, it is not of divine origin, but only a human opinion.[70] Berthold especially charges the Enlightenment

66. Ibid., 124.
67. Ibid., 129.
68. Ibid., 136.
69. Ibid., 141.

theologians with such eisegesis in their *moralization* of scripture. According to Berthold, such an approach aims at the marginalization of the doctrinal content of the Bible. Such a movement began with Jean-Jacques Rousseau (1712–78). After a critique of Kant, Berthold especially deals with Heinrich Eberhard Gottlob Paulus (1761–1851), who destroys all historical certainty with his plea for a complete disregard of patristic tradition. This, of course, fits his agenda to re-create the true face of early Christianity.[71] Paulus's "violent psychological historical scholarship . . . destroys the literal sense and the authenticity of history":[72]

> Such a rule contradicts every use of grammar among educated and uneducated people. To explain the words or writing of somebody else means . . . to expose what the author meant when he used the words in question. Whoever attaches a meaning to the sentences of a writer, which he did not express, does not explain him but only expresses the interpreter's own thoughts through the author's words. . . .[73]

Should Catholics Read the Bible?

A major problem Catholic exegetes faced in their work was overcoming the prejudice that Catholics do not read scripture. It was not only Protestants who charged Catholics with being ignorant of the holy book, but many Catholics also were hesitant to buy and study the many new, approved vernacular translations. Knowledge of the holy books was insufficient even among the clergy. Thus, in 1768, a pastoral letter of the bishop of Ypern admonished that a necessary part of the revival of the priesthood must be a better understanding of Holy scripture. Every day, a priest should read at least one chapter from the New Testament, the bishop states, and the priest should always have a Bible at hand to engage with the word of God. Likewise, superiors of

---

70. Ibid., 142–43.
71. Ibid., 146–52.
72. Ibid., 163. "Mit gleicher Conjectural-Kritik, afterpsychologischen Ansichten und Raisonnement (dies soll Schrift-Exegese seyn!) fährt Paulus fort, die Wunder Christi, und der Aposteln natürlich, ob es ihm schon nicht gelingt, auslegen zu wollen, und die biblischen Thatsachen nach seinem vorgesetzen Plane gewaltthätig mit philosophischen Hypothesen zu verdrehen."
73. Ibid., 182.

monasteries were instructed to implement this originally Tridentine idea of reading scripture more frequently.[74] The Catholic Enlightenment went even a step further, motivated by similar requests from Jansenists, maintaining that the laity also should read the Bible.

Among the academic treatments of Bible reading in German theology, a few stand out, which we will introduce in more detail. Adam Joseph Onymus (1754–1836), professor of exegesis at the University of Würzburg, tackled the issue in his history of Bible reading, published in 1786. The aim of this little book was to take away the fear many Catholics still had of reading scripture. Consequently, he demonstrated, in the first part, the decay of active scripture reading, beginning with the ancient Israelites. He made the reader acquainted not only with the main books of the Bible, but also with the main currents of Jewish theology and biblical history.[75] He clarified that a private reading of scripture has always been a rare occurrence, but that even the first Christians knew the holy scriptures predominantly from listening, and that the texts remained unexplained until under Origen, the first commentaries came into existence:

> Now, not only was the food offered but also made edible and digestible. This preparation, that is commenting, soon became *en vogue*; the most able minds regarded it is as the pinnacle of their efforts. . . .[76]

But it was "arbitrary allegory" that impeded the further flourishing of exegesis in Christianity, argued Onymus. One presupposed the literal meaning of the text, although it was often not at all clear what that literal meaning really was.[77] Onymus saw the origin of allegory not in Judaism, but in Oriental philosophy, particularly in Gnosticism. That St. Paul and Jesus himself used allegory was, of course, not mentioned by him. With the sixth century, he sees the end of good scriptural scholarship. The decline of scripture reading was, in his eyes, due to the impact of the barbarians, because priests were deprived of the

---

74. *Instructio Pastoralis Rev. D. Episcopi Iprensis ad universum clerum* (Ypern: 1768), 11.
75. Adam Joseph Onymus, *Entwurf zu einer Geschichte des Bibellesens* (Würzburg: 1786), 1–15.
76. Ibid., 22.
77. Ibid., 24.

tranquility needed to study scripture, and began to lose knowledge of the sacred languages: the Bible became a "closed" book.[78] When the barbarians, who could not read or write, accepted Christianity, the Christian message became more exteriorly oriented. While the first Christians listened to the words of scripture, these men preferred exterior rites. A pure doctrine thus became mixed with superstition, which soon also affected the liturgy. Scripture reading ceased with the introduction of the Latin rite, because now, everybody prayed individually, separated from the priest.[79] Dogmatic theology also had, for Onymus, tremendous negative influence, because it became a system of thought that neglected scripture. Theologians have left their most important source behind and built a well with holes, which can hold no water, as Onymus put it. The Bible does not fit into a scholastic system, Onymus explained. While the teachings of the Bible are clear and simple, they are only understandable in the context of its entirety, and are oriented toward action. Scholasticism is useless and complicated:

> After scholasticism had given up explaining scripture it forgot the simple language of revelation and filled everything with the inventions of dialectics. The simplest terms were imbued with the language of Aristotle. The most complicated differentiations increased conceptual darkness and confusion. . . . Now it became difficult to distinguish revelation from reason and the essential doctrines from the nonessential ones.[80]

This call to a renewal of theology and a conversion in how theology treats sacred scripture is very similar to the program the Second Vatican Council set out in *Dei Verbum* 23: "Sacred theology rests on the written word of God, together with sacred tradition, as its primary and perpetual foundation."

The Salzburg Augustinian Thaddäus Surer (1745–1803), who was a student of the eminent exegete Aloysius Sandbichler (see the chapter on him and Jakob Hess in this volume), argued very similarly.[81] His

---

78. Ibid., 39.
79. Ibid., 52–88.
80. Ibid., 92.
81. Thaddäus Surer, *Das Bibellesen in den ältesten Zeiten* (Salzburg: 1784). Surer left the order in 1789

little brochure was published because the Archbishop of Salzburg, Hieronymus Colloredo, who, in a pastoral letter of 1782, publicly encouraged his flock to read the Bible, allowed it to circumvent the intransigent book censor, who considered it Jansenist.[82] Archbishop Colloredo (1732–1812) had stated that one could not encourage the laity enough to read the holy scripture, which was the real treasure house of all Christian knowledge and all sober morals. Once Bible reading was established, the pastoral letter continued,

> the common man will think with more clarity, and become more enlightened, and will no longer stick to prejudices and superstition but be open to solid Christian catechesis . . . and be motivated to civic virtues . . . and it helps the unhappy and depressed. . . . May this divine book be more valuable and more precious to you than all treasures of the world. May it become the source in which you find daily light, consolation and strength to do good. . . .[83]

Surer based his argument about the necessity of reading scripture on a text of St. John Chrysostom—namely, his third homily on the resurrection of Lazarus—and thus defeated the argument of his opponents that his stance would contradict tradition. It was a smart strategic move to rely on an important father such as Chrysostom (as well as nineteen others), especially because he demonstrated that Chrysostom was convinced that without reading scripture, one cannot be saved—which was, indeed, in direct contradiction to the famous anti-Jansenist bull *Unigenitus* (1713).[84]

His Augustinian confrere Aloysius Sandbichler did not share his enthusiasm. He emphasized that it was wrong to regard the Bible as the only rule of faith for the first Christians, as his Protestant peers argued. The first Christians indeed read the Bible with immense industriousness and found in it the "waters of eternal life," but they did

and under the name "Franz Wadler" became a clockmaker in Nuremberg, where he died in 1803. Thaddäus Surer, *Freymüthige Beleuchtung des Glaubensbekenntnisses des Pietro Gianonne und der Mönchsgelübde* (Nuremberg: 1790), ix.
82. Surer, *Freymüthige Beleuchtung*, v–viii.
83. *Sr. Hochfürstlichen Gnaden des Hw. Herrn Hieronymus Joseph Erzbischofs und des H. R. Reichs Fürsten zu Salzburg . . . Hirtenbriefe gesammelt* (Salzburg: 1782), pastoral of June 29, 1782, nu. 22, 58–59. Johann Michael Bönike (1734–1811) was most likely the author of this pastoral.
84. Surer, *Das Bibellesen*, 21.

so with special care. Although it was the first rule of faith, it was not the only one. As much as the first Christians listened to the word of God, they listened to the church. Thus, while the question whether the first Christians read the Bible can easily be answered, it is, in Sandbichler's eyes, much more important to realize how they read it.

The first answer to this is that it was read out loud in the congregation, very much like in the Jewish synagogue, and at home one reflected about what one had heard. A necessary prerequisite for this was that it was accessible in the vernacular. Therefore, many translations were done over the next centuries.[85] But Sandbichler also amasses a number of quotations from the fathers that show their appreciation and interest in augmenting the reading of holy scripture by the laity.[86] He certainly laments that this use has stopped, but he does not address the historical roots of it; rather, he embraces the imperial decree of August 10, 1781, which allowed the entire Christian world to read any Catholic vernacular Bible that the imperial censors had approved as well as Prince Bishop Colloredo's decree of 1782. For Sandbichler, the "justified" causes that led the fathers of Trent to so much caution regarding translations no longer exists.[87] He defends the allegorical interpretation of scripture, but also stresses the knowledge of the original languages, of biblical archeology, poetry, and a healthy higher criticism. But he rejects Theodore of Mopsuestia (350–428), who had polemicized against allegory.[88] For Sandbichler, Theodore was almost a Socinian, because he downgraded mysterious sayings of the Bible and understood them merely literally—just like Hugo Grotius, Wohlzogen, Semler, or Teller, argues Sandbichler.[89] The fathers unanimously defend—besides the literal meaning—a mystical meaning of scripture. He affirms the classical Augustinian rule that the literal meaning is the basis for the mystical interpretation and that such a mystical meaning can only be certain of the New Testament.[90]

85. Aloysius Sandbichler, *Lasen die ersten Christen die heilige Schrift? Und wie lasen sie dieselbige?* (Salzburg: 1784), 5–19.
86. Ibid., 35–40.
87. Ibid., 47.
88. Ibid., 70–118.
89. Ibid., 118.

Nevertheless, he agrees that Origen often went too far when he saw an allegory in everything. Against such an abandonment of the literal sense, the Church preferred the hermeneutic of St. Irenaeus.[91] Thus, it is clear to him that the first Christians did not read the Bible "blindly," as his Protestant peers argued, but with "certain principles."

The Supernatural in the Bible

Of course, one of Germany's most pressing questions for exegetes who followed in the footsteps of modern criticism was how they should deal with the biblical descriptions of supernatural events. Perhaps the boldest statements came from the Carmelite Thaddäus Dereser (1757–1827).[92] Dereser's main principles for exegesis were part of the mainstream Enlightenment and probably learned from his Würzburg teachers Franz Berg (1753–1821) and Franz Oberthür (1745–1831).[93] In 1789, this professor at the University of Bonn, who later embraced the French Revolution, but was reconciled with his church, published a little book on the temptations of Christ, according to Matthew 4:1–11.[94] He states against his critics: "I am quite far from the untamed freedom to undermine all miracles of the Old and New Testament and to present them all as natural occurrences, as certain zealots say."[95] On the contrary, Dereser claims that he defends every miracle which is *defensible,* and for which reasonable proofs are possible. If biblical miracles can be explained naturally, "it is absolutely impossible that I regard them as miraculous only because older theologians, whose knowledge of science and exegesis was inferior, have regarded them as such."[96]

---

90. Ibid., 125–32.
91. Ibid., 139–44.
92. Anonymous, *Katholische Betrachtung eines Köllnischen Theologen über die Scriptursätze des P. Thadaeus a S. Adamo* (Erfurt: 1785).
93. Cf. Franz Oberthür, *Idea Biblica Ecclesiae,* 6 vols. (Würzburg: 1790–1821). Thaddäus Anton Dereser, *Entstehung und Einweihungsgeschichte der kurkölnischen Universität zu Bonn . . .* (Bonn: 1786), 59–60; Hans Werner Seidel, "Bibelwissenschaftliche Arbeit und Forschung an der Katholisch-Theologischen Fakultät der Universität Breslau," *Jahrbuch der Universität Breslau* 10 (1965): 7–45.
94. Thaddäus Dereser, *Die Versuchungsgeschichte Christi, erklärt und von Widersprüchen gerettet* (Bonn: 1789).
95. Ibid., 20.
96. Ibid., 20.

Dereser agrees that a critical reader who is used to reading "old stories" with "a sentiment for historical probability" will be puzzled by certain elements of the temptation account. The first problem is, according to him, the initial improbability that Jesus, after the beginning of his public ministry, initiated by his baptism, would go for forty days into seclusion. Why would he have to prepare for his preaching if he was the Son of God? If he had desired to reflect on his ministry, the complete fasting would have impeded the full use of reason, argues the Carmelite. Can a human being fast completely for forty days? A miracle cannot be invoked to explain the abstinence from food and water since it would have been unnecessary, useless, and even harmful, Dereser argues. It would have been harmful because it would have favored the errors of suicidal people, who would—in imitation of Jesus—starve themselves to death. Equally problematic is that the devil appears as a person. If he appeared as the devil, how could Jesus have listened to him even for just one second? Why does he want to know from Jesus whether he is the Son of God?

> Was he not present when the angel spoke to Mary: The fruit of your womb will be Son of the most high? (Luke 1:35) Did he not witness that Jesus was born without the help of a man by a virgin? Did he not hear the thunderous voice from heaven that solemnly declared him to be his son at his baptism in the Jordan River? . . . Did he not hear about all this? He, who according to all theologians, has his spies everywhere?[97]

Moreover, Dereser asks whether Jesus would have sinned if he had responded to the devil's doubt and had transformed stones into bread, since it would have only manifested his divinity. Also, if it is sin to turn stone into bread for a personal reason—namely, to prove to the devil his divine status—then the miracle of not needing to eat falls into the same category. How credible is it that Jesus was kidnapped by the devil and placed on the roof of the temple, since ancient sources witness that it was covered with big nails? Likewise, one cannot argue for a literal reading of the devil showing Jesus all the kingdoms of the earth. Interestingly, Dereser approvingly quotes to this effect Voltaire's

97. Ibid., 7–8.

L'Evangile de la Raison, his *Melange Philosophiques*, his *Sermon de Cinquante*, and Karl Friedrich Bahrdt's letters *Über Die Bibel Im Volkston: Eine Wochenschrift von Einem Prediger Auf Dem Lande.* Dereser is also critical about the traditional location of the temptation of Christ.

When Jesus rejects performing the miracle of turning stones into bread, he does so in reference to Deuteronomy 8, the story in which God admonishes the Israelites in the desert to remember that God would feed them with manna. "And thus he taught you that humans cannot only live of bread but from everything Jehovah's command produces."[98] In this context, however, it only means that God instructed them to eat the plant juice available in the desert which previous generations disregarded, according to Dereser. Therefore, Jesus seems to imply that a miracle is not necessary because nature provides enough to survive—herbs, roots, insects, honey, and so on. In the second temptation, Jesus was brought to a high building next to the temple and not shown "all" kingdoms, but only a number of prospering kingdoms. Moreover, Dereser argues, the Greek word used for "showing" can also mean showing with words.[99]

But why did Jesus go to the desert in the first place? Dereser agrees that the most rational explanation is that Jesus wanted to prepare for his preaching and to reflect on his future deeds. Since he was also human, he could do so, despite his divine omniscience: "He does what every reasonable man should do. . . ."[100] However, he does not defend the claim that Jesus actually fasted for forty days. One has to interpret "fasting" as "eating little," but not "nothing." When the Gospel of Luke claims just that—namely, that he did not eat or drink anything—then Luke only used an idiom that was in use at the time for regular or severe fasting, but not total abstinence from all food and drink. For Jesus, such fasting meant becoming acquainted with a life of sacrifice and material need. Moreover, it was a real physical training to be able to teach over long durations without need of food or water. Fasting in imitation of Christ can, therefore, not pertain to all people, but only to

98. Ibid., 15.
99. Ibid., 18.
100. Ibid., 19.

the small class of those who follow in his ministry and whose service demands similar endurance.[101]

Dereser, however, does not explain the "devil" away by invoking superstition. Instead, he argues that the temptation of Christ is a parallel to the temptation of Adam and Eve in paradise, which Dereser believes was a "hieroglyphical poem that was only later put in written form without changing the images." Just as Eve was deceived under the mask of a seemingly well-intentioned angel (the snake is a symbol for the evil angel—an idea Dereser borrows from Ernst Friedrich Rosenmöller and Jacques Vernet), so was Jesus. However, since the appearance of the devil is, for an increasing number of people, unintelligible, Dereser also gives another interpretation: that of a dream. Interestingly, he cites as reference the ancient writer Theodore of Mopsuestia. To interpret the temptation story in this way seemed, for him, the best solution to avoid contradictions. Thus, the temptation was more of an inner temptation and not so much an event caused by an evil being. Jesus fasted a long time in the desert and felt the temptation: "Should I not change these stones into bread?" Another time, he went to Jerusalem and walked on the roof of a building and thought when he looked down: "How would it be, if I fell down and remained unhurt?" The third temptation happened when he happened to be on a hill: "Should I not pronounce to all that I am the earthly Messiah my nation expects?"[102] Dereser makes clear that among Catholic theologians, a view that denies the existence of a personal devil will find no acceptance, despite the fact that Oriental languages often personify things so that one cannot deduce that the account was about a personal encounter with the devil. This interpretation he sees in accordance with the claim of Hebrews 4:15—that Jesus was tempted in everything, like humans, but humans are usually not tempted by personified demons.

A similar provocative work was Dereser's *Sentences on the 19th Chapter*

---

101. Ibid., 21–24.
102. He refers here to Heinrich Corrodi, *Beyträge zur Beförderung des vernünftigen Denkens in der Religion* (Frankfurt: 1782), issue 3, 89; and *Stromata: eine Unterhaltungsschrift für Theologen* (Duisburg: 1787), issue 2, 106.

of the Book of Genesis (1784).[103] It was heavily attacked by conservative theologians. An anonymous defense, however, praised Dereser as a bringer of light into the Catholic darkness of prejudice and ignorance:

> Believe it, dear citizens of Bonn and Cologne: There was no rain of fire and sulfur on Sodom, only lightening destroyed it. The snake did not talk with Eve—that is mere *metaphorical* language. Lot's wife did not turn into a pillar of salt; she died, was mummified according to Egyptian tradition and her body sunk in the Dead Sea.[104]

Dereser's main point in this book is that the most important way of getting access to holy scripture was the knowledge of Oriental languages.[105] For some of his critics, such as the ex-Jesuit Hermann Goldhagen (1718–94), that was impractical. He even complained that for his interpretation, Dereser had translated the book of Genesis from the original Hebrew text and had not used the Latin Vulgate. Consequently, he thought the Carmelite would hold contempt for the Council of Trent and its recommendation of the Latin text. Yet, the author of Dereser's defense (possibly Dereser himself) quotes a number of approved Catholic writers who understand Trent's canon not as an exclusion of the Hebrew or Greek text at all. Francois Feller (1735–1802), the aggressive anti-Enlightener, thought it unwise of Dereser to publish his account of the Sodomites in the vernacular since it was embarrassing for the faithful: "Too bad that this simple and scrupulous Abbé was not born 3000 years earlier; he would have certainly warned Moses not to write about such topics."[106]

Moreover, Feller rejects Dereser's attempt to make the account intelligible and to show that God used for his punishments natural

---

103. Thaddäus Anton Dereser, *Scriptursätze aus dem Grundtexte des ersten mosaischen Buches, mit Anmerkungen über etliche Ausdrücke im XIX. Kap.* (Bonn: 1784).

104. Anonymous, *Katholische Betrachtung eines köllnischen Theologen über die Skriptursätze des P. Thaddäus vom H. Adam* (Frankfurt and Leipzig: 1785), 1; Francois Feller, "Review of Dereser, *Scriptursätze,*" *Journal historique et littéraire* 159 (1784, October 15): 256–64. Another review was published in the Catholic journal *Mainzer Monatsschrift von geistlichen Sachen* 1 (1785): 315–19. A naturalist explanation of the demise of Sodom and Gomorrah in a thunderstorm is also given by the Benedictine Augustine Calmet in his literal commentary on Genesis; see Calmet, *Commentarium Literale in omnes ac singulos tum veteris cum novi testament libros* (Augsburg: 1734), 1/1:160–61.

105. Thaddäus Anton Dereser, *Necessitas linguarum orientalium ad S. Scripturam intelligendam, vindicandam ac dogmati fidei inde probanda* (Cologne: 1783).

106. *Katholische Betrachtung,* 5.

causes such as a thunderstorm, and not fire and brimstone. Of special importance was, however, Dereser's account that the Catholic Church "deceived herself" for centuries about the true meaning of many Bible verses, but that the Lutherans had brought progress into this scholarly desert.[107] Goldhagen's claim that Dereser broke the first and most important rule of exegesis is interesting: that the interpreter of holy scripture should not deviate from the literal meaning without necessity. For the defense, however, it is argued that a literal meaning has to be unearthed by explaining and analyzing Oriental idioms and not just by looking at the plain language, which might be misleading.[108] Goldhagen's argument against the use of the Hebrew Bible consisted mainly of referring to St. Jerome's statement that most Hebrew words were ambiguous and the language itself uncertain. How, then, the anonymous defender asks, could he have translated the Bible if it was so uncertain? "What we can deduce [from St. Jerome's statement] is that men who undertake such a Herculean task should not be bothered by stupid censors."[109]

Another argument of Goldhagen's is the permanent use of the works of the Protestant exegete Johann David Michaelis, who would undermine the divinity of Christ with his naturalist explanation of the Old Testament miracles, to which the anonymous defender responds: "Christ will remain true God even if Lot's wife did not turn into a pillar of salt."[110] Dereser shows that the term "to become a pillar of salt" means, in Egyptian, "to die" or to "perish," so that this meaning is preferable to a literal reading. Likewise, it was problematic for conservative theologians that Dereser gave up the idea that an exegete always had to explain the Bible according to the unanimous consensus of the fathers, since this criterion was used against Enlighteners, but not against conservative theologians. Soon after the first defense of Dereser, another pamphlet defended him, yet more moderate in style.[111] Here, Dereser's view that a verse can be interpreted differently

107. Ibid., 9.
108. Ibid., 13.
109. Ibid., 14.
110. Ibid.

if it does not pertain to morals or faith is supported, but he nowhere denies the ideal of exegesis, which is to interpret texts about faith and morals according to the unanimous meaning of the fathers.[112]

Enlightened Hermeneutics and Theological Reading of Scripture

For Clemens Baader (1762–1838), the Augustinian Aloysius Sandbichler[113] was one of the most enlightened and erudite Catholic theologians of his time.[114] He attempted to avoid what he considered the extreme of Dereser's rationalism and that of earlier uncritical over-allegorizations of scripture by combining higher criticism and theological interpretation.

Sandbichler relies heavily for his rules for a common hermeneutics of Old and New Testament on his Catholic colleague from Vienna, Johann Jahn (1750–1816), who, in his eyes, went too far in his naturalist explanations of scripture.[115] Sandbichler, who writes in a clear and non-technical German, distinguishes between a grammatical, a historical, and a historical-theological explanation of scripture. Moreover, he argues for the necessity of biblical hermeneutics against the criticism of the Catholic Enlightener Engelbert Klüpfel (1733–1811),

111. *Zwote katholische Betrachtung . . . die Erwägungen welche Herrn Goldhagen zu Mainz . . . und Herr Pater Feller . . . zu machen beliebten wider die Scriptursätze des P. Thaddäus vom H. Adam* (Frankfurt: 1785).
112. Dereser, *Notiones Generales Hermeneuticae Sacris Vetris Testamenti* (Bonn: 1784), §17: "Nec non & aliae regulae Interpreti Biblico observandae sunt, inter quas prima est: *Textus, cui ceu fundamento, Fidei dogma, & doctrina morum innituntur, exponendus est juxta mentem oecumenicorum Ecclesiae Conciliorum, atque secundum unanimem SS.PP. consensum, a quo in rebus Fidei & Morum recedere nefas est.* Utrumque hic extremum est vitandum, ne aut nihil, aut nimium sapere videamur. Fieri non potest, ut Ecclesia, sanctique Patres ad unum omnes circa mysteria Fidei ac praecepta morum errent; secure igitur hac in materia sententiam illorum amplectimur. At in caeteris falli possunt; imprudenter igitur in verba eorum semper juratur. Quapropter si agatur de antilogiis conciliandis, de figenda chronologia, de serie historica, de rebus ad historiam naturalem aut Physicam pertinentibus; cum laude vestigia antecessorum relinquuntur, ubi alius modus faelior ac convenientior a Recentioribus inventus est. Sana enim ratio, ac principia melioris philosophiae, illi solummodo caecum assensum praebere imperant, qui gaudet privilegio non errandi. Qui vero hoc de integra Expositorum turba circa memoratas materias evinces? Parcius ergo communem Interpretum viris objiciendam meminerint."
113. On his life, see Anonymous, "Denkschrift auf den sel. Herrn Alois Sandbichler," *Neue Quartalschrift für katholische Geistliche* 7 (1833): 1–14; Adolar Zumkeller, "Sandbichler, Aloys,"in *Biographisch-Bibliographisches Kirchenlexikon* (Nordhausen: Bautz, 1994), 8:1303.
114. Niklas Raggenbass, *Harmonie und schwesterliche Einheit zwischen Bibel und Vernunft. Die Benediktiner des Klosters Banz: Publizisten und Wissenschaftler in der Aufklärungszeit* (St. Ottilien: EOS, 2006), 245.
115. Aloysius Sandbichler, *Darstellung der Regeln einer allgemeinen Auslegungskunst von den Büchern des alten und neuen Bundes* (Salzburg: 1813).

who had contested its usefulness because of its use by Socinian or rationalist critics of the Bible. For the Freiburg theologian, the permanent tradition of the Church was relevant—but he saw that one also needs a hermeneutic to understand this tradition.[116] For Sandbichler and Jahn, the fate of exegesis took a turn for the worse when the influence of Origen increased, and with him, a less literal but more mystical interpretation of the texts. Both see an important counterpart to this trend in the ancient Antiochian interpretation. Augustine masterfully formulated the historical interpretation in *De doctrina christiana*, but even he lacked a system of rules for his hermeneutics (as did Jerome). Only the religious controversies of the Reformation made it necessary to reflect with more serenity on such rules.[117] Just like Sandbichler, Jahn explicitly praises the earlier attempts of their Catholic peers Josef Monsperger (1724–88),[118] Stefan Hayd (1744–1802),[119] Adam Vizer (dates unknown),[120] Christoph Fischer (d. 1791),[121] and Gregor Mayr (1754–1820).[122] Among Protestant scholars, Sandbichler likes, especially, Johann August Ernesti (1707–81),[123] Gottlob Wilhelm Meyer (1768–1816),[124] Georg Friedrich Seiler (1733–1807), and Karl Gottlieb Bretschneider (1776–1848).[125]

What is the meaning of scripture? Every word corresponds to a concept, and from sentences, arise meanings. The author conveys this meaning through the original connection of concepts. The main rule for an interpreter consists in learning the use of the language of the ancient reader; from this rule, all others are deduced:

---

116. Engelbert Klüpfel, *Commonitorium S. Vincentii Lerinensis* (Vienna: 1790); see also the criticism of Klüpfel by Altmann Arigler, *De Studio Biblico* (Vienna: 1809) and his *Hermeneutica Biblica Generalis* (Vienna: 1813).
117. Sandbichler, *Darstellung der Regeln*, 9–11. Sandbichler also refers for his outline of the history of hermeneutics to Ernst Friedrich Karl Rosenmüller, *Handbuch für die Literatur der biblischen Kritik und Exegese* (Göttingen: 1797–1800), part 4, 23–164.
118. Joseph Julius Monsperger, *Institutiones hermeneutica V. T.: praelectionibus academicisaccomodata* (Vienna: 1776/84).
119. Stefan Hayd, *Hermeneutica in Sacros Novi Testamenti libros* (Augsburg: 1777).
120. Adam Vizer, *Praenotiones hermeneuticae N. T.* (Tyrnau: 1777).
121. Christoph Fischer, *Institutiones Hermeneuticae N. T.* (Prague: 1788).
122. Gregor Mayr, *Institutio Interpretis Sacri* (Vienna: 1789).
123. Johann August Ernesti, *Institutio Interpretis N. T.* (n.p.: 1761).
124. Gottlob Wilhelm Meyer, *Versuch einer Hermeneutik des alten Testaments*, 2 vols. (Göttingen: 1779–80).
125. Karl Gottlieb Bretschneier, *Historisch-dogmatische Auslegung des N. T.* (Leipzig: 1806).

> Hermeneutic is therefore nothing arbitrary. It relies on necessary and immutable laws, which are not invented arbitrarily and *a priori*, but depend on the fact which use of language the author and his contemporaries, his countrymen and people, applied.[126]

Following in the footsteps of Protestant theologian Johann August Ernesti, Sandbichler and Jahn agree that language is determined not only by time, but also by geography, religion, and science, as well as ecclesiastical and state reforms, common use, and public morals. Despite the fact that words can have different meanings, the sentence can have only one meaning, unless the author wanted to express himself ambiguously. A biblical writer must have written just like a profane author if he wanted to be understood.[127] The use of a dead language can be established by comparison with other languages: in the case of Hebrew, with Chaldean, Syriac, and Arabic.[128] While an author can think of several meanings of the words he is using, he must think of the one and only meaning of the sentence he has in mind when he puts the words together in context. The Holy Spirit certainly knew all possible meanings beforehand, but "can the Holy Spirit be indifferent if one assumes all these meanings against the context of the speech . . . ? He let the authors write in a human language and therefore must have wanted these authors to obey the laws of human language."[129] By using the rules of language, the biblical author had to apply the contemporaneous use of words. If another meaning can be established with the same rule, one has to weigh the reasons why one meaning can be more probable than another.

This does not mean that the exegetical meaning is also objectively true—for example, that the Jews called Jesus a blasphemer is true—but it is libel for Sandbichler.[130] If a meaning could not have been intended or imagined by the author or his first readers, then this meaning must be false. This is always the case if one imports a new use of language into the original text. Only prophecies are exempt from this rule,

126. Sandbichler, *Darstellung der Regeln*, 14–15.
127. Ibid., 15–19.
128. Ibid., 26.
129. Ibid., 20.
130. Ibid., 21.

because often even the prophets themselves did not understand the meaning of their words.[131] If one has established the true meaning, one can still encounter difficulties; for example, one could wish that this meaning was not the genuine meaning of the text because it contradicts certain prejudices. Here, one must abstain from doing violence to the text and check if only a *prima facie* contradiction exists.[132] Such obstacles can come into being if the meaning of the text contradicts perfectly certain knowledge of history; then, one has to see whether a contradiction really exists. If a difficulty arises from the doubtful meaning of words or idioms, one has to have recourse to the use of language and to archeology. For Sandbichler, exegesis was able to resolve many obstacles over the last decades, especially in understanding the prophets. When the prophets used different time forms (*tempora verborum*) almost arbitrarily, one was able to show that profane poets did the same and that one should not attribute a special meaning to it.[133]

If the meaning of a sentence is the representation of something else, or an image for it, one calls such a meaning *sensus mediatus* or mystical sense.[134] Sandbichler differentiates it in a historical, prophetic, and moral sense. While Sandbichler agrees with Johann David Michaelis (1717–91) that an indirect (*mittelbar*) prophetic sense can be established, he also acknowledges the problems Michaelis and Johann Wilhelm Rau have pointed to—especially, Origen's excessive use of the anagogical meaning of scripture.[135] Origen's method, which seems to exclude, at times, any historical meaning, is extreme, but so is the exclusion of any allegorical meaning. The latter would have to assume that sayings of the prophets, which talk about their extraordinary actions and signs, and likewise of Jesus (for example, his cursing of

---

131. Ibid., 21–22.
132. Ibid., 23: "Es folgt nun gar zu leicht auch ein Versuch, einen solchen geheimen Wunsch zur Wirklichkeit zu bringen. Kann man nicht zeigen dass die Schwierigkeit nur anscheinend ist, so verfährt man oft mit den gewaltsamsten Mitteln, die exegetische Wahrheit des erforschten Sinnes, wo nicht gänzlich umzustossen, was man meistentheils nicht kann, doch zu verdunkeln."
133. Ibid., 25.
134. Ibid., 26.
135. Johann David Michaelis, *Entwurf der typischen Gottesgelartheit*, 2nd ed. (Göttingen: 1763); Johann Wilhelm Rau, *Fremüthige Untersuchung über die Typologie* (Erlangen: 1784).

the fig tree [Matt. 21:18–20; Mark 11:12–14]) have to be taken literally. Similarly, the history of the Old Covenant, especially of its sacrifices, has to be read in connection to their fulfillment in Christ's ultimate sacrifice on the cross.[136] The detection of such an indirect meaning is not arbitrary. Among the certain indications that such a meaning is intended is the explicit explanation of a certain action or description as image (as when Moses explains certain rites), or if an action is reported that had a certain symbolic meaning (e.g., when it is said that the prophet Jeremiah was three years naked), or when a wise man undertakes or commands an action that would be meaningless without indicating something higher (e.g., some liturgical rites of the Old Covenant or the sacraments of the New Covenant). Last, but not least, one can give a text an allegorical meaning for the purpose of spiritual edification, so that the text speaks to the contemporary listener.[137]

It is important that Sandbichler explicitly rejects a number of interpretations, because these explanations "de-bible" (*entbibeln*) holy scripture, or rob it of its supernatural character.[138] The most important of these is the *mythological* interpretation. While Sandbichler does not deny that ancient Israel had a mythology (e.g., about the angels), he rejects the notion that biblical texts are *only* mythological narratives, like accounts found in Greek and Roman literature. Since such conclusions are made on the grounds of mere exterior analogies of these accounts and without proper proof, and because the texts of the Bible are connected to historical facts and not to imaginary times, like the Greeks, this approach cannot be applied properly. The *psychological* interpretation is very similar, which claims that the biblical authors believed they really narrated true stories, but were themselves deceived. Kant is subsumed under a *moral* interpretation, because it is completely arbitrary.[139] Only a proper knowledge of the context of

---

136. Sandbichler, *Darstellung der Regeln*, 31.
137. Ibid., 31–32; on the allegorical interpretation for spiritual edification: "Dieser ist der sogenannte *zugewandte* Sinn, an sich selbst so wenig ein wahrer Sinn, als er es nicht war, wenn die Griechen aus Homer Verse verschiedentlich anwandten. Die Homiletiker bedienten sich nachher desselben vor anderen; sie mögen es; aber *ne quid nimis et circumspecte!*"
138. Ibid., 32.

a text, of the object of a speech or narrative, and the reason why an author wrote, can help to unveil the true intention of the writer.[140] For the reconstruction of a context, Sandbichler suggests the consultation of concordances and analysis of parallel texts.[141]

Sandbichler concedes that not every citation of Old Testament verses in the New Testament should be used to construct a positive proof, because sometimes formulas such as "so that the word of scripture was fulfilled" were sometimes just that—formulas; for example, when the New Testament quotes in order to correct a certain view or uses it to construct an *argumentum ad hominem*. Whether such a quotation can be used to construct a proof derives solely from the content compared with the intention of the person who cited it. For example, one can state that when Jesus uses Psalm 110 in Matthew 22:43-44, he wants to stress his identity as Messiah.[142]

The analogies in teachings or the sum of teachings of each biblical writer, as well of all, can also help the exegete, especially if, otherwise, errors in religion or morality would be accepted. An example for this is when God prescribed morally bad actions:

> One has to avoid two extremes. First, that one assigns a meaning to a verse that opposes the clear and distinct analogy of the Bible's teachings. Second, that one imposes on the words and sentences of sacred scripture a meaning under the pretext of the analogy of teaching [*Analogie der Lehre*], which hermeneutic principles cannot justify.[143]

For a Catholic exegete, this means to also take church tradition into consideration, but does not mean to interpret the Bible according to church dogmas or theological opinions. Yet, how is one to interpret the tropological idioms—that is, words that were given a new meaning beyond their original one? While originally, such idioms were

---

139. See, for example, Heinrich Eberhard Gottlob Paulus (1761–1851), *Philologisch-kritischer und historischer Commentar über das Neue Testament*, 4 vols. (Lübeck: 1800-04) to which Sandbichler reacted with his *Stimme des Rufenden in der Wüste*, 3 vols. (Linz: 1805-14). Sandbichler, *Darstellung der Regeln*, 34.
140. Sandbichler, *Darstellung der Regeln*, 40–43.
141. Ibid., 46–52.
142. Ibid., 52.
143. Ibid., 54–55.

necessary because of the limitations of language, later, they were used for a poetical improvement of language. Knowledge of the languages and cultures of the Orient is necessary for differentiating idioms from words that should be translated literally, in order to avoid problematic interpretations such as those found in Origen, who "smelled everywhere an allegorical or anagogical meaning."[144] Sometimes, reverence for the mysterious teachings of the New Testament can mislead the exegete and make him assume a group of words constitute an idiom. Nevertheless, as a rule, one should, argues Sandbichler, assume a literal meaning unless necessity urges a deviation from it—for example, if the literal meaning would lead to an absurd or contradictory meaning. As an example, Sandbichler refers to Matthew 19:12, when Jesus talks about castration. Sandbichler consequently rejects Heinrich Paulus's claim that this rule could not always apply, so that one should rather look for a literal meaning even if it was farfetched, rather than assuming an idiom.[145]

It is noteworthy how Sandbichler tries to resolve contradictions in verses. This is especially the case when a moral of the Old Testament contradicts the New Testament, but one has to assume "that revelation revealed certain teachings, even in morality, only gradually in their more explicit dimensions."[146] One has to discern whether a teaching is clearly put forth or not. If the contradiction only pertains to *obiter dicta*, one should not see it as contradiction. If a contradiction appears in prophetic texts, one has to remember first that prophets sometimes made threats under the condition that no change of heart would occur; second, that prophecies about future events can apply to different times and contexts; three, that prophecies are mostly not propositions about future events, but commands about proper behavior; and four, that such utterances are often only depictions and allegories.[147] More

---

144. Ibid., 58.
145. Ibid., 60: "Vielleicht wollten die Erfinder dieser Regeln, die den tropischen Sinn als einen nicht litteralen, unmittelbaren von dem litteralen unecht unterschieden, sagen, man habe ohne dringende Ursache nicht auf einen tropischen zu denken. Da hatten sie Recht; aber sie hätten auch beysetzen sollen, eine eigentliche Bedeutung sey, ohne Zwangursache, nicht mit einer weit hergesuchten, die dem Worte sonst auch zukommen könnte, zu verwechseln, und eine solche Zwangursache konnte nur der Zusmmenhang u. s. w. seyn."
146. Ibid., 84.

complicated are contradictions between historical verses, but most can be solved by realizing that the authors used different sources and names for the same things, locations, or persons. "The biblical authors wrote like others their history, and although they were guided and assisted by God, this does not mean that they were prevented from every alleged contradiction...."[148]

Accommodation and the Farewell to the Devil

In his posthumously published essays, Johann Jahn, who had taught at the University of Vienna until he resigned his chair due to heavy attacks based on his defense of historical criticism, gives us a remarkable insight into his thought as an exegete. He deemed it possible to divulge his view on *accommodation* only posthumously.[149] The accommodation theory is, in his eyes, the centerpiece of enlightened criticism, but he nevertheless rejects the dogmatic accommodation whose growth he sees among rationalists, and which desires to undermine the true teachings of the New Testament. Such *dogmatic accommodation* would see the doctrine of the resurrection as a problematic, time-bound idea of first-century Judaism.[150] Accommodation means that Jesus and the writers of the books of the New Testament used the common prejudices and conceptions of the common people, such as the differentiation between minor and major commandments, or the descent of an angel into the pool of Bethesda, and that they used popular concepts in a different sense than they were understood, such as the kingdom of heaven.

Moreover, it means that Jesus and the apostles interpreted the Old

147. Ibid., 85: "Zweytens beziehen sich die Weissagungen oft auf verschiedene Zeiten und Zeitumstände. Dieses verstanden die Juden von den Prophezeiungen des Messias deren einige auf seinen Zustand der Erniedrigung in diesem Leben bis zum Tode, andere auf den Zustand seiner Erhöhung nach der Auferstehung ... gingen ... Drittens. Es sind Vorsagungen zukünftiger Dinge, was oft gesprochen wird, sondern Befehle wie man sich zu verhalten hätte."
148. Sandbichler, *Darstellung der Regeln*, 86.
149. Johann Jahn, *Nachträge zu seinen theologischen Werken* (Tübingen: 1821), 15–60; ibid., "Was that Jesus während der vierzig Tage von seiner Auferstehung bis zu seiner glorreichen Auffahrt?", 1–15; "Was lehret die Bibel vom Teufel?", 61–251; cf. Hermann Pottmeyer, "Die historisch-kritische Methode und die Erklärung zur Schriftauslegung in der dogmatischen Konstitution 'Dei Filius,'" *Annuarium Historiae Conciliorum* 2 (1970): 87–111.
150. Jahn, *Nachträge*, 15–16.

Testament in the common way of the time and attached to certain verses an allegorical meaning. Thus, they talked "as if they would accept" the "errors" of rabbinic exegesis.[151] The first preachers of the Gospel did not preach against every error; this would have been impossible or even disadvantageous because the eradication of an error can also shake the belief in a neighboring belief—for example, a criticism of the existence of the devil could undermine the belief in God. Jesus and the apostles thought that it was better to undermine those errors that do not threaten the essential message of Christianity, and to criticize them indirectly by contrasting them with positive core doctrines of their religion.[152] Due to polemics between the fathers (as between St. Jerome and St. Augustine), the accommodation was sometimes driven too far, only in order to defeat the opponent. "But if the oldest and most erudite fathers accepted accommodation interpretations of the New Testament, then we only follow in their footsteps if we find such a stance in holy scripture. . . ."[153] However, if the fathers used this method in order to deceive others, we cannot follow them.

Jahn rejects mysticism and rationalism because both abuse scripture as their handmaid.[154] He laments that not many Catholics, who appropriately use the *grammatical-historical* interpretation, as he calls it, are able to situate the Bible in its context. The aim of his treatise on the devil is to "encourage Christians in their faith in holy scripture, who are offended by the temptations of the devil, the possessions of demons, which the Bible portrays, and who began" to doubt their faith, since they were asked to believe such things.[155] Jahn makes clear that ancient Jews not only believed in the devil and his fallen angels, but in all kinds of demons and evil spirits. They arrived in Israel through Egypt, Greece, and Rome, and through the Zoroastrians of Persia. During the Babylonian Captivity (586–539 BCE), the Jews accepted great

151. Ibid., 17.
152. Ibid., 18.
153. Ibid.
154. Ibid., 61.
155. Ibid., 63.

parts of their teachings on spirits.[156] According to Jahn, the Bible always differentiates between fallen angels, demons, and the devil. A crucial difference is that evil spirits and demons do not seduce or tempt, but have only *effects* on the body. He goes even so far as to state that before the Babylonian Captivity, there are no literary traces of any belief in a devil and his realm of evil spirits. Under the influence of Greek culture, Jews merged their Babylonian beliefs with the beliefs of the Greeks, and thus created a complex system of theories about evil spirits. This, however, must not lead the interpreter to a denial of the existence of a realm of evil spirits, since "the teaching of heaven, hell and the resurrection of the body originally migrated from the followers of Zoroaster into the writings of the Jews."[157]

For the principle of accommodation, it is much more important whether Jesus and the apostles mentioned such spirits only marginally, whether they presupposed such popular beliefs and did not want to cause uproar by rejecting them, or whether they taught about them with authority as they did about heaven, hell, and the resurrection. That the early fathers acknowledged that Jesus and the apostles did not reject superstitious beliefs on several occasions warrants our belief in their same stance toward demons. Nevertheless, Jahn reminds the reader that if two incompatible concepts about the same thing, effect, or action appear in the words of the same person or in the writings of the same author, one of them must be a condescension to the more ordinary popular beliefs and language, and thus an accommodation.[158] From Matthew 15:2–20 and Mark 7:2–23, where Jesus teaches that the source of moral impurity is in the heart or soul of the person and does not come from the outside, he observes Jesus' obliviousness about any devilish temptations. Jesus does not mention that sin comes from somebody else other than the human person. Thus, Jahn feels justified in saying that this is a good argument that, for Jesus, the devil does not play any role in sinful behavior, and that when he mentions him, he

---

156. Ibid., 65, with reference to Johann Friedrich Kleuker, *Anhang zum Zend-Avesta* (Riga: 1781), 1[2]:65–66, 253–54.
157. Jahn, *Nachträge*, 79.
158. Ibid., 80.

does so in consideration of the Israelites, and thus accommodates his teaching to them.[159] Whenever Jesus talks about the devil's deeds, he does not want to make his listeners believe that the devil has this or that effect on the world. Likewise, it should not be taken literally when the Gospels (Matt. 26:14–16; Mark 14:10–11) report the devil having taken possession of Judas. When they talk about the "devil in him," the apostles only denounce the nastiness of his crime.[160] When the first letter of John mentions that the devil tempts people and that everybody who sins is a child of the devil, he does not want to give an explanation about the origin of evil (1 John 5:18), but wants to encourage his readers in a time of turmoil and persecution. Thus, John uses the common language about the devil. His readers could easily identify, Jahn thinks, these remarks as accommodations, especially when he says in 1 John 2:1: "My children, I am writing this to you so that you may not commit sin. But if anyone does sin, we have an Advocate with the Father, Jesus Christ the righteous one."

According to Jahn, John's pictures of the devil in the book of Revelation are important metaphors, but they do not "contain a truth, nothing real."[161] Also here, the intention of the author was to demonstrate through the image of the devil, what Christians could expect, but not some speculative truth about demonology. Less convincing is Jahn's argument that the description of the devil renders itself null and void because he seems to be the sovereign of the world, since as a creature, he could not be present in the entire world in order to tempt it, and be, simultaneously, the prosecutor who charges sinners at God's tribunal, day and night.[162] Also, the letter of St. James (James 1:13–15) clearly states, according to Jahn, that sin originates in human concupiscence, in the disorder of human sensuality. He does not mention that the devil tempts people, and from this Jahn deduces that St. James vehemently rejects that the devil has anything to do with the origin of evil in everybody's lives.[163] St. Paul buttresses this

159. Ibid., 81–82.
160. Ibid., 90.
161. Ibid., 97.
162. Ibid., 99.

witness. As the root of sin, he mentions the sensuality of human beings, concupiscence, and the weakness of the flesh, not the temptation of the devil. Even his autobiographical comment that he had a sting of the devil in his body (2 Cor. 12:7) is, for Jahn, a clear sign that all talk about devils is just an accommodation to please popular demand, but not a real teaching about the origin of sin and evil. One could not really believe that an angel of Satan hit St. Paul, states Jahn. The accommodation in this verse, is therefore "undoubtable."[164] It would be even more problematic if one took St. Paul literally, when he talks about Satan being an instrument for the conversion of sinners. How could, asks Jahn, the enemy of God be an instrument of salvation? (1 Cor. 5:5).

But how should one then interpret the temptation story of Jesus? One could, of course, circumvent any problems by stating that the temptation was only interior and psychological. This, of course, entails that Jesus was uncertain about his mission and his status as the Son of God, which, for Jahn, does not conform to the dignity of Jesus. Moreover, the text does not give any indication that the situation described happened within the mind of Jesus. Since he must have told his disciples about it, he would have had to tell them if it had only been a dream. Of course, one could also regard the story as a myth with a historical kernel of truth. However, one can dismiss this option because myths do not come into existence so quickly—just within a few years of the codification of the Gospels. Even more complicated is the theory that the tempter was not Satan, but a high priest from Jerusalem, because such a man would have never demanded worship from another Jew. Instead, Jahn believes that the *diabolos* was indeed the prince of this world, because his depiction fits what Jews believed. Jahn remarks that the temptation stories are unique, because the devil appears in human form and goes with Jesus from the desert to the holy city of Jerusalem onto the roof of the temple, then to a high hill. "Such things one will not find anywhere else in the Bible said about the

163. Ibid., 106–8.
164. Ibid., 129.

232

devil, and it is in itself very improbable."[165] If Jesus had realized that the person who tempted him the first time was the devil, why did he follow him to the second and third temptations? In other contexts, the devil is portrayed as shrewd, but here he seems to be a "very dumb devil,"[166] who does not see that no religious Jew would follow his temptations:

> A Jew knew that God had given his forefathers in . . . Arabia manna and quails, but that he never turned stones into bread; how could a pious Jew, even if he had the power to work miracles, be tempted to turn stones into bread? The religious Jew knew the plan of divine providence, and trusted it. He was instructed by the example of his forefathers not to test God . . . for example, by jumping from the roof of the southern temple hall. . . . In the third temptation the devil appears as the prince of the world, as the god of this world . . . and he is short-sighted enough to hope to be worshiped by a Jew if he promises him all realms of the world.[167]

If he knew that the Jews thought him to be the father of lies, why would he try to tempt one of them? If he did not know, why did he not know? Jahn's explanation begins by directing attention to the beginning of the story. All three accounts mention that Jesus was "driven by the spirit" or the "holy spirit" into the desert, where he was tempted. In Revelation 17:3; 20, and 21, visions happen because "in the spirit," the visionary is guided by God to a mountain. The end of the narrative proves much more conclusively, however, that the story was a dream—namely, Matthew 4:11: "Then the devil left him, and angels came and attended him." *Diakonein*, the serving of food and drink, would not make sense if the previous temptations did take place in actual locations, because Jesus would have had plenty of opportunity to take or buy food. Especially for a trip to Jerusalem, he would have had to bring food. Another hint that the story was a dream is the remark about the very high mountain on which Jesus was placed and from which he could see the realms of the world. If his explanation was true, it would be the only dream Jesus ever talked about. The first temptation obviously means that miraculous power should never be

165. Ibid., 140.
166. Ibid.
167. Ibid., 141.

used for private purposes; the second one that one should never bring oneself with full intention into danger and test God; the third that all power, all glory has to be rejected for the one true religion.[168]

A last example of Jahn's enlightened exegesis is his view on what Jesus did between the resurrection and the ascension. Jahn is convinced the term "he appeared" cannot mean that Christ became miraculously visible. In Jahn's explanation, "appearing" means coming. Jesus came to his disciples in his earthly, resurrected body. From the fact that he was resurrected from the grave and wore clothes, Jahn deduces that the resuscitated Jesus must have received the clothes from the gardener. This would also explain why Mary Magdalene did not recognize Jesus and thought him to be the gardener. Moreover, due to his passion, his voice was different and still suffering from what he had endured. Jesus did not "appear" to those who doubted him or crucified him, because they would have arrested him and would have tried to kill him again. This, however, would have made the consolation of his followers and the strengthening of their faith impossible.[169]

Inspiration and Miracles

Miracles and divine inspiration are, for Jahn, inherently connected. The divine assistance in preservation from error is what Jahn calls inspiration. It is differentiated from revelation because it does not give new content to the writers, does not teach them anything new, but only preserves them from falling into error. Jahn relies here, surprisingly, on the seventeenth-century Jansenist theologian Louis Ellies Dupin (1657–1719).[170]

In order to verify a divine inspiration, a miracle is necessary—a divine legitimization. The Hebrew rabbis knew about divine inspiration and made it part of their theology. This can especially be seen in how they treated the prophets, whose office was oral and had divine

168. Ibid., 142–51.
169. Ibid., 1–15.
170. Dupin, *Dissertation preliminaire ou prolegomenes sur la Bible*, book 1, ch. 2, §7. Louis Ellies Dupin, *A Compleat History of the Canon and Writers of the Books of the Old and New Testament, by Way of Dissertation . . .* (London: 1694), 54–55.

authority, but whose sayings were written down much later. This presupposes divine assistance for the process of codifying their words. Other divine messengers received the explicit command to write down certain messages. "From this the Hebrews deduced rightly that God must have foreseen that these men would write the pure truth without error or that he preserved them from it."[171] The New Testament confirms the inspiration and flawlessness of the Old Testament. Jesus never questioned the faith of the Old Testament, only some teachings. That even the apostles accepted the divine inspiration of the Old Testament can be seen from the fact that all early communities read these texts in their liturgies.[172] The ancient deniers of the divine origin of the Old Testament, who claim that Jesus used the principle of accommodation and just conceded to the general opinion of the Jews about their holy scriptures in order to obtain entrance into their theological circles and gain a hearing are, for Jahn, unconvincing since Jesus takes a similarly high view of the Hebrew Bible (Matt. 26:24–31; Luke 22:37). Since Jesus and the apostles did not define to what extent the scriptures were divinely inspired, the early church discussed this quite diversely. While some have a maximalist understanding and extend inspiration to all words (Justin Martyr, Athenagoras), others have a more restricted view that seems similar to Jahn's (Clement of Rome, Dionysius of Alexandria). Jahn argues that even defenders of a maximalist view, such as St. Augustine and St. Jerome, sometimes concede mistakes in the Bible about historical or scientific facts and refer in these sentences to a weaker level of inspiration. He accepts again Dupin's judgement:

> Every Christian then ought to believe that all the canonical books of the Old and the New Testament were written by the inspiration of the Holy Ghost, who has guided the thoughts and the pen of those who wrote them in such a manner, that they have not fallen into any error concerning religion, faith, good manners, and the historical matters of fact on which religion is established. So that every Christian is obliged to believe what is contained in those books, and no person has liberty of denying or

171. Jahn, Einleitung, 1:95.
172. Ibid., 1:96–101; reference to Dupin, A Compleat History, book I, ch. V, 47–51.

doubting any of the truths of this nature that are established on such a foundation.[173]

It was the scholastic theologians who adopted maximalist terminology and extended it to the entirety of scripture so that one had, in the end, two parties. The first extended inspiration: (a) to the motivation and decision of the writer to write such-and-such, (b) to the choice of subjects, (c) to the choice of words, (d) to the choice of order of themes, and (e) to the choice of order of each word. The second school remained convinced that inspiration only protects from falling into error. In 1587, a controversy broke out in the Netherlands since most universities defended the stronger first opinion, while Leonhard Lessius SJ (1554–1623) and Jean Hamelius (du Hamel) (1554–89) of Louvain defended the weaker version. Following William Estius's (1542–1613) charge, it was censored because they argued that not every word in scripture had to be inspired, nor that every single truth or sentence in it had to be immediately inspired by the Holy Spirit, and that some books, such as Second Maccabees, are books of human industriousness and only regarded as sacred because they do not contain any error. Later Jesuit theologians such as Cornelius à Lapide, Bellarmine, Suarez, and Bonfrerius, but also theologians such as Huet, Dupin, Calmet, Serry, and others, disregarded the censoring of Lessius and disseminated this idea. Likewise, Henry Holden argued that everything that is not essentially connected with doctrine was not inspired.[174] Jahn realized that, in Protestantism, the strict and strong meaning of inspiration was increasingly marginalized. First, it was reduced to the meaning of scripture; then, to the meaning of a doctrine; then, to certain prophecies, until it was given up, "so that now only a few still defend it until today . . . while some others argue the books only have divine authority because they contain among

---

173. Dupin, *A Compleat History*, book I, ch. II, section V, 52; Jahn, *Einleitung*, 1:106.
174. Henry Holden, *Divinae Fidei Analysis [1652]* (Paris: 1757), 53: "[A]uxilium special divinitus praestitum auctori cujuslibet scripti, quod pro verbo Dei recipit Ecclesia, ad ea solummodo se porrigat, quae vel sint pure doctrinalia, vel proximum aliquem aut necessarium habeant ad doctrinalia respectum; in iis vero quae non sunt de instituto scriptoris, vel ad alia referuntur, eo tantum subsidio Deum illi adfuisse judicamus, quod piissimis caeteris auctoribus commune sit." Jahn, *Einleitung*, 1:114.

many other things *also* divine truths. Thus, they overlook that the original divine doctrine has to have been written down with divine infallibility, if a book should have divine authority."[175]

Conclusion

Catholic exegetes of the Enlightenment were motivated by the Council of Trent's insistence on the value of holy scripture for a Christian's life. Nevertheless, they were discontent with how low the knowledge of Oriental languages had sunk, and how the analysis of the literal meaning of the Bible had been forgotten. Inspired by the achievements of their Protestant peers, these men wrestled with new ideas about philological criticism and the value of the church fathers for interpretation, but left the question unanswered of how historical research and theological interpretation are related to each other. While most left historical criticism and theology unrelated, Sandbichler attempted to connect the two. This is quite understandable if one considers the fate of exegetes such as Isenbiehl or Jahn, who were both censored and lost their teaching positions because of their exegetical opinions. Nevertheless, these theologians prepared the way for appreciating holy scripture as the treasure house and source of life for the entire church. Without their preparatory work, the many Catholic vernacular editions of the Bible could not have been printed, and thus could not have supplied the Romantic revival with its source of inspiration. Last, but not least, it was also Catholic engagement with the Bible that brought about several revivals, some of which developed forms of Catholic pietism and affiliations with Evangelicalism.[176]

---

175. Jahn, *Einleitung*, 1:111.
176. Cf. Johannes Altenberend, *Leander van Ess (1772-1847): Bibelübersetzer und Bibelverbreiter zwischen katholischer Aufklärung und evangelikaler Erweckungsbewegung* (Paderborn: Bonifatius, 2001).

10

The Conundrums of Eighteenth-Century Catholic Biblical Scholarship and J. L. Isenbiehl's Interpretation of Isaiah 7:14

In 1546, the fourth session of the Council of Trent passed the *Decree on the Edition and the Use of the Sacred Books.* The Council fathers regarded this to be a necessary response to the many translations and scripture commentaries in circulation that, in their view, confused the faithful and could potentially draw them to Protestantism. In order to ensure that the faithful would use only proper commentaries or translations, certain rules for official publication permissions were implemented. More importantly, this decree stated a hermeneutic principle for all Catholic theologians—in particular, for exegetes. This principle affirmed the continuity of teaching of faith and morals between the church of old and the church of the Tridentine reform, and admonished consistency with the fathers of the church. The decree read:

> [I]n order to restrain petulant spirits, [the Council] decrees, that no one,

relying on his own skill, shall,—in matters of faith, and of morals pertaining to the edification of Christian doctrine,—wresting the sacred scripture to his own senses, presume to interpret the said sacred scripture contrary to that sense which holy mother Church,—whose it is to judge of the true sense and interpretation of the holy scriptures,—hath held and doth hold; or even contrary to the unanimous consent of the fathers; even though such interpretations were never (intended) to be at any time published. Contraveners shall be made known by their Ordinaries, and be punished with the penalties by law established.[1]

In the eighteenth century, in the midst of the rise of historical criticism, the question was discussed anew as to what extent a scripture scholar must follow the fathers. The case of Johann L. Isenbiehl, who not only lost his university chair in exegesis in Mainz, but also was imprisoned for going against the consensus of the fathers, exemplifies this theological discussion. Isenbiehl had claimed to have explored a literal or historical interpretation of Isaiah 7:14 that made the traditional typological or allegorical interpretation of the verse redundant. In the following paragraphs, I will first reconstruct the place of literal meaning for post-Tridentine Catholic exegesis, and then discuss eighteenth-century concepts of theological freedom in interpreting scripture. This contextualization suggests Isenbiehl emerging as a theologian who went beyond Muratori's concept of theological freedom, thus pushing Catholic Enlightenment forward, relying on the tools of historical criticism alone while bracketing tradition. Consequently, it will become clear that Isenbiehl's censoring did not happen because he used a literal interpretation or Michaelis's historical-critical method, but because he rejected the consensus of the fathers and tradition. As such, his case is exemplary to demonstrate the complex methodological and theological issues Catholic exegesis had faced between 1750 and 1800.

---

1. "Decretum de Editione et Usu Sacrorum Librorum," according to the translation of James Waterworth, *Canons and Decrees of the Council of Trent* (London: C. Dolman, 1848), 19–20. For the original Latin, see Heinrich Denzinger and Peter Hünermann (eds.), *Enchiridion Symbolorum. A Compendium of Creeds, Definitions and Declarations of the Catholic Church* (San Francisco: Ignatius, 2012), DH 1507.

Losing and Finding the Literal Meaning of Scripture

The medieval commentaries on scripture usually based their mystical interpretations, whether allegorical or typological, on a careful reading of the literal meaning of the text.[2] During the sixteenth century, this emphasis on the literal meaning was still very much adhered to by Catholic exegetes in their often remarkable commentaries (e.g., Maldonatus). Over the course of the seventeenth century, however, literal emphasis had steadily declined, and thus it was fitting that the ingenious French Oratorian Richard Simon (1638–1712) attempted to recover it with modern philological tools. His attempts, however, were associated with Spinozism, and, consequently, mostly ignored by his Catholic peers.[3] Simon's confrere, the Oratorian Bernard Lamy (1640–1715), even stated in his *Apparatus Biblicus* (1696) that the church fathers had neglected, not ignored, the literal sense because it was their motivation to mold the faithful into saints, not scholars (*non doctors . . . sanctiores*).[4]

Despite these singular efforts to re-emphasize the importance of the literal meaning of the Bible, exegesis in Catholic universities continued to decline markedly in favor of controversial and polemical theology for yet another generation. The fear that an emphasis on the literal meaning of the text would indirectly help Protestant causes was too great.[5] Apart from quarrels with Protestantism, the controversies with Jansenism also affected the place of scripture in Catholic theology.

---

2. Literature on medieval exegesis and its respect for literal interpretation is legion. One can begin by consulting Jane Dammen McAuliffe et al., eds., *With Reference for the Word. Medieval Scriptural Exegesis in Judaism, Christianity and Islam* (Oxford: Oxford University Press, 2003), as well as Alan Hauser et al., eds., *A History of Biblical Interpretation*, vol. 2 (Grand Rapids: Eerdmans, 2003).

3. See Sascha Müller, *Kritik und Theologie: christliche Glaubens- und Schrifthermeneutik nach Richard Simon (1638–1712)* (St. Ottilien: EOS, 2004).

4. Bernard Lamy, *Apparatus Biblicus. Nova Editio* (Lyon: 1696), lib. II, ch. 8, 395.

5. For a contemporary's view, see Gallus Cartier OSB (d. 1777) of Ettenheimmünster, *Tractatus theologicus de Sacra Scriptura* (Freiburg: 1736), praefatio: "Deplorandam sane nonnullorum nostri aevi Theologorum indolem, qui neglecto hoc tam salubri & firmandae nostrae Religioni adeo necessario sacrae Scripturae studio, utpote unde potissimum solida argumenta nostrae fidei eruuntur, rerum non adeo utilium sectantur cognitionem." See also Sebastian Merkle, *Die kirchliche Aufklärung im katholischen Deutschland* (Berlin: Reichl, 1910), 74–75; F. J. Crehan, "The Bible in the Roman Catholic Church From Trent to the Present Day," *Cambridge History of the Bible* (Cambridge: Cambridge University Press, 1963), 3:199–237; Richard H. Popkin, *The Third Force in Seventeenth-Century Thought* (Leiden: Brill, 1992), 30–32.

Against the Jansenists, the bull *Unigenitus* (1713) condemned the proposition that the reading of the Bible was necessary for everyone's salvation. This, however, could be interpreted as a new Catholic marginalization of scripture. The Reform Benedictines of St. Maur desired to refute such allegations and supported their member Augustine Calmet OSB (1672–1757), as well as his disciples, in demonstrating the centrality of scripture for the Catholic faith. Calmet re-emphasized the literal meaning of the text. His monumental "literal" commentary on all books of the Old and New Testament energized many to delve into scripture, and it became one of the most widely read commentaries in the Catholic world.[6] From the middle of the eighteenth century onwards, there was an explosion of interest among Catholics in Oriental languages, biblical archeology, and exegesis—in which Calmet had played an enormous role.[7]

The Maurists, and in particular Calmet's work, were the result of a successful implementation of the Tridentine Reforms and its rediscovery of scripture as the source of ecclesial life.[8] The other important reason for this revival was, however, the lively discourse with the Enlightenment in which Simon, Lamy, Calmet, and others engaged. While the first cautious exchanges with Enlightenment criticism had been on historiographical issues, soon, this engagement began to spread to other disciplines of theology too. Open-minded theology departments, religious orders, bishops, and rulers throughout Europe attempted to implement such a dialogue with the spirit of the times and supported the renewal of Catholic exegesis.[9] While most Catholic exegetes merely re-emphasized the literal meaning—or historical meaning, as it now increasingly was called—and more clearly

---

6. Augustin Calmet, *Commentaire litteral sur tous les livres de l'Ancien et du Nouveau Testament* (Paris: 1724–26).
7. See Marius Reiser, "Catholic Exegesis between 1550 and 1800," in Ulrich L. Lehner, Richard Muller, A. G. Roeber (eds.), *Oxford Handbook of Early Modern Theology* (Oxford: Oxford University Press, 2016), forthcoming.
8. See Louis Châtellier, *The Religion of the Poor: Rural Missions in Europe and the Formation of Modern Catholicism, c. 1500–c. 1800* (Cambridge: Cambridge University Press, 1997) and Guy Bedouelle, *The Reform of Catholicism, 1480–1620* (Toronto: Pontifical Institute of Mediaeval Studies, 2008).
9. Calmet knew the achievements of modern archeology and criticism, but he was not a critically-minded exegete, as Bertram Schwarzbach suggests in "Dom Augustin Calmet. Man of the Enlightenment Despite Himself," *Archiv für Religionsgeschichte* 3 (2001): 135–48.

re-established it as the basis for any further mystical interpretation, a few desired to minimize mystical interpretations as a whole.[10]

By stressing the literal meaning of the text and using the tools of textual criticism, however, one could arrive at interpretations that would contradict the consensus of the fathers. This was a serious theological conundrum. In swift succession, the Protestant world of scholarship presented the Catholics with a number of new challenges. Many Protestant scholars claimed that hitherto obscure scriptural passages could now be interpreted literally, which would render mystical interpretations at least questionable. At the same time, others confronted their Catholic peers with the uncomfortable reality that even the consensus of the fathers had erred in some biblical interpretations. Catholic theologians, therefore, pondered how to resolve this problem while nevertheless remaining faithful to the decrees of the Council of Trent. Catholic Enlighteners did not view Trent's decision as an impediment for research, but rather attempted to develop a hermeneutic of continuity that allowed them to follow both the Council and the findings of their research. Nonetheless, there seemed to be boundaries that no theologian was supposed to cross.

Muratori and the Moderate Freedom of the Exgete

It is the great achievement of Ludovico Muratori (1672–1750), the friend of Pope Benedict XIV (1740-58), to have outlined those boundaries. In his *On the Moderation of Our Cleverness in Religious Matters* (1714), he painted a picture of how far a theologian's freedom in academic research could go, and where he had to be obedient to tradition and church rulings. This inspired generations of eighteenth- and nineteenth-century Catholic theologians to engage with modern thought and culture, although the limitations Muratori envisioned would soon be regarded as too narrow.[11]

---

10. See the general remarks of Benedict Stattler, *De Locis Theologicis* (Ingolstadt: 1777), 110: "Sensus mysticus nunquam sine literali bene tamen literalis sine mystico esse protest . . . Sensus mysticus in literali fundari debet, id est, inesse rebus sensu literali expressi, ceu signis suis." See the insightful reflections of Benedict Werkmeister, "Ueber den mystischen Sinn," *Jahrschrift für Theologie und Kirchenrecht der Katholiken* 2 (1809): 259–376.

Muratori was unhappy about the state of Catholic exegesis, but instead of simply arguing in favor of the superiority of the literal meaning of the text, he distinguished that every literal meaning of scripture was either proper [*proprium*] or figurative [*figuratum*]. While his theological hero St. Augustine had defended the view that a passage could have several literal meanings, others denied this. Muratori, therefore, attempted a reconciliation of both positions:

> One has to suppose then that the Holy Spirit wanted/intended [voluisse] to express one literal sense (not excluding the mystical one), either in proper or figurative words. Because the words of scripture can sometimes be obscure [obscura] as to their literal meaning, and can be interpreted in various ways, it is often not certain whether one should understand it properly or figuratively: therefore it is licit to apply to such a passage different literal interpretations.[12]

In order to give the theologian as much freedom as possible, and to guarantee that he would not be slandered as a heretic if he applied such a different explanation, Muratori insisted that "every one of these [interpretations]—as long as it does not violently contort scripture, and does not contradict scripture, tradition or reason in other aspects—can be regarded as suitable [convenire], can be laudable [laudari] and permissible [tolerari]."[13]

Any interpretation could be used because the one and only literal meaning the Holy Spirit intended was not evident [evidenter]. Such liberality in interpretation, however, was not licit for passages where such meaning was evident or pertained to faith and morals. For these, one "can have only one literal meaning and explication rather than many, because the church transmits the one and only intended full [germanum] meaning God has put in such a pasage," because the church received such meaning through divine instruction, tradition, and the unanimous consensus of the fathers:

---

11. Ludovico Muratori, *De ingeniorum moderatione in religionis negotio* [1714] (Augsburg: 1779).
12. Muratori, *De Ingeniorum Moderatione*, lib. I, ch. 22, 231.
13. Ibid.

> Therefore it is forbidden to deviate in the interpretation of such passages from the church and the tradition of the fathers. In other scriptural passages, however, where no salvific doctrine is entailed, and where the meaning is not certain, or where it is obscure and where a diverse literal interpretation seems convenient [commode], the opinion of St. Augustine and others is correct: Such a passage allows several different literal interpretations, which one can and must tolerate [posse ac tolerari debere].[14]

For Muratori, it was clear that Trent had decreed a non-negotiable principle of theology—namely, that of a continous teaching tradition, but whose terminology and implications had to be interpreted.

The scholar from Modena decided to interpret Trent's decree in favor of the largest possible freedom for the theologian. This was a direct rejection of a narrow understanding of the Tridentine rule, which argued that in *all* biblical questions, the consensus of the fathers had to be followed. If one followed such an inflexible traditionalism, Muratori stated, the Church could not participate in any fruitful dialogue with science, history, philosophy, or philology. In physics, Catholic teaching would be rendered irreconcilable with Copernicus,[15] and any meaningful advances in biblical scholarship would be made impossible. Muratori, instead, argued that Trent did not disallow or anathemize historical, mathematical, astronomical, philosophical, or other investigations, whose results deviated from the fathers, but that it admonished scholars to receive their authoritative words in humility and obedience if (and only if) they pertained to faith and morals. Consequently, the Council did not so much tame the "boldness" of creative intellects, but restricted the excessive zeal [zelum exuberantem] of those who abused the authority of the fathers for inopportune [importune] teachings or explanations that did not "belong to the edification of Christian doctrine" [aedificationem Doctrinae].[16] Trent's decree was, therefore, in Muratori's opinion, no

---

14. Muratori, *De Ingeniorum*, lib. I, ch. 22, 231.
15. Ibid., lib. I, ch. 23, 237.
16. Ibid., lib. I, ch. 23, 238.

straitjacket for the freedom of the theologian, but a protection against narrow-minded traditionalists:

> Thus the Council fathers have embraced most wisely the principle through which the unity of faith is maintained and the freedom of genius [ingeniorum libertatem] is not diminished. For they realized well that as long the veracity of scripture and the doctrine of the true faith were ascertained . . . one was not allowed to denounce [litem intendere][17] the diverse opinions of interpreters in things that do not pertain to faith and morals and to the edification of Christian doctrine.[18]

For this, Muratori relied on Francois Veron SJ (1578–1649) and his *De Regula Fidei Catholicae* (1645). According to Veron, one did not have to accept the motives and proofs behind the consensus of the fathers and definite teachings of the Church, and could consequently deviate from patristic commentaries.[19]

In reflections on the methodology of exegesis, the Augustinian exegete Alois Sandbichler of Salzburg (1751–1820) expressed agreement with Veron.[20] Both Veron's and Muratori's viewpoints were discussed in eighteenth-century textbooks as the "recent" view [recentior], and were contrasted with the old one, which was called "traditionalist," although there were certainly variations.[21]

As a characteristic proponent of the latter view, one could arguably name the ex-Jesuit Hermann Goldhagen (1718–94), who also was the fiercest critic of Isenbiehl. In his many publications, a positive word about contemporary biblical scholarship is difficult to find, especially not in reference to Protestants. Goldhagen differed from the Carmelite Thaddaeus Dereser (1757–1827) and other enlightened German

---

17. Literally, "to charge with a crime."
18. Muratori, *De Ingeniorum*, lib. I, ch. 23, 238.
19. Francois Veron (1578–1649), *De Regula Fidei Catholicae* [original edition: 1645] (Valentia: 1801), c. 1, p. 4, nr. 5, 22: "Unde generaliter dicimus, eorum quae continentur in capitibus, id solum et totum esse de Fide, quod definitur, seu (ut loquuntur Iuristae) solum dispositivum arresti seu conteni in capite aut canone de Fide, motivum vero arresti, seu eius probationes, non sunt de Fide. Ratio est, quia primum solum proponitur credendum, et proprie definitur, non autem motivum seu probationem."
20. Aloys Sandbichler, *Abhandlung über die zweckmässigen Mittel den hebräischen und griechischen Grundtext dem Wortsinne nach richtig zu verstehen* (Salzburg: 1791), 556.
21. See Thaddaeus Dereser OCD, one of the most important Catholic German exegetes of the eighteenth century, in his *Notiones Generales Hermeneuticae Sacrae Veteris Testamenti* (Bonn: 1784) 17.

Catholic exegetes, not in the opinion that the three dimensions of a mystical interpretation (allegorical, analogical, tropological) were as important as the knowledge of the literal or historical meaning of a text, but in his unwillingness to admit that a number of traditionally mystically explained verses have only a literal meaning, and therefore to concede mistakes of the fathers.

Moreover, Goldhagen differed from Dereser in his reluctance to concede that theologians, with the help of mystical interpretations, read dogmatic ideas into the text that the literal meaning could not justify.[22] Against Aquinas, Goldhagen was even convinced that the mystical interpretation could be used for a dogmatic proof.[23] To Goldhagen, scholars who so much as questioned whether a text could have several meanings or a possible mystical reading were Socinians[24] or Crypto-Protestants, because their emphasis on the literal text, the concepts the human author used, and their historical context echoed Protestant writers such as Siegmund Jakob Baumgarten (1706–57)[25] and Georg Lorenz Bauer (1755–1806).[26]

Johann David Michaelis's Hope for Catholic Exegesis: Johann L. Isenbiehl

One exegete, in particular, embodies the strife between these conflicting interpretations of Trent regarding agreement with the fathers—namely, Johann Lorenz Isenbiehl (1744–1818). While the Catholic Church chastised Isenbiehl, Protestant exegetes received his ideas with enthusiasm. Wilhelm Gesenius's (1786–1842) commentary on Isaiah, published in 1823, which marked the beginning of modern historical scholarship on this biblical book, stated that Isenbiehl had been the *first* exegete to defend in a sophisticated work the historical

---

22. Hermann Goldhagen, *Introductio in Sacram Scripturam Veteris ac Novi Testamenti* (Mainz: 1765), 1: 148–50; see for example Dereser, *Notiones Generales Hermeneuticae* 18.
23. Goldhagen, *Introductio*, 157–58. Cf. STh I, q. 1, art. 10.
24. Ibid.
25. Siegmund Jacob Baumgarten, *Unterricht von Auslegung der heil. Schrift* (Halle: 1759), 55–87.
26. Georg Lorenz Bauer, *Entwurf einer Hermeneutik des Alten und Neuen Testaments* (Leipzig: 1799), 96.

meaning of Isaiah 7:14, independent of any connection to the New Testament.[27]

When Isenbiehl accepted a chair as professor for exegesis at Mainz in 1773—one of the most tolerant Catholic states in the Holy Roman Empire—his friend Johann Gertz (1744-1824) reminded him that a Catholic principality might not be prepared to accept the historical-critical method that had been victorious in Protestant theology: "Mainz is not Göttingen."[28] Lorenz Isenbiehl, however, was naïve enough to expect the small, hitherto Jesuit University of Mainz to become, within weeks of his arrival, as open-minded as his alma mater, Göttingen.[29]

Isenbiehl was born in 1744, undertook studies in the seminary in Mainz, and was ordained a priest in 1769. Almost immediately, he was sent as *missionarius* to the small Catholic parish of Göttingen, where he was allowed to continue his studies. Under the direction of Johann David Michaelis (1717-91), one of the fathers of modern orientalism, Isenbiehl studied Oriental languages and exegesis.[30] It was here that Isenbiehl learned to read the Bible according to the historical-critical method. Michaelis vehemently rejected mystical interpretations, and Isenbiehl adopted his master's teaching that every type and image in

---

27. Wilhelm Gesenius, *Philologisch-kritischer und historischer Commentar über den Jesaja I* (Leipzig: 1821), 309–10. I am indebted in my interpretation to Marius Reiser, *Bibelkritik und Auslegung der Heiligen Schrift* (Tübingen: Mohr Siebeck, 2007), 277–328. Still very helpful in understanding the history of the interpretation of Isa. 7:14 is Laurenz Reinke's *Die Weissagung von der Jungfrau und vom Immanuel Jes. 7:14-16. Eine exegetisch-historische Untersuchung,* (Münster: 1848).

28. On Gertz, see Franz Rudolf Reichert, "Johann Gertz (1744-1824). Ein katholischer Bibelwissenschaftler der Aufklärungszeit im Spiegel seiner Bibliothek," *Archiv für Mittelrheinische Kirchengeschichte* 18 (1966): 41–99. For an overview of Isenbiehl's time in the theology department in Mainz, see Philipp Anton Brück, *Die Mainzer theologische Fakultät im 18. Jahrhundert* (Wiesbaden: F. Steiner, 1955), 41–59.

29. Sascha Weber, "Mainz ist nicht Göttingen. Der Mainzer Kurstaat und die Affäre Isenbiehl (1773-1780)," *Archiv für Mittelrheinische Kirchengeschichte* 61 (2009): 211–28; Norbert Jung, *Der Speyerer Bischof Andreas Seelmann (1732-1789)* (Mainz: Selbstverlag der Gesellschaft für mittelrheinische Kirchengeschichte, 2002), 22–26, 624–61; Marius Reiser, *Bibelkritik und Auslegung der heiligen Schrift* (Tübingen: Mohr Siebeck, 2007), 277–330; Franz Rudolf Reichert, "Trier und seine Theologische Fakultät im Isenbiehlschen Streit (1773-1779)," in *Verführung zur Geschichte. Festschrift zum 500. Jahrestag der Eröffnung einer Universität in Trier,* ed. by Georg Droege et al. (Trier: NCO-Verlag, 1973), 276–301.

30. For a recent study of Michaelis's methodology, see Michael C. Legaspi, *The Death of Scripture and the Rise of Biblical Studies* (Oxford: Oxford University Press, 2010).

a biblical text can have only one meaning, because otherwise, it would be impossible to explain such an image with certainty.[31]

It must be noted that Michaelis did not dismiss the possibility of a double meaning of a verse, but he reserved those for idioms or mysteries. One could not, he argued, accept a double meaning without necessity.[32] Michaelis liked his disciple, as is evident in a review of Isenbiehl's first publication about the Syrian diacritical point for verbs. The young priest had been so enchanted with exegesis, particularly with Syriac studies, that he wished to bring the riches of the Syriac tradition back into the bosom of the Church. Michaelis, not a man whose praise one could easily win, commended Isenbiehl's zeal for studying Oriental languages and his boldness in investigating a new theme. The idea of studying the diacritical points came to Isenbiehl in the summer of 1772, when he attended a seminar by Michaelis on Dathe's new Syriac Psalter.[33] Michaelis had high expectations of his Catholic master student: "A Catholic who focuses on Syriac can have some advantages over a Protestant. It will be much easier for him to visit Rome, and to improve his knowledge by studying the inexhaustable treasures of the Vatican Library and by conversing with Syrians. For the sake of the improvement of academic scholarship I hope that Mr. Isenbiehl will be able to enjoy such advantages." To the professor in Göttingen, Isenbiehl was a "lucky genius," who could "import the German way of thinking to Rome," and "of whom one can expect much."[34]

After the suppression of the Society of Jesus, the University of Mainz discharged all but one Jesuit from professorial duties. With Isenbiehl, the university wanted to bring the newest, most current method of exegesis to Mainz. On November 26, 1773, Isenbiehl informed his

31. Johann David Michaelis, *Entwurf der typischen Gottesgelahrtheit*, 2nd ed. (Göttingen: 1766), 45. Cf. ibid., 47: "Um dieser Ursachen willen kann ich auch denen nicht beytreten, die beynahe in einem jeden Vorbilde erstlich das Geheimnis Christi und denn das Geheimnis der Kirche suchen . . ."
32. Michaelis, *Entwurf*, 46–51.
33. Johann August Dathe, *Psalterium Syriacum* (Halle: 1768).
34. Johann Lorenz Isenbiehl, *Beobachtungen von dem Gebrauche des syrischen Punkti diacritici bey den Verbis* (Göttingen: 1773). Johann David Michaelis, *Orientalische und Exegetische Bibliothek* 4 (Göttingen: 1773): 45–52, at 47–48. A similar version of this review was also published in *Göttingische Anzeigen von gelehrten Sachen* 1 (1773): 185–86.

former teacher Michaelis that he had begun a lecture cycle on the Hebrew Bible, which had about thirty students, ten of whom were members of religious orders. Until then, in Mainz, there had been "not only no desire to study Hebrew, but also no desire for erudition."[35] Isenbiehl was expected to lecture on Syriac, Chaldean, Arabic, and Hebrew grammar. Since he embodied the critical method of Michaelis, even before his arrival, a number of colleagues suspected him of being a heretic. Unfortunately, Isenbiehl did not pay much attention to the misgivings of his colleagues, believing that no one with reason and common sense could reject the Enlightenment. On January 12, 1774, he informed Michaelis that he had come up with a new explanation for Matthew 1:22:

> I cannot wait to communicate to you a new explanation of Matt. 1:22 . . . the words of Isaiah were quoted only *ob analogiam signi prophetici*. . . . The Evangelist made this historic reflection, not in an historical style, but with the help of a biblical quotation. In the same way he described the distress of the mothers of Bethlehem with biblical words in chapter 2:17–18 . . . I was already because of this explication regarded a half-heretic, and consequently forced to communicate my thoughts in print. . . .[36]

Students had reported Isenbiehl's "suspicious" exegesis, because it shed doubt on whether Isaiah 7:14 was a prophecy about Christ's miraculous birth. Moreover, Isenbiehl's decision to defend himself in print was probably not the wisest, because his 140 theses about the Gospel of Matthew (April 1774) did not pass censorship. He was now officially under investigation for heresy. The Archbishop Elector continued to protect his exegete, but would have preferred that he had taught the traditional, allegorical, or typological explanation of scripture until the university reforms had been brought to a successful conclusion and the university had become part of the enlightened

---

35. Staats- und Universitätsbibliothek Göttingen: 2°Cod ms Michaelis 323, fol. 424v.
36. Staats- und Universitätsbibliothek Göttingen: 2°Cod ms Michaelis 323, fol. 425f, Isenbiehl to Michaelis of January 12, 1774.

scientific community.[37] For Isenbiehl, this would have been contrary to his conscience, and therefore a drama was soon to unfold.

This drama began with the death of the Archbishop Elector Breidbach-Büresheim in June 1774. Not even Karl von Dalberg (1744–1817), the Mainz stadtholder of Erfurt, could protect Isenbiehl any longer.[38] The conservative cathedral chapter took control of the diocese until the election of a new bishop and dismissed both Isenbiehl and two of his enlightened colleagues. The ex-Jesuit Hermann Goldhagen, who had made a name for himself, not only as an exegete, but especially as editor of an anti-Enlightenment journal, was put in charge of hiring new professors for the university and the colleges of Mainz.[39] The new Archbishop and Elector, Friedrich Karl Erthal (1719–1802), did not return to the Enlightenment-friendly politics of his predecessor, because he had promised the Cathedral chapter that he would hire only conservative teachers.[40] At this point, Isenbiehl was punished for his exegetical teachings with a two-year re-education in the seminary of Mainz, where he was expected to learn the "orthodox interpretation of scripture." Isenbiehl's career was over—before it had really begun. His bishop would not grant him leave to teach in the universalist Philanthropinum in Dessau, and no other theology department in the Reich dared to hire him.[41]

When Isenbiehl informed his teacher Michaelis about his dismissal on November 1, 1774, he stated that he was content with studying

---

37. Brück, *Die Mainzer theologische Fakultät*, 46. Allegorical interpretation is the interpretative approach in which "biblical persons and incidents become representative of abstract virtues or doctrines," while a typological interpretation is the interpretation "whereby parts of the Hebrew Bible are read as foreshadowing and prediction of the events of the Gospels" (James L. Kugel and Rowan A. Greer, *Early Biblical Interpretation* (Philadelphia: Westminster Press, 1986), 80–81).

38. For the interregnum, see Heribert Raab, "Das Mainzer Interregnum von 1774," *Archiv für Mittelrheinische Kirchengeschichte* 14 (1962): 168–93.

39. On Goldhagen's journal, see Franz Dumont, "Wider Freygeister, Protestanten und Glaubensfeger: Hermann Goldhagen und sein 'Religions-Journal,'" in *Von 'Obscuranten' und Eudämonisten': gegenaufklärerische und antirevolutionäre Publizistik im späten 18. Jahrhundert*, ed. Christoph Weiss (St. Ingbert: Röhrig, 1999), 35–76. For the life and works of Goldhagen, see also Johannes Hompesch, *Hermann Goldhagens Religionsjournal* (PhD Thesis, Cologne: 1923).

40. Weber, "Mainz" 219; Raab, "Interregnum," 177–79.

41. Reichert, "Trier und seine theologische Fakultät" 281; Brück, *Die Mainzer theologische Fakultät* 47. On the Philanthropin see Jörn Garber, *Die Stammutter Aller Guten Schulen. Das Dessauer Philanthropinum und der Deutsche Philanthropismus 1774-1793* (Tübingen: Max Niemeyer Verlag, 2008).

in the seminary, but was most upset about the loss of his salary. He hoped that the new book about Isaiah 7:14, which he had finished on October 24, 1774, *New Attempt about the Prophecy of Immanuel,* would bring him some monetary help.[42] He lamented not being able to travel to libraries or to visit other scholars, but he tried to be content: "In the meantime I want to enjoy the grace of the Elector; and if it becomes a punishment, I want to regard it as grace, and keep working secretly."[43] He had to learn to regard the treatment of the Elector as a grace sooner than he probably anticipated, because the Archbishop Elector—unbeknownst to Isenbiehl—had begun an official investigation of his writings on the suspicion of heresy. Even his letters were now censored or confiscated, so that he had to warn his teacher Michaelis to send the letters instead to a friend, "Mr. Trattenig, Bailiff of his Em. Count Metternich," who then smuggled them to Isenbiehl.[44] Michaelis must have written a touching account to his former student, because Isenbiehl responded on December 28, 1774 that he was moved to see how seriously and personally his teacher was taking the whole affair. Michaelis's letter was a sign to him of "sympathy and friendship." Isenbiehl advised him not to worry: "I am content and happy."[45] His optimism made him believe that within two years, he would teach again. He even made plans to engage with French scholars, e.g., Paul Foucher (1704–78), in Paris.[46]

The freedom from preparing lectures allowed Isenbiehl to concentrate on revisions and a substantial enlargement of the first draft of the *New Attempt.* The few people who saw the first draft of 1774 included, of course, Michaelis, but also the auxiliary bishop of Trier, Johann Nikolaus von Hontheim (1701–90), who spearheaded the German Febronian movement; the exegete Gertz; auxiliary bishop Seelmann of Speyer (1731–89); Abbot Rautenstrauch (1734–85) of Vienna; and the enlightened theologian Franz Oberthür (1745–1851)

---

42. Staats- und Universitätsbibliothek Göttingen: 2°Cod ms Michaelis 323, fol. 429.
43. Staats- und Universitätsbibliothek Göttingen: 2°Cod ms Michaelis 323, fol. 429.
44. Staats- und Universitätsbibliothek Göttingen: 2°Cod ms Michaelis 323, fol. 430.
45. Staats- und Universitätsbibliothek Göttingen: 2°Cod ms Michaelis 323, fol. 433.
46. Staats- und Universitätsbibliothek Göttingen: 2°Cod ms Michaelis 323, fol. 434–434v.

of Würzburg.[47] An informal inquiry as to whether the theology department of the University of Vienna would permit the printing of his book was negative, despite the positive response of Rautenstrauch, its chair person. The department called the book erroneous, false, and imprudent. In a letter to his teacher Michaelis on May 15, 1775, Isenbiehl complained: "I want to try one more time to get the book officially approved. If I do not receive permission, I want to publish the book without it. . . . Whoever reads my publications in the future will change his viewpoint, just as I converted all those who read my previous material. . . ."[48] Only after repeated attempts to get the book past the censors failed did Isenbiehl decide, in 1777, to sell the manuscript and get it published without official permission. To publish a theological book without proper censorship approval was illicit and such behavior, of course, caused a scandal.[49] The proscription decree of the Elector of Mainz of March 9, 1778, emphasized that the book had not been approved by the censorship commission and contained "many" offensive and false propositions.[50] It had been forbidden in order to protect the faithful from a book that mistreated scripture and "deviated from its meaning as laid out by the church fathers."[51] Trent's decree, which we discussed in the beginning of this chapter, had been invoked. The question of whether the interpretation of a verse was a truth of faith—because Isenbiehl never doubted the virgin birth or the Incarnation—was not asked by Isenbiehl's superiors, but only by his defenders. Within a year, the book was proscribed, the author in jail, and within two years the papacy had officially condemned its exegesis for the entire Church.[52]

---

47. Isenbiehl sent these men his finished manuscript again in 1777. Their letters of approval are reprinted in *Le Brets Magazin zum Gebrauch der Staaten- und Kirchengeschichte* 7 (1783): 22–36.
48. Staats- und Universitätsbibliothek Göttingen: 2°Cod ms Michaelis 323, fol. 435f.
49. The best exegetical analysis of the Isenbiehl controversy is Reiser, *Bibelkritik* 277–330. It replaces the earlier account of Felice Montagnini, "L'interpretazione di Is 7, 14 die J.L. Isenbiehl," in Alberto Vaccari and Augustin Bea, eds., *Il messianismo: atti della XVIII Settimana biblica* (Brescia: 1966), 95–105.
50. *Religions-Journal* 3 (1778): 192–96.
51. Ibid., 196.
52. See the complete bibliography of the pamphlets written around the Isenbiehl controversy in Jung, *Weihbischof Seelmann*, 919–22.

The Problem: Young Woman or Virgin?

The seventh chapter of Isaiah recounts the so-called syriac-ephraimitic war.[53] Around 734 BCE, the kings of Aram and Israel wanted to force Ahaz, the king of Judah, to join their coalition against the Assyrians. Isaiah met his king and offered him a guarantee of divine assistance, after Ahaz had refused the offer of a sign, "either in the depth, or in the height above" (Isa. 7:11). The prophet admonished Ahaz not to weary God:

> Therefore the Lord himself will give you this sign: the virgin (*ha-almah*) shall be with child, and bear a son, and shall name him Immanuel. He shall be living on curds and honey by the time he learns to reject the bad and choose the good. For before the child learns to reject the bad and choose the good, the land of those two kings whom you dread shall be deserted. (Isa. 7:14–16)[54]

The Septuagint reads *he parthenos* for *ha-almah*, the Vulgate has *virgo*. The Gospel of Matthew then picks up this theme in 1:22–23 after the angel has appeared to Joseph and instructed him not to abandon his spouse Mary, because her child has been conceived through the Holy Spirit and is not the result of infidelity.[55] The child shall receive the name Jesus, and Matthew continues:

> All this took place to fulfill what the Lord had said through the prophet: "Behold, the virgin shall be with child and bear a son, and they shall name him Emmanuel," which means "God is with us." (Matt. 1:22–23)

The quotation from Isaiah 7:14 could be understood as the continuing speech of the angel proclaiming a direct relationship between the prophet's words and the events surrounding Jesus' birth. However,

---

53. Stuart A. Irvine, *Isaiah, Ahaz, and the Syro-Ephraimitic Crisis* (Atlanta: Scholars Press, 1990).
54. Translations of Biblical texts follow the New American Bible, Revised Edition (NABRE) [2011].
55. Matthew 1:18–21: "Now this is how the birth of Jesus Christ came about. When his mother Mary was betrothed to Joseph, but before they lived together, she was found with child through the holy Spirit. / Joseph her husband, since he was a righteous man, yet unwilling to expose her to shame, decided to divorce her quietly. / Such was his intention when, behold, the angel of the Lord appeared to him in a dream and said, 'Joseph, son of David, do not be afraid to take Mary your wife into your home. For it is through the Holy Spirit that this child has been conceived in her. / She will bear a son and you are to name him Jesus, because he will save his people from their sins.'"

Christian tradition decided that Matthew had provided a divinely inspired commentary to the angel's words.[56] Yet, the Christian tradition was not homogenous in its understanding of Isaiah, but instead recognized two different (main) interpretations of the verse in question. One understood Isaiah 7:14 as *direct* prophecy about the birth of Jesus, while the other saw in it a contemporary *image* for the birth of Jesus, and thus a typology.

Isenbiehl rejected both and taught, instead, that Isaiah 7:14 had no connection to Jesus or to the New Testament. This was read as a direct assault on the authority of the Gospel of Matthew, which was, after all, a divinely inspired book that was believed to have had God as its primary author. If one took Isenbiehl literally, Matthew must have erred; but the Christian tradition claimed that the Bible, as God's inspired word, was infallible. However, Isenbiehl did not intend to attack Matthew's authority and, in fact, had defended the literary integrity of the entire book against the English exegete John Williams (1727–98), who claimed that the first two chapters of Matthew had been written by someone else.[57] In Matthew 1:22, Isenbiehl claimed, the evangelist had *not* intended to interpret the prophet Isaiah, but only to compare two events from salvation history—the promulgation of the birth of Christ and the promulgation of divine help at a time of war and devastation. Both events had in common that two divine messengers, Isaiah and Gabriel, confirmed the authenticity of their mission by means of a miracle—namely, the pregnancy of an unmarried woman.[58] The main argument against Isenbiehl's thesis was that it contradicted both the consensus of the church fathers and Matthew's own words. Even the eminent historian of Lutheran theology, Emmanuel Hirsch (1888–1972), conceded that orthodox Lutherans in the eighteenth century would have come to the same conclusion as Isenbiehl's Catholic critics.[59]

56. Reiser, *Bibelkritik,* 277–78. See the already concise overview of Richard Simon, *Kritische Historie des Textes des Neuen Testamentes. Herausgegeben von Johann Salomo Semler* (Halle: 1776), 438–43.
57. John Williams, *A free enquiry into the authenticity of the first and second chapters of St. Matthew's Gospel* (London: 1771). Williams was a nonconformist English divine, and it seems that Isenbiehl was among the first to refute his claims with a monograph.
58. Isenbiehl, *Neuer Versuch,* 190–233.

Isenbiehl's Interpretation in Detail

According to Isenbiehl, the Christian tradition acknowleged two interpretations of the verse. One saw it as a literal prophecy of the birth of Christ; the other one as a typology of Christ. While the first one has more authority, since it is the opinion of the fathers, the latter and more recent one had better arguments, but was also "more confusing."[60] Jerome (347–420) had mentioned the latter disapprovingly for the first time in his Isaiah commentary, but without condemning it as heretical.[61] Isenbiehl points to this fact and to the rediscovery of this reading by Grotius (1583–1645), who had made this interpretation almost universally accepted.[62] Exegetes in the eighteenth century, especially Catholics, increasingly accepted Grotius's interpretation, because it could be reconciled with the late medieval concept of a double literal meaning of scripture. Such reconciliation means that Old Testament verses have a historical frame of reference, but can and must be re-connected to Christ through the New Testament (examples are Hos. 11:1/Matt. 2:15; 2 Sam. 7:14/Heb. 1:5). This *typological exegesis* was also preferred by Calmet, who called it the "healthier interpretation."[63] Also, one of the most notable Catholic works of apologetics of the seventeenth century, Pierre-Daniel Huet's (1630–1721) *Demonstratio Evangelica* (1679), defended a typological reading of Isaiah 7:14. This string of remarkable authorities was a crucial element of Isenbiehl's defense because such a typological reading was just like his own interpretation in contradiction to the consensus of the fathers.[64]

---

59. At Reiser, *Bibelkritik,* 283.
60. Isenbiehl, *Neuer Versuch,* 17.
61. Reiser, *Bibelkritik* 287. Jerome, *Commentarius in Isaiam III* 7, 714 (CCL 73/1, 105, linea 83).
62. Isenbiehl, *Neuer Versuch* 20. On Grotius see Richard Simon, *Historia Critica Commentatorum praecipuorum V. & N. T.* (Gosslar: 1713), 510–15; Richard Simon, *Histoire Critique des principaux commentateurs du Nouveau Testament* (Rotterdam: 1693), 807–8.
63. Augustin Calmet, *Dissertationes ac Disquisitiones: Excerptae ex Commentario Literali in Omnes Veteris Testamenti Libros* (Tyrnau: 1773), 8:83–117 (Dissertatio in illud Isaiae, at 87). On Calmet see Arnold Ages, "Voltaire, Calmet and the *Old Testament.*" *Studies on Voltaire and the Eighteenth Century* 41 (1966): 87–187. For Grotius's interpretation, see H. J. M. Nellen, "Growing Tension between Church Doctrines and Critical Exegesis of the Old Testament," in *The Old Testament. The History of Its Interpretation,* ed. Magne Saebo (Göttingen: Vandenhoeck & Ruprecht, 2008), 2:802–26, at 813.

Anthony Collins (1676–1729)—during the height of deism[65]—began to dismiss even the typological reading of Isaiah 7:14. He argued in 1724 that a prophecy could *only* be fulfilled if it was literal. A typological or allegorical prophecy would, therefore, be nonsensical. Since Isaiah 7:14 was about Isaiah's own son or the king's, it could not be fulfilled in Jesus Christ. Hermann Samuel Reimarus (1694–1768) later referred to Collins's hermeneutic principle in his explanation of the prophecies, and even Baron d'Holbach (1723–89) relied on him in his *Histoire critique de Jesus Christ,* which was condemned by the papacy in 1778, the same year that the Isenbiehl scandal surfaced. Isenbiehl probably knew of Collins's principle and of d'Holbach, but if he did, he disguised this fact perfectly in his writings.[66] The words in Isaiah in their "plain drift and design of the prophet, literally, obviously and primarily understood," refer to a young woman in the days of King Ahaz. The birth of her boy was a sign of hope and comfort for the people of God. A fulfillment of this prophecy over 700 years later could not have been an appropriate sign for Ahaz, thought Collins and Grotius—a view Isenbiehl adopted.[67]

Isenbiehl consequently rejected the notion that a mystical meaning might lie beneath the literal meaning of Isaiah 7:14. As he saw it, the only two arguments that could be made in favor of such an interpretation—first, that the term "virgin" fits better Mary, the Mother of God, than the wife of a prophet; and second, that the the son of the prophet was not named Immanuel—could not be defended.[68] The first argument can be dismissed, reasoned Isenbiehl, because nothing

64. Isenbiehl, *Neuer Versuch,* 132; Pierre-Daniel Huet, *Demonstratio Evangelica,* 3rd ed. (Paris: 1690), propositio VII, n. 15, 351–69.
65. For Collins's methodology see Henning Graf Reventlow, *The Authority of the Bible and the Rise of the Modern World* (London: SCM, 1984), 354–83.
66. Anthony Collins, *A Discourse of the Grounds and Reasons of the Christian Religion [1724]* (London: 1741), 38. Cf. Reiser, *Bibelkritik,* 288–89. For a recent reprint of the main passages of Collins regarding prophecies, see John Drury, *Critics of the Bible 1724-1873* (Cambridge: Cambridge University Press, 1989), 21–45; and for a commentary, see Hans W. Frei, *The Eclipse of Biblical Narrative. A Study in Eighteenth and Nineteenth Century Hermeneutics* (New Haven and London: Yale University Press, 1974), 66–85.
67. Collins, *A Discourse* 38; ibid. 39: "This prophecy [is] therefore not being fulfill'd in Jesus according to the literal, obvious, and primary sense of the words as they stand in Isaiah, it is supposed that this, like all the other prophesies cited by the Apostles, is fulfill'd in a secondary, or typical, or mystical, or allegorical sense." Cf. Isenbiehl, *Neuer Versuch,* 60.
68. Isenbiehl, *Neuer Versuch,* 158.

in the expressed thoughts of Isaiah warrants that he wanted to express the notion of a miraculous virgin birth.[69] Isenbiehl supported his argument with the second-century translations of Aquila of Sinope, Symmachus, and Theodotion, who have *neanis* instead of *parthenos*. Moreover, the definite article in *ha-almah* might indicate that the prophet was pointing to a young woman when he spoke the words of his prophecy, Isenbiehl argued.[70] He rejected the second argument, because he found it incomprehensible that the Israelites would have kept the prophecy in the text, had it not been somehow fulfilled in the birth of a boy at the time of Ahaz, even if he had received a different name.[71] After showing that the verse does not suggest a deeper mystical meaning, Isenbiehl expressed his conviction that God would primarily reveal himself in the literal meaning of a text:

> Why cannot God talk in the way humans talk, when he talks to humans? This certainly would be appropriate. Did he not have the intention in his revelations that humans would understand him . . . ?[72]

The Gospel of Matthew cannot be used against his interpretation, argued Isenbiehl, because the verse Matthew 1:22, "All this took place to fulfill what the Lord had said through the prophet," does not imply that Isaiah 7:14 is a prophecy about Christ. He then introduced a number of distinctions of what "fulfillment" can mean, relying on the work of his fellow Catholic exegete, the Jesuit Juan Maldonado (1533–88), as well as on Augustine Calmet's literal commentary.[73]

Maldonado had analyzed what the verb could mean and arrived at

69. Isenbiehl, *Neuer Versuch*, 159: "Ein wahrer Sinn ist ohne Zweifel der, welcher die Sache so vorstellet, wie sie ist, und wie der Prophet dieselbe im Gemüthe gehabt hat. Nun die Begriffe des Propheten können wir nicht anderst als aus seinen Ausdrücken erkennen. Ein wahrer Sinn ist also derjenige, welcher mit der eigenthümlichen Bedeutung derjenigen Wörter genau übereinstimmt, die Jesaias gebrauchet hat, um seine Gedanken auszudrücken. Allein der Gedanke von einer jungfräulichen Mutter ist gewiss nicht ausgedrücket . . . er ist also nicht der wahre und noch weniger ein wahrer Sinn; er ist falsch."
70. Isenbiehl, *Neuer Versuch* 45–54; Franz Sedlmeier, "Jesaja 7, 14. Überlegungen zu einem umstrittenen Vers und zu seiner Auslegungsgeschichte," in *"Geboren aus der Jungfrau." Klarstellungen*, ed. Anton Ziegenaus (Regensburg: Pustet, 2007), 3–43, at 27–28 shows that Isenbiehl simplifies here and that the fathers who stated that *almah* means "also" virgin were right.
71. Isenbiehl, *Neuer Versuch*, 161.
72. Ibid., 35.
73. Augustin Calmet, *Commentaire litteral sur tous les livres de l'Ancien et du Nouveau Testament* (Paris: 1724–1726).

THE CONUNDRUMS OF CATHOLIC BIBLICAL SCHOLARSHIP

four different meanings. First, it can mean a literal fulfillment; second, an allegorical fulfillment; third, a fulfillment can mean that something similar had happened; fourth, it could mean something that happened in the past that also occurs frequently in the present. Isenbiehl insisted that the third meaning must be the correct explanation of Matthew 1:22, although his two authorities never applied their findings to this particular verse.[74] Consequently, according to Isenbiehl, Matthew only wanted to point out a parallel between the births of the two boys.[75] This does not mean that Isenbiehl had given up his belief in the virgin birth of Jesus Christ, but only that he prefered not to base it on a questionable verse from Isaiah, but rather on the teaching tradition of the Church. He reasoned that, therefore, his construal did not contradict the rule of the Council of Trent.[76] Another argument in Isenbiehl's favor is his analysis of Matthew 13:34–35 ("He spoke to them only in parables, to fulfill what had been said through the prophet . . ."), where Jesus' way of speaking is connected to Psalm 78:2. For Michaelis, this is Matthew's way of describing how Jesus used similar ways of preaching to the prophets of old.[77] Isenbiehl thought that, just as Matthew attempts to describe Jesus' preaching analogous to accounts in the Old Testament and not as fulfillment, so too one must understand Matthew 1:22.

Isenbiehl was aware that such a new reading requires the text to become "alien," since one has to overcome traditional hermeneutic presuppositions that find Jesus everywhere in the text, because one's mind is already occupied with his story.[78] He furthermore questioned that a doctrinal truth (virgin birth) of Christianity should be built on the verses Isaiah 7:14 or Matthew 1:22, because in the long history of their use to prove the fulfillment of the Old Testament in the New Covenant, this had not convinced the Jews, was never undisputed,

---

74. Isenbiehl, *Neuer Versuch,* 232–44.
75. The virgin birth cannot be proven through these verses anyway, Isenbiehl assures the reader. Isenbiehl, *Neuer Versuch,* 242.
76. Isenbiehl, *Neuer Versuch,* 132–35.
77. Ibid., 288; Michaelis, *Deutsche Uebersetzung des Alten Testaments, 6: Psalmen* (Göttingen: 2nd ed. 1782), 185.
78. Isenbiehl, *Neuer Versuch,* 3.

and has never converted a substantial number of people. Isenbiehl therefore felt that enlightened Catholic theologians should abandon the use of these verses as dogmatic proofs, in order to avoid indirectly feeding into the arguments of the enemies of religion:[79]

> What I say here is not imagination, but my own experience. I know a number of free-thinkers who would have been filled with zeal for religion, but who began to doubt when they heard the propositions ... and alleged arguments with which some try to prove the most important truths of faith. ... Proofs, which do not stand the test of a thorough investigation, harm our cause more than that they are useful. ... Therefore I would not put our prophecy in the category of those from whom one can prove the fulfillment in the Christian Religion.[80]

Hermeneutic of Suspicion or Fruitful Criticism

Isenbiehl rejected the exegesis of tradition, because he felt that not every exegetical commentary should be considered as truth of faith, even if it had been given by the fathers, but that it must be subject to certain restrictions, e.g., it had to have been accepted by *all* the fathers. In the case of Isaiah 7:14, however, he disregarded the consensus of the fathers, because none had interpreted the verse merely historically, and while he tried to conceal this fact by a number of sophisticated arguments, his opponents centered their criticism on this very fact.[81] Isenbiehl's rejection of the fathers was based on a hermeneutical principle that became, during the eighteenth century, a standard presupposition in exegesis—namely, that the literal meaning of the text was primary and that, therefore, all mystical interpretations must be open to critical investigation.

Isenbiehl argued that although some passages of the Bible contain double meanings, it would be "stupid" to suspect that all of scripture was in need of such a double interpretation. Instead, because of the

---

79. Isenbiehl, *Neuer Versuch*, 5.
80. Ibid., 5–6.
81. Ildephons Schwarz, *Anleitung zur Kenntnis derjenigen Bücher, welche den Candidaten der Theologie ... wesentlich nothwendig und nützlich sind* (Coburg: 1804), 1: 170–71 stated that the Church should have been grateful to Isenbiehl for his defense of the Gospel of Matthew and should not have overreacted, since he had never questioned a dogma of faith, just the proper exegesis of a verse.

multitude of "very confused, and all too indeterminate, tasteless and superficial"[82] mystical interpretations, Isenbiehl came up with the rule that all (!) mystical readings must be viewed as "suspicious and allegedly false."[83] Apart from this "hermeneutic of suspicion" about mystical interpretations, Isenbiehl's methodology rested on the presupposition that one should try to understand the Old Testament independently from the New Testament, and as a revelatory document and piece of literature in its own right.

If mystical interpretations misinterpreted a text, it is important to note what Isenbiehl understood by "false." A *false meaning* was, for Isenbiehl, that which the inspired author did *not* intend or which the Holy Spirit did not prescribe. Such false meanings, produced by allegorical or typological readings, might be useful for ascetcism and spiritual exercises, but not for exegetes, he stated. Moreover, he made clear that one should not maintain the interpretation of the fathers out of wrongful reverence or traditionalism, but take it seriously when they expressed that they only escaped to a mystical meaning when the literal meaning seemed impenetrable to them. If one took such statements of the fathers literally, then exegetes could legitimately recover the literal meaning of Biblical texts and one could shelve the mystical interpretations for such a verse.[84] It seems that Isenbiehl echoes Muratori here, and one can presume that he has read him.[85]

---

82. Isenbiehl, *Neuer Versuch,* 152.

83. Ibid., 153: "If we want to consider scripture without regard to its divine nature merely as a piece of human reason and creativity, we cannot deny that it can have a double meaning. . . . This, however, is not an advantage which helps us to find traces of its divine origin, nor is it seldom that one would look for such cases in vain. The fables . . . have under the appearance of the letters something hidden, which a theologian would call mystical meaning. As foolish as it would be to state a double meaning for all profane scriptures, it is equally foolish to state that all verses of holy scripture have a double meaning. Old and new writers have conceived a mass of such mystical explanations that one can formulate this rule: every mystical meaning must look suspicious, and is allegedly false."

84. Isenbiehl, *Neuer Versuch* 154.

85. Muratori, *De Ingeniorum,* lib. II, ch. 5 290, quoting Alphonsus de Castro, *Adversus Omnes Haereses Libri XIIII* (Paris: 1541) 14: "There are people . . . who are so affected [afficiuntur] by the writings of others, that when they vaguely realize that somebody deviates from the opinion of these writers in the smallest degree [digito transverso], they immediately call it heresy. . . . I therefore confess that I cannot withhold my anger [iracundia] whenever I see people addicted to the writings of men. . . . Such people want to regard the writings of men as if they were divine promulgations [divina oracula], and that one must receive them and show them the honor that one is only obliged to give to holy scripture."

To Isenbiehl, a *true meaning* was that which "describes a thing as it is and as the prophet had it in mind."[86] Since one can deduce the concepts of the prophet only through his expressions, a true meaning must be congruent with the idiosyncratic use of words one finds in Isaiah. However, the idea of a virginal mother cannot be found there; thus, this concept cannot be part of the true meaning of the verse. "The two thoughts: she will conceive by losing her virginity and give birth; *and* she will conceive and give birth without losing her virginity *cannot* be conjoined in a proposition."[87] Isenbiehl's opponents rejected this view and insisted that the New Testament with Christ's self-identification as the Son of God gave legitimacy to read Isaiah in the light of his incarnation and to give this verse a new meaning. For Isenbiehl, such an argument was flawed: with its help, one could dismiss any intrinsic historical meaning of the Old Testament because a Christian would view the New Covenant as always superior.[88] Instead, Isenbiehl argued that the value of a meaning had to be derived from its clarity, simplicity, and its congruence with the object and "natural judgement."[89] The clearest, simplest, and most natural explanation was, therefore, to assume that the Israelites would have purged the Isaiah 7:14 verse from scripture, if contemporary readers had not believed that its prophecy had been fulfilled.[90] To assume that all prophecies of the Old Testament pointed to Christ, as typological interpretation at this time usually assumed, was in Isenbiehl's view, arbitrary:

> If this were true, then all prophecies would be about Christ, and all writings of the prophets a permanent allegory. Who dares to say that? In Isaiah we do not find a word, not an expression . . . from which one could suspect that it is a type for Christ.[91]

---

86. Isenbiehl, *Neuer Versuch* 159.
87. Ibid., 160.
88. Ibid.: "Der Werth des Sinnes wird nach dem Werthe des Gegenstandes geschätzet: und jene des neuen Bundes sind ohne Widerspruch schätzbarer, als etwas verlegenes aus dem alten. Aber nach dieser Schätzungsart könnte man bey einem geringen und niedrigen Gegenstand niemals einen vortrefflichen Sinn und Gedanken haben.
89. Ibid.
90. Isenbiehl, *Neuer Versuch,* 161.
91. Ibid., 162.

Isenbiehl's enemies, especially Goldhagen, argued that Isenbiehl's "critical hermeneutic" of suspicion toward any mystical interpretation was heterodox. In a remarkable book that boldy defended Isenbiehl, most likely written by another biblical theologian, it was shown that criticism as the art of discernment must be at the core of exegetical work.[92] The person cited to defend this statement was none other than the celebrated and universally admired Prince-Abbot of St. Blasien, Martin Gerbert (1720–93), who was above any suspicion of heterodoxy. In his *Exegetical Theology*, Gerbert had developed seven rules of true and "fruitful" criticism. While the ability to discern whether a manuscript was true or forged was part of a "therapeutic" criticism, hermeneutic criticism relied first, not only on the knowledge of the language of the text, but on the use and patterns of the spoken language [*viam ac rationem in omnia orationis schemata*] as well as its allusions and hidden meanings [*arcanas intentiones*] and idioms. Second, a reader desiring to understand a text must know rhetoric in order to distinguish in a text true from false claims, allusions from descriptions, and to understand specific rhetorical patterns. Third, in order to judge not only singular words and idioms correctly, a reader must combine "natural and artificial logic" [*logica tam naturals . . . artificialis concurrere debet*].[93] This means that the reader's mind must be actively present to discern the right meaning of words, sentences and paragraphs, in order to draw the right conclusions. Fourth, the reader has to pay close attention not only to the historical circumstances of the text, but also to the coherence of the text. Fifth, the reader always has to have the intention [*finis*] of the author in front of him. This intention can be deduced from an entire longer text, or from texts that explain each other, or from those in which a doctrine is specifically entailed. This nexus between texts helps the reader to find the "true meaning" of the text. Sixth, one has to explain the words of scripture *first and foremost literally*

---

92. Anonymous, *Katholische Betrachtungen über die zu Mainz, Heidelberg und Strassburg wider den Isenbiehlischen Versuch vom Emmanuel ausgebrachten Censuren* (Frankfurt and Leipzig: 1778), 10–13.
93. Martin Gerbert, *Principia Theologiae Exegeticae* (St. Blasien: 1757), 183. These rules are not contained, as the *Katholische Betrachtungen* claimed, in Gerbert's *Apparatus ad eruditionem* but in his exegetical theology. Another example of a positive view of criticial theology is Eusebius Amort, *Demonstratio Critica Religionis Catholicae Nova, Modesta, Facilis* (Venice: 1744).

and not figuratively, unless something absurd would follow.[94] Thus far, Isenbiehl is presented as someone who followed the distinguished Martin Gerbert's advice in explaining scripture. However, this could only be defended by omitting, as the anonymous defender did, the seventh rule of exegesis. This seventh rule states that when there seem to be multiple meanings, such a text must be read *christologically*. Such an allegorical or typological meaning has apodactic force if it is found in scripture and tradition.[95] This last rule was the point where Isenbiehl deviated.

But how did the anonymous defender resolve the problem of Isenbiehl's deviation from the *consensus* of the fathers? He agreed that an article of faith must be explicitly named in holy scripture, or, if it is only alluded to in scripture, has to be acknowledged as such by the church. If an article of faith is not entailed in scripture at all, then it must be contained in tradition—namely, in the consensus of the fathers of the first five centuries, e.g., by demonstrating that they unanimously rejected the opposite as heretical. However, one also has to read the fathers as "scholars, as ascetics, as homilists . . . and in this regard they are private men [Privat-Männer], who explain obscure scripture passages according to their own insights and according to the reasons that seemed most likely to them. . . . In these opinions, everyone is permitted to deviate from their opinions and to hold a different one . . . until he is declared . . . a heretic."[96] Thus, for the defender, it was not a deviation from a truth of faith, since Isenbiehl did not question the virgin birth, but only deviated from the explanation of a scriptural passage. He went against the consensus of the fathers, not with the intention of heresy, but of legitimate theological dissent.

The Theological World and Isenbiehl's Book

The *New Attempt* was published at the end of October 1777 (although its cover states 1778) and was forbidden in Mainz in March 1778. By April,

---

94. Gerbert, *Principia Theologiae Exegeticae*, 183: "In sensu proprio scripturae verba sumenda, nec ad tropos recurrendum, nisi alias absurdum aliquod sequeretur."
95. Ibid., 183–84.
96. *Katholische Betrachtungen*, 15.

it was forbidden in Speyer, Worms, and Fulda. Soon, Trier, Cologne, Salzburg, Prague, Vienna, Würzburg, Passau, Chur, Paderborn, Hildesheim, and Regensburg followed suit. In Mainz, the proscription decree was even promulgated from all pulpits of the archdiocese.[97] While in Vienna, the highest Court of the Empire, the *Imperial Aulic Council,* had already proscribed the book on July 2, 1778, the Archbishop of Mainz asked for further theological clarification and requested evaluations from the theology departments of Trier, Salzburg, Münster, Heidelberg, as well as from the Sorbonne in Paris. The whole world disputed about his book while Isenbiehl remained silent.

As an example of the reports of the theology departments, which argued almost identically, I want to single out Strasburg as typical. Strasburg's report is also worthy of note because this theology department heavily emphasized a new argument against Isenbiehl—the argument from the perspective of Christian worship as a *locus theologicus.* The report of the Strasburg department highlighted that the liturgy itself is ample proof that the Church understood the prophecy infallibly as a prophecy fulfilled in Christ. The Roman Missal as well as the Ambrosian and Mozarabian liturgies use the verse in the mystical sense, either allegorical or typological. The Strasburg theologians also declared that the consensus of all theologians at all times would qualify the prophetic explanation as a truth of faith.[98]

Moreover, Isenbiehl's explanation, the Strasburg theologians point out, was, in substance, derived from Socinian sources (specifically, Socinus in his *Lectiones Sacrae* and Crell in his *Opera exegetica*),[99] although they acknowledged that some ancient rabbis had taught it. To Isenbiehl's argument that the Church had never given the verse a definite interpretation, the Strasburg theologians countered with Bossuet's response to Richard Simon that it was not wise of the Church

---

97. Weber, "Mainz" 222–23; Reichert, "Trier und seine theologische Fakultät" 283.

98. *Judicium Theologorum Argentinensium de Libro Germanico Vulgato: J. L. Isenbiehl, Neuer Versuch . . .* (Mainz: 1778), arg. III, 37. The theologians meant Benedict XIV, "De Festis Beate Mariae Virginis. Liber Secundus. Caput Primum," in Benedict XIV., *Opera Omnia vol. 8 [De Sacrosancto Missae Sacrificio]* (Venice: 1767), 178.

99. *Judicium Theologorum* 72: "Substantiam ergo Systematis sui Auctor ex Socinianis hausit." Grotius is treated here as Socinian. Cf. ibid. 62–72.

to decide undisputed truths, which are held in good faith by the faithful.[100] The Strasburg theologians also heavily criticized Isenbiehl for his disrespectful treatment of the fathers. He had conceded that one could construct a proof for a doctrinal proposition or a certain biblical interpretation from the witness of the fathers. If several fathers declared that

> the universal church believed this or that teaching, then it would be as infallible as the whole church is infallible. If they lived in the first centuries and witnessed that something was taught by the Apostles, it is as certain as if it was written in the canonical books of the New Covenant. . . . Not a single father of the church states that his opinion is the meaning the entire church embraces or the meaning the Apostles held. That our prophecy is about Jesus Christ is not even regarded as the belief of particular churches. Can one really make use of witnesses for proof, if they do not witness to anything at all?[101]

The theologians of Strasburg argued that such a view of tradition was *minimalistic.* Following this approach, no dogmatic proofs could be made at all. Moreover, they insisted that Isenbiehl's restrictions were arbitrary and contradicted the Council of Trent's declaration about the explanation and interpretation of holy scripture. The theologians regarded Isenbiehl's rejection of Irenaeus—who explicitly speaks about the apostles' belief in the prophecy as a *philosophical reflection*—as proof of Isenbiehl's sophistry.[102]

Likewise, Isenbiehl's assertion that Trent's rule for interpreting Scripture was not part of the deposit of faith, but just a *pastoral* command that was rejected, since it had been explicitly included in the profession of faith of Trent. Isenbiehl's attempt to cite Pierre-Daniel Huet as an example of another theologian who *contradicted* the fathers without magisterial repercussions was similarly unsuccessful with the Strasburg theologians, because Huet had at least held a typological view of the prophecy.[103] For the theology department, the case was

---

100. *Judicium Theologorum Argentinensium,* 75. Cf. Joseph Gass, *Strassburger Theologen im Aufklärungszeitalter, 1766–1790* (Strasbourg: 1917), 38–43.
101. Isenbiehl, *Neuer Versuch,* 123–24.
102. *Judicium Theologorum Argentinensium,* 84–106.
103. *Judicium Theologorum Argentinensium,* 131, 135. Isenbiehl, *Neuer Versuch* 139–40.

clear. Isenbiehl's minimalist historical interpretation of Isaiah 7:14 that excluded any christological dimension, along with the insistence that the Evangelist Matthew was wrong, were *heretical* viewpoints. The Sorbonne came to an almost identical conclusion on August 1, 1778.

It is important to note that two theological worlds collided here. One allowed a certain amount of freedom of theological research, while the other regarded the patristic interpretation as a revealed truth of faith. Abbé Louis of Strasburg, who, in an article for Goldhagen's journal, explained the verdict, proves this. Abbé Louis deemed Isenbiehl's doctrine to be heretical because it directly opposed what had always and everywhere been believed in the Catholic Church. It was a "catholic truth of faith" that Isaiah predicted in Isaiah 7:14: (1) the Messiah, who (2) is Christ, and that (3) Matthew recognized this. "This is so obviously [*aperte*] contained in scripture and tradition that according to unanimous consensus [*omnium consensu*] it has to be regarded as revealed [*revelatae*]."[104] Isenbiehl's book was heretical because it denied these three claims. According to the Strasburg faculty department, everyone who contradicts the unanimous consensus of the fathers, contradicts tradition, and is, therefore, a heretic [*haereticum esse*].[105] When confronted with the question as to whether the department had judged Isenbiehl too harshly, Abbé Louis responded on May 7, 1778:[106]

> The academics [in Germany] imagine that a teaching is only heretical if its opposite . . . was explicitly defined by the Church . . . but this opinion is false. For a teaching to be heretical it is sufficient that the tradition of the Church was always against it. It is not necessary for the Church to have defined the opposite.[107]

The problem with this statement was, of course, that the opinion Jerome reported from the fourth century was never rejected as

104. "Kurzgefasste Erläuterung der Censur, welche die löbliche theologische Facultät zu Strassburg . . . über die drey vornehmsten Sätze des Isenbiehlschen Versuches . . . gefällt hat," *Religionsjournal. Beylagen* 1 (1778—24 July): 205–18, at 210.
105. "Kurzgefasste Erläuterung der Censur," 216.
106. "Antwort welche der oft belobte Hr. Professor Louis zu Strasburg . . . gegeben hat," *Religionsjournal. Beylagen* 1 (1778—29 August): 222–24.
107. "Antwort welche der oft belobte Hr. Professor Louis," 222–23.

heretical. Thus, Isenbiehl had communicated: "The Holy Fathers were not accustomed to anathematizing everyone who did not share their opinion . . . they excluded only those from their community who had argued against explicit revelation, true tradition."[108] Louis, however, had a narrower understanding of tradition and was able to dismiss this argument because he embraced wholeheartedly what Charles Du Plessis d'Argentré (1673–1740) had already stated in his *Elementa Theologica* (1702). According to this learned doctor of the Sorbonne, and later bishop of Tulle, everything that was known through perpetual and universal tradition as being contained in scripture, was of divine and Catholic faith, and had the highest claim to being defined doctrine.[109] Also, the question whether it could be an article of faith that one had to understand a text this or that way was answered in this work.[110] For this purpose, du Plessis d'Argentré differentiated between two kinds of texts. One kind was understandable by itself [*per se apertus*]; the other through the perpetual or continous tradition of the Church, whereby the tradition that explained a text of the second category belongs to the deposit of divine faith.[111]

Isenbiehl's anonymous defender did, of course, cite Muratori and his view in defense of the German exegete, but it should be clear that two irreconcilable theologies clashed in this case. The charge of the theology departments that Isenbiehl would marginalize Mary with his exegesis was rejected with a referance to Muratori. According to the latter, Mary would despise it if mere "opinions" (e.g., the interpretation of Isaiah 7:14) were treated as if they were of divine origin.[112] Louis and the theology faculties of Mainz, Heidelberg,

---

108. *Katholische Betrachtungen*, 30.
109. Charles Du Plessis d'Argentré, *Elementa theologica, in quibus de autoritate ac pondere cujuslibet argumenti theologici . . . disputatur. Postremo etiam accedit, cum de fide divina, tum de summa Ecclesiae authoritate in proscribendis nominatim et damnandis perversis quibuscumque scriptis, tractatio* (Paris: 1702), 329: "Respondeo: quaecumque in Scriptura sacra contineri, perpetua & universali Ecclesiae Traditione constat, ea esse de fide divina simul & catholica."
110. Du Plessis d'Argentré, *Elementa theologica*, 330–31: "An fidei divinae & catholicae dogma esse possit, hunc vel illum Scripturae sacrae locum hoc vel illo sensu intelligendum esse; seu, an sit a Deo revelatum, quisnam sit sensus germanus singulorum Scripturae locorum, & ubinam extet illa revelatio?"
111. Du Plessis d'Argentré, *Elementa theological*, 331.
112. *Katholische Betrachtungen*, 24.

Strasburg, Paris, and Salzburg were not about to listen to Muratori, especially not when they were charged with a sin against charity in denouncing a book.[113] They were equally unimpressed that in defense of Isenbiehl, he even quoted Cornelius Jansen (1535–1638) who, as the founding father of Jansenism, was certainly above any suspicion of laxism, in defense of Isenbiehl. The bishop of Ypres had stated that from the words of the prophecy in Isaiah alone, one could *not* conclude that the virgin would conceive as virgin and give birth as virgin, and that, therefore, the verse was *worthless* for a dogmatic defense of the perpetual virginity of Mary.[114] The Würzburg theologian Franz Oberthür (1745–1851), one of Germany's most ardent Catholic Enlighteners, nevertheless, defended Isenbiehl:

> I have not found the least of what could be regarded as heresy. . . . It is not orthodoxy to believe a proposition because some hold it and declare: this is the opinion of the Church (*communis theologorum*)! Instead, one has to prove with arguments that it is the opinion of the Church. To hold such a proposition is *reasonable orthodoxy*, and it is this, what the Church asks of every Catholic. *Sit rationale obsequium vestrum.* . . . (Rom. 12:1)[115]

Apart from a few anonymous theologians and some Catholic Enlighteners or Reformers, who were already suspected of schism or heresy (Ruatenstrauch, Oberthür, Hontheim, etc.), nobody came to a defense of Isenbiehl. His critics used this situation to portray the author as a freethinker and wanted the book condemned not just by a few German bishops, but by the pope himself. The denunciation was sent to Rome, and the Holy Inquisition began a formal investigation of the *New Attempt* and its author.

Censoring and Condemnation

Isenbiehl had been arrested on December 28, 1777, and remained for two months in the Cathedral prison in Mainz. He rejected all requests

---

113. *Katholische Betrachtungen* 8; Muratori, *De ingeniorum*, lib. II, ch. 5.
114. Cornelius Jansen, *Commentariorum in Suam Concordiam ac totam Historiam Evangelicam* (Leuven: 1606), c. 8, 53–54. Cf. *Katholische Betrachtungen* 23.
115. *Magazin zum Gebrauch der Staaten- und Kirchengeschichte* 8 (1783), 25–28, at 26.

to explain his theses and to answer the charges of heresy, unless he would be released from prison in order to draft a response in peace and tranquility. Only after he finally recited the Creed in front of the Cathedral chapter was he allowed to leave the prison for an internment in the abbey of Eberbach, where he was imprisoned from February 1778. The abbot there treated Isenbiehl badly because he assumed this would amuse the Elector.[116] All attempts by Karl von Dalberg to get Isenbiehl acquitted or even released on a bail of 1,000 Talers—an enormous sum—failed. After an unsuccessful attempt to escape the monastery, Isenbiehl was again imprisoned in Mainz until he finally recanted.[117]

Many historians have wondered why Isenbiehl published his book and whether he was really so naïve as to expect no repercussions. One could have found the answer quite easily in the *New Attempt*. There, the Mainz exegete states that he published the thoughts of his lectures because men of faith and learning (Hontheim,[118] Rautenstrauch, Gertz, Michaelis) encouraged him to do so. Moreover, he insists on his academic, and, especially, his Christian (!) freedom to make his opinions public, even if they did, as he put it, "clash with contemporary school opinions, they are presented in the freedom which Christ has given us and which neither church nor state can take away from us."[119]

---

116. Dom- und Diözesanarchiv Mainz: Bestand 12/1, Nr. 153; Haus-, Hof- und Staatsarchiv Wien, Mainzer Erzkanzler Archiv, Geistliche u. Kirchensachen 81, letter of F. Adolphus, abbot of Eberbach, to the Elector of February 15, 1778 (I thank Mr. Sascha Weber for bringing this letter to my attention). Helmut Mathy, "Isenbiehl, Johann Lorenz," *in Neue Deutsche Biographie* 10 (1974) 191–92; Brück, *Die Mainzer theologische Fakultät* 58.

117. Isenbiehl did not want to escape to Utrecht, as his friend Dalberg suggested, although there were "plenty good Catholics and freedom." Dalberg to Oberthür on August 18, 1778, Universitätsbibliothek Würzburg, Nachlass Oberthür, Passivkorrespondenz, at Jung, *Seelmann* 638. For the relationship Dalberg-Isenbiehl see Ferdinand Koeppel, "Karl von Dalbergs Wirken für das Hochstift Würzburg unter Franz Ludwig von Erthal," *Zeitschrift für Bayerische Landesgeschichte* 20 (1957): 253–98.

118. Hontheim was ferociously attacked for his sympathy with Isenbiehl's book by his own bishop, as well as by the papal nuncio, and this ultimately led to his downfall. He defended himself by insisting that he had only received a part of the manuscript, and that he had relied on the unpublished review of Philipp Cordier (1716–1779), a Jesuit theologian in Trier, who had not identified any heresy in Isenbiehl's *New Attempt*. Cordier made clear that he disagreed with Isenbiehl, as one could see from his book *Religio christiana ex prophetis antiquis demonstrata* (Trier: 1775), 28–36, but defended Isenbiehl against the charge of heresy. Cf. Reichert, "Trier und seine Theologische Fakultät," 292. Cf. Ulrich L. Lehner, "Johann Nikolaus von Hontheim and his *Febronius*," ch. 6 of this volume.

119. Isenbiehl, *Neuer Versuch,* preface.

The investigation by the Holy Inquisition in Rome seemed initially to take a good course. In order to judge the book fairly, Isenbiehl's *New Attempt* was translated into Latin and Italian.[120] Then, however, the Franciscan censor Guiseppe Antonio Martinelli (1717–88) judged the entire work [*doctrina*] to be downright heretical. A second report, probably by Michele di Petro (1747–1821) denied this qualification. Although the censors were required to consult prior decisions about the book issued by Catholic theology departments, e.g., the decisions of the departments of the Sorbonne-Paris, Heidelberg, and Mainz, they could not have considered the one university report that defended Isenbiehl (at least initially), issued on April 21, 1778, by the theology department of Salzburg, because it was filed in German—despite the fact that the original was, of course, in Latin.[121] It seems that either some mysterious conspiracy or simple negligence successfully silenced the one voice that was favorable to the author.

The consultors of the Roman Inquisition did not follow Martinelli and did not consider the entire teaching [*doctrina*] of Isenbiehl "heretical." Instead, they decided that only certain propositions were to be censored and rejected ten qualifications of the censors as too harsh or unfounded.[122] Nevertheless, these were still considered "*falsa*," "*temeraria*," "*perniciosa*," and "*haeresi proxima*," but they were convinced that Isenbiehl's book was only *conducive* to heresy, not intrinsically heretical. Pope Pius VI (reign 1775–99) affirmed this assessment in his brief *Divina Christi Domini Voce* on September 20, 1779, and condemned the possession or reading or dissemination of the book with the punishment of excommunication. According to the pope, it

---

120. Burkard, "Schwierigkeiten," 311 also points out that the consulters were unable to read Hebrew and therefore could not follow Isenbiehl's argumentation.
121. Burkard, "Schwierigkeiten," 312. This is remarkable since the original report of the Salzburg theology department was of course in Latin (of April 21, 1778). The original (first) report is reprinted in *Katholische Betrachtungen* 169–208. Moreover, it was signed by the dean of the department, Simpert Schwarzhueber OSB, who himself was a renowned Mariologist and not in the least suspicious of heterodoxy or modernist leanings. However, on September 10 the department wrote a new, more thorough report, which now harmonized with the other, negative voices (Gass, *Strassburger Theologen* 54).
122. The rejected qualifications included "piarum aurium offensivas," "simplicium seductivas," "Theologis et Patribus injuriosas," contumeliosas," "periculosas," "de haeresi suspectas," "haeresique faventes," "praesertim vero Socianismo," "ipsumque sapientes," "erroneas," "damnatisque alias ab Ecclesia persimiles, atque damnandas." Burkard, "Schwierigkeiten" 309.

contained a poison [*venenum*] that could easily lead the reader to a complete irreverence toward the fathers and to an interpretation of scripture accoridng to personal whim [*spiritus privatus*]. He explicitly invoked the Council of Trent's hermeneutical rule and complained that Isenbiehl, in his cleverness, did not feel the urge to surrender to tradition.[123] It is remarkable that *Divina Christi Domini Voce* is the only magisterial teaching or exhortation regarding biblical exegesis between the Council of Trent and Pius IX's *Syllabus of Errors* (1864) that has been included in the *Enchiridion Biblicum*, the official collection of magisterial texts on the Bible. It reads:

> A terrible insult to Catholics has been published. They have heard stated publicly that the prophecy concerning the divine Emanuel, sprung from a virgin, in no way, neither literally nor typologically, refers to the Mother of God's virginal begetting of him, which all the prophets announced. It has nothing to do with the true Immanuel, Christ the Lord. And this when St. Matthew testifies expressly that the remarkable prophecy was fulfilled in that wondrous mystery of religion. Yet it is claimed that the Holy Evangelist does not recall it as a fulfillment of the prophecy, but a mere passing mention or allusion. On hearing this, pious people have been horror-struck. Scripture and also tradition, as it has come down to us from the constant agreement of the fathers, is being undermined with utter shamelessness. . . . We, therefore, . . . with the plenitude of apostolic power, condemn the said book . . . as containing doctrine and statements that are respectively false, rash, scandalous, dangerous, erroneous and favoring heresy and heretics. It is our wish and decision that hereafter the said be forever considered condemned and disapproved of.[124]

After such a universal condemnation, Isenbiehl could no longer withhold his recantation if he did not want to be imprisoned for life. Thus, he submitted to the Holy See and signed his recantation, denouncing his own book on Christmas Day 1779, and was

---

123. Dominik Burkard, "Schwierigkeiten bei der Beschäftigung mit der päpstlichen Zensur im ausgehenden 18. Jahrhundert am Beispeil der Causa Isenbiehl," in *Verbotene Bücher. Zur Geschichte des Index im 18. und 19. Jahrhundert*, ed. Hubert Wolf (Paderborn: Schöningh, 2008), 299–316.

124. The translation can be found in Pius VI, Brief "Divinia Christi Domini Voce (1779), in Dennis Murphy, ed., *The Church and the Bible. Official Documents of the Catholic Church* (New Delhi: 2007), 36. For the Latin original see *Enchiridion biblicum Documenta ecclesiastica Sacram Scripturam spectantia* (Naples/Rome: 4th ed. 1965), 31–32. As usual in collections like the *Enchiridion*, the letter is substantially shortened, here by almost two-thirds. The entire text, so it seems, was only published in a Protestant journal, namely August Schlözer's *Briefwechsel* vol. 6 , issue 37 (1780): 346–51 and hitherto no one has really paid much attention to it.

consequently released from prison on December 30, 1779, rehabilitated and given the position of a canon in Amöneburg. However, because of some bureaucratic error, his book did not appear on the *Index of Forbidden Books* until 1783. There was no chance that he would ever be permitted to work as a professor again and, apart from a two-volume introduction to theology he produced in 1787, he never again took up his pen for academic purposes.[125]

The case of Isenbiehl shows that the Catholic Church did not agree with Isenbiehl's critical hermeneutical stance on Isaiah 7:14, which the father of modern liberal Protestant theology, Johann Salomo Semler (1725–91) expressed thus: "Jesus is everything that he was and what he has done . . . regardless of whether the verse in Isaiah is said about his birth or not."[126] It would be another forty years until another Catholic theologian, Peter Alois Gratz (1769–1849) of Tübingen, would cautiously build on Isenbiehl's insights, incorrectly believing that the times had changed. In 1821, he too lost his chair over this matter.[127] It is an irony of history that today, Isenbiehl's historical method has become the standard academic approach to Isaiah 7:14, although there is still some discussion as to whether the verse refers to the prophet's or the king's son.[128]

---

125. Johann Lorenz Isenbiehl, *De Rebus Divinis tractatus*, 2 vols. (Mainz: 1787). These volumes are a patristic explanation of holy scripture. A review of Isenbiehl's *De Rebus Divinis* can be found in the *Mainzer Monatsschrift für Geistliche Sachen* 3 (1787), 404–7; ibid., 408–16 Isenbiehl's defense against a (different) critical reviewer. When his friend Gertz informed him in 1783 about events in the scholarly world, Isenbiehl answered sarcastically: "You want to entertain me with scholarly matters? You should have written about onions, garlic and soup herbs . . . since I am now responsible for the economy of this chapter . . . and no longer an author, a scholar, a Biblicist or reader of the fathers, but a farmer, gardener and cook! Gosh, what a metamorphosis." At Weber, "Mainz," 227.

126. At Richard Simon, *Kritische Historie des Textes des Neuen Testamentes. Herausgegeben von Johann Salomo Semler* (Halle: 1776), 443.

127. Peter Alois Gratz, *Historisch-kritischer Kommentar über das Evangelium des Matthäus* (Tübingen: 1821), 56. For Gratz, the meaning of Isaiah's verse was first of all historical, but he conceded that it was at the same time also an *unconscious* prophecy about the future, unknown to the author. Thus, by some divine providence, unknown to the prophet, the utterance of Isaiah was also and even more completely fulfilled in Christ. Norbert Wolff, *Peter Alois Gratz (1769-1849). Ein Theologe zwischen 'falscher Aufklärung' und 'Obscurantismus'* (Trier: Paulinus-Verlag, 1998), 229, 246 missed that Gratz knew Isenbiehl's work.

128. Reiser, *Bibelkritik* 319; Martin Rösel, "Die Jungfrauengeburt des endzeitlichen Immanuel," *Jahrbuch für biblische Theologie* 6 (1991): 135–51.

Magisterial Implications

The Isenbiehl controversy provides the historical context of why Catholic exegetes over the next generations became worried about emphasizing the historical-literal reading of a text, and rather left this approach to their Protestant peers. It also shows that the papacy did not reject historical criticism per se, as it was perceived by many, but rather a historical/literal approach that claimed to be the only legitimiate approach to scripture, in particular if such an approach was against the "consensus of the fathers." "Consensus" was understood as the *moral,* yet universal harmony of the fathers in their interpretation of a certain verse and considered part of the universal belief of the church.[129] The papal decision to censor Isenbiehl can only be regarded as a clear rejection of the historical-critical method *as* it was known and practiced by Johann Salomo Semler (1725–91) or Johann August Ernesti (1707-81), who both insisted that *only* the historical, grammatical sense should be regarded as the licit meaning of a text passage, and that the authority of the fathers was hermeneutically inadmissable.[130]

Besides Gratz, a number of other Catholic exegetes fell victim to such policy, Johann Jahn of Vienna (1750-1816) being the most prominent one. Jahn, who was, in the first third of the nineteenth century, arguably the most prominent Catholic Old Testament scholar, faced in 1805 a similar choice as Isenbiehl—to publicly write and teach according to "common belief," but rejected because he "could not consciously tell . . . a lie."[131] Like Isenbiehl, he dismissed the fathers as "fallible interpreters," and argued against the Augustinian Engelbert Klüpfel (1733-1811) that the diversity of opinions among the fathers was much greater than usually conceded, and that no reference to

---

129. Franz Vogl, *Die heilige Schrift und ihre Interpretation durch die heiligen Väter der Kirche* (Augsburg: 1836), 106–10; cf. Georg Michael Wittmann, *Principia catholica de sacra Scriptura* (Regensburg: 1793). On moral certainty, see Sven Knebel, *Wille, Würfel und Wahrscheinlichkeit* (Hamburg: Meiner, 2000).

130. Hermann Joseph Pottmeyer, "Die historisch-kritische Methode und die Erklärung zur Schriftauslegung in der dogmatischen Konstitution *Dei Filius* des I. Vatikanums," *Annuarium Historiae Concilium* 2 (1970): 87–111, at 98.

131. Johann Jahn, *Nachträge zu seinen theologischen Werken* (Tübingen: 1821), vii; cf. Johann Jahn, *Enchiridion Hermeneuticae Generalis* (Vienna: 1812).

their authority could ever replace historical-philological work.[132] The censoring of theologians who saw the historical-critical approach as the only legitimate—or at least, supreme—approach to scripture intimidated Catholic biblical scholars who, understandably, withdrew to "safe" research areas and left the field to their Protestant peers, with the result that Catholic exegesis began to become irrelevant for academic discourse.

While Vatican I did not show much understanding for the relevance of independent historical exegesis, it understood that the Bible was a book of the church and that there was no way to adequately understand its content except through the Church.[133] Catholic exegesis was bound through the text of *Dei Filius* to the scriptural meaning the church has held and holds. Yet, until 1943's *Divino Afflante Spiritu*, Catholic theologians would have to fear the possibility of being dismissed from teaching positions or being denied the permission to publish if they went beyond these boundaries of research and established historical interpretations independent from tradition.[134]

The Isenbiehl episode was also a step in the direction of a central theological magisterium under the guidance of the popes. The Council of Trent had promulgated a reform decree about scriptural interpretation that aimed at restricting abuse and libertinist interpretation. It maintained that the meaning of scripture, as it was held by the Church (tradition), was normative and that it was the duty of the Church, bishops, and theologians (*doctores et magistri*), to ensure

---

132. Pottmeyer, "Die historisch-kritische Methode," 100. Cf. Wendelin Rauch, *Engelbert Klüpfel. EIn führender Theologe der Aufklärungszeit* (Freiburg: 1922), 79–86; 149–55.

133. Pottmeyer, "Die historisch-kritische Methode," 110. Joseph Ratzinger, *Traditionsbegriff*, 47 at ibid.: ". . . dass, gleichwie es ein Wächteramt der Kirche und ihrer geistbegabten Zeugenschaft gibt, so auch ein Wächteramt der Exegese besteht, die den Literalsinn erforscht und so aller Gnosis entgegen die Bindung an die Sarx des Logos hütet. Insofern gibt es dann so etwas wie eine Eigenständigkeit der Schrift als eines selbständigen und in vieler Hinsicht durchaus eindeutigen Masstabes gegenüber dem kirchlichen Lehramt."

134. As was the case in Germany with Joseph Schnitzer in 1908. See Manfred Weitlauff, *Der "Fall" des Augsburger Diözesanpriesters und Münchener Theologieprofessors Joseph Schnitzer (1859-1939)* (Augsburg: Verlag des Vereins für Bistumsgeschichte 2011). Henning Graf Reventlow, "Katholische Exegese des Alten Testamentes zwischen den Vatikanischen Konzilien," in *Die katholisch-theologischen Disziplinen in Deutschland, 1870-1962*, ed. Hubert Wolf (Paderborn: Schöningh, 1999), 15–39, at 22: "Noch 1938 war die Situation offenbar unverändert. Überall ist von seiten der Exegeten das Bemühen zu spüren, in dem Netz der Direktiven Schlupflöcher zu finden, die eine, wenn auch eingeschränkte Bewegungsfreiheit erlauben."

(*iudicare*) that exegesis did not contradict it (*contra sensum ecclesiae*). In the aftermath of Trent, however, tradition seems to have become subservient to the Magisterium.[135] On the eve of Vatican I, for some Catholic theologians of the so-called Roman school (e.g., Perrone), which heavily influenced Vatican I, the Magisterium is even identified with tradition.[136] Vatican I reiterated Trent's formulation in the dogmatic constitution *Dei Filius* (1870), but turned it positively so that it stated that the true meaning of sacred scripture was the one the Church held and holds (*tenuit ac tenet*) and that the Church alone had jurisdiction to judge about the right scriptural interpretation. "Church," however, no longer included ordinaries and theologians,[137] as it did at Trent, but meant the *central* magsterium of the pope, and *iudicare* dogmatic decision-making.[138] Consequently, critics saw in the latter, the end of "autonomous scriptural scholarship."[139] However one interprets the development from Trent to Vatican I, with the censoring of Isenbiehl, the papacy entered the stage of modern exegetical controversy, and took the stance that scriptural interpretation needs the fathers and tradition, rejected the possibility of an autonmous historical-critical approach, and claimed the right to have the decisive say in defining the boundaries of exegesis.[140]

Catholic exegesis did not recover from the consequent narrowing of academic freedom until the eve of Vatican II, when theologians began

135. Hans Kümmeringer, "Es ist Sache der Kirche, *iudicare de vero sensu et interpretatione scripturarum sanctarum*. Zum Verständnis dieses Satzes auf dem Tridentinum und Vaticanum I," *Theologische Quartalschrift* 149 (1969): 282–96. This article is the text of a seminar paper written under the direction of Joseph Ratzinger, who recommended it for publication (see ibid., 282).
136. Walter Kasper, *Die Lehre von der Tradition in der Römischen Schule* (Freiburg: Herder, 1962), 179–81.
137. For the wider context of this important development, see Klaus Unterburger, *Vom Lehramt der Theologen zum Lehramt der Päpste?: Pius XI., die Apostolische Konstitution "Deus scientiarum Dominus" und die Reform der Universitätstheologie* (Freiburg im Breisgau: Herder, 2010).
138. Kümmeringer, "Es ist Sache der Kirche," 294–96. Pottmeyer, ""Die historisch-kritische Methode."
139. Reventlow, "Katholische Exegese des Alten Testamentes zwischen den Vatikanischen Konzilien," 18. The question of whether something like "autonomous exegsis" is possible or desirable has to be left out here.
140. The encyclical *Providentissimus Deus* (1893) recovered more freedom for the exegete and made some concessions to a historical-critical approach to scripture, but most of them were withdrawn or relativized during the Modernist crisis and in *Spiritus Paraclitus* (1920). Only *Divino Afflante Spiritu* (1943) opened Catholic theology to historical-critical methodology and more importantly to the hitherto rejected *Formgeschichte*. Hans-Josef Klauck, "Die katholische neutestamentliche Exegese zwischen Vatikanum I und Vatikanum II," in *Die katholisch-theologischen Disziplinen in Deutschland, 1870-1962*, ed. Hubert Wolf (Paderborn: Schöningh, 1999), 39–71.

276

to push open the door, *Divino Afflante Spiritu* (1943) had cautiously[141] opened for historical criticism, and turned it into a "floodgate" (H. J. Klauck).[142] This new approach to scripture was deeply attractive, even for the young Joseph Ratzinger during his studies of theology in Freising after World War II: "The candid questions from the perspectives of the liberal-historical method created a new directness in the approach to sacred scripture and opened up dimensions of the text that were no longer perceived by the all-too-predetermined dogmatic reading. The Bible spoke to us with new immediacy and freshness." Yet, he realized that this frankness could lead to a "flattening" of the Bible, which had to be "compensated for by obedience to dogma. A characteristic fruitfulness came from the balance between liberalism and dogma."[143] It is this characteristic fruitfulness, so it seems, that Catholic theologians aim to recover by rejecting some of the positivist presuppositions of the historical-critical method and rediscovering tradition as an interpretive key to scripture in what they call "theological interpretation."[144] Pope Benedict XVI, well aware of Isenbiehl and his approach, believes that historical-critical exegesis cannot provide a convincing interpretation of the prophet's words in Isaiah 7:14 and that a christological reading is the only valid one.[145] Marius Reiser, on whom the pope relies, however, does not share such a narrow interpretation, but instead embraces the modern view that interprets the verse as a sign of hope for Ahaz's contemporaries, but states that the verse has an *additional* ("mitgemeint") prophetic meaning due to its oracular character. He

---

141. Robert B. Robinson, *Roman Catholic Exegesis since Divino Afflante Spiritu. Hermeneutical Implications* (Atlanta: Scholars Press, 1988).

142. Klauck, "Die katholische neutestmentliche Exegese." The image used here is Klauck's.

143. Joseph Ratzinger, *Milestones: Memoirs, 1927-1977* (San Francisco: 1998), 52–53.

144. See especially Henri de Lubac, *Medieval Exegesis. The Four Senses of Scripture* [Exégèse médiévale, *1954-64*], 3 vols. (Grand Rapids: Eerdmans, 1998–2009); Joseph Ratzinger, "Schriftauslegung im Widerstreit. Zur Frage nach Grundlagen und Weg der Exegese heute," in *Schriftauslegung im Widerstreit,* ed. Joseph Ratzinger (Freiburg: Herder, 1989), 15–44; Joseph Ratzinger/Pope Benedict XVI., *Jesus von Nazareth,* 3 vols. (Freiburg: Herder, 2006/12).

145. Joseph Ratzinger/Pope Benedict XVI, *Jesus of Nazareth. The Infancy Narratives* (New York: Image, 2012), 48: "So the sign would need to be sought and identified within the historical context in which it was announced by the prophet. Exegesis has therefore searched meticously, using all the resources of historical scholarship, for a contemporary interpretation—and it has failed." Ibid., 51, a reference to Reiser, whom Benedict XVI has quoted frequently in his *Jesus*-books.

seems to embody the combination of "liberalism and dogma" mentioned above when he reasons: "The prophet's prediction is like a miraculously formed keyhole, into which the key of Christ fits perfectly."[146]

146. Marius Reiser, *Bibelkritik und Auslegung der Heiligen Schrift* (Mohr Siebeck: Tübingen, 2007), 328.

11

Apocalypse 2014—Post-Tridentine Catholic Exegesis of Revelation: The Futurist Commentary of Alphonsus Frey (1762)

The book of Revelation—or the Apocalypse of John—the last book of the New Testament, has intrigued interpreters for the last two thousand years due to its cornucopia of images. Should it be read as a book that describes the historical persecution of the early Christians, or as a book predicting the future—this has been and continues to be the main question for its interpreters. This chapter focuses on the futurist commentary of Alphonsus Frey of 1762 on the book of Revelation, which predicted the end of the world for 2014. His approach will be compared to other post-Tridentine approaches to Revelation, in order to show the wider developments in Catholic exegesis that led, in the eighteenth century, to the abandonment of futurism.

Post-Reformation Interpreters

The majority of Protestant interpreters of Revelation adopted an historicist view that saw the main events of Christian history up to the interpreter's time foretold in the prophetic images of the text. A common feature of all forms of historicist interpretation was the "year–day principle", according to which, one day in prophetic time corresponds to a literal year.[1] Catholic exegetes, however, can be categorized into at least two groups—*preterists* or *futurists*.[2] For preterists, most of the Apocalypse was already fulfilled. The futurists, however, argued that only a small part of the prophecies had been fulfilled, usually chapters 1–3.[3] In Catholic exegesis of the sixteenth century, one can identify a gradual marginalisation of the multiple senses of scripture in favor of a strengthening of the literal meaning of a textual passage. For the book of Revelation, this occurred as a strategic move to defend Catholic doctrine against Protestant critics: one had to prove that the Church of Rome was not the Whore of Babylon, and the pope not the Antichrist. Moreover, the text had not only to coincide with the interpretation of exegetes, but also be consistent with dogma and tradition. Jean-Robert Armogathe observes:

> The texts served as the scriptural proof that dogma demanded. It was required of the texts of the Bible not only that they provide a foundation to dogma but also that they anticipate their own literal reading. The debate around Revelation was especially strained. How was it possible to retain at the same time a literal reading and a dogmatic reading of a text that we now know . . . belongs to a very particular genre. The historical interpretation was judged incomplete, the mystical interpretation dangerous.[4]

1. Kenneth G. C. Newport, *Apocalypse and Millennium: Studies in Biblical Eisegesis* (Cambridge: Cambridge University Press, 2000), 9. On this principle, see also William H. Shea, *Selected Studies on Prophetic Interpretation* (Washington: n.p., 1982), 56–93.
2. A "counter-historicist" school certainly existed in Catholicism as well, but seems never to have had much support (Newport, *Apocalypse and Millennium*, 80–82). Charles Walmsley OSB (1722–97), *The General History of the Christian Church . . . deduced from the Apocalypse of St. John* (n.p.: 1771) can serve as an example for this strain of interpretation.
3. Newport, *Apocalypse and Millennium*, 16. Jean-Robert Armogathe, "Interpretations of the Revelation of John: 1500–1800," in *Encyclopedia of Apocalypticism* , ed. John J. Collins and Bernard McGinn (New York: Continuum, 1998), 2:185–203.
4. Armogathe, "Interpretations," 187.

The Spanish Jesuit Alphonsus Salmeron (1515–85) seems to have been the first Catholic exegete to argue that Revelation describes primarily the early church, and is consequently hailed as the father of preterism. Only from Revelation 9 onwards did he see a connection to the contemporary church, in which Christ reigns spiritually.[5] Also, Luis de Alcazar SJ (1554–1613), in his *Investigation of the Hidden Meaning of the Apocalypse*, stressed the historical context of the book.[6] His was the first preterist commentary on Revelation, and as such understood almost the entire book (chapters 5–20) as a treatment of early church history. Only chapter 20—about the millennium, the thousand-year reign of the faithful with Christ (Rev. 20:5)—was to be understood about the present time, and almost nothing about the future. "Alcazar is unusual in the extent to which he was prepared to apply the preterist logic consistently; for him the whole book of Revelation related to the past."[7] Many interpreters of all denominations followed Alcazar's lead—most prominently, Hugo Grotius (1583–1645), and in Catholic circles, Jacques-Bénigne Bossuet (1627–1704).[8]

Bossuet, whose commentary became one of the most widely read in the Catholic world, complained that most contemporaries read the book of Revelation as universal admonition to do penance and to prepare for the return of Christ. If this were the only dimension in which the book could be read, Bossuet argued, then the author, John, would not deserve a place among the prophets.[9] Instead, a rediscovery of the prophetic dimensions of the book has to be undertaken.[10] Bossuet found evidence for such a historical-prophetic reading, especially in the prophesied fall of the pagan Roman Empire by Alaric (d. 410) in Revelation 17 and 18. He even went so far as to see in this

5. Alphonsus Salmeron, *Disputationum in Epistolas canonicas et Apocalypsin* (Madrid: 1602), 4:462, describes the possibility (*non inutilis*) of identifying the first apocalyptic (666) beast with Mohammed. See also Franz S. Tiefenthal, *Die Apokalypse des Johannes* (Paderborn: 1892), 54–55; Edward Elliott, *Horae Apocalypticae 3rd. ed.* (London: 1847), 4:450–90.
6. Luis de Alcazar, *Vestigatio arcani sensus in Apocalypsin* (Antwerp: 1614).
7. Newport, *Apocalypse and Millennium*, 72.
8. Tiefenthal, *Die Apokalypse*, 57; Armogathe, "Interpretations," 195–96.
9. Jacques-Bénigne Bossuet, *L'apocalypse avec une explication* (Paris: 1689), 10. For an overview of Bossuet, see also Elliott, *Horae Apologeticae*, 4:456–61.
10. Bossuet understands prophets foremost as foretellers of future events.

event the key to understanding the entirety of the book.[11] Only chapter 11, about the return of Enoch and Elijah, had yet to be fulfilled.[12] Bossuet agreed with Alcazar that one is not obliged to follow the church fathers in their musings about images or metaphors, unless they teach unanimously a truth of faith or morals.[13] He was convinced that the historical meaning of the text was not accessible to the fathers, because they never exhausted the literal meaning of the text. Moreover, Bossuet made clear that even if one demonstrates that a literal prophecy has been fulfilled in the past—namely, in the first centuries of the church's existence—that such a prophecy could still contain a prophecy about the future.[14] As a consequence of such an interpretation, Bossuet did not identify the apocalyptic green horse (Rev. 6:8) with Islam, or the Antichrist with Mohammed.[15] Instead, he understood chapter 8 to be about the persecution of Jews under the emperors Trajan and Hadrian, in the context of the Bar-Kochba insurrection.[16] He interpreted chapter 9 as an attack of Jewish heresy against Christianity and about the fall of Rome. In Bossuet's opinion, chapter 10 concerned the persecutions under the Roman Emperors. Diocletian (244–311) is therefore the apocalyptic beast whose name is 666, because "Diocles Augustus" in numbers equals 666.[17] The apocalyptic woman in chapter 12 is the church, and her son, Emperor Constantine the Great. Chapter 14 portrays the destruction by Alaric and Attila, and so forth.[18] The "millennium," in which the church enjoys peace and tranquillity, is the period in which the church lives now, but according to chapter 20, right before the end of the world, Satan will be liberated for a short time and allowed to persecute the church. Bossuet rejected the idea that this was already happening.[19] Despite the certitude with which Bossuet identified historical events

---

11. Bossuet, *L'apocalypse*, 22–24.
12. Ibid., 25.
13. Ibid., 29–31.
14. Ibid., 39.
15. Ibid., 136–37.
16. Ibid., 150.
17. Ibid., 269; Didacus, *Enchiridion Scripturisticum*, 518.
18. Bossuet, *L'apocalypse*, 273.
19. Ibid., 358.

as being predicted by the biblical book, he explicitly warned about a mathematical "calculation" of the times mentioned in the book, because the numbers are "secret numbers" (*nombre mystique*), whose full meaning one cannot understand.[20] Bossuet's commentary was, of course, not only written to better understand Revelation, but also served a theological strategy—namely, to refute Protestant interpretations that identified the apocalyptic beast with the papacy.[21] Augustine Calmet OSB (1672-1757), Louis Dupin (1657-1719), and Jacques-Philippe Lallemant SJ (1660-1748) were also preterists, in Bossuet's sense.[22] Calmet, likewise, believed that the Antichrist would come as a real person, and that figures such as Antiochus and Nero only prefigured him. For the French Benedictine, he will be a religious and political leader who will wage real war.[23] The Jansenist Isaac-Louis de Sacy (1613-84) rejected a chiliast reading in his 1667 translation of Revelation.[24]

Quite different was the approach of fellow Jesuit Francisco Ribera (or Ribeira) (1537-91), who can be credited as the first prominent Catholic futurist with his commentary on Revelation of 1590. As a futurist, he argued that only a small portion of the book relates to the past, and the largest part to future events. The millennium of Revelation 20 is the time between Christ's death and the coming of the Antichrist. However, for Ribera, the saints will rule in heaven and not on earth. For Ribera, the Antichrist will be a real person, but unlike Salmeron, he did not see him as Muslim or in any way connected to Islam, but instead as a Jew. He would, therefore, be expected to rebuild the temple of Jerusalem. Unlike Frey, whose explanation we will encounter below,

---

20. Ibid., 206.
21. Noteworthy is that Bossuet ended his book with reflections about chiliasm, especially Protestant chiliasm, and renewed his belief in a spiritual reading of Rev. 20. Bossuet, *L'apocalypse*, 378-85.
22. Louis Ellies Dupin, *Analyse de l'apocalypse, contenant une nouvelle explication simple & littéraire de ce livre,: avec dissertations sur les millenaires, sur l'état des ames aprés la mort, sur le purgatoire, sur le jour du jugement, et sur d'autres matieres importantes de la religion* (Paris: 1714); Augustin Calmet, *Commentaire litteral sur tous les livres de l'Ancien et du Nouveau Testament*, vol. 8 (Paris: 1726); Jacques-Philippe Lallement, *Réflexions morales sur le Nouveau Testament*, vol. 12 (Paris: 1725).
23. Augustin Calmet, *Dictionarium Manuale Biblicum* (Augsburg: 1775), 1:77; cf. Newport, *Apocalypse and Millennium*, 73; Tiefenthal, *Die Apokalypse*, 58.
24. Isaac-Louis de Sacy, *Die heilige Schrift erkläret aus den heiligen Vätern ... des neuen Bundes zwölfter Band* (Augsburg: 1803).

Ribera did not regard the 1260 days in which the two witnesses of Revelation 11 (Elijah and Enoch) would prophesy as a mystical time frame, but as literally three and one-half years, during which the Antichrist would persecute the Christians.[25]

Ribera was also among the first who rejected reading into Revelation a mystical meaning (*mysticos quidem sensus non attingemus*), because such commentaries already existed. If he had written in the same manner, it would have meant "bringing wood into the forest" (*ligna in silvam ferre*). The historical meaning, however, which is most "obscure" and "neglected by all" (*obscurissimus & magna ex parte ab omnibus neglectus*) must be elucidated, he argued. Revelation should consequently be read like any other prophetic book, and as such the historical meaning—that is, the historical proof of what was foreseen—had to be established.[26] In his 1627 commentary, Cornelius a Lapide (1567–1637) followed the role model set by his fellow Jesuit, but remained quite cautious and critical of any immediate expectation of the end times. He rejected the preterism of Alcazar and thought the end of the world would come around the year 2000, but wisely added that nothing sure and definite could be said about this and rejected any mathematical computations, especially about the role of Islam in eschatological affairs.[27] Like Ribera and Frey, Lapide was convinced that Babylon in chapter 17 was not the Christian Rome of the present, but the pagan Rome of the future that had apostatized from the faith. According to his logic, at the appearance of the Antichrist, the Christian Roman Empire will cease to exist, and Rome will become a sea

---

25. For Ribera's account of the apocalypytic woman, see Ribera, *In sacram*, 236–37; on Apoc. 11 and computation, ibid., 118. Cf. the tendentious but learned account of Edwin LeRoy Froom, *The Prophetic Faith of Our Fathers: The Historical Development of Prophetic Interpretation* (Washington: Review & Herald, 1948), 2:484–505; Elliott, *Horae Apocalypticae*, 4:456.

26. Francisco Ribera, *In sacram beati Joannis Apostoli & Evangelistae Apocalypsin Commentarii* (Lyon: 1593), proemium, 3.

27. Jean-Robert Armogathe, "Per Annos Mille: Cornelius a Lapide and the Interpretation of Revelation 20:2–8," in *Millenarianism and Messianism in Early Modern Europe: Catholic Millenarianism: From Savonarola to the Abbe Gregoire*, ed. Karl A. Kottman (Dordrecht: Kluwer, 2001), 45–52. Armogathe calls Cornelius's stance a "mitigated millenarianism, urging the moral necessity of hastening one's conversion being conscious that the ages to come draw us nearer than ever to the end of the world" (ibid. 51). See also Roberto Osculati, "Hic Romae: Cornelio a Lapide commentator dell' Apocalisse al Collegio Romano," in *Storia e figure dell'Apocalisse fra '500 e '600*, ed. Roberto Rusconi, (Rome: Viella, 1994), 315–29.

of sin, tyranny, and vice. Yet, he also reported opinions, such as that of Aureolus, who understood the Babylon of Revelation to correspond to Islam, the beast to Egypt and its Turkish sultan, and that of Aretas and Capinsachius, who understood Babylon to stand for Turkish Constantinople.[28] Another reserved futurist was Jesuit Cardinal Robert Bellarmine (1542-1621), who believed, like Ribera, that the Antichrist was an individual Jew, and attacked the year–day principle that seemed to favor Protestant interpretations. Nevertheless, Bellarmine's main point, so it appears, was that if the Antichrist had reigned in the Catholic Church, one would expect a uniform date of the beginning of his reign among Protestant interpreters. Since such a unanimous consent was far from being established, he dismissed such interpretations as figments of imagination.[29]

While the commentary of the Flanders Carmelite Didacus a S. Antonio (1681-1763) admitted that the book contains many obscure prophecies that no one may ever clearly penetrate, it also stated that it is certainly (*clarissima*) a book that encourages patience and perseverance in persecution.[30] The Benedictine Gervasius Bulffer (1714-92) of Ettenheimmünster followed the idea of Didacus in his 1773 futurist commentary, although he does not mention him. In it, Bulffer rejected the notion that Revelation talks at all (!) about past events.[31] He provided a translation into the vernacular with a short commentary on each verse. Bulffer called Revelation the only "prophecy of the law of grace" (*einzige Weissagung des Gesetzes der Gnade*). According to Bulffer, there is no trace of a history of persecution in Revelation—instead, everything is about the future of the church and

---

28. Lapide, *Commentarius,* 196–97.
29. Bellarmine, "*Controversia de Summo Pontifice,*" book 3, ch. 3. 635–36 at Armogathe, "Interpretations," 190; Froom, *Prophetic Faith,* 2:497. There is also Bellarmine's view of John Damascene's interpretation of Mohammed as the Antichrist, see Newport, *Apocalypse and Millennium,* 73–76.
30. Didacus a S. Antonio, *Auctuarium Scripturistici* (Brussels: 1748), 4:414. Archives of the Order of the Discalced Carmelites of the Flemish Province in Belgium, *Series Superiorum et Religiosorum C.D.,* archive nr. B 0169. Letter of Jean-Pierre Debels of 15 October 2012. On the contemporaneous exegete Leonardus a S. Martino, see also Chr. de Backer, *Leonardus a S. Martino.* In *Nationaal Biografisch Woordenboek* (Brussel: Paleis der Academien 1977), 7:508–11.
31. Gervasius Bulffer, *Geheime Offenbarung, oder einzige Weissagung des neuen Testamentes* (Augsburg: 1773). Manuscripts of Bulffer can be found in the Badische Landesbibliothek Karlsruhe; see Karl Preisendanz, *Die Handschriften des Klosters Ettenheimmünster* (Karlsruhe: 1932), 48–52.

its battle with the Antichrist.[32] Consequently, Revelation is understood as an introduction to a theology of grace and a book of perpetual consolation.[33] More outspoken as futurist was Johann Hyacinth Kistemaker (1754–1834) of Münster. He was a propagator of the traditional reading of scripture and rejected the achievements of historical criticism. The fathers, and the fathers alone, were for him the authoritative interpreters of scripture. Bossuet was consequently rejected, and criticised for limiting Revelation almost entirely to the past.[34] Likewise, he discarded the interpretation of Johann Gottfried Eichhorn (1753–1827) and Leonhard Hug (1765–1846) that certain images had no other meaning than decoration (*Ausschmückung*), because he saw behind this move the danger of labelling a part of scripture a "mere product of human ingenuity."[35]

Among Catholic futurists of the eighteenth century, a growing number interpreted Revelation—certainly influenced by Protestant commentaries—as foretelling the downfall of the Church and the papacy around 1800. Drue Cressener (c. 1638–1718), an Anglican minister, identified the Catholic Church as the fourth apocalyptic beast (cf. Daniel 7; Rev. 13:5, 8) and the beginning of its 1,260-year reign with Justinian the Great, sometime in the sixth century. Consequently, a major blow to the papacy was expected to happen around 1800, and he seems to have been the first to argue for that position.[36] Accordingly, he stated:

> And then since the last Vial ends with the destruction of the Beast, this is a new confirmation of that which has been elsewhere advanced, viz. that the first appearance of the Beast was at Justinian's recovery of the Western Empire from which time to about the year 1800 will be about 1,260 years. . . . And that which remains for the ruin of the great City Babylon . . . is the conversion of all the Roman Church except a tenth part of it.[37]

---

32. Bulffer, *Geheime Offenbarung*, preface.
33. Ibid., 166–74.
34. Johann Hyacinth Kistemaker, *Sendschreiben der Apostel* (Münster: 1823), 2:478.
35. Kistemaker, *Sendschreiben*, 2:481.
36. Drue Cressener, *A Demonstration of the First Principles of the Protestant Applications of the Apocalypse* (London: 1690), VIII–IX; cf. Froom, *Prophetic Faith* 2:592.
37. Drue Cressener, *The Judgements of God Upon the Roman-Catholick Church, from Its First Rigid Laws for*

The Scottish preacher Robert Fleming (c. 1660–1716) followed in Cressener's footsteps. In 1701, Fleming produced a discourse on the rise and fall of the papacy, in which he sided with the prediction that a disastrous strike against the papacy would take place around 1800.[38] Much like Frey's work, Fleming's discourse found a broad audience at the time of the fulfillment of such prophecies, particularly in 1793 and 1848. William Lowth (1660–1732) estimated that the end of the reign of the beast would come in 1866, and likewise, predictions about the French Revolution of 1789 and the execution of Catholic kings were frequently uttered throughout the century, usually by Protestants.[39] In 1720, the Berlin preacher Johann Christian Seitz claimed that the Antichrist would appear in the 1720s, but slightly changed his view after 1735.[40]

An important yet continuously overlooked work of German apocalypticism, written by arguably one of the most esteemed theologians of the time, is the account of the Benedictine Prince Abbot Martin Gerbert (1720–93) of St. Blasien in the Black Forest. He was an erudite theologian, who not only corresponded with Protestant theologians, but even asked them for advice in interpreting scripture. The correspondence Gerbert maintained with the reformed minister Johann Jakob Hess in Zurich between 1783 and 1793, which also included personal visits by Hess to the abbey, reveals just that.[41] Gerbert's two volumes, *The Church Militant* (1789), even impressed

Universal Conformity to It, Unto Its Last End. . . . In Explication of the Trumpets and Vials of the Apocalypse, Upon Principles Generally Acknowledged by Protestant Interpreters, (London: 1689), 309.

38. Robert Fleming, *Discourses on Several Subjects. The First Containing a New Account of the Rise and Fall of the Papacy. The Second Upon God's Dwelling with Men. The Third Concerning the Ministerial Office. The Fourth Being a Brief Account of Religion As It Centres in the Lord Jesus Christ* (London: 1701); Froom, *Prophetic Faith* 2:642–43.

39. David S. Katz, "The Occult Bible: Hebraic Millenarianism in Eighteenth-Century England," in *The Millenarian Turn, Millenarian Contexts of Science, Politics and Everyday Anglo-American Life in the Seventeenth and Eighteenth Centuries*, ed. James E. Force and Richard H. Popkin (Dordrecht: Kluwer, 2001), 119–32; Froom, *Prophetic Faith*. 2:724.

40. Corrodi, *Critische Geschichte*, 3:122–25; Anonymous (i.e., Johann Christian Seitz), *Ausführlicher Beweis, daß I. die zween Apoc. XI gedachte Zeugen zwey einzelne Personen, II. daß solche Moses und Elias in Person seyen . . . : von J. C. S. Dienern der großen Gemeinde Ps. 40:10* (n.p.: 1721); Johann Christian Seitz, *Mathematischer, das ist himmelfester und sonnenclarer Beweiss, daß die 3 1/2 und 1260 Tage der Zeugen Apoc. 2 . . . natürliche Tage seyn* (n.p.:1735).See an overview of the treatment of Revelation in the German Enlightenment (limited to Protestant authors) in Gerhard Meier, *Die Johannesoffenbarung und die Kirche*, WUNT 25 (Tübingen: Mohr Siebeck, 1981), 448–83.

41. Arthur Allgeier, "Der Briefwechsel von J. J. Hess mit Martin Gerbert," *Zeitschrift für die Geschichte*

Cardinal Giuseppe Garampi (1725–92). It was through the cardinal that, in February 1790, Pope Pius VI received a copy of this work.[42] In *The Church Militant*,[43] he gave, like Walmsley, a counter-narrative of church history, of the persecution of Catholicism, the tribulations and successes over time, and demonstrates that the millennial reign of Christ is not a literal time span of 1,000 years, but the timely existence of the church on earth from the beginning to the second coming. For this view, he relied on Ribera.[44] In Gerbert's judgement, the rejection of the light of the church through radical Enlighteners, Febronianists, Jansensists, and Gallicans, and their "false" or "hellish" light, were clear indicators of the time in which Satan will be released (Rev. 20:7).[45] The Antichrist that he expected would be a singular person, a *"vero singulare monstrum hominis . . . diabolum incarnatum."*[46]

The reason why Revelation contains future references was believed to be, as Walmsley argued, to give

> a tolerable intelligence of transactions that will touch us so nearly and will be more terrible and trying to human nature than any that have ever happened. By a previous, though imperfect, knowledge of dreadful calamities, we are warned to prepare for them. An impending evil . . . is less alarming when foreseen and expected.[47]

What Frey offered, however, is not a simple Catholic futurism, but like Walmsley, a counter-historicism that viewed the book as partly fulfilled and partly about the future.

des Oberrheins 56 (1943): 504–49. Zentralbibliothek Zürich: FA Hess (1741) 181, Bd. 14–19 (17 letters).

42. Arthur Allgeier, "Martin Gerbert and Karl Theodor von Dalberg. Beiträge zu den Schlußkapiteln der Geschichte des Bistum Konstanz," *Freiburger Diözesanarchiv* 69 (1949): 66–91.

43. Martin Gerbert, *Ecclesia Militans*, 2 vols. (St. Blasien: 1789).

44. Gerbert, *Ecclesia Militans*, 1: ch. 9, 37–44.

45. Ibid., 2: ch. 62, 366; cf. vol. 1:111–17. For a telling description of the Enlightenment, see Martin Gerbert, *De Sublimi in Evangelio Christi*, vol. 3 (St. Blasien: 1793), 143: "Sed deteriora monstra aetas nostra tulit, quae necdum Bossuetus (ex quibus iam cerberus infernalis templum Dei, et sanctorum eius invasit) nata ad praeparanda antichristi tempora Voltaire, Helvetius, Rousseau, Diderot, Dalembert, Rainald etc."

46. Martin Gerbert, *Ecclesia militans regnum Christi in terries* (St. Blasien: 1789), 2:262.

47. Walmsley, *The General History*, 269. Walmsley distinguishes seven "ages" of church history, while only the sixth is the age of the church militant on earth (shorter reflections on pp. 525–32), and the seventh the "age" of eternity (532–33).

The Clandestine Futurist: Alphonsus Frey (1700–63)

Alphonsus Frey was born on December 3, 1700, in Nollenden, Swabia (Germany), entered the Benedictine Abbey of Ochsenhausen, and died there on August 13, 1763. Unfortunately, we do not know anything about his education or academic life, apart from the fact that he was professor of Oriental languages and exegesis in his monastery, and seems to have become intrigued by the book of Revelation in the 1760s. His unfinished ten-volume commentary on Revelation, as it seems his only book, circulated in many manuscripts throughout the Catholic south of Germany because it predicted with alleged accuracy the fate of the church until the second coming of Christ in 2014. Until at least 1803, this work stood in the abbey's library and could be consulted, but was lost soon afterwards.[48] A one-volume summary written in the 1780s survived, which Frey's student Bruno Bischoff (1739–92), also professor of Oriental languages in the same monastery, had crafted for easier use by students.[49] Only in 1822 and 1832 was Frey's work translated and published.[50] An extract from the "prophecies" of Frey, written by an eighteenth-century hand, is kept in the Staatsbibliothek Stuttgart. The monk's interpretation is far from applying historical-critical scholarship. Instead, Frey provided a good example of an eisegesis—of reading one's own expectations and ideas into the text—and is one of the few examples of a clandestine Catholic futurist, that is, of a secretly circulating manuscript which sees Revelation in great part as a futurist vision. For Frey, the end of the world was bound

48. Franz Xaver Christmann, *Roms unglückliche Sechser: Oder Beleuchtung des bekannten Verses "Semper sub sextis perdita Roma fuit"* (Constance: 1803), 164–67.
49. Leopold-Sophien Bibliothek Überlingen: Ms 14, *Synopsis septem sigillorum ac septem tubarum apokalypseos.* Bischoff is also the author of *Interpretatio sibi specietenus adversa complurium cum Animadversionibus in Librum Geneseos* (Ulm: 1772). On Bischoff, see Georg Geisenhof, *Kurze Geschichte des vormaligen Reichsstifts Ochsenhausen in Schwaben* (Ottobeuren: 1829), 203. Staatsbibliothek München: Clm 27057 (1,011 pages) contains only the first eight chapters of Frey's commentary and thus only the historical narrative, not the futurist prophecies. Ibid., Clm 27089 is identical with the manuscript in Überlingen.
50. Alphons Frey, *Erklärung der Offenbarung des hl. Johannes als prophetischer Schlüssel zu den Schicksalen der Kirche und der Staaten. Das ist: Fragmente und Ahnungen einer Universalhistorie der christkatholischen Kirche von der Sendung des heiligen Geistes bis zum Ende der Zeiten,* 2 vols. (Ulm: 1822; 2nd. ed., 1832). Since Frey's commentary begins with ch. 4 of Revelation, the interpretation of the first chapters was taken from works of Johann M. Sailer, while the missing chapters 12–20 were commented on by an anonymous contemporary. I excluded these later texts from my analysis.

to the Holy Roman Empire. Like Gerbert, who probably knew this text, the tendencies among German bishops to become independent from Rome were signs of a soon-to-happen apocalyptic catastrophe. The crisis of the German *Reichskirche* was, for him, the key to understanding world and salvation history. Frey's work is, therefore, also a good example of how biblical interpretation can be contextualized and abused for one's own politico-ecclesiastical worldview.

Frey divided Revelation into four parts. The first describes the context of the churches in Asia (chapters 1–3), the second (chapters 4–11) deals with the conferrals and withdrawals of God's grace over time, while the third part (chapters 12–14) describes the apocalyptic battle with the dragon and its persecutions, and the fourth part contains the way to heaven through the tribulations at the end of times (chapters 15–22). Unfortunately, only Frey's musings about the second part have survived. Bischoff mentioned that Frey also consulted the church fathers, Bossuet, Calmet, Didacus de S. Antonio OCD, Cornelius a Lapide SJ, and most importantly John Gerard Kerkherdere (1673–1738), a widely forgotten Habsburg historian, whose *Prodromus Danielicus* (1711) provided Frey with the computational means to calculate the time frame of Revelation.[51]

For Frey, the main question for interpreting Revelation was whether the prophecies of the book have already been fulfilled, as the historicists claimed, or whether most of them are yet to be fulfilled, as the futurists argued.[52] Frey attempted a somewhat conciliatory middle way by arguing with St. Jerome that even if a prophecy foretold an event of the past, it can still contain innumerable more prophecies for the future.[53] He saw his work as differing from other commentaries, because he dared to compute an exact and applicable timetable for this biblical book. Such historical dates were, for Frey, the hermeneutical

---

51. Johann Gerard Kerkherdere, *Prodromus Danielicus sive Novi Conatus Historici, Critici, in celeberrimas Difficultates Historiae Veteris Testameni, Monarchiarum Asiae &.* (Leuven: 1711).
52. Alphons Frey, *Erklärung der Offenbarung des hl. Johannes als prophetischer Schlüssel zu den Schicksalen der Kirche und der Staaten. Das ist: Fragmente und Ahnungen einer Universalhistorie der christkatholischen Kirche von der Sendung des heiligen Geistes bis zum Ende der Zeiten* (Kirchdorf: 1831), 1:iv.
53. Frey, *Erklärung*, 1:iv. Leopold-Sophien Bibliothek Überlingen: Ms 14, *Synopsis septem sigillorum ac septem tubarum apokalypseos*, fol. 3–4: "Apocalypsis est prophetica, infinita futurorum mysteria continens in quam si plurima fuerint dicta, plura semper dicenda restabunt."

key to understanding Revelation. Moreover, he was convinced that he was the first interpreter to give a reasonable explanation of who the first and second apocalyptic beasts are, and that he was the first to make a distinction between the final persecution and the Antichrist.[54]

The Seven Ages of the Church (Revelation 6–7)

In Frey's account, the sixth chapter of Revelation depicts the glory and misery of the church. The seven seals on the scroll correspond to special graces and to the seven ages of the church, as Joachim of Fiore had envisioned them. The first seal is a prefiguration of the primitive church (33–70 CE), the second one signifies the church battling paganism for 242 years between 70 and 312. The third age is the 277-year conflict with teachers of heresy between 312 and 589. The fourth identifies the roughly 165 years of protection of the church in the Roman Empire and the first attacks on her by "Saracens" and icon destroyers, between 587 and 754.[55] The fifth age is the time of transition of grace from the Eastern to the Western Roman Empire, from the Eastern Church to the Roman Church and comprises the time between 754 and 1314, 560 years. The sixth age is the time of apostasy, which according to Frey, began with John of Jandun (1285–1323),[56] Marsilius of Padua (1275–1343), John Wycliffe (1320–84), and Jan Hus (1369–1415), and consequently, lasts from 1314 to 1481—about 167 years. The seventh age is the time in which apostasy in the West increases, especially through the "heresies" of Martin Luther (1483–1546) and John Calvin (1509–64).[57]

Frey saw this historical narrative buttressed by the four apocalyptic riders and their horses in Revelation 6. The first horse is white and symbolizes the church, while the rider is the Holy Spirit, who with his weapons, bow and arrow, defeats his enemy, Judaism.[58] The red second

54. Frey, *Erklärung*, 1:v–vii.
55. Leopold-Sophien Bibliothek Überlingen: Ms 14, fol. 63.
56. Not in the Überlingen manuscript, only in the printed translation. See Frey, *Erklärung*, 1:61.
57. Frey, *Erklärung*, 1:60–61.
58. Ibid., 1:66. The crown the rider receives shows that the grace of God was transferred from Judaism to the Roman Empire. Frey, *Erklärung*, 1:67; Leopold-Sophien Bibliothek Überlingen: Ms 14, fol. 69.

horse, which destroys peace on earth, signifies paganism, which tries to eradicate the church, and its rider the Roman emperor.[59] The black third horse is ridden by Satan himself and symbolizes the attack on Christianity by heresy.[60] After the third seal is broken (Rev. 6:6), a voice among the animals complains about the price of corn and the request not to damage olive oil or wine, which Frey interpreted as the prayer of the church to preserve its teachings (wine) and doctrinal definitions (oil).[61] It was clear to the Benedictine that this prayer was heard, since the church battled successfully with many heresies between 312 and 589.[62] Frey dated the beginning of the end of the black horse to the launch of the persecution of heretics in the year 518 under Justinian the Great (482–565), and its culmination in 589. In the pale or green horse of Revelation 6:7–8 Frey saw the attempts of Satan to eliminate the church in the Roman Empire through Islam[63] and the iconoclastic emperors Leo Isauricus (714–41) and Constantine V Copronymus (741–75).[64] When the Eastern churches at the Council of Hieria (754) rejected icons and relics, they apostatized from the true faith and were subjected to the punishment of God in the form of Islamic persecution.[65] The name of the rider of the fourth horse, "death", is proof that one should see in him the symbol of the Saracene Caliphate [*Caliphatu Saracenorum*].[66] Since the Caliph's theology denies, like all Islamic theology, the triune God and all sacraments, which are the

---

59. Leopold-Sophien Bibliothek Überlingen: Ms 14, fol. 73–75.
60. Leopold-Sophien Bibliothek Überlingen: Ms 14, fol. 78: "Haeretici solam allegant scripturam ad instar judiciis in materia credendorum." The scale that Satan holds in his hand (Rev. 6:5) means that the heretics ponder God's words with reason alone and disregard the weight of doctrinal decisions. This interpretation of the scale was not new, as Cornelius a Lapide also used it, as Frey admits (Leopold-Sophien Bibliothek Überlingen: Ms 14, fol. 78. Cornelius a Lapide, *Commentarius in Apocalypsin Apostoli*, 2nd ed. (Venice: 1717), 92).
61. Frey, *Erklärung*, 1:75.
62. Leopold-Sophien Bibliothek Überlingen: Ms 14, fol. 81–83.
63. Leopold-Sophien Bibliothek Überlingen: Ms 14, fol. 86: "Apostasia a Christo per Mahoemdam introducitur." On Islam as the continuation of ancient Arianism see Frey, *Erklärung*, 1:87; Leopold-Sophien Bibliothek Überlingen: Ms 14, fol. 92. See the chart in Froom, *Prophetic Faith*, 2:530, 786–87, which shows that many early modern interpreters saw Islam as an apocalyptic enemy of Christianity.
64. With the introduction of Islamic doctrines and forced conversion (*violentiam armarum; armis cogeret*), Satan wanted to rob Christians of the knowledge of Christ and his true church. See Leopold-Sophien Bibliothek Überlingen: Ms 14, fol. 87. Frey, *Erklärung*, 1:82. Frey, *Erklärung*, 1:85.
65. Frey, *Erklärung*, 1:88; Leopold-Sophien Bibliothek Überlingen: Ms 14, fol. 93.
66. Leopold-Sophien Bibliothek Überlingen: Ms 14, fol. 97.

paths to salvation, Islam "is the religion of death" [consequente Mahomedismus est religio mortis].[67] Also, politically, the Caliph's government is connected to death as its dominion brought destruction to formerly prosperous areas, so that Frey stated that Islam is also, in this respect, a religion that "contributes to the destruction of the human race" [ad destructionem generis humani].[68]

Frey dated the beginning of the fifth seal to 754, when grace was withdrawn from Emperor Copronymus and transferred to the king of the Franks, Pippin (d. 768), and the final execution of the seal to 775, when Copronymus and Caliph Al-Mansur (714–75) die.[69] Since, according to the next verse, the saints receive a white garment and power (Rev. 6:10–11), Frey assumed that this indicated the beginning of the thousand-year reign of the saints on earth and the limitation of the full powers of Satan.[70] For Frey, the historical proof for his claim was that by 775, the most important enemies of the faith had been eliminated in Western Europe, and also around this time (768) Charlemagne assumed the throne as the new protector of Christianity.[71] The Spanish Reconquista obviously fits into Frey's historical outline, especially the 807 victory over the Saracen fleet and the victory at the battle of Clavijo in 844 "with the help of St. James."[72] Although in Frey's view, Islam continued to be a powerful force for several centuries, he saw its power broken by the year 1300.[73] Revelation 6:11 nevertheless mentions another wave of persecution during this time, which for the Benedictine would be executed again by the Ottomans.[74] This persecution, according to Revelation 13:42, lasts forty-two prophetic months, and since some months in the old calendars had only 29 days, these amount to 1,239 prophetic days,

67. Leopold-Sophien Bibliothek Überlingen: Ms 14, fol. 98.
68. Frey, Erklärung, 1:93; Leopold-Sophien Bibliothek Überlingen: Ms 14, fol. 99.
69. Frey, Erklärung, 1:105–6; Leopold-Sophien Bibliothek Überlingen: Ms 14, fol. 110–11. On the commonplace theory of a translatio imperii, see Werner Goez, Translatio imperii: ein Beitrag zur Geschichte des Geschichtsdenkens und der politischen Theorien im Mittelalter und in der frühen Neuzeit (Tübingen: Mohr, 1958).
70. Frey, Erklärung, 1:114; Leopold-Sophien Bibliothek Überlingen: Ms 14, fol. 122.
71. Frey, Erklärung, 1:119; Leopold-Sophien Bibliothek Überlingen: Ms 14, fol. 127.
72. Frey, Erklärung, 1:120; Leopold-Sophien Bibliothek Überlingen: Ms 14, fol. 130.
73. Ibid.
74. Frey, Erklärung, 1:133–34; Leopold-Sophien Bibliothek Überlingen: Ms 14, fol. 139–40.

which equal 1,239 years.[75] Consequently, this persecution that was to begin in 775 would continue until 2014.[76]

The earthquake, solar eclipse, red moon, and sixth seal described in Revelation 6:12 are, according to Frey, a prophecy about the fate of East and West. While the East declined more and more, the West was able to rise,[77] but was brought to a halt by Satan. The Benedictine dated the beginning of this age to about 1314, when Ludwig the Emperor (1282–1347), with the help of Marsilius of Padua and others, began to undermine papal authority, and when the Byzantine Empire allied with the Ottomans.[78] The sun that eclipses is, therefore, the papacy, because the popes receive the light of grace from Christ, but now the "shadow" of Wycliffites, Lutherans, and Calvinists, as well as anti-papists, overshadows their influence.[79] The red moon signifies the Roman Empire because, as the real moon receives its light from the sun, so the Roman Empire is enlightened by the papacy. Once the Roman Empire begins to shy away from a consequent defense of the papacy, it sinks into bloody battles and wars. This prophecy Frey saw fulfilled in the Hussite Wars in the West, and in the East by the persecution of Christians under the Ottomans.[80] Nevertheless, the apostasy and martyrdom of Christians in the East is compensated by gains for Christianity in the West, and in Asia and America.[81] Grace is more and more withdrawn from Europe (Rev. 6:14) and given to Spanish/Portuguese America (*ab Europa in Americam recedere incepit*).[82] As source for his knowledge about Christianity in Asia and America, the monk relied on Cornelius Hazart SJ (1617–90).[83]

---

75. Frey, *Erklärung,* 1:136.
76. Ibid., 137; Leopold-Sophien Bibliothek Überlingen: Ms 14, fol. 139–43.
77. Frey, *Erklärung,* 1:148–49.
78. Frey, *Erklärung,* 1:149–55; for Gregor XI, see Leopold-Sophien Bibliothek Überlingen: Ms 14, fol. 162–63.
79. Frey, *Erklärung,* 1:156; Leopold-Sophien Bibliothek Überlingen: Ms 14, fol. 164.
80. Frey, *Erklärung,* 1:160–61. Cf. Leopold-Sophien Bibliothek Überlingen: Ms 14, fol. 164.
81. Frey, *Erklärung,* 1:163; Leopold-Sophien Bibliothek Überlingen: Ms 14, fol. 164.
82. Leopold-Sophien Bibliothek Überlingen: Ms 14, fol. 173. The manuscript does not mention Hazart but the "communio historiographorum opinio".
83. Frey, *Erklärung,*1i: 163; Cornelius Hazart and Ulrich Dirrhaimer, *Kirchen-Geschicht der gantzen Welt absonderlich der vergangnen und nunmehr verflossnen zwey-hundert Jahren: in welchen enthalten wird die Gelegenheit der Landen Art und Manieren der Religion der Innwohnern,* 4 vols. (Vienna: 1678/84; Munich: 1701/02; 1725).

The seventh chapter of Revelation describes the good effects of penance, symbolized by the four angels who are commanded to stop the four winds, which resemble evil spirits and persecution.[84] Frey dated the beginning of this process of penance to around 1400, when St. Vincent Ferrer began to preach.[85] For Frey, the second angel in Revelation 7:2–3 was the guardian angel of the Holy Roman Empire that arises like the sun in the east, and because the sunrise signifies the papacy, it brings true faith. Frey saw such a resurgence of the guardian angel in the time of Emperor Sigismund (1368–1437), when he burned Jan Hus (1369–1415) at the stake in Constance and united the realm in resistance against the Ottomans.[86] Because of these sincere reform attempts, the church received (Rev. 8:1) "half an hour" of silence in heaven, which means a time of peace in the midst of the tribulation after the Council of Basel (1431). Alphonsus Frey dated this "break" to 1481, the year in which Mehmed II the Conqueror (1432–81) died, and when the ecclesiastical reforms seemed to bear first fruits.[87] This half an hour, however, is not to be taken literally, but signified, according to Frey, the span of a human life, approximately 35 or 36 years, so that the next tribulation must occur around 1517—the beginning of the Protestant Reformation.[88]

The Demise of the Church (Revelation 8)

When in chapter 8, the seven angels are given seven trumpets (Rev. 8:2), the seven punishments for sin and apostasy are indicated. The first trumpet is the sign that Europe is robbed of its faith; with the second, it is taken from America; with the third, the political order of the church is destroyed; with the fourth, the spiritual power of the church is diminished; with the fifth, the doctrine of the Antichrist rises to power; with the sixth, his dominion begins. The seventh trumpet,

---

84. Frey, *Erklärung*, 1:174;
85. Ibid., 175–76; Leopold-Sophien Bibliothek Überlingen: Ms 14, fol. 190.
86. Frey, *Erklärung*, 1:177; Leopold-Sophien Bibliothek Überlingen: Ms 14, fol. 191–92.
87. Frey, *Erklärung*, 1:180–81; Leopold-Sophien Bibliothek Überlingen: Ms 14, fol. 207–8.
88. Frey, *Erklärung*, 1:182; Leopold-Sophien Bibliothek Überlingen: Ms 14, fol. 212–13.

however, signifies judgement day and the destruction of the Antichrist.[89]

Europe is robbed of its faith because it had become unworthy of it. The guardian angel of America (Rev. 8:3) therefore implores God to receive this grace instead, around 1490.[90] The fire that this angel brings to earth is the spirit of evangelization (*viri Apostolici inflammati*) that had died in Europe with Luther, Beza, Calvin, and Zwingli, and was reignited by Sts. Ignatius of Loyola, Francis Xavier, Francis de Sales, Charles Borromeo, Theresa of Avila, and Maria Magdalena de Pazzi.[91] "There were peals of thunder, rumblings, flashes of lightning"—the conversion of America and India brought about major signs and major effects of grace (Rev. 8:5):

> What is similar between a conversion and an earthquake is that dry land becomes in both instances a lake, mountainous land plain, and very much in the same sense the spreading of the Gospels has transformed America. Pagan America has been transformed into a fruitful region, which—after accepting the yoke of Christ—bears the fruits of penance and holiness.[92]

When in chapter 8, verse 6, the angels "prepare" to blow the trumpets, this was, for Frey, the last admonition to do penance. He dated this event between 1500 and 1501.[93] The first trumpet, which results in "hail and fire mixed with blood" (Rev. 8:7) points to the apostasy of the Reformation [*falsissima Lutheri dogmata*].[94] After hail and fire, one-third of the land is burned (Rev. 8:7), which, for Frey, equaled the loss of about one-third of Europe to the churches of the Reformation.[95] At the outbreak of the Reformation, one "could hear" the sound of the first trumpet, which lasted until 1648, or about 131 years.[96]

---

89. Leopold-Sophien Bibliothek Überlingen: Ms 14, fol. 217.
90. Frey, *Erklärung,* i: 184–85; Leopold-Sophien Bibliothek Überlingen: Ms 14, fol. 218–20 with a detailed account.
91. Frey, *Erklärung,* i: 187.
92. Leopold-Sophien Bibliothek Überlingen: Ms 14, fol. 224: "America enim arido paganismi superstitioni priori addicta, in terram valde fructissimam conversa fuit . . ." cf. Frey, *Erklärung,* 1:188–89.
93. Frey, *Erklärung,* 1:190.
94. Leopold-Sophien Bibliothek Überlingen: Ms 14, fol. 226.
95. Leopold-Sophien Bibliothek Überlingen: Ms 14, fol. 227–29.
96. Frey, *Erklärung,* 1:206.

With the second trumpet, the grace of faith is taken from India and America.[97] After the sounding of the second trumpet, a huge mountain falls burning into the sea (Rev. 8:8). While the mountain symbolizes great power, the fire symbolizes heresy. "The meaning must be the following: A power, stained by error, has come into the sea and has gained control over it. As a consequence, 'a third of the creatures of the sea died.'"[98] For Frey, this loss of life symbolized the loss of the true faith, and the powers that reign over the sea are England and the Netherlands, both Protestant powers.[99] The reason why God would withdraw his grace from the American Indians, however, was because the Spanish and Portuguese—whom God had sent with the purpose of spreading the Gospel—did *not* act righteously. The colonial powers were not driven by a desire to save the Indians spiritually, namely, to "free them from the servitude of the devil and to offer them the freedom of becoming children of God" [*a servitute demonis liberare ac in libertatem filiorum Dei afferre*], but by a burning desire for gold [*auro et avaritio sordide*]. They imposed on the native population an almost unbearable burden [*jugum vix tolerabile*]. They did not set a good example, but were instead cruel and scandalous in their behavior [*crudelitate graviter offenderunt . . . scandali permoti*].[100] The defeat of the Spanish Armada, the first sounding of the second trumpet, was God's punishment for Spain's sins and its reluctance to do penance.[101]

With the third trumpet, "a large star burning like a torch fell from the sky. It fell on a third of the rivers and on the springs of water" (Rev. 8:10). The sounding is, again, a divine judgement, this time over the worldly power of the Roman emperors and it occurs in 1700. The only reason why God had continuously saved the Holy Roman Empire was because it did not entirely defect from the Catholic faith. Habsburg's "*pietas austriaca*" had saved the empire.[102] The star that falls is, first

---

97. Frey, *Erklärung*, 1:211; Leopold-Sophien Bibliothek Überlingen: Ms 14, fol. 233 has instead of India America.
98. Frey, *Erklärung*, 1:212.
99. Leopold-Sophien Bibliothek Überlingen: Ms 14, fol. 235–36.
100. Leopold-Sophien Bibliothek Überlingen: Ms 14, fol. 236–37.
101. Frey, *Erklärung*, 1:216.
102. Ibid., 219–25; Leopold-Sophien Bibliothek Überlingen: Ms 14, fol. 240–47. For the concept "pietas Austriaca" see Anna Coreth, *Pietas Austriaca* [1959] (West Lafayette: Purdue Univ. Press, 2004).

and foremost, Spain, thought Frey, with the death of the last Spanish Habsburg heirs, Charles II (1661–1700), in 1700.[103] That people die from the bitterness of the water signified, for Frey, the series of wars of succession that followed the death of Charles II.[104] After the sounding of the fourth trumpet, "a third of the sun, a third of the moon, and a third of the stars were struck, so that a third of them became dark. The day lost its light for a third of the time, as did the night" (Rev. 8:12). This indicated for the Benedictine a diminishing of the church's power [potestas ecclesiastica decrescere incipit], which he identified with the peace negotiations between Habsburg and Prussia during the first Silesian Wars (1740ff), in which Prussia desired a secularization of church property. "Catholics resisted it, but many lukewarm Christians desired it. The Protestants will not cease to enforce it, and it will be the punishment of our sins."[105] The third part that falls into darkness is the German Reichskirche:[106]

> The meaning of this sacred text is therefore as follows: a decree of secularisation will be issued and immediately a third of the papal Church will be suppressed with all its clergy, and bishops in the Holy Roman Empire.... However, how will this suppression be executed with the help of such a secularisation decree? After the promulgation of this decree all spiritual goods will be forfeited, including the dioceses and ecclesiastical principalities, the sovereignty and landownership of the monasteries will be taken away and the clergy will only have left meagre pensions.[107]

The sun, which symbolizes the light of Christ, becomes dark because the preaching of the Gospels and the celebration of the sacraments will face serious obstacles.[108] All this will happen around 1775, because this

---

103. Frey, Erklärung, 1:230.
104. Ibid., 232.
105. Ibid., 235; Leopold-Sophien Bibliothek Überlingen: Ms 14, fol. 249–50.
106. Didacus interprets this verse as a description of future persecution and confusion brought about by Judaism, which introduces a wrong understanding of scripture for a false Messiah. Didacus, Enchiridion, 475.
107. Frey, Erklärung, 1:234–35; cf. Leopold-Sophien Bibliothek Überlingen: Ms 14, fol. 252–53. Staatsbibliothek Stuttgart: Cod. Don. 435, p. 4: "Tunc enim in Imperio Romano Ecclesiae romano catholicae regimen abrogabitur: episcpatus omnes secularizabuntur: Parochi catholici a suis Parochiis amovebantur: Religiosi ordines dissolventur, et haec omnia in odium et destructionem fidei animarum detrimentum et exitium sempiternum."
108. Frey, Erklärung, 1:237; cf. Staatsbibliothek Stuttgart: Cod. Don. 435, p. 4–5: "Hinc lux fidei, et claritas Christianae virtutis jam hoc tempore magnam patitur Eclipsin, peccatis nostris...."

is the year in which the dragon that was captive will be set loose after his thousand-year-long captivity (Rev. 20).[109] It is noteworthy that Frey predicted this correctly, as many European monasteries—in the Holy Roman Empire, almost all (after 1802)—and other Church institutions such as ecclesiastically run universities, were dissolved in a process called "secularization" between 1773 (papal suppression of the Jesuits) and 1803.

The Anti-Catholic Emperor and the Pseudo-Pope (Revelation 9)

Alphons Frey's exegesis then brought him to his own time. Consequently, he could no longer look into history for proof of his reading of Revelation. Regarding Revelation 9, he therefore reflected first on the methodological question of how he could properly interpret this chapter, since it pertained to future events. After all, 2 Peter 1:20 admonishes that no prophecy could be interpreted according to one's own whim alone, and no historical facts could be used to buttress his claims.[110] Consequently, he regarded his interpretation of Revelation 9ff as mere "Muthmaßungen" (assumptions), rather than "truths."[111]

After the fifth angel blows the fifth trumpet, a star falls from Heaven and the key to the abyss is handed over to this star (Rev. 9:1). The first sound of this trumpet would be heard, according to Frey, around 1800. It would signal the end of the Catholic Holy Roman Empire, the

---

109. A detailed discussion of the apocalyptic schedule with the biblical citations as references is given in Frey, *Erklärung*, 2:91–103; Leopold-Sophien Bibliothek Überlingen: Ms 14, fol. 315–28. Leopold-Sophien Bibliothek Überlingen: Ms 14, fol. 253 on the millenarian expectation and the computation of 1775.

110. Second Peter 1:20–21: "Know this first of all, that there is no prophecy of scripture that is a matter of personal interpretation, for no prophecy ever came through human will; but rather human beings moved by the Holy Spirit spoke under the influence of God."

111. Frey, *Erklärung*, 2:2. An extract of the original Frey manuscript from the Ducal Library of Donaueschingen contains parts of his interpretation of ch. 9 of *Apoc*. It was written, most likely copied for the monks of his monastery, before 1800 since the introduction refers explicitly to "our future". Staatsbibliothek Stutgart: Don 435, entitled: "Extractus ex Manuscripto exegetico R. P. Alphonsi Frey Benedictini Ochenhusani de Secundo Christi Adventu." The cover is entitled "Prophetia . . . Alphonsi Frey". This account demonstrates that the later translation and summary manuscript have not been altered in order to vindicate Frey. This pre-1800 account confirms Frey's belief that around 1800, a great distress would affect the church. Staatsbibliothek München: Clm 27057 (1,011 pages) contains only the first eight chapters of Frey's commentary and thus only the historical narrative, not the futurist prophecies.

beginning of an anti-Catholic empire and a pseudo-papacy (*Imperium Acatholicum et Pseudo-Papatus*).[112] The apocalyptic "star" is a *"homo terrenus,"* a man of the earth, who will neither care for religion nor hope for eternal bliss, but see his ultimate goal solely in worldly success. The imperial crown[113] will be transferred to him after the death of the last proper Habsburg heir around 1832.[114] This man will be given the key to the abyss (Rev. 9:1) and he will be permitted to use his power against the papal See and set up a pseudo-papacy.[115]

The abyss was, for Frey, an image for the apostasy from the true faith through the Qur'an and Talmud.[116] The key the worldly person received is the intellect

> ... or the science to explain the Qur'an. ... This godless emperor will be an apostate Muslim (*Memeluck*) . . . and he will focus all his thoughts to motivate his entire realm to apostasy as well. He will attempt to do this with ... at first sight reasonable arguments from the Qur'an, Talmud and other Jewish writings.[117]

The decrees of the new anti-Catholic emperor are identified as "smoke" (Rev. 9:2), since they are natural signs of an emerging new religion (*secta*), of a rapidly spreading fire.[118] Among the new beliefs

112. Leopold-Sophien Bibliothek Überlingen: Ms 14, fol. 260. For Walmsley, *The General History*, 197, the man who opens the bottomless pit is Martin Luther: "Luther therefore opened the door to Hell, and there issued out a thick Smoke. . . . What can this thick smoke be but a strong Spirit of Seduction, which had been hatched in Hell. . . ."
113. Leopold-Sophien Bibliothek Überlingen: Ms 14, fol. 261.
114. Staatsbibliothek Stutgart: Don 435, p. 2: "Terra est homo terrena diligens, corde terrae, non coelo affixus, Deum, veraque religionem non curans, spem omnem beatitudinis abjicens, ultimum suum finem in terrenis ac temporalibus solummodo ponens: verbo homo haereticus, vel apostata, adeo ut sensus hujus versus sit: quod corona imperialis transferatur in Principem acatholicum, mortuo nimirum ultimo Imperatore, salten e sanguine materno a Rudolpho I Habsburgico descendente quod juxta opinionem auctoris eveniet circa annum Christi 1832." Franz II (1768–1835) died in 1835; however, he had abdicated the Imperial crown already in 1806. "Ein Mensch . . . der alle Begierden an die Erde, an das Irdische heftet, der sich um Gott, um die wahre Religion nichts bekümmert, sein ewiges Heil nicht suchet, und sein letztes Ziel ins Gegenwärtige setzet" (Frey, *Erklärung*, ii: 3). Leopold-Sophien Bibliothek Überlingen: Ms 14, fol. 261: ". . . seu devolvetur in principem acatholicum, qui religionem et ea quo sunt Dei, aspernabitur, et ea, quo sunt mundi nimium sectabitur."
115. That the translator of the 1822/31 edition identified this "homo terrenus" in a footnote with Napoleon I (1769–1821), and the described attacks on the church by Napoleonic church policy, including the imprisonment of Pope Pius VI (1775–99) and Pius VII (1800–23), cannot surprise.
116. Frey, *Erklärung*, 2:3–4; Leopold-Sophien Bibliothek Überlingen: Ms 14, fol. 262.
117. Frey, *Erklärung*, 2:4–5. Not in the Überlingen manuscript.
118. Leopold-Sophien Bibliothek Überlingen: Ms 14, fol. 263: ". . . id est permissa credendi ac scribendi libertate ex eodem Pseudo-Papatu obscura fidei dogmata prodibunt. . . ."

of this new religion would probably be that: (1) Jesus was not divine; (2) all visible ecclesiastical power should be abolished; (3) all spiritual power should be taken from the church—as a consequence, church holidays will cease to exist, and the invocation of the saints will be stopped; and (4) instead of Christianity, a new cult will be erected (*falsam et pestiferam sectam substituerunt*),[119] which will be a syncretism of Judaism, Islam, and heresy (*Mohametismus et haeresis conjungentur et in unum coalescent*).[120] The universal persecution of Catholicism and the establishment of this new cult would begin around 1800 and continue until 1980. Then, in 1980, the Antichrist would manifest himself through false dogmas and demonic miracles.[121]

This persecution, which would begin around 1832, would be similar to the persecution of the Israelites by the Egyptians, and the five months it lasts (Rev. 9:10) should be understood as 147.5 years, since each month corresponds to a series of 29 months.[122] The priests of this new religion are compared to locusts with the power of scorpions (Rev. 9:7).[123] That these are wearing crowns indicated to Frey that the new religion would find state support, and their humanlike appearance meant that they would appear to be rational and prudent (*prudentia ponderare videbuntur*).[124] According to Revelation 9:8, the clergymen of this new religion will have hair "like women's hair," which indicates their effeminate characteristics (*molles ac effeminati*) and their false doctrine.[125] This persecution will almost extinguish the church,

119. Leopold-Sophien Bibliothek Überlingen: Ms 14, fol. 264.
120. Staatsbibliothek Stuttgart: Cod. Don. 435, p. 5. Cf. Frey, *Erklärung*, 2:8; Staatsbibliothek Stuttgart: Cod. Don. 435, p. 2–3: "Perversissima Dogmata: 1.) Christum non esse Deum, quoniam multi seductores exierunt in mundum, qui non confitentur Jesum Christum venisse in carne. Hic est seductor et Antichristus 2 Joann.: hi seductores sunt praecursores Antichristi; et Papatus iste per antonomasiam est bestia secunda apoc. 13:7 descripta. 2.) Mariam non esse Matrem Dei. 3.) Invocationem SStorum prodesse hominibus non posse. 4.) Nullam inesse summo pontifici, episcopis, ceterisque rectoribus ecclesiae potestatem. 5.) Neque Christum pollere postetate invisibile ad regendam, neque sanctos ad protegendam ecclesia." The fundamental beliefs of the pseudo-patriarch who perverts the fundamental Catholic dogmas are according to Frey: "1. qua Abaddon tollet Sacram Scripturam. 2. qua Apollion Symbolum nicaenum. 3. qua exterminans jus canonicum et omnes constitutiones ecclesiasticas, durabitque hoc ab anno Christi 1832 1/2 usque ad A. 1980. toto hoc tempore patietur Ecclesia persecutionem grandem illam, quam Christus praedixit Math 24:21. . ."
121. Staatsbibliothek Stuttgart: Cod. Don. 435, p. 6.
122. Frey, *Erklärung*, 2:12. Leopold-Sophien Bibliothek Überlingen: Ms 14, fol. 266.
123. Leopold-Sophien Bibliothek Überlingen: Ms 14, fol. 266; Staatsbibliothek Stuttgart: Cod. Don. 435.
124. Frey, *Erklärung*, 2:14–15. Cf. Leopold-Sophien Bibliothek Überlingen: Ms 14, fol. 268.

wherefore its leader, Apollyon, can be called the exterminator (Rev. 9:10) or the new Lucifer or "Afterpapst."[126]

With the sound of the sixth trumpet (Rev. 9:13–14), it becomes clear that the West has accepted this new religion. This trumpet announces the coming of the Antichrist: "Then the sixth angel blew his trumpet, and I heard a voice coming from the [four] horns of the gold altar before God, telling the sixth angel who held the trumpet, 'Release the four angels who are bound at the banks of the great river Euphrates.'" The gold altar was, for Alphonsus Frey, the church, insofar as it is the true church; the four horns, the four ways of worshipping—namely, adoration (*latreuticum*), thanksgiving (*eucharisticum*), prayer for the satisfaction of sin and punishment (*satisfactorium*), and petitionary prayer for future benefits (*impetratorium*). From these four, the altar receives a fourfold voice which requests judgement from God over the West, which has abandoned the church.[127] The Euphrates symbolizes the Holy Roman Empire, while the four angels that are bound (Rev. 9:14) signify the four devils (*mali angeli*) that destroyed Rome between 400 and 476.[128] As long as the empire was worthy of the angels' protection, they were bound. But now, the voice from the altar, the voice of the church, is heard, which cries for help because the empire has adopted a heresy after the sounding of the fifth trumpet. The release of the angels must mean the "sentence of excommunication for the Emperor," thought Frey. "These four devils will bring unrest to the empire . . . the emperor will not usurp this or that right of the church but he will attempt to suppress ecclesiastical power, the papal state and the city of Rome."[129] The punishment for this will be the suppression of the Holy Roman Empire (*ruina Romani imperii*).[130]

The three apocalyptic riders that carry out the persecution of the

---

125. Frey, *Erklärung*, 2:16. Cf. Leopold-Sophien Bibliothek Überlingen: Ms 14, fol. 269.
126. Leopold-Sophien Bibliothek Überlingen: Ms 14, fol. 271; Staatsbibliothek Stuttgart: Cod. Don. 435, p. 4. Frey, *Erklärung*, 2:19.
127. Frey, *Erklärung*, 2:21–23; Leopold-Sophien Bibliothek Überlingen: Ms 14, fol. 274–76; ibid. "Quatuor sacrificandi ritus in Ecclesia receptos designant, videlicet sacrificium Latreuticum, Eucharisticum, Satisfactiorium, & impetratorium."
128. Frey, *Erklärung*, 2:23, 42; Leopold-Sophien Bibliothek Überlingen: Ms 14, fol. 277.
129. Frey, *Erklärung*, 2:45.
130. Leopold-Sophien Bibliothek Überlingen: Ms 14, fol. 279.

faithful (Rev. 9:17) are the forces that had continuously attacked the church—namely, paganism, Judaism, and Islam.[131] Unlike the persecutors of the past, the future ones will not be content with Christians rejecting their beliefs, but only with their complete destruction.[132]

The Return of Enoch and Elijah and the Arrival of the Antichrist in 1980 (Revelation 11–13)

"Then I saw another mighty angel come down from heaven wrapped in a cloud, with a halo around his head; his face was like the sun and his feet were like pillars of fire" (Rev. 10:1). This angel is not a real, but a moral angel [angelum mysticum],[133] because he signifies more than one person. Instead, according to Alphonsus Frey, he signifies the remaining faithful clergymen, because after the destruction of the empire, the Antichrist will sit in God's temple and demand worship.[134] The small scroll the angel holds (v. 2) contains the message of the second coming of Christ; his two feet are Elijah and Enoch, who give the convocation of clergy prophetic power.[135] For 1,260 days, each day representing a year, the prophets will preach repentance (Rev. 11:3) in the spirit of Enoch and Elijah.[136] Yet, by "2014 the church will be banished, proscribed and practically eliminated from the empire," while the Eastern Christians are subdued by the "yoke of Mohammedanism."[137]

The reason for the computation of 1980 can be found in Revelation 13. It gives a description of the two apocalyptic beasts. The first has seven heads, of which one is wounded, but healed. The wound was the attack by Islam, but it healed because the Ottoman Empire recovered from the Crusades. Of the second animal, the text says that it had two horns like the lamb, but it talked like a dragon. For Frey, this animal

---

131. Leopold-Sophien Bibliothek Überlingen: Ms 14, fol. 280.
132. Frey, Erklärung, 2:55.
133. Leopold-Sophien Bibliothek Überlingen: Ms 14, fol. 290.
134. Frey, Erklärung, 2:68.
135. Leopold-Sophien Bibliothek Überlingen: Ms 14, fol. 292. Frey, Erklärung, 2:71–72.
136. Leopold-Sophien Bibliothek Überlingen: Ms 14, fol. 306.
137. Leopold-Sophien Bibliothek Überlingen: Ms 14, fol. 305.

represented current heresies. While the first animal had the number 42, this one had the number 666. The first one is Magog, the second Gog. The first signifies unbelief, the second heresy. Nevertheless, neither of these two animals can be called the Antichrist, because the devil will call the two together, so that "the Antichrist will do miracles and appear to prove that he is the true Messiah."[138] He will manifest himself after the second animal has done its work for 666 years. If one assumes its beginnings in 1314, the reign of Ludwig the Emperor, then one arrives at the year 1980.[139] Frey showed that the word "Ludovicus" either in German or in Latin numbers, always equals 666.[140] In 1980, both beasts will be forged into one, with the appearance of the Antichrist.[141]

The returned prophets Enoch and Elijah will be killed by him after preaching repentance for 33 years, consequently in 2013. For Frey, their murder will indicate the destruction of sacred Rome, most likely by the Ottoman Empire.[142] After three and a half days of happiness for the murderers, the prophets will rise again and be assumed into heaven (Rev. 11:11–12). At this moment, an earthquake will shake the city, destroy it and kill 7,000. This event marks the liberation of the faithful (Rev. 11:13). All this Frey seemed to understand literally.[143] Then, after 33.5 years of domination by the Antichrist, he is destroyed in 2014.[144] The seventh trumpet follows, with which Christ's kingship is restored. After God had given the East 700 years' time in which to repent (753–1453), and similarly the West (1314–2014), his universal kingship comes to Earth.[145] The *church militant* will be united with the *church triumphant* and her enemies will be destroyed. This union will take place, according to Daniel 12:11–12, forty-five years after the defeat of the Antichrist—in Frey's opinion, in 2059 (Rev. 11:14).[146] Only

---

138. Frey, *Erklärung,* 2:108.

139. Ibid., 2:110; Leopold-Sophien Bibliothek Überlingen: Ms 14, fol. 331–32.

140. Frey, *Erklärung,* 2:111. Andreas Helwich (c. 1572–1643) has calculated that some papal titles such as "vicarius filii dei" also equal 666 (see Froom, *Prophetic Faith,* vol. 2, 605–8).

141. Frey, *Erklärung,* 2:120.

142. Ibid., 2:117; Leopold-Sophien Bibliothek Überlingen: Ms 14, fol. 334–35.

143. Frey, *Erklärung,* 2:118; Leopold-Sophien Bibliothek Überlingen: Ms 14, fol. 337.

144. Staatsbibliothek Stuttgart: Cod. Don. 435, p. 7.

145. Frey, *Erklärung,* 2:120.

then will fire fall from heaven, consume the earth and signal the last judgement, which is followed by the creation of a new heaven and a new earth (Rev. 21).[147] Yet, about the date of the new creation and the resurrection of the flesh, nothing certain is revealed.[148]

Conclusion: The Enlightenment as Enemy?

Frey was not the only one who saw in the eighteenth century, and especially the Enlightenment, a time of decline of Christianity, and possibly the end of all times. The French clergyman Remy Pothier (1727–1812) published his apocalyptic account for the first time in 1773, with the result that it was immediately forbidden by state censorship, because it was so offensive.[149] Also, Pothier believed that the Roman Empire would end in 1800, and that the reign of the Antichrist would follow around 1880, after the fall of the Ottoman Empire in 1873.[150] Anti-Enlightenment forces translated the book into Latin in 1797, and into German in 1798.[151] Also, Bishop Marc Antoine Noé (1724–1802) expected the progress of impiety and de-Christianisation, and had prepared a speech for the National Assembly of the French clergy in 1785, later published as his *Discours sur l'état futur de l'Église* in 1788. He had based his text on Revelation and predicted a future of persecution and terror for faithful Catholics.

Noé's contemporary Claude Fauchet (1744–93) believed quite the opposite, and his 1788 reading of Revelation expected positive progressive changes.[152] Fauchet's analysis was not unique, as Catholic

146. Frey, *Erklärung*, 2:127; Leopold-Sophien Bibliothek Überlingen: Ms 14, fol. 348. Staatsbibliothek Stuttgart: Cod. Don. 435, p. 6.
147. Frey, *Erklärung*, 2:128; Staatsbibliothek Stuttgart: Cod. Don. 435, p. 8.
148. Frey, *Erklärung*, 2:134; Staatsbibliothek Stuttgart: Cod. Don. 435, p. 9.
149. Remy Pothier, *Ouvrage sur l'apocalypse par un prêtre François* (Cologne: 1776). The endorsement letter of Pius VI, ibid., as unpaginated appendix. Bart Van der Herten, *Het begin van het einde. Eschatologische interpretaties van de Franse revolutie* (Leuven: Leuven University Press, 1994), 78–81. *Revue de Champagne et de Brie 7* (1895): 674; *Dictionnaire de Bibliographie Catholique* (Paris: 1838), 1:237.
150. Pothier, *Die Offenbarung*, 46.
151. Remy Pothier, *Die Offenbarung des heiligen Johannes. Der prophetische Schlüssel zu den Schicksalen der Kirchen, und der Staaten bis ans Ende der Zeiten* (Augsburg: 1798). German translation of Remy Pothier, *Compendium Operis in Apocalypsin, ex quo habetur prophetiae intelligentia* (Augsburg: 1797). See the critical remarks of Sandbichler about this approach in *Oberdeutsche allgemeine Literaturzeitung* CIX (September 14, 1801), 509.
152. Marc Antoine Noé, *Discours sur l'état futur de l'Église* (n.p. 1788); Claude Fauchet, *De la religion*

theologians, who were open to the changes of the Enlightenment, including the achievements of historical criticism, increasingly read Revelation as a historical document containing a document of consolation for the early Christians, and gave up the notion of an apocalyptic battle with the alleged arch enemy of faith, the Enlightenment.[153] Computational attempts as to when the world would end were given up, and allegorical readings of the text discontinued. However, a few Catholic theologians attempted to bridge theological exegesis as it was done by the fathers and modern historical criticism, the Augustinian Aloysius Sandbichler (1751–1820) being the most prominent. Realizing a "flattening" of Revelation, and inspired by the work of the Reformed theologian Johann Jakob Hess (1741–1828), he conceived an "enlightened" salvation history, which could be reconciled with a new millenarian perspective. It is through Sandbichler that the Catholic Tübingen school received the impetus to develop a new "salvation history"—and so, reading Revelation becomes, indeed, a key to understanding the formation of modern Catholic theology.[154]

nationale (Paris: 1789), ch. 4; R. Hermon-Belot, "God's Will in History: The Abbe Gregoire, the Revolution and the Jews," in *Millenarianism and Messianism in Early Modern Europe: Catholic Millenarianism* (Dordrecht: Kluwer, 2001), 91–100.

153. Johann Babor, *Uebersetzung des Neuen Testaments mit erklärenden Anmerkungen* (Vienna: 1805), 3:65; Benedict Feilmoser, *Einleitung in die Bücher des Neuen Bundes (1810)*, 2nd. ed. (Tübingen: 1830), 565.
154. See the chapter on Johann Jakob Hess in this volume.

12

Apocalypse, Enlightenment, and the Beginning of Salvation History: The Ecumenical Friendship of J. J. Hess and A. Sandbichler

Reading and interpreting the book of Revelation has been one of the most controversial tasks in Catholic exegesis after the Council of Trent. While most followed the preterist interpretation of Jacques-Bénigne Bossuet (1627–1704)[1] and saw in the biblical book predominantly a history of ancient times—in particular, of the persecution and the final victory of the church—some remained convinced that it contained mostly information about the future state of the church. This future could, argued the futurists, be deduced from the text and a timetable of events constructed.[2]

1. Jacques-Bénigne Bossuet, *L'apocalypse avec une explication* (Paris: 1689). For an introduction, see Jean-Robert Armogathe, "Interpretations of the Revelation of John: 1500–1800," in *Encyclopedia of Apocalypticism*, 2:185–203. For Catholic futurists, the chapter "Apocalypse 2014" in this volume.
2. See, for example, Francisco Ribeira, *In sacram beati Joannis Apostoli & Evangelistae Apocalypsin Commentarii* (Lyon: 1593).

In the eighteenth century, interpretations changed dramatically. Futurism receded almost entirely and only made a comeback after the reign of terror during the French Revolution. Preterist interpretations were now preferred, and many exegetes attempted to build on the insights of Bossuet and improve his historical commentary. Yet, some Catholic thinkers, who due to the increased quality of biblical scholarship during the eighteenth century became weary of simplistic preterist or futurist readings of Revelation, began to wonder whether a sound middle way between futurism and preterism existed—one that did justice to the theology of the book. In the German-speaking lands, the most prominent theologian of such a new approach that led to the introduction of "salvation history" into Catholic theology was the Salzburg Augustinian Aloysius Sandbichler (1751–1820). In this chapter, I want to discuss how Sandbichler developed this new view through the mediation of his Reformed friend Johann Jakob Hess (1741–1828). Compared to other enlightened Catholics, many of whom have garnered fame for their exegesis (such as Hug, Feilmoser, etc.), Sandbichler emerges as the only theologian who developed a systematic salvation history in order to prevent a rationalist flattening of the Book of Revelation.

Catholic Enlighteners and the Book of Revelation

During the eighteenth century, Catholic theologians all over Europe began a constructive dialogue with the Enlightenment process and developed new paradigms for theological reflection. Their attempts to make Catholic doctrine intelligible to their culture and defend it against radical attacks can be described as "Catholic Enlightenment." The spectrum of Catholic Enlighteners was considerable. One could indeed find thinkers who argued against marriage as a sacrament or for the abolition of the hierarchy, yet most intended a reform of the theological disciplines with, rather than against, the church. In the last quarter of the eighteenth century, Catholics in biblical studies especially began to find intellectual orientation in the historical criticism of their Protestant peers. In order to understand

Sandbichler's middle way, it is necessary to look at the main proponents of such an enlightened Catholic exegetical approach. They all attempt to historicize the biblical accounts, and reject any millenarianism.

Three main tendencies changed the Catholic understanding of Revelation in and during the Enlightenment. First, following Protestant interpreters, Catholics slowly reversed "the traditional Danielic vision of world-historical descent through four monarchies" and replaced it with the gradual ascent of reason or a more progressive hope, as outlined by the Marquis de Condorcet (1743–84) in his *Sketch for a Historical Picture of the Progress of the Human Mind* (1795).[3] Second, with this new, more optimistic, yet historical interpretation, chiliast and futurist interpretations fell under suspicion.[4] Third, the developments of historical-critical exegesis and the rise of comparative religious studies enabled Catholic exegetes to reassess Revelation as a book written for a specific historical context. Catholic exegetes such as Johann Jahn (1750–1816) followed in the footsteps of Protestants such as Johann August Ernesti (1707–81), who rejected any mystical reading of the text in his influential *Institutio interpretis Novi Testamenti* (1761). Ernesti argued that an exegete's sole job was to find the *sensus grammaticus* or *sensus literalis*, through a thorough historical and philological understanding of the text.[5] Jahn, arguably the most famous Catholic exegete of the early eighteenth century, stated that

3. Robin Barnes, "Images of Hope and Despair: Western Apocalypticism, 1500–1800," in *The Continuum History of Apocalypticism*, ed. Bernard McGinn et al. (New York, 2003), 143–84. See, for example, Claude Fauchet, *De la religion nationale* (Paris: 1789), ch. 4; R. Hermon-Belot, "God's Will in History: The Abbe Gregoire, the Revolution and the Jews," in *Millenarianism and Messianism in Early Modern Europe: Catholic Millenarianism: From Savonarola to the Abbe Gregoire*, ed. Karl A. Kottman, (Dordrecht: Kluwer, 2001), 91–100.
4. Heinrich Corrodi (1752–98), a reformed minister from Zurich, provided a highly critical account of chiliasm, on which many Catholic theologians relied. Heinrich Corrodi, *Kritische Geschichte des Chiliasmus*, 3 vols. (Frankfurt: 1781).
5. Johann August Ernesti, *Institutio Interpretis Novi Testamenti* (Leipzig: 1761), ch. 1, nr. 14–15, 10–11: "Eius porro observatio propria est Grammaticorum, quorum artis maxima et praecipua pars in eo versatur, ut quid verbum quodque tempore quoque, apud scriptorem quemque, in forma denique loquendi quaque, sonuerit, diligenter exquirant. Unde sensus literalis idem *grammaticus* dicitur, immo verbum *literalis* est latina interpretatio *grammatici*: nec minus recte historicus vocatur, quod, ut cetera facta, testimoniis et auctoritatibus contineatur. . . . Itaque nullus alius sensus est [!] nisi grammaticus, eumque Grammatici tradunt."

Revelation contained images of the devil, which although meaningful, were mere images of evil and not of a demonic reality.[6]

Johann Babor (1762–1846), a celebrated professor of biblical hermeneutics in Olmütz, Bohemia, whose works were endorsed by his Protestant peers, states in the commentary to his translation of the New Testament that dogmatic decisions are "irrelevant" for the historical-critical evaluation of a text:

> If one wants to judge the aim and content of a book, one has to use the principles which are available for poetic and symbolic books. One must not disregard the imagination and mode of description of the Hebrew prophets of old.[7]

If one uses the Hebrew prophets and prophecies as a key to understanding Revelation, then an important differentiation has to be made, Babor argued. One group of such accounts conveys a message to the prophet in clearly understandable words, the other through symbols and mysteries. Prophets who were told future events in the latter mode must, therefore, have had supernatural help to explain the otherwise obscure clues. Revelation falls into the same category. It is the symbolic story of how Christianity will be victorious over paganism and Judaism. Nothing in it is about the future.[8]

Johann Leonhard Hug (1765–1846), professor of exegesis in Freiburg, Breisgau, states in his important introduction to the New Testament (1808), which was also translated into English,[9] his dissatisfaction with most Catholic interpretations of Revelation. In fact, he says, for no other book of the Bible have exegetes produced such distorted interpretations. This he explains by the fact that, since the perdition of the ancient Jewish state, the Jewish way of thinking and writing has been forgotten so that Christians became unable to properly

---

6. Jahn, *Nachträge zu seinen theologischen Werken,* ed. Ernst Gottlieb Bengel (Tübingen: 1821), 97: "In der Offenbarung Johannis ist zwar der Teufel mit seinen Dienern sehr geschäftig, und spielet eine grosse Rolle; allein es ist hier alles bloss in Bildern dargestellt, die zwar etwas bedeuten, aber in sich selbst eben so, wie die gedichteten Parabeln, keine Wahrheiten enthalten, nichts Reelles haben ..."

7. Johann Babor, *Uebersetzung des Neuen Testaments mit erklärenden Anmerkungen* (Vienna: 1805), 3:65.

8. Babor, *Uebersetzung,* 3:115, also with references to Vergil's *Aenid* and Plato's *Timaeus.*

9. Johann Leonhard Hug, *Introduction to the Writings of the New Testament* (London: 1837).

understand the images of the text.[10] Only the recovery of ancient Judaism, as was done by the historical schools of the eighteenth century, suddenly opened the possibility to understanding Revelation yet again. Hug considered the commentary of his Protestant peer Johann Gottfried Eichhorn (1753–1827) to be the most important tool of his time for beginning a proper exegesis of Revelation.[11] Following Eichhorn, Hug understands all numbers in the text no longer as symbolic or mystical, but as literal descriptions. Hug is also convinced that not all images found in the text are important, such as the detailed descriptions of plagues (hail, diseases, etc.), because these were just parallels to the Egyptian plagues of the book of Exodus. Likewise, falling stars belong to the vocabulary of both the orient and prophets predicting bad fate, and therefore should not be taken too seriously.[12] Only two historical events can be connected to the book of Revelation, argues Hug. Apart from the victory of Christianity, it is the destruction of the Jewish temple and the demise of Rome. For Hug, the book is a mere work of consolation, written in the time of the Emperor Domitian (81–96 CE), and contains no references to future events:[13]

> John . . . could encourage Christianity, incite its professors to constancy in these trying times, that they might maintain their religion, and transmit it to those brighter days when it would rise nobly and triumphantly over every adverse fortune, erect its altars in every nation, and become the religion of the world.[14]

Peter Alois Gratz (1769–1849), a member of the Catholic Tübingen School and friend of Johann Sebastian Drey (1777–1853) and Johann B. Hirscher (1788–1865), was one of the most outstanding Catholic

---

10. Johann Leonhard Hug, *Einleitung in die Schriften des Neuen Testaments* (Tübingen: 1808), 2:404–23 (Revelation throughout the patristic time), at 428. An introduction to the four Gospels appeared already in 1797. For Hug's life and works, see Erwin Keller, *Leonhard Hug: Beiträge zu seiner Biographie* (Freiburg: n.p., 1973).

11. Johann Gottfried Eichhorn, *Commentarius in Apocalypsin Joannis*, 2 vols. (Göttingen: 1791); Johann Gottfried Eichhorn, "Ueber die innern Gründe gegen die Aechtheit und Kanonicität der Apokalypse," *Allgemeine Bibliothek der biblischen Litteratur* 3 (1791): 571–645.

12. Hug, *Einleitung*, 2:434.

13. Ibid., 2:441.

14. The translation is taken from Hug, *Introduction*, 673. For the German original, see Hug, *Einleitung*, 2:442.

exegetes of the nineteenth century. Gratz follows almost entirely the lead of Hug, stressing that Revelation is a historical book, written for a concrete set of circumstances and contains no hints about future events and no justification for any millenarian interpretation.[15] Like Hug, Gratz argued that the main purpose of the book is to provide consolation for persecuted Christians, the promise of their liberation and victory, punishment of the persecutors (4–9), and the destruction of paganism (10–19). Concerning the 1,260 days in which the apocalyptic woman of Revelation 12 will be persecuted and the 42 months (according to Rev. 13:5) during which the apocalyptic beast will rule, Gratz comments that these are mystical numbers as in the book of Daniel, and point to a short time. "This is after all the main purpose of the Apocalypse, namely to console the Christians of that time and to give them hope that the time of persecution will not last very long."[16] Consequently, he conceives Revelation 20 as the messianic government of the world before the end of the world. The 1,000 years of Christ's reign have to be understood as a prophetic-mystical depiction of the eternal victory of God contrasted with the short 3.5 years of persecution.[17]

The last example is that of Heinrich Braun (1732–92), who published a remarkable translation of the New Testament in the 1780s.[18] The best way of reading Revelation, this Catholic Enlightener explained, was to assume the fulfillment of all its prophecies. In his eyes, applying the images of the text to more recent historical events creates an unscientific "could-be" exegesis of the text.[19] Also, Braun preferred Bossuet's historicist approach, and stated that the book's aim is to give hope and consolation to the first persecuted Christians.[20] Its obscurity

---

15. Peter Alois Gratz, "Reflexionen über die Offenbarung Johannis," *Theologische Quartalschrift* 8 (1826): 587–605, at 591.
16. Peter Alois Gratz, "Meine Ansicht von Kapitel 4–20 der Apokalypse," in *Theologische Quartalschrift* 11 (1829): 3–38, at 21.
17. Gratz, "Meine Ansicht," 36.
18. Heinrich Braun, *Die göttliche heilige Schrift des neuen Testamentes in lateinischer und deutscher Sprache . . . nach dem Sinne der heiligen-römisch-katholischen Kirche . . . erläutert von Heinrich Braun . . .* vol. 3 (Augsburg: 1788).
19. Braun, *Die göttliche Schrift*, 3:405.
20. Ibid., 3:405.

comes not so much from the text, but from the reader who is unacquainted with the "spirit of Hebrew Poetry"[21] and who does not look for the hermeneutical key where it could be found—namely, in the historical context of the biblical book.[22] One should, said Braun, assume that the prophecies of Revelation have been fulfilled, but also, understand them as a key to conceiving the second coming, as Jesus' words in Matthew 24:25 about the destruction of Jerusalem can provide a key to understanding the last judgment.[23]

From Rationalism to *Heilsgeschichte*: Johann Jakob Hess

The above-described trends in Catholic theology, with their omission of eschatology as a theological category, led some to its rediscovery. The merging of Enlightenment Catholicism and Reformed "covenant" theology (or federalism) paved the way for a salvific (*heilsgeschichtliche*) theology, which found its earliest expression in the works of Alois Sandbichler, and later systematically refined in the works of Bernhard Galura (1764–1856) and Friedrich Brenner (1784–1848). After centuries in which the kingdom of God had been identified with the institutional Church, and despite a profound biblical analysis of "thy kingdom come" in the *Roman Catechism* of 1566,[24] Catholics found their way back to this biblical paradigm only through the mediation of the Reformed Swiss theologian Johann Jakob Hess, who had recognized the kingdom of God as the main theme of the Gospels and differentiated three stages: a preparatory stage from creation to the birth of Christ, a main stage from Jesus' birth to the end of the world, and the final fulfillment in Heaven.[25]

---

21. Braun endorses here Herder's views in Johann Gottfried Herder, *Vom Geist der ebräischen (sic!) Poesie*, 2 vols. (Dessau: 1782). For an appreciation of Herder, especially for bringing the *parallelismus membrorum* alive, see Aloysius Sandbichler, *Erläuterungen der biblischen Geschichte nach Herrn Johann Jakob Heß besonders zum Gebrauche für katholische Leser* (Salzburg: 1794), 1:344–45.
22. Braun, *Die göttliche Schrift*, 3:406.
23. Ibid.
24. *The Catechism of the Council of Trent*, translated by John McHugh and Charles Callan (Rockford, IL: 1982), 522–24.
25. See Peter Müller-Goldkuhle, *Die Eschatologie in der Dogmatik des 19. Jahrhunderts* (Essen: Ludgerus, 1966), 25–78; on Galura, see Theodor Filthaut, *Das Reich Gottes in den katechetischen Unterweisungen* (Freiburg: Herder, 1958), passim, but especially Leonhard Hell, *Reich Gottes als Systemidee der*

Federal theology stresses the covenant with God as the centerpiece of dogmatic theology, which manifests itself in history. Johannes Cocceius (1603–69) is credited with conceiving one of the most influential federal theologies, which helped his followers to better integrate "history and the realities of human existence" into a scripture-based theological reflection. "Federal theology should thus be seen as an attempt to establish a correlation between revelation and history, between eternity and time—an attempt to recognize the historical character of the divine revelation of salvation history."[26] Hess became acquainted with federal theology through Johann H. Heidegger's (1633–98) *Medulla theologiae Christianae* (1697) during his studies in Zurich under Johann Jakob Bodmer (1698–1783) and Johann Jakob Breitinger (1701–76). He was also influenced by Nathaniel Lardner (1684–1768), Charles Bonnet (1720–93), and took up ideas and challenges put forth by Johann David Michaelis (1717–91) and Johann August Ernesti.[27] From Bodmer and Breitinger, Hess received the idea of a practical or pragmatic historiography that is not so much interested in educating the intellect of the reader, but rather, in connecting him and his character with the virtues and characters of history. These thinkers saw historiography as the mindful interpretation of personal actions. Johann Lorenz Mosheim (1694–1755) was probably the main proponent of such a biographical-historical approach, which gradually marginalized orthodox Lutheran and Reformed dogmatic theology.

Nevertheless, until the eighteenth century, no pragmatic biographical study of the life of Jesus had been written, until Hess began working in 1764 on a "human" history of Jesus, which aimed at being pleasant reading and a useful textbook without too many supernatural elements.[28] While Hess was certainly influenced by

Theologie: historisch-systematische Untersuchungen zum theologischen Werk B. Galuras und F. Brenners (Mainz: M.-Grünewald-Verlag, 1993).

26. Willem J. van Asselt, *The Federal Theology of Johannes Cocceius (1603-1669)* (Leiden and Boston: Brill, 2001), 1–2.

27. Friedhelm Ackva, *Johann Jakob Hess (1741-1828) und seine Biblische Geschichte. Leben, Werk und Wirkung des Zürcher Antistes* (Frankfurt et al.: Peter Lang, 1992), 25–43; on Michaelis, see Michael C. Legaspi, *The Death of Scripture and the Rise of Biblical Studies* (Oxford: Oxford University Press, 2010).

28. Ackva, *Johann Jakob Hess*, 44–54.

Cocceius, he did not share the anti-rationalist starting point of his exegesis—namely, that of grace and election—but preferred natural reason, just as Joseph Butler (1692-1752) had done.[29] In 1768, the first two parts of his *History of Jesus' Last Three Years* (*Geschichte der drey letzten Lebensjahre Jesu*) were published. But only five years later, Hess changed his view that one should understand Jesus only from his moral, political, and psychological context.[30] Reading Locke's *Reasonableness of Christianity* (1695) obviously changed his mind. He had now arrived at the conclusion that God was leading humanity through history. The newfound insight into the intelligibility of history echoed also Christian Wolff's (1679-1754) and Bonnet's desire for a demonstration of a connection of all things (*nexus rerum*), as well as a better appreciation of Cocceius.[31] Unlike Cocceius, however, Hess believed he could trace God's footprints with reason alone.

Hess was convinced that if one follows Jesus' life through the hermeneutic lens of a divinely conceived scheme of salvation history, then the human life of Jesus becomes less important than his teachings, passion, and death.[32] Hess used the terms "theocracy" or "Kingdom of God" to articulate his new vision for a biography of Jesus, in which the question of how far the fate of Jesus describes the nature and reality of the kingdom of God becomes central.[33] This approach is then further

29. Ackva, *Johann Jakob Hess*, 77–78; 86; 173.
30. For the previous, more moralist approach, see Johann Jakob Hess, *Geschichte der drey letzten Lebensjahre Jesu* 2nd ed. (Zurich: 1773), 1:xxiv; 2:xxxvii-xxxix. For Hess, only those accounts that cannot be explained by human or natural causes should be regarded as miraculous (2:xiii-xiv); for example, the resuscitation of a dead person or the healing of a person born blind. Moreover, the miracle worker has to convey that he is sent by God and preach certain propositions. For Hess's discussion of miracles, see the second volume Hess, *Geschichte der drey letzten Lebensjahre*, 2:vii-viii: "Wunderwerke sollen Werke seyn, aus welchen sich sicher schliessen lässt, dass der, sie sie verrichtet, von Gott abgeordnet oder bevollmächtigt sey, um einen gewissen Auftrag an die Menschen von besonderer Wichtigkeit zu besorgen."
31. Ackva, *Johann Jakob Hess*, 76; cf. James Jakob Fehr, *"Ein wunderlicher nexus rerum": Aufklärung und Pietismus in Königsberg unter Franz Albert Schultz* (Hildesheim: Olms, 2005).
32. Hess, *Geschichte der drey letzten Lebensjahre Jesu*, 3:iii-lvi, viii-ix: "Nun erst dann, wenn er diese Geschichte nicht bloss als ein abgebrochenes Stück der Weltgeschichte, auch nicht bloss als eien Reihe moralischer und anderer Auftritte, dergleichen man in einer jeden Völkergeschichte antrift, und also auch nicht bloss als die Privatgeschichte eines grossen Mannes ansieht, sondern als ein solches Werk der Fürsehung, das durch die ganze vorhergehende Geschichte dieses Volks gleichsam angebahnet war, und die Ausführung jenes göttlichen Entwurfes seyn solte, welcher, so eingeschränkt und national er Anfangs zu seyn schien, doch das ganze Menschengeschlecht umfasste. Wenn er sie von dieser Seite ansieht, erst dann wird er sich für alles in derselben interessiren, erst dann mit rechter Theilnehmung sie lesen."

explored in his *The Kingdom of God* (*Von dem Reiche Gottes*) (1774).[34] According to his pragmatic salvation history, one will not find any inner-Trinitarian speculation in his works, since the kingdom of God is nothing but the "continuous guidance of human affairs for the purpose of the most enduring highest possible divine bliss."[35] Consequently, the human being is the center of such an approach.

For Hess, the concept of the kingdom of God has practical implications. By trusting in such providential guidance, humans can overcome, so he is convinced, sensual pleasure and improve their morals. The "Kingdom of God" becomes an "institution of education" (*Erziehungsanstalt*). Such divine pedagogy can be seen throughout biblical history, wherefore Hess reconstructs a coherent outline of biblical providential history. Instead of offering a dry theological analysis, Hess invited his readers to assume the persona of a pious Israelite and to tread with him through the history of God's chosen people.[36] His account was, nevertheless, attacked, especially because in the eyes of conservative theologians, he appreciated the rationalist explanations of demonic possession. On the other side, rationalist theologians, especially proponents of the so-called mythical school of biblical interpretation, spearheaded by Georg Lorenz Bauer (1755–1806), rejected his use of the Old Testament as "history."[37]

The first Catholic who took Hess's theological agenda seriously was the Salzburg Augustinian Alois Sandbichler, who had to battle

33. Hess, *Geschichte der drey letzten Lebensjahre Jesu*, 3:l–lii; Johann Jakob Hess, *Die Schriften des Neuen Testamentes*, (Lebensgeschichte Jesu, 2. Teil) (Zurich: 1828), 3:liii–liv: ". . . die Schicksale unsers Herrn . . . stellen ihm [the reader] das in seiner wahren Beschaffenheit und Wirklichkeit dar, was zur Anbahnung des in diesen Schriften so oft genannten Reiches Gottes, oder Reiches der Himmel erforderlich war; sie . . . waren das wirksamste Mittel zur Herbeiführung dessen, was schon der Geist der Weissagung von einem einst aufzurichtenden Gottes- oder Messiasreiche hatte erwarten heissen." See also Ackva, *Johann Jakob Hess*, 90–101.
34. Johann Jakob Hess, *Von dem Reiche Gottes. Ein Versuch über den Plan der göttlichen Offenbarungen und Anstalten*, 2 vols. (Zurich: 1774).
35. Johann Jakob Hess, *Von dem Reiche Gottes*, 2nd ed, (Zurich: 1781), 1:361: "Und da nach dem gesundesten Begriffe, ein göttliches Reich nichts ander ist, als eine fortgehende Leitung der menschlichen Angelegenheiten, dadurch die grösstmögliche dauerhafteste Glückseligkeit (hier oder dort, oder beyder Orten) unter Gott . . ."
36. Jakob Hess, *Von dem Reiche Gottes* (Zurich: 1781), 1:242; cf. Ackva, *Johann Jakob Hess*, 121–31.
37. Ackva, *Johann Jakob Hess*, 143; 158. An example for a contemporary Lutheran orthodox critic see [Johann F. Teller], *Gedanken eines sächsischen Predigers über die Geschichte der drey letzten Lebensjahre Jesu* (Leipzig: 1774); [Johann F. Teller], *Nöthige Erinnerungen über Herrn Johann Jakob Hess Geschichte der drey Lebensjahre Jesu* (Frankfurt and Leipzig: 1774).

ferocious attacks because of his positive engagement with the views of a Reformed theologian.[38] Later, Bernhard Galura followed in Sandbichler's footsteps; however, in a systematic and not in an exegetical fashion, synthesizing Hess, Sandbichler, and Kant.[39]

The First Catholic Biblical Salvation History

Sandbichler was never afraid of engaging with Enlightenment thinkers. He even stated publicly that a good Catholic theologian should read Herder, Lessing, and Semler, and could find pearls of wisdom in their works, even if their views on revelation were ultimately inadequate.[40] He began exchanging letters with Hess in 1791, and thus initiated a correspondence that lasted at least until 1812. While Sandbichler embraced much of modern biblical criticism and saw Ernesti, Eichhorn, and Michaelis as heroes of exegesis, he was quite critical of their alleged naturalism.[41] For him, the application of the most recent exegetical findings never excluded the possibility of an allegorical reading or the existence of miracles. Instead, the Augustinian attempted to walk a middle way between the extremes of rationalist exegesis on the one side, and an overemphasis on allegory and disregard for philology and history on the other. He did this in full submission to the tradition of the church, but nevertheless pointed out

38. Sandbichler, *Erläuterungen der biblischen* Geschichte, 1:2. Johann T. Reutemann, *Bemerkungen über die von dem Herrn J. Jac. Hess . . . herausgegebene Lebens-Geschichte Jesu* (n. p.: 1802); Johann T. Reutemann, *Kurzgefasste Demonstration und Belehrung an den Herrn Joh. Jac. Hess . . . dass Jesus kein gemeiner blosser purer Mensch . . . sey* (n.p.: 1802). The papers of Sandbichler, which have unfortunately never been analyzed, are preserved in the University Library of Salzburg. There are 15 files with smaller theological manuscripts (M II 364), six manuscript volumes of his salvific history *Historia consiliorum divinorum* (M I 254), which have never been published, and 11 files of reviews (M I 408).

39. Ackva, *Johann Jakob Hess*, 266–67. Others, who followed Galura's ideas were Dobmayer, Thanner, Hirscher, and Stapf, while Scheeben, Kleutgen, and Staudenmaier criticized the centrality of his Kingdom of God idea. See Hell, *Reich Gottes als Systemidee der Theologie*, 4; on Dannenmayr's work as historical theologian, see ibid., 181–82. Hell also argues that the Augustinian Engelbert Klüpfel was a main influence on Galura (194–95). A synthesis of biblical theology and German idealism regarding the concept of "Kingdom of God" was attempted by Ignaz Thanner (ibid., 195). For the best treatment of this idea in Kant, see Alfred Habichler, *Reich Gottes als Thema des Denkens bei Kant* (Mainz: Grünewald, 1991).

40. Aloysius Sandbichler, *Revision der Augsburger Kritik über gewisse Kritiker. Freymüthige Betrachtungen über wichtige von Obscuranten entstellte Religionsgegenstände nach den Bedürfnissen unserer Zeit* (Salzburg: 1792), 340–42.

41. Letter to Hess of August 20, 1792, Zentralbibliothck Zurich: ΓA Hess 1741, 181y, 278.

that many propositions his critics claimed to be part of tradition were, instead, mere school opinions, and thus could not be part of the deposit of faith. This angered many intransigent ex-Jesuits: "I must be happy if I can escape the *auto da fe* that is prepared for me ... but I cannot defend something as truth of what I am not convinced—whatever the consequences."[42]

For example, the Augustinian presupposed Moses' authorship of some parts of the Pentateuch, but added that Moses built his books on older fragments, which, in his view, did not diminish the divine status of the writings.[43] He also conceded that it would not contradict any doctrine of faith to dispute the historicity of the Great Flood.[44] He saw himself not as "the man who explains miracles out of the Bible, where they really are," but who does not see the need to concede them, where "mediated natural causes" can be assumed,[45] or where fables are told—for example, the story about Lot's wife being turned into a pillar of salt.[46] Sandbichler's hermeneutic begins with Ernesti's insight that the literal meaning of the text is crucial. A verse can have, however, an accommodated meaning, but such was, in his eyes, usually rare. He also rejected as impossible to prove that a verse could have four different meanings, according to the four senses of scripture. "With such a principle ... one can read into the Bible ... whatever one desires ...," he exclaimed.[47] After centuries of neglecting or marginalizing the literal and historical meaning of scripture, for Sandbichler, it was "time to arm ourselves with the sword—the two-bladed sword—of *literal meaning* against the enemies of religion."[48] He was convinced that only

---

42. Letter to Hess of June 29, 1792, Zentralbibliothek Zurich: FA Hess 1741, 181x, 193. Sandbichler refers here to the two volumes of essays in which he targeted the Catholic anti-Enlightenment, *Revision der Augsburger Kritik über Kritiker*, 2 vols. (Salzburg: 1791/92), and in particular, so it seems, the teaching about papal infallibility.
43. Sandbichler, *Erläuterungen der biblischen Geschichte*, 1:12.
44. Ibid., 1:22–23.
45. Ibid., 1:27.
46. Ibid., 1:45.
47. Ibid., 1:272; 274: "Ich verehre Väter, und Theologen, die zur Auferbauung manches aus der Bibel nehmen, was buchstäblich nicht in ihr steht—aber Leute, die mir so etwas als Bibelsinn mit Gewalt für Wahrheit aufdringen wollen—bedaure ich zum wenigstens—oder verabscheue sie gänzlich, so bald ich sehe, dass sie es nicht aus blossem Missverstande thun— ... sie ist nur da, der wilden Einbildungskraft wildes Spiel zu verschaffen und die Bibel dadurch herabzuwürdigen."
48. Sandbichler, *Erläuterungen der biblischen Geschichte*, 1:275.

318

a sound philological and historical reading of scripture could defend revelation against its critics. "Hyperorthodox people," who are easily offended, were, therefore, not his target reading audience, as he conceded himself.[49]

In his first letter to Hess of June 5, 1791, he confessed his debt to the Swiss theologian:

> Long have I loved you—held you in high esteem—how could I not? So much have I learned from your writings, so that I can say that my little knowledge of scripture derives predominantly from Michaelis's and your writings. You have taught me to look at scripture according to its great, overarching divine plan. Before that I had looked only at singular passages; I saw hardly any coherence and connection. The Bible remained despite all efforts to understand it a closed book for me. But your *The Kingdom of God* tore away the curtain, and I made since then attempts in exegesis . . . for which I would not have had the eyes before. This occurred to me, occurred to others—and of this intellectual transformation [*Ideenumschaffung*] among us Catholics you are the author. May God give that many of us do not close their eyes to this . . . enlighten or turn away from [confessional, U. L.] prejudice. . . . Yet, divine providence will lead to a good outcome. Contradiction always has to surface where truth rises—this is my consolation and I walk my way . . . as you walk ahead it does not seem so dangerous anymore and I will follow you—certainly with smaller, inadequate steps.[50]

On May 26, 1793, Sandbichler assured Hess that an increasing number of Catholic "Bible friends" see in the Swiss writer now a "leader" in the fight against the rationalist destruction of biblical theology.[51] In another letter of 1811, he explained why his interpretation of scripture, attacked by anti-Enlighteners—"hyperorthodox fanatics," as he called them—as heretical and dangerous, was also despised by "Christian naturalists and deists." Sandbichler's acceptance of the Bible as the revealed word of God ran against the deists' "anti-Christian principles. That's why they take offense at the words of our faith."[52] Taking the Bible seriously as a document of the history of God's salvific

49. Ibid., 1:525.
50. Zentralbibliothek Zurich: FA Hess 1741, 181v, 116.
51. Zentralbibliothek Zurich: FA Hess 1741, 181z, 111.
52. Letter of Sandbichler to Hess of January 4, 1811, Zentralbibliothek Zurich: FA Hess 1741, 181bk, 420.

will entailed a rejection of rationalist approaches to exegesis that saw, in every supernatural event or revelation, an accommodation of the divine to the uneducated, unenlightened spirit of antiquity:

> One can do nothing better than to refute such assassinations with history, although some evil people take great efforts to destroy even that with their hermeneutic of accommodation. Yet, this mendacious hermeneutic has to go—because it must become evident to every unbiased person that one does not have *more* legitimization to find the intended meaning of the authors of Biblical history than of any other history.[53]

An Enlightened Millenarianism

Since Hess had not applied his historical, pragmatic method to the book of Revelation (it was published only posthumously), Sandbichler—encouraged by Hess—undertook this challenge in 1794. He admitted openly that until the eighteenth century, most interpreters did not fully understand the book because they did not possess the grammatical or historical tools to fathom it. "Were not also the other prophets veiled in darkness until we were able in our own times to penetrate their literal sense . . . ?"[54] Sandbichler wrote his treatise after several readings of the book and after comparing it carefully with similar writings of the Old Testament—in particular, the prophets, and consulted exegetical commentaries only afterwards. Most Catholic commentaries, he stated, were useless—except Calmet's[55] and Bossuet's, which pay more attention to the literal meaning of the text. He saw, therefore, a particular need among Catholics for a "literal-historical interpretation (independent from dogmatic definitions)," because allegorical interpretations of Revelation were sometimes used for upholding "dangerous doctrines." Sandbichler also refrained in his work from citing exegetical authorities—first, because he believed that he gave sufficient arguments for each of his interpretations, and second, because he felt

---

53. Letter of Sandbichler to Hess of May 26, 1793, Zentralbibliothek Zurich: FA Hess 1741, 181z, 111.
54. Sandbichler, *Erläuterungen der biblischen Geschichte*, 2:preface.
55. Augustin Calmet, *Commentaire litteral sur tous les livres de l'Ancien et du Nouveau Testament* vol. 8 (Paris: 1726).

that a mere accumulation of citations would distract from the original text.[56] The Augustinian emerges here as a quite self-confident scholar, who trusted in his own reasoning more than the authority of his peers.

Sandbichler took the poetic elements of Revelation seriously, and thus had no problem seeing the natural catastrophes described in the text as representing political affairs: boiling pots as wars, and thunderstorms, solar or lunar eclipses, or earthquakes as revolutions.[57] However, he did not follow the rationalist trend of Eichhorn in viewing the biblical imagery as offensive to reason (e.g., the description of the heavenly Jerusalem). "If Milton or Klopstock use such descriptions we don't dislike them . . . ,"[58] but if a biblical writer uses them, they are suddenly offensive, writes the frustrated friar. Sandbichler also reflected on the method of accommodation and made clear that not everything that rebels against our modern understanding can be degraded to a "Jewish figment of imagination, or an image"[59] because such an interpretation does violence to the prophets. This does not mean that he rejected the differentiation of image, idiom, and so forth; but he thinks some go too far—for example, when they reject the future conversion of the Jews or the millennial realm of Christ. One cannot avoid all "offenses" of scripture. According to Sandbichler, one of the main objections against Revelation is that the book seems to describe "what must happen soon" (Rev. 1:1). *En tachei*, however, he explained, does mean the sequence of things, so that one can assume that John saw, in a short and fast sequence, all future epochs of the world. As such, he only saw the main events, but not the secondary causes and the times between the epochs.[60] "This is how poets . . . work . . . they put centuries together and compress them."[61] He also defended the author of Revelation against the charge of anthropomorphism, and made clear that his description of the heavenly Jerusalem might

56. Sandbichler, *Erläuterungen der biblischen Geschichte*, 2:preface.
57. Ibid., 171. Sandbichler refers here to Michaelis and Eichhorn, but also to his Catholic peer Johann Babor, *Altherthümer der Hebräer* (Vienna: 1794), 295.
58. Sandbichler, *Erläuterungen der biblischen Geschichte*, 2:145.
59. Ibid., 393.
60. Ibid., 153.
61. Ibid., 154.

be "philosophically" much more coherent than a deist description of Heaven that disregarded the bodily nature of human beings and only paid attention to immaterial souls. Sandbichler, thus, clearly rejected any Platonist substance dualism, and instead embraced a more holistic, biblical view of the person.[62]

One of the most astonishing idiosyncrasies of Sandbichler's book is his treatment of hell and the final victory of Christ over all of his enemies—a centerpiece of eschatology. If the kingdom of God is the moral governance of God over all of his creatures, how do his enemies fit into this scheme—in particular, the damned in hell? If, according to Psalm 109, all enemies of God will be subdued and God will be all in all (1 Cor. 15, 20-29), who are these enemies of the kingdom of God if they are in hell? For Sandbichler, the enemies of the kingdom must be immoral rational beings.[63] The problem that arises then, is how death as the last enemy (1 Cor. 15:26) can be overcome by Christ. Does this not contradict the eternity of hell? Does one have to assume that the immoral inhabitants of hell will be simply annihilated?

Sandbichler rejected this option because it contradicts the Catholic tradition of the eternity of hell. Then, however, he made a stunning suggestion. He proposed that demons and other rational immoral beings in hell could morally and intellectually advance. Scholastic thinkers seem to agree that they cannot, yet "scripture seems to suggest here and there the opposite . . . —and reason presumes it anyway."[64] Even if the punishments for the damned are eternal—do they exclude the possibility of improvement? Sandbichler assumed that such could be the case if one understood "punishment" in the right sense—as a punishment that aims at the improvement of the person (*poena medicinalis*). If the damned could be improved so that they would reject and curse their bad deeds, would not also their physical misery end, Sandbichler asked.[65] All punishments God has sentenced them to would cease, due to their moral improvement, yet

---

62. Ibid., 147.
63. Ibid., 7.
64. Ibid., 8.
65. Ibid., 9.

their fate would not change. Such "advanced" damned persons would still be unhappy compared to those in Heaven and remain prisoners, but would now consider their imprisonment as just. In this way, they would subject themselves indeed to Christ and give up their inimical stance. If one wants to take St. Paul literally—that the enemy death has to be defeated—then one can argue, since there are grades of happiness in Heaven as well, that there could be grades among the damned in which death and its consequence (the separation from God), understood as physical evil, cease to exist.[66]

How then did he envision the positive counterpart, the resurrection of the flesh? Interpreting Revelation 20:4-5, 12; and 1 Corinthians 15:23, Sandbichler argued that one can distinguish two resurrections. One is the particular resurrection of the saints, the martyrs and witnesses to Christ on one side, and after a thousand years, the rest of the faithful on the other side. Until the millennium comes to an end, the resurrected saints are reigning with Christ and preach his word in a physically perceptible way.[67] He cautioned his readers, however, not to think of a political earthly reign of Christ, but rather of a priestly one. The resurrected saints are priests rather than kings:

> The Saints, who will be resurrected by Christ into his millennial realm, will have an immortal and transfigured body. This body, however is not entirely transfigured as if it would not be in need of further perfection . . . this perfection will happen in the universal resurrection . . . in which the sensual is gradually transformed into the spiritual.[68]

After the universal resurrection follows the universal judgment (Rev. 20:4-6). The images of thrones and judges, sheep and trumpets were, for Sandbichler, just that: signs, which indicate a "great event" and want to capture the "new feeling of the resurrected."[69] With Johann David Michaelis, he rejected interpreting Revelation as the story of ecclesiastical decline and the papacy as apocalyptic beast, but also rejected identifying the witnesses of Revelation 9 as Luther and Calvin,

---

66. Ibid., 2:10.
67. Ibid., 18.
68. Ibid., 21.
69. Ibid., 23.

instead of Elijah and Enoch.[70] Likewise, he discarded a simplistic allegorical interpretation that makes these two witnesses the abstract ideas of scripture and tradition, or natural and positive revelation, because such interpretations only "serve the mindset" of the interpreter and do not explain the text itself.[71] Sandbichler believed that the description of the two witnesses has Old Testament parallels and has to be understood as foretelling the future. Since both witnesses are sent to Jerusalem, he assumed that their main task will be to convert the Jews. Consequently, he assumed that a new Christian community will arise there and build a new temple. It is this new Jewish-Christian church that is identified with the apocalyptic woman in Revelation 12.[72]

The city of Rome, as portrayed in Revelation 18, is, for the Augustinian, a neo-pagan Rome which will oppress the church.[73] Due to its persecutions, the number of Christians will dramatically decrease so that at the end, there will only be a few good Christians left.[74] For Sandbichler, the apocalyptic beast of the earth from Revelation 12:11–17 is priestly power. In Sandbichler's time only a few attempted to start such a false religion with forged miracles, like Alessandro Caligiostro (1743–95);[75] however, in the end times, the Augustinian was convinced, many would attempt just that. In those days, the "light of science" will be extinguished, so that the founders of new cults will be able to obscure their deception. The prophets of this new religion will be "atheists" *and* superstitious![76] They will bring about false miracles. The culmination of these false miracles will be the forged resurrection of their leader. The 42 months of persecution Christians have to endure from this new religion parallels the 3.5 years in Daniel 12 (persecution

70. Ibid., 41–42.
71. Ibid., 43.
72. Ibid., 48–50.
73. Sandbichler, *Erläuterungen der biblischen Geschichte*, 2:62; Johann David Michaelis, *Anmerkungen für Unglehrte zu seiner Uebersetzung des neuen Testaments* vol. 4 (Göttingen: 1792), 118.
74. Sandbichler, *Erläuterungen der biblischen Geschichte*, 2:73.
75. Cf. John V. Fleming, *The Dark Side of the Enlightenment: Wizards, Alchemists, and Spiritual Seekers in the Age of Reason* (n.p.: W. W. Norton, 2013).
76. Sandbichler, *Erläuterungen der biblischen Geschichte*, 2:79, 101. For the occult tendencies of the eighteenth century, see Paul Kleber Monod, *Solomon's Secret Arts. The Occult in the Age of Enlightenment* (New Haven: Yale University Press, 2013).

of the Jews under Antiochus). Whether one should therefore take 42 months literally "remains to be seen by the generations after us," Sandbichler commented.[77] After the punishment of these enemies, universal peace will be restored. Sandbichler assumed that the beginning of Christ's reign on earth will be connected with the conversion of the Jews. He endorsed Fredrick Wilhelm Hezel's (1754–1824) idea that such a conversion would be possible if one could improve the "taste of Jews and teach them proper biblical theology, but while such political and religious measures might fail, Revelation seems to give hope to really expect such a 'revolution' (*Umwälzungen*)."[78]

Sandbichler was a rare exception in not dismissing the millennial reign of Christ as allegorical. Yet, he made clear that his account did not support the millenarian expectations of fanatics because he believed this reign to be of "saints" (*hagioi*), or in Hebrew, *kadischim*. This word does not designate properly canonized saints, but means the faithful, and thus their reign will be an earthly realm, similar to others in which religion can be disseminated and grow through morality, peace, and happiness. It will be a powerful reign with many signs, but be structured according "to the way of nature":

> And now I ask! How can the millennial realm . . . be offensive? A theocracy was already visible in the Old Testament . . . and at the beginning of Christianity . . . but resurrected Saints and Jesus as visible king! I have explained . . . that these Saints are the faithful and Christ as King means the effects of his in the realm of the world. . . .[79]

The chiliasts misunderstood this theocracy as a merely earthly affair, and in Sandbichler's eyes overlooked that the regents of this kingdom will be *priests* who make "Christ visible." This future realm has nothing to do with the presence of a king like at a royal court, yet something sensually perceptible will indicate the presence of Christ, the *kabod Jahwe*.[80] The friar assumed that most millennial interpretations had

77. Sandbichler, *Erläuterungen der biblischen Geschichte*, 2:82.
78. Ibid., 98. Sandbichler praises the achievements of Moses Mendelssohn (1729–86) and Salomon Maimon (1753–1800) for the "improvement of . . . Jewish taste," ibid., 98–102.
79. Ibid., 107.

been rejected because of chiliast abuses and misinterpretations, and because some churches used Revelation for their own propaganda.[81]

An unsophisticated reader could indeed see Sandbichler as a supporter of political theocracy, and thus a danger to society and church. Thus, it cannot come as a surprise that a number of influential ex-Jesuits convinced the Court in Vienna to proscribe his book in the Habsburg Lands in 1796.[82] The fear of the censors was not entirely ungrounded. In 1815, Thomas Pöschl (1769–1837) read Sandbichler's account as buttressing his own apocalyptic teachings for a Reawakening Movement, which came under heavy attack from the Catholic Church. Sandbichler tried to correct Pöschl, but gave up: "In this man is something holy, something that only needs polishing."[83]

At the end of these thousand years, faithlessness and immorality will again increase, and a new anti-Christian time will arrive because the reign of Christ was "all too sensual," and thus taken for granted, and ultimately dismissed as unimportant. Satan, who is now liberated (Rev. 20), will wage war, but the seducers Gog and Magog will ultimately perish in fire.[84]

Sandbichler showed that his interpretation of the millennial realm was in accordance with Justin Martyr and Lactantius and similar to that of the Madrid Jesuit Juan de Ulloa in his *De primis et ultimis temporibus seu de principio et fine mundi*,[85] who had considered such a position as "not improbable."[86] Sandbichler argued that the church has never clarified the exact heresy or mistake of millenarianism. Was it that the saints are raised from the dead or that there will be an earthly realm?[87] The first cannot contradict dogma, since it is not a contradiction that

80. Ibid., 108.
81. Ibid., 110–11.
82. Letter of Sandbichler to Hess of November 23, 1796, Zentralbibliothek Zurich: FA Hess 1741, 181ae, 131.
83. Theodor Wiedemann, *Die religiöse Bewegung in Oberösterreich und Salzburg beim Beginne des 19. Jahrhunderts* (Innsbruck: 1890), 100–101. For Pöschl's autobiography in the context of gender studies see Edith Saurer, "Die Autobiographie des Thomas Pöschl: Erweckung, weibliche Offenbarungen und religiöser Wahn," in *Die Religion der Geschlechter. Historische Aspekte religiöser Mentalitäten*, ed. Edith Saurer (Vienna: Böhlau, 1995), 169–212; cf. Peter Barden, "Pöschl, Thomas," in *Biographisch-Bibliographisches Kirchenlexikon* (Nordhausen: Bautz, 1994), 7:775–77.
84. Sandbichler, *Erläuterungen der biblischen Geschichte*, 2:117–24; 2:128–29.
85. (Augsburg: 1719), disp. 3, c. 3, p. 1–3.
86. Sandbichler, *Erläuterungen der biblischen Geschichte*, 2:397.

some might be resurrected earlier[88] than others, and also the reality of an earthly kingdom is attested by scripture (e.g., Dan. 7). Could it be that some regard this doctrine as heretical because the kingdom of Christ lies in the future? Only if one disregards that this future aspect only pertains to the visible (!) development and fruition of this kingdom—in other respects, the kingdom of God has already existed since Jesus' resurrection, Sandbichler explained. The future kingdom, however, will be the perpetuation of the invisible one and will last until the day of judgment. Is it, asked Sandbichler, that some theologians have their problems with millenarianism because the kingdom of Christ is going to be an earthly one and not wholly invisible? Yet, if one conceives this future kingdom according to the theocracy of the Old Testament—namely, that the power of God disseminates slowly, reaching nation after nation ("auf alle Völker der Erde nach und nach sich ausbreitend vorgestellt wird"), and if one eliminates everything "rough" and sees the goal of this realm and its effects in morality and so forth alone—why could it not be part of faithful Catholic theology? After all, Sandbichler stated that the providential reign of God extends from earthly existence into the supernatural.[89] The Augustinian friar believed that the thousand-year reign of Christ was rejected so vehemently on account of some extreme, rough, and anthropomorphic concepts propounded by the millenarians. He embraced a reign of Christ and his saints with physical effects, but a moral-spiritual influence on the physical world, stressed that his interpretation was based on a "literal" understanding, and showed that it does not contradict the common, more figurative understanding.[90] "I let the future citizens of the realm of Christ taste political and physical bliss

---

87. Sandbichler, *Erläuterungen der biblischen Geschichte*, 2:401. Cf. Johann David Michaelis, *Einleitung in die göttlichen Schriften des Neuen Testaments*, 2nd ed. (Göttingen: 1788), 2:1648.

88. Sandbichler rejects the notion of a thousand-year-long "sleep" of the saints. Sandbichler, *Erläuterungen der biblischen Geschichte*, 2:404.

89. Sandbichler, *Erläuterungen der biblischen Geschichte*, 2:403: "Was soll es demnselben an seiner Glaubwürdigkeit verschlagen, dass es zum Theile irdisch, und nicht bloss geistig ist? Es ist doch den Führungen Gottes angemessen, im irdischen anzufangen, und so dann nach und nach ins Ueberirdische überzugehen."

90. Sandbichler, *Erläuterungen der biblischen Geschichte*, 2:416.

according to their moral standing. . . ."[91] Sandbichler made clear that he followed his own insights despite the criticism of many of his peers:

> I went my own way—that is true. The opinions that many theologians hold and elevate to dogmas did not hold me back. Instead I examined them and chose what I considered true . . . I was also not afraid of the easily foreseeable contempt, the mockery and the gloating smiles of those, who regard due to some principles a literal and historical explanation of the Apocalypse as the infeasible, fatuous enterprise of a fanatic.[92]

Conclusion: Salvation History

With Aloysius Sandbichler, salvation history entered into Catholic theology. The new paradigm was received enthusiastically by the Catholic Tübingen School and has ever since provided a critical lens for Catholic systematic theology.[93] That this reorientation of Catholic thought is grounded in the Catholic Enlightenment and a commentary on the book of Revelation of 1791 has been undeservedly forgotten.

For Sandbichler, Revelation is the history of the church of all times, of its battle with powerful empires, but also of its final perseverance.[94] Sandbichler, the forerunner of modern biblical theology, was also a child of the Enlightenment—the religious Enlightenment—and he valued its effects on the state of theology. Only the religious Enlightenment of the eighteenth-century scholars, he believed, began the rediscovery of the simplicity and beauty of the Gospels, because they had learned to discern Revelation and human additions to the deposit of faith.[95] According to Sandbichler, Revelation also teaches that the church should not fear changes in the world, not even revolutions, because they ultimately help in the dissemination of her message. Instead, the providential reign of God through history that Revelation admonishes us to accept, as Sandbichler outlined, is a sign of hope for a further increase of the "true" church of Jesus Christ. That

91. Ibid., 2:416.
92. Ibid., 2:517–18.
93. See, for example, Grant Kaplan, *Answering the Enlightenment. The Catholic Recovery of Historical Revelation* (New York: Crossroad, 2006).
94. Sandbichler, *Erläuterungen der biblischen Geschichte*, 2:288.
95. Ibid., 2:349.

the Augustinian learned this insight from his Reformed friend Hess shows that the confessional divide of the eighteenth century was more permeable than historians have led us to believe, and that during the religious Enlightenment, a fruitful inter-confessional enrichment was possible.

13

Moses and Apollo:
The Beginnings of Comparative
Religionsgeschichte in Catholic Exegesis

The comparative study of religions and the applications of insights found therein to exegesis was a fruit of the Enlightenment. It is, however, usually forgotten that this "new science" originated in the work of a devout Catholic, namely Giambattista Vico (1668–1744), arguably the most original Catholic Enlightenment thinker.[1] Nevertheless, Vico's approach only slowly disseminated among his Catholic peers. In fact, by the end of the eighteenth century, most Catholic Enlighteners were more aware of comparative studies produced by their Protestant peers than those of Vico. Moreover, due to the enormous pressure on exegetes to conform to standards of orthodoxy, this discipline was a minefield for researchers. One could easily find one's books censored, and even be imprisoned and deposed from one's teaching position. The case of Michael Wecklein

---

1. Cf. Guy Stroumsa, *A New Science: The Discovery of Religion in the Age of Reason* (Cambridge, MA: Harvard University Press, 2010).

(1771–1840) is yet another example of the complete destruction of a theologian's life.[2]

A Danger for the Students of Münster

On April 27, 1806, the vicar general of Münster in Westphalia, Franz von Fürstenberg (1729–1810), himself an enlightened priest, prohibited the theology students of the diocese from continuing to attend the lectures of Michael Wecklein for "known reasons inherent in the Christian-Catholic system of doctrine." The students, however, loved their teacher and desired to study with him, but were warned that by doing so, they would forfeit any chance of being ordained to the priesthood.[3] The president of the Royal Prussian Chamber, von Vincke, was furious because he regarded such measures as overstepping episcopal authority and requested, on the same day, an immediate withdrawal of the prohibition. Fürstenberg answered instantly, stating that he had already asked the government a year before to dismiss Wecklein and presented documentation with the reasons for such a measure. Only because this meeting—as well as another on April 23, 1806, with the Prussian State Minister von Massow—had no effect, his conscience obligated him to prohibit students from attending Wecklein's lectures:

> Therefore it is impossible for me to take a step back, since I have done it with great caution and only after all other means proved to be without effect. . . . I am willing to accept whatever consequences might come, but my conscience will be my witness that I did what I was obliged to do for God, the church and myself.[4]

This solemn statement deserves our attention. One wonders what

2. There is an exhaustive reconstruction of the case, however with less emphasis on Wecklein's theology and his critics and without reference to his letters to Franz Oberthür. Ton Meijknecht, "De Zaak Wecklein 1806," *Nederlands archief voor kerkgeschiedenis* 56 (1976): 450–62; 57 (1977): 62–94; 222–37.

3. Landesarchiv Nordrhein-Westfalen, Abteilung Westfalen/Münster: Verein für Geschichte u. Altertumskunde Westf., Abt. MS—Nachl. Franz Bernh. Jos. v. Bucholtz, Nr. 1072, Promulgation of April 27, 1806.

4. Landesarchiv Nordrhein-Westfalen, Abteilung Westfalen/Münster: Verein für Geschichte u. Altertumskunde Westf., Abt. MS—Nachl. Franz Bernh. Jos. v. Bucholtz, Nr. 1072, Letter of Fürstenberg of April 27, 1806 to von Vincke.

Wecklein had taught to infuriate the enlightened Fürstenberg so much. After all, Wecklein, born in 1778 in the diocese of Würzburg and a priest since 1801, had written a most distinguished dissertation under the direction of the famous Catholic Enlightener Franz Oberthür (1745–1831). Oberthür was one of the most creative Enlighteners and most prolific writers, and worked his entire career for a better integration of biblical knowledge into systematic theology.[5] He was no rationalist or radical, but certainly pushed Catholic theology to its limits, thus forcing his peers to acknowledge the validity of modern thought and new forms of theological discussion. One of the ideas he fought for was the acknowledgement of anthropology, and thus humanity, as a main category of theological reflection: "Humanity one can only find in Christianity, and what does not contribute . . . to the augmentation of true, pure humanity does not belong to the essential core of Christianity."[6] Moreover, it was Oberthür who got Wecklein his professorship in Münster a few years earlier, a position that a number of academics had politely declined. Why did the relationship between Fürstenberg and Wecklein sour? Why did the vicar general perceive Wecklein, whom the dean of the cathedral chapter had personally invited to apply for the position, as a threat to the orthodoxy of his future priests?

Naturalist Exegesis and "Private" Scholarship

An anonymous report about Wecklein, written for von Fürstenberg, goes into detail. By invoking the Council of Trent, it declares that a "Catholic Christian is not allowed to interpret holy scripture according to their individual insight or phantasy. He is not allowed to interpret supposedly dark or hard to grasp verses according to individual whim."[7] According to the denunciation in this report, Wecklein did

---

5. Surprisingly, to date there has been only one book on Oberthür: Otto Volk (ed.), *Franz Oberthür: Persönlickeit und Werk* (Neustadt: Degener, 1966).
6. Franz Oberthür, *Theologische Enzyklopädie* (Augsburg: 1828), 1:36.
7. Landesarchiv Nordrhein-Westfalen, Abteilung Westfalen/Münster: Verein für Geschichte u. Altertumskunde Westf., Abt. MS—Nachl. Franz Bernh. Jos. v. Bucholtz, Nr. 1072, Promemoria, nr. 7.

just that. His critics saw in his ability to not only engage the patristic tradition of interpretation, but also the modern historical-critical method, a spirit that was dangerously "private" and contrasted it with the "Catholicity" of traditional exegesis. In particular, Wecklein's expressions about the revelatory character of the Old Testament, the moral contradictions found therein, and the statement that Moses had "sold" the Israelites his own law as divine commands, were considered highly offensive. Wecklein's comment in a seminar that an "immediate revelation of God was impossible" was considered especially heretical.[8] According to this report, Wecklein attempted to "accommodate" the Bible to a "rationalist creed" (*Vernunftglauben*), whose main characteristic was "modern hermeneutics."[9] A few examples are cited for the latter. When Wecklein taught his archeology seminar, he supposedly explained that the walls of Jericho collapsed during a storm and not due to the procession of the Israelites around them, or that the appearances of Jesus in locked rooms could be explained by the fact that he sneaked into the room before anybody could see him. The miracles of Moses during the Exodus were not supernatural, but merely happy coincidences, while Sodom and Gomorrah were not destroyed by fire and brimstone, but by a volcanic eruption. Likewise, Uzzah was not struck down dead by God for touching the holy ark, but died of a stroke or fell under the cart carrying the ark (1 Sam. 7:1). He also taught that Jacob's deathbed prophecy over Judah (Gen. 49:10), namely that the scepter would not be taken away until the coming of Shiloh, was a later addition. In his "Encyclopedic Theology" seminar, he had taught that the book of Revelation was a poetic-historical account rather than a mere vision, while the Song of Songs was only the "idyllic poem . . . of an Oriental in love." A mystical explanation of these writings, especially the Song of Songs, was rejected by Wecklein, because it was not also used in the interpretation of profane writings. It was considered outright heresy that he saw the seduction of Adam

8. Landesarchiv Nordrhein-Westfalen, Abteilung Westfalen/Münster: Verein für Geschichte u. Altertumskunde Westf., Abt. MS—Nachl. Franz Bernh. Jos. v. Bucholtz, Nr. 1072, Promemoria, II.
9. Landesarchiv Nordrhein-Westfalen, Abteilung Westfalen/Münster: Verein für Geschichte u. Altertumskunde Westf., Abt. MS—Nachl. Franz Bernh. Jos. v. Bucholtz, Nr. 1072, Promemoria, III.

and Eve by the serpent, their fall and punishment as a Hebrew "idea" to interpret the arrival of evil in the world,[10] just like Pandora's box.[11] His detailed explanation of sexual events in the Bible was also criticized. After all, he was educating theologians and not "future anatomists."[12] In other lectures, he was charged with denying the existence of the one true religion and church, and instead professing a pluralism, according to which there was no subjective religion without error, and that these religions lead in a process of objective perfectibility to the ultimate truth about the divine. Therefore, he came to the conclusion that "we must tolerate each other, regardless of what religion."[13] Wecklein's explanation of the Last Supper was no less controversial because according to him, Jesus expressed in it his command for "universal tolerance and fraternization."[14] It cannot surprise that Wecklein was accordingly branded as a disciple of Gotthold Ephraim Lessing (1729–81) and his play *Nathan the Wise*. Wecklein's lectures were considered products of theological snobbery and seen as contemptuous of Catholic teaching.[15] "Even respectable Protestants" would reject Wecklein's talk of the "great man of Nazareth"—as he called Jesus.[16]

"Liberal" Prussians and "Bigoted" Catholics

So far, we have considered the charges against the man; now, however, we have to look more deeply at his work and his intentions to judge whether the accusations were accurate or just senseless slander. As I outlined above, Wecklein always supported the goals of his teacher, Oberthür, and even tried to find subscribers for his *Idea Ecclesiae* in

10. Today, one would call it an etiology.
11. Landesarchiv Nordrhein-Westfalen, Abteilung Westfalen/Münster: Verein für Geschichte u. Altertumskunde Westf., Abt. MS—Nachl. Franz Bernh. Jos. v. Bucholtz, Nr. 1072, Promemoria, cc.
12. Landesarchiv Nordrhein-Westfalen, Abteilung Westfalen/Münster: Verein für Geschichte u. Altertumskunde Westf., Abt. MS—Nachl. Franz Bernh. Jos. v. Bucholtz, Nr. 1072, Promemoria, IX.
13. Landesarchiv Nordrhein-Westfalen, Abteilung Westfalen/Münster: Verein für Geschichte u. Altertumskunde Westf., Abt. MS—Nachl. Franz Bernh. Jos. v. Bucholtz, Nr. 1072, Promemoria, V, citation of Wecklein.
14. Landesarchiv Nordrhein-Westfalen, Abteilung Westfalen/Münster: Verein für Geschichte u. Altertumskunde Westf., Abt. MS—Nachl. Franz Bernh. Jos. v. Bucholtz, Nr. 1072, Promemoria, VIII.
15. Ibid.
16. Ibid.

his little Franconian hometown of Gerolzhofen near Schweinfurt, but nobody was interested in theology anymore. A disillusioned Wecklein wrote to his teacher: "The answer I always received was: 'Today theology has no good reputation any more.'" The reason for this was a proud philosophy, Wecklein reasons, which looks with contempt on every textual or positive science such as exegesis. "A few years ago people at least still read some more liberal Protestant theologians, but now they even throw those into the dust [of oblivion]." A good example was his own reading circle, consisting of pastors and priests, which voted 14 to 6 against buying theological books, and instead for belletristic books.[17]

Unlike most theologians of the day, Wecklein had mastered Hebrew, Aramaic, Greek, and even Arabic.[18] This was an enormous plus when the dean of the Münster Cathedral, Count von Spiegel, asked Oberthür if he had a student who would be interested in becoming a professor in Münster. Oberthür suggested Wecklein to the university, who instantly agreed to the offer. However, in November 1805, Spiegel still hoped also to lure Oberthür to Münster to begin something like an ecumenical theology department, in which Protestant students could attend Catholic and Protestant classes alternately. Such a united theology department had existed in Würzburg since 1805.[19] Nevertheless, the bishop of Münster had not been asked about the final appointment of Wecklein, on October 17, 1805, by the university and the Prussian state to professor of biblical exegesis and Oriental languages, and it seems that Spiegel had not properly informed him. Spiegel disliked the chair of exegesis, Hyacinth Kistemaker (1754–1834), and was interested in hiring somebody of a different mindset—someone embodying the Enlightenment. Wecklein also had to defend himself for being Franconian, since the Prussian government began preferring Prussian-born academics for its positions. Nevertheless, the "resident alien"

17. Universitätsbibliothek Würzburg: Nachlass Oberthür, De-20, Letter of Michael Wecklein to Oberthür of January 30, 1805.
18. Ibid.
19. Universitätsbibliothek Würzburg: Nachlass Oberthür, De-20, Letter of Michael Wecklein to Oberthür of November 10, 1805: "Herr Domdechant setzt sein ganzes Vertrauen auf Sie, er wünscht Sie wären in 1/2 Jahr hier. . . ."

was initially so enchanted with the enlightened atmosphere in Prussia, that he was no longer homesick for Würzburg: "I do not want to see Franconia any more. The liberal and clear-sighted [*helldenkende*] government of Prussia and my continuous contentedness remunerates me for everything."[20] On December 5, 1805, only a few weeks before Wecklein's demise began, he wrote to Oberthür with enthusiasm:

> May Divine Providence grant that I may be most useful as a professor. My lectures have begun with great success—may this continue forever! I have at least the best hopes. . . . My vocation and dealing with theological issues diminishes all other troubles and all homesickness for the fatherland and relatives.[21]

Despite the pressure that a new academic position with the obligation of teaching a variety of courses entailed, he even found the time to find a publisher for Oberthür's multivolume *Biblical Anthropology*.[22] Yet, he perceived that Fürstenberg was no longer an Enlightener, like Spiegel. "A certain party," of conservatives, he already indicates, "entirely bigoted," was a public enemy of Spiegel.[23] In Münster, Wecklein enjoyed taking walks, and attending "concerts and many comedies." He had 104 students in dogmatic theology, 96 in encyclopedic theology, and at least 60 in Hebrew antiquities, while Spiegel and Westphalia's Governor (Oberpräsident) von Vinck, arrange "protection for me and enable me with freedom of expression and thought":[24]

> I am constantly so content and healthy as I never was before in my life. . . . The lifestyle here, the food and also the lodging facilities I like much better than in Würzburg. . . . There are plenty of vegetables, meat, milk, butter, etc., . . . and what is especially wonderful—one drinks here more wine and finer drinks than in Würzburg.[25]

20. Universitätsbibliothek Würzburg: Nachlass Oberthür, De-20, Letter of Michael Wecklein to Oberthür of November 10, 1805; ibid., of December 5, 1805: "Meine Franken habe ich, ich sollte fast sagen, vergessen: denn noch habe ich weder nach Gerolzhofen noch nach meinen Geschwistern ein Schreiben ergehen lassen."

21. Universitätsbibliothek Würzburg: Nachlass Oberthür, De-20, Letter of Michael Wecklein to Oberthür of December 5, 1805.

22. Universitätsbibliothek Würzburg: Nachlass Oberthür, De-20, Letter of Michael Wecklein to Oberthür of December 17, 1805.

23. Ibid.

24. Universitätsbibliothek Würzburg: Nachlass Oberthür, De-20, Letter of Michael Wecklein to Oberthür, undated, probably of late December 1805 or early January 1806.

This optimism came to an abrupt end. A friend had informed Oberthür about a pending investigation of Wecklein, and so, the student explained to his teacher that the man who denounced him to Oberthür's friend was publicly known as a "religious fanatic, of whom one can expect to . . . spread untrue rumors without prior critical inquiry."[26] Moreover, he claimed, he had been instructed by Spiegel and Vinck to work against "the increasing Jesuitism and . . . spurious theology [After-Theologie]." He showed his intention to do this with shrewdness, but it was almost impossible because his colleagues were all "ex-Jesuits."[27] According to Wecklein, his only heresy was that he read in his lecture course on Hebrew antiquities a few sentences by Heinrich Paulus; the fact that he quoted a Lutheran theologian was reason enough to question his orthodoxy! Moreover, he acknowledged that some fanatics would call it heretical that he explained the six days of creation not as six twenty-four-hour days, but as epochs of time. It did not help his case that he also lectured about variants of the Bible and did not embrace the theory that the Holy Spirit protected every letter of the Bible from error. His view that "God does not exist in space and time" was equally misunderstood, so that his colleagues thought he did not believe in heaven or hell, the Incarnation or the Real Presence, although Wecklein had stated such only for natural religion. "What happened? Soon . . . the clergy set off the public against me. . . ." A report was sent to Berlin without his knowledge and the clergy was portrayed as causing public unrest. "All my students say in the interrogations only good things about me."[28] After all, he followed standard textbooks in his lectures, such as Thomas Tychsen's *Grundriß einer Archäologie der Hebräer* (1789) or Engelbert Klüpfel's *Institutiones theologicae dogmaticae* (1802–3).[29] In order to avoid trouble, he had abstained from using the more progressive and sophisticated writings of Oberthür.[30] That Wecklein was surprised about his dismissal is

25. Ibid.
26. Universitätsbibliothek Würzburg: Nachlass Oberthür, De-20, Letter of Michael Wecklein to Oberthür of January 12, 1806.
27. Ibid.
28. Ibid.
29. Anton Pieper, *Die alte Universität Münster 1773-1818* (Regensburg: 1902), 45.

obvious from a letter to his teacher Oberthür of 1805. In it, he expresses his blind trust in Spiegel's protection: "He is extremely liberal, and under his protection I have to fear nothing."[31]

Persecution of the "Liberal Method"

Between January 3 and March 7, 1806, about thirty interrogations were conducted, many of them over four hours long, to find out whether the charges against Wecklein were correct. Since Wecklein announced in the printed university catalogue for the summer semester lectures on biblical hermeneutics and the first two books of the Pentateuch, the vicar general intervened, as mentioned above. Wecklein had to stop lecturing, officially because of a lack of students, who were too intimidated to come to the seminars of their beloved teacher.[32] Despite the prohibition on teaching, Wecklein remained officially a member of the department and of the institute for Oriental languages until 1816, when he was finally moved to a position in the philosophy department as lecturer for history and literature, and in 1818 appointed librarian of the University of Bonn.

Already in 1805, an outline of Wecklein's lectures had been printed without his knowledge or approval in the *Quartalschrift für Religionslehrer* of Natorp in Essen. An anonymous Protestant theologian had sent it, together with a letter, to the editor of the journal.[33] This author attested that every theologian, regardless of denomination, could only applaud Wecklein's acumen and attempts to teach theology in accordance with the needs of the time.[34] Yet, praise always also draws condemnation. Soon afterwards, Wecklein's "liberal method" was attacked by Marcellinus Molkenbuhr (1741–1825), a prominent conservative theologian and provincial of the Saxonian Franciscans,[35]

30. Universitätsbibliothek Würzburg: Nachlass Oberthür, De-20, Letter of Michael Wecklein to Oberthür of November 3, 1805.
31. Ibid.
32. Pieper, *Die alte Universität Münster 1773–1818*, 45–46.
33. I was unable to obtain a copy of this journal.
34. Marcellinus Molkenbuhr, *Neue Auslegungsart der heiligen Schrift des alten Testaments. Empfohlen von dem Herrn Michael Wecklein. . . .* (Dorsten: 1806), vi.
35. Molkenbuhr, *Neue Auslegungsart*; Winfrid Cramer, "Molkenbuhr, Marcellinus" in *Neue Deutsche Biographie* 17 (1994): 731.

and five other priests in Münster began preaching against Wecklein's theories from the pulpit.[36] Now, the professor had to defend himself against the charge of deviating from common Christian doctrines. In the newspaper *Westfälischer Anzeiger* Nr. 23 of March 21, 1806, he made clear:

> I have explained some biblical passages, from which only theological nonsense could extract a miracle, in an unstrained way. . . . Those miracles, however, which are truly important and which should be acknowledged as such, I have demonstrated in a much more profound way than Catholic exegetes have done thus far.[37]

According to Molkenbuhr, however, not a single miracle remains in Wecklein's framework. For the Franciscan, Wecklein embodied what the exegete had once confessed—that theologians can bring about "disaster"; however, unlike Molkenbuhr, he saw such a danger only if the theologians were "only half-enlightened and floating between light and darkness."[38] Wecklein was responsible for much of the uproar himself: instead of slowly introducing his students to more modern views about the Bible, he shocked them from the first week of the semester with his approach. When he explained in the first week, without preparing the minds of his listeners, that Balaam's donkey had not talked, or that Jericho's walls had not collapsed after the procession of the Israelites, he made a big mistake. Soon after, the theologian had drawn the attention of the entire city; everybody talked about the "unorthodox propositions" of the new professor.[39] Molkenbuhr denied that Wecklein's theses were still in the realm of school opinions, and thus permissible to be taught. Moreover, he found that Wecklein denied important truths of faith—for example, that a revelation from God could not be immediate, because God was unapproachable by

---

36. Molkenbuhr, *Neue Auslegungsart*, vii.

37. At Molkenbuhr, *Neue Auslegungsart*, ix: "Ich habe manchen Bibeltext, aus dem nur der theologische Unsinn ein Wunder heraus zaubern konnte, in einer andern ganz ungezwungenen Verbindung dargestellt. . . . Jene Wunder aber, auf die es vorzüglich ankommt, und welche wirklich als solche anzusehen sind, auf eine gründlichere Art erwiesen, als er vor mir so manche andere katholische Exegeten gethan haben."

38. Michael Wecklein to Spiegel on August 5, 1829, at Ton Meijknecht, "De Zaak Wecklein 1806," *Nederlands Archief voor Kerkgeschiedenis* 56 (1976): 450–62, at 462.

39. Molkenbuhr, *Neue Auslegungsart*, xii.

humans. Wecklein's attempts to reason about the radicality of revelation and the salvaging of divine transcendence could indeed be seen as undermining the church's deposit of faith: if God revealed himself through the mediation of men and women who, because of their insight, speak in the name of God intelligibly and have a flawless character, then this was awfully close to Spinoza's concept of revelation in the *Tractatus Theologico-Policticus*, chapter 7: the deeds of prophets and apostles no longer needed to be seen as supernatural![40]

"Sane Principles" for Exegesis

Following the assaults on his person and the rumors about his lectures, Wecklein felt pressured to present his exegesis publicly. He therefore published his *Ideas for a More Liberal Interpretation of the Old Testament* shortly after his troubles began. He states that his book also became necessary because his students did not understand his lectures, since they lacked the knowledge of "sane" exegetical principles with which to interpret the Old Testament (*saniora principia deesse*).[41]

By about 1785, Wecklein explained, exegesis had improved greatly. Elements of this change were a better study of philology, a more accurate understanding of ancient dialects, multiple variants of the text, chronology, archeology, secular history, and other auxiliary sciences. Finally, one was able to be more certain (*certius*) about finding the intention of the author.[42] Wecklein praised especially Matthias Flacius's *Clavis S. Scripturae* (1567), Wolfgang Franz's *Tractatus theologicus novus de interpretatione* (1708), Johann Conrad Dannhauer's *Hermeneutica* (1654), Valentin Löscher's *Breviarium exegeticae* (1715), and Jacob Rambach's *Hermeneutica Sacra* (1725)—all Protestants.[43]

Nevertheless, Wecklein criticized his Protestant colleagues because their scriptural scholarship was too much informed by systematic

40. Ibid., xiii.
41. Michael Wecklein, *Momenta praecipua ad liberaliorem V. T. interpretationem* (Essen: 1806), preface.
42. Wecklein, *Momenta*, 5–6.
43. Cf. Torbjörn Johansson, et al. (eds.), *Hermeneutica Sacra: Studien zur Auslegung der Heiligen Schrift im 16. und 17. Jahrhundert* (Berlin: De Gruyter, 2010); John Sailhamer, *Introduction to Old Testament Theology: A Canonical Approach* (Grand Rapids, MI: Zondervan, 1995), 230f.

dogmatic theology and a wrong concept of inspiration, which entailed that *every word* was inspired.[44] A sober exegesis of the Old Testament was also impeded by neglecting the historical context (*quam quod illud ex indole aetatis, qua scriptores vixerunt, explicare negligebant*) and using later concepts to explain earlier ones—that is, as if the prophets would have had the same knowledge of nature, theology, philosophy, or psychology.[45] For example, when the ancient writers talked about the soul or the human spirit (*de anima, de spiritu hominis*), contemporary authors understood these terms as eighteenth-century concepts (*hodie nos utimur*).[46] A similar mistake can be made in the exegesis of the New Testament. In fact, Wecklein calls it the gravest "sin" an exegete can commit (*gravissime porro peccabant*), to presuppose that all theological concepts (*notiones*) handed over from Christ and the apostles must also have been preached, and therefore found in the text.[47] This is, of course, an attack on a hermeneutic that reads scripture within the context of scripture (and tradition), and especially a christological reading of the Old Testament—a view Molkenbuhr defended.[48] If, for example, Genesis 1 taught that the human person was created in the image of God (*imaginem Dei formatum*), then the question was what this actually meant. Most exegetes of previous generations understood this according to the concepts of St. Paul and not according to the concepts of the "ancient and rude people" (*prisci et rudes*) who wrote it down.[49]

The new way of reading scripture was, for Wecklein, predominantly a German Enlightenment achievement. His champions were Döderlein, Eichhorn, Hezel, Herder, and Paulus.[50] They provided exegesis with a variety of wonderful resources, and especially the method of comparing ancient Hebrew texts with Greek and Roman texts and cultural artefacts in order to detect differences and parallels in style.[51]

---

44. Wecklein, *Momenta*, 8.
45. Ibid., 8–9, refers to Georg Lorenz Bauer, *Hermeneutica sacra veteris testamenti* (Leipzig: 1797), 258.
46. Ibid., 9.
47. Ibid.
48. Molkenbuhr, *Neue Auslegungsart,* 17.
49. Wecklein, *Momenta,* 10. Other examples ibid., 10–11.
50. Cf. Henning Graf Reventlow, *History of Biblical Interpretation,* trans. Leo G. Purdue (Houston Mill, GA: Society of Biblical Literature, 2010), 4:123–230; Gottlob Wilhelm Meyer, *Geschichte der Schrifterklärung seit der Wiederherstellung der Wissenschaften* (Göttingen: 1809), vol. 5, passim.

As secondary sources, Wecklein recommended to his readers Johann G. Herder's *Geist der hebräischen Poesie* (1783), Johann Heinrich Justus Köppen's six volumes of annotations to Homer (1787ff), Johann Gottfried Eichhorn's *Urgeschichte* (1790f), Martin Gottfried Herrmann's *Handbuch der Mythologie*, W. Friedrich Hezel's *Geist der Philosophie und Sprache der alten Welt* (1794), and Woltmann's *Grundriss der älteren Menschengeschichte* (1797), among others.[52] All of these books not only stress a strong philological and historical analysis of texts, including a comparison of ancient and biblical ones, but also emphasize the study of culture. Wecklein seems to have been among the first Catholic exegetes who tried to integrate these authors into Catholic circles, and also make the study of culture fruitful for Catholic thought.[53]

Wecklein believed that the idea of immediate divine causation and revelation came about among uncultured people who were ignorant of intermediate and secondary causality. Consequently, when ancient societies believed that natural events were caused by the gods—for example, explaining Ganymede's disappearance by the fact that he was kidnapped by Zeus—one must ascribe the same belief to the Hebrews, when they talk about the assumption of Elijah and Enoch.[54] When ancient miracles happen, like that of the wounded Aeneas not falling into the hands of the enemy, but being guided by Apollo through fog, then such events have to be compared with biblical accounts, such as the story about Hagar and Ismael, who were supposed to have died in the desert, but on whom God had mercy after hearing their prayers.[55] Likewise, conscience and dreams are described by the ancients as given by God instead of looking for psychological explanations. Cain's sudden remorse after killing his brother and his conversation with God in Genesis 4, or Isaiah's prophecy about Cyrus being the messiah, have to be seen as narratives that elucidate this problem. A reason why God could not influence one's conscience or dreams, however, is not

51. Wecklein, Momenta, 11–12.
52. Ibid., 14–16. Molkenbuhr boasts that he has read not a single of the named authors. See Molkenbuhr, Neue Auslegungsart, 23.
53. Cf. Michael Carhart, The Science of Culture in Enlightenment Germany (Cambridge, MA: 2007).
54. Wecklein, Momenta, 18.
55. Ibid., 19.

given.[56] It seems that, for Wecklein, the ancient worldview that sees God at work in the entire world is at fault. After all, ancient scribes also saw the virtues as deriving from God, as the story about Noah and the flood in Genesis 6 negates human activity and responsibility.[57] Wecklein sees the same divinization at work in specific titles, such as "Sons of God." One should not understand it literally, because after all, Homer had already given worldly princes the same title, just as the Hebrews did with their kings (Ps. 2:7).[58] This was, of course, easily misunderstood, in the sense that Wecklein could have meant that just as the Homeric heroes were human beings, Jesus was a human being, because both the heroes and Jesus share the same title.[59]

A second principle is that whatever God cannot do immediately or directly, he can do through messengers. A comparative study of the Bible could prove the widespread belief in divine messengers, and thus provide a cultural proof for the Catholic doctrine on angels.[60] When Abraham is admonished in a dream (Gen. 22) to sacrifice his son Isaac for the glory of God, Wecklein asserts that the patriarch had erred. He had not counted on the fact that God could reveal his will also through weaknesses, erroneous prejudices, and human opinions.[61]

Molkenbuhr criticized that such an interpretation led to the reading of Abraham committing three errors: first, when he believed God had commanded him to sacrifice his son; second, when he believed God had named a special mountain for the sacrifice; and finally, when he believed God commanded him to sacrifice the ram instead.[62] Abraham

---

56. Molkenbuhr, *Neue Auslegungsart,* 19–20.

57. Ibid., 21.

58. Wecklein, *Momenta,* 21.

59. Molkenbuhr, *Neue Auslegungsart,* 51.

60. Wecklein, *Momenta,* 22–23. He also argues that by reason alone one could prove the existence of angels, since there must be a scale of continuously better and more perfect beings until the most perfect being is reached (Quis enim de dogmate dubitat, cujus veritatem ipsa adeo ratio adcontinuandam entium imperfectiorum seriem ad ens perfectissimum usque, Numen supremum dictum, tam necessario postulat.). The necessity of this proof was of course attacked as an infringement upon God's freedom; see Molkenbuhr, *Neue Auslegungsart,* 52. In his interpretation, Wecklein seems to rely on Ernst Christian Stahl, "Versuch über die Erscheinungen Jehovas," in *Eichhorn's Bibliothek der Biblischen Litteratur* 7 (1795): 156–80. This essay contains a letter from Stahl in which he outlines a future academic treatment of the topic.

61. Wecklein, *Momenta,* 24: "Lucide hinc apparet, Deum per hominum adeo imbellicitates, praejudicia, opiniones suam ipsis voluntatem manifestasse, eos docuisse et virtutem eorum probasse; quae veritas, nostris etiamnum temporibus, tot hominum satis confirmatur."

is instructed in Genesis 21 about the fate of Sodom and Gomorrah; Wecklein sees here a parallel to Homer, according to whom Athena appeared to Odysseus and gave him advice.[63] The angel that struck the Assyrians in 2 Kings 19:35 is a parallel to Homer's Apollo striking the Greeks because they did not honor his priest.[64] The black death that Apollo sends to Troy is a parallel to 2 Kings 19:35, where the angel of the Lord strikes the Assyrians.[65] Yet, despite these sophisticated parallels, there remains an inherent problem. On the one hand, Wecklein believes in the reality of biblical angels; on the other, he explains the divine messengers in Homer as figments of imagination. One cannot have one's cake and eat it too. Since Wecklein is otherwise surprisingly consistent, it seems to me that he added the proof about angels to secure himself from criticism or to demonstrate the value of his theology for apologetics; otherwise, one has to assert contradictions in his method. Moreover, Wecklein never asks the question of what should and could be compared in ancient religions. If the black death in Troy was no miracle, then a parallel in the Old Testament could hardly qualify as such, unless there is a significant difference, such as different literary genres—a valid point of criticism raised by Molkenbuhr.[66]

The third rule of comparative exegesis is that in ancient times, human actions and emotions, especially passions such as wrath or sadness, are ascribed to God.[67] However, Moses, David, and the prophets already had "better notions" about the sanctity of God, his justice and mercy, and used such words only to accommodate their message to the common people.[68] While this does not yet sound problematic, one could easily interpret Wecklein's comment to mean that the wrath of God or his punishment of sinners is part of anthropomorphic imagery. However, one could then, like Molkenbuhr,

62. Molkenbuhr, *Neue Auslegungsart*, 55–56.
63. Wecklein, *Momenta*, 27–28.
64. Ibid., 27.
65. Ibid.
66. Molkenbuhr, *Neue Auslegungsart*, 73.
67. Wecklein, *Momenta*, 28–29.
68. Ibid., 30.

argue that the logic of damnation should be rejected, because God's justice would only be an anthropomorphic image.[69] Moreover, in such an anthropomorphic image, God would also be charged with evil actions—for example, that he "hardened Pharaoh's heart" (Exod. 4:21).[70] Whatever good or evil happened was, in ancient times, always attributed immediately to God, whether as reward or punishment, without assuming a natural cause or cooperation on the part of human beings. Wecklein sees this in the *Odyssey*, especially in book 3:133, when Zeus uses winds to wreck ships as punishment. Therefore, according to Wecklein, Hebrews and Greeks seem to have the same basic views about divine action.[71] That Enlightenment theology had not automatically brought about a better understanding or more appreciation of Judaism can be seen from Wecklein's statement that the "uncultivated" people thought that sacrifice alone would justify them, regardless of their interior disposition—namely, a life of integrity. This opinion he also holds of pre-Mosaic Judaism.[72]

A fourth finding of comparative theology is that divine beings descend from heaven and visit humans. In the *Odyssey*, Athena visits Erechtheus (Book 8:81), or in Ovid's *Metamorphoses,* Jupiter and Mercury visit Philemon and Baucis (Book 8:640) and bless them for their hospitality. Wecklein asserts that one finds similar accounts in Genesis, not only when God walks around in paradise (Gen. 2), but also when he destroys Sodom and Gomorrah.[73]

Consequently, such parallels between secular and sacred writings

---

69. Molkenbuhr, *Neue Auslegungsart,* 73.

70. Wecklein, *Momenta,* 32–34.

71. Ibid., 38: "Conveniunt in eadem opinione, cum Graecis, Hebraei. Probos Deus praemiis terrenis afficit, opibus, honore, corporis firmitate et sanitate, longaevitate, omnibusque prosperitatis generibus, a cunctis eos calamitatibus defendit, et singularem eorum curam habet. Improbos econtra afficit poenis, egestate, ignominia, morbis, aliisque adversitatibus obruit. Delicta poena sequitur comes. Sententia haec per omnes V. T. libros obvia est.".

72. Ibid., 43–44: "At sicut populi inculti, qui Deum ex suo modulo metiuntur, cultum divinum ritibus solum externis et donis imprimis peragi, se vero per ejusmodi oblationes, supremo reru arbitro, digniores reddi existimant; ita ii, qui ad altiorem naturae divinae cognitionem penetrarunt, sacrificiis et ritibus externis pretium omnino nullum statuendum esse judicant, nisi animi pietas et vitae integritas accedat. Ad hanc maturiorem cognitionem denique, post Mosem, etiam Hebraei pervenerunt. Davides, Assaphus, Salomo, necnon Prophetae unanimi consensu assidue declararunt, sacrifica sine interna mentis sanctitate et probitate nullius esse apud Deum pretii."

73. Ibid., 45–46.

have to be taken into consideration in an interpretation, especially if a similar event is described, if the sources are from the same time period, and so on.[74] Wecklein assumes that the notions and opinions of people change; despite the fact that people who are secluded from others cling to their traditions, they still adopt new ideas, so that one can observe a gradual mutation of their concepts. This happened to the Hebrews, so that wrong concepts of earlier generations were replaced with more purified, newer ones.[75]

In order to understand the concepts of the ancient Hebrews, one has to consult the opinions and laws of the ancient peoples with whom Israel stood in contact and from whom Israel probably learned.[76] This is certainly a sign of the appreciation of history, as the Catholic exegetes Dom Calmet, Richard Simon, and many others have demonstrated, but Wecklein's nemesis Molkenbuhr comments: "Such research is neither recommended by holy scripture, nor by the fathers, nor by the church."[77] In defense of Molkenbuhr, one has to say that since he believed Moses was the most ancient writer, in his view, all pagan writers wrote after the Babylonian exile. Thus, it was counterintuitive to learn from later writers about Moses. Instead, Molkenbuhr relied on Tertullian's idea that the pagans learned their wisdom from the Hebrews.

Among the peoples from whom the Israelites learned were the Egyptians, especially because Moses was educated by them at the royal court and from whom he received much of his knowledge, even regarding legislation.[78] Molkenbuhr also interjects here and insists that Moses learned more from the Medianites where he spent more of his lifetime—but he does not see that by admitting this, he refutes

74. Ibid., 49: "Ubi in lectione scriptoris profani aliqua cum scriptore sacro occurrit similitudo, considerandum est, an vera sit similitudo satisque similia sint loca; id est, an sit in utroque eadem res idemque factum, non modo verbum idem, ut judicium tuto fieri possit."
75. Ibid., 50: "Et quamquam populi a societate cum aliis seclusi, qui insuper non multum temporis in studio litterarum consumunt, notionibus suis a majoribus acceptis firmiter adhaereant, nec facile ab iis recedant: successu tamen temporis aliquam saltem mutationem illos subire, majorem interdum claritatem accipere, falsas, quae admixtae fuerant, ideas amittere, inter omnes constat."
76. Ibid., 51.
77. Molkenbuhr, *Neue Auslegungsart,* 91.
78. Wecklein, *Momenta,* 51.

his own argument, because then, the knowledge of Medianite culture would be helpful in better understanding Moses.[79] Even the mutual exchange (*mutuum commercium*) between Israelites and Babylonians, which Wecklein considers crucial, is disregarded by the Franciscan.[80]

Although Wecklein concedes that the authority of scripture might be endangered by his more liberal interpretation (*liberaliorem interpretationem*), it is by no means destroyed. It can appear "suspicious and dangerous" (*suspectam et periculosam*), but in reality it only resolves the problems Voltaire, Paine, and others have pointed to in their acerbic biblical criticism.[81] By demonstrating that the content of holy scripture was accommodated to the cultural state of the human beings who heard God's revelation, Wecklein defended divine revelation against its critics and reinstated the authority of scripture.[82] Wecklein even embraces Gotthold Ephraim Lessing's concept that revelation is "educatio totius generis humani per providentiam divinam a primordiis mundi incepta, et per saecula sequiora continuata."[83] Consequently, revelation works gradually, wherefore one cannot expect breadth and purity (*amplitudo et puritas*) from the Old Testament. With the help of the great teachers Moses, the prophets, and Jesus, God brings this concept of revelation to perfection.[84] For example, it was against "healthier moral doctrine" (*saniori doctrinae*

79. Molkenbuhr, *Neue Auslegungsart*, 94–96.
80. Ibid., 98; Wecklein, Momenta, 51–52: "Per mutuum dein commercium, quod Israelitae cum Babyloniis habuerunt, dum collapsa republica exules sub iis vivebat, philosophiam chaldaicam (si excellenti hoc nomine digna videtur) caram factam esse, quis, qui Danielem legerit, non videt? Ideas vero Persarum, a quibus Babylonia demum Cyro duce occupata est, Hebraeis non ignotas fuisse, e capite XLV Isaiae, cujus author Jehovam, qui lucem et tenebras formavit, bonum quoque ac malum producere ait, luculenter apparet."
81. Cf. Bertram Eugene Schwarzbach, *Voltaire's Old Testament Criticism* (Geneva: Droz, 1971).
82. Wecklein, *Momenta*, 53: "Per liberaliorem V. Testam. interpretationem, cum revelationem divinam in his libris contentam indoli ac statui primorum hominum accomodatam ese ostenditur; ipsa vindicatur revelatio et majorem adipiscitur authoritatem; ergo et S. Scriptura ceu depositum hujus revelationis. Surrexere quondam revelationis derisores, qui S. Scripturam hanc ob causam exponebant, quod sint in ea loca quam plurima sibi repugnantia, fabulae, conceptus Deo indigni; qupd extollantur facta hominum valde turpia, et vituperentur quae merentur bonorum aestimationem. Erant praecipui ex hac classe Voltairius et Painius, praeter alios multos Gallos et Anglos; ut omittam recentiores ex omni fere hominum ordine frequentes. At quidquid hi in lucem protulerint, et etiamnun proferant, suam fatentur ignorantiam, etsi defectus morales in S. Scriptura esse obvios et puram npn ubique narrari historiam, libenter concedimus. Neque enim quid sit revelatio, neque quid praestare debeat haud sat bene distinguere nesciunt."
83. Ibid., 54–55.
84. Ibid., 55.

morali) that Abraham lied about Sarah being his sister or that Jacob deceived Esau.[85] Jesus, instead, worked (*elaboravit*) for a purer and subtler Jewish religion, but his simple doctrine has been eclipsed by "unexperienced" (*imperitis*) doctors of the church. These read the Old Testament without any knowledge of antiquities, invented things, and had the wrong concept that every word of scripture was "quasi infused" by God, and in the end interpreted the Old Testament against the New Testament.[86] These doctors—and Wecklein does not seem to think of ancient heretics, but rather of fathers of the church, and especially scholastic theologians—have, as one could see in their dogmatic textbooks (*compendiis dogmaticis*) and homilies, taught again an anthropomorphic God whose benevolence one could gain through sacrifices (*oblationes*), and that sins would be forgiven, according to merit. Last, but not least, they also neglected true piety and a "sincere emendation of the heart."[87] It is remarkable how Wecklein rejects with this one sentence a tradition of almost two thousand years, and charges generations of his peers with blind ignorance.

Since much of the Old Testament was composed in a pre-literary time, the texts were orally transmitted. When they were written down, the narratives were enlarged, and many transformed into miraculous accounts (*vertuntque in miracula*). This is just like the origin of the ancient myths—for example, about the origin of humanity and its founders, of a Golden Age, and so on—and so, one has to see and interpret scripture in this light.[88] Myths, Wecklein insists, however, are not just fables but ancient narrations, which are substitutes for physical, moral, or natural human facts, or a philosophical concept, and are only presented as miraculous due to the incapacity of the human mind.[89] From this account, it becomes clear that Wecklein relies on Christian Gottlob Heyne's account of myth.[90] Also, the belief that

---

85. Ibid., 56.
86. Ibid., 57.
87. Ibid., 57.
88. Ibid., 59.
89. Ibid., 59–60: "Mythi non sunt fabulae, sed priscae narrationes; quae vel factum physicum aliquod, vel factum morale in natura humana, vel conceptum philosophicum supponunt; sed pro modulo imperfectioris hominum rudium cognitionis, et pro sincera animi eorum indole, miraculose propositae."

without proper knowledge of the classics, and especially classical mythology, one could not properly interpret the Old Testament was taken from Heyne.[91]

There are truths in the Old Testament that are not contained in any Greek or Roman writer, namely about the "ens supremum, unicum, omnipotens, sanctum et individum mundi moderatorem" or that whatever happens to a human being hardly ever has to do with his merits.[92] However, Wecklein concedes that through his more liberal method, a number of biblical passages will be dismissed, which were used by dogmatic theologians to prove the dogma of the creation of the universe, the reality of grace, original sin, the existence of angels and demons, of the Trinity, of Purgatory, of the resurrection of the dead in the way described by St. Paul, and the expectation of a Messiah in the person of Jesus of Nazareth:

> However, we do not need such deficient arguments, above which the truth of the dogmas is constructed. There is other support from the New Testament and the perpetual teaching tradition of the church.[93]

The historical facts in the Old Testament gain more certitude through the new method, especially since it gives nature and history back its causality, and thus increases the trustworthiness of the accounts. The more miracles, the less wise God must be, who is forced to interfere; the fewer miracles, the more awe they inspire in humans.[94] Moreover, miracles that seem to have no final moral aim or contradict the moral law must be rejected.[95] Most narratives of miracles in the Old

---

90. Heyne bases his thoughts on the origin of language. See Marianne Heidenreich, *Christian Gottlob Heyne und die alte Geschichte* (Munich: Saur, 2006), 429–48; Axel Horstmann, "Mythologie und Altertumswssenschaft Der Mythosbegriff bei Christian Gottlob Heyne," *Archiv für Begriffsgeschichte* 16 (1972): 60–85.

91. Peter Bietenholz, *Historia and Fabula: Myths and Legends in Historical Thought from Antiquity to the Modern Age* (Leiden: Brill, 1994), 285–86; Christian Hartlich and Walter Sachs, *Die Entstehung des Mythosbegriffs in der modernen Bibelwissenschaft* (Tübingen: Mohr Siebeck, 1952), 11–19.

92. Wecklein, *Momenta,* 60–61.

93. Ibid., 61.

94. Ibid., 62.

95. Ibid., 63: "Quod tamen maximum mihi semper visym est momentum, erat disharmonia factorum ejusmodi mirabilium cum fine morali, quem providentiam divinam per omnes, quos in rebus humanis permittit aut immediate efficit, casus proponere sibi oportet. Ad finem hunc rationabilem, vel rectius moralem, quidquid accidit, quidquid sub specioso revelationis nomine

Testament contain so many "obvious" disharmonies that they have to be rejected as human inventions.[96] "Such is utterly unworthy of God!" reasons Wecklein.[97] This concept, which sees in the Old Testament and in the traditional way of explaining scripture a way of omitting secondary causality and introducing a deus ex machina, rests, it seems, on the work of the Protestant theologian Johann Christoph Döderlein (1745–92), who thought that it was possible that the accounts of the Flood, the Tower of Babel, and the destruction of Sodom could be explained naturally.[98]

Are there then any miracles left in Wecklein's Bible? The exegete does not reject all miracles or the notion that God could use extraordinary means to admonish, teach, or deter people from a sin, but that not *all* accounts of miraculous events were true miracles, but instead one should speak of an ordinary and an extraordinary providence, and thus distinguish between primary and secondary divine causality: Natural events have an aim that is congruent with divine providence.[99] Because of this belief in providence, the accounts from Abraham to Jesus deserve proper attention. By appealing to providence, Wecklein tries at the end of his book to defend himself as an orthodox theologian. By invoking the concept of sacred history or *Heilsgeschichte,* he migrates the miraculous from nature to history. This is an important parallel to the work of Aloysius Sandbichler (see the chapter on him in this volume), who projected a salvific theology, but was never censored.[100]

Conclusion

Marcellinus Molkenbuhr argued forcefully that Catholics could not

posteris traditum, dijudicamus: cui si congruit, ceu divinum admittimus; si repugnat, ceu fraudulentum rejicimus, saltem humanum existimamus."
96. Ibid., 64: "ad alendam hominum curiositatem . . . ad mitigandam Israelitarum pertinaciam . . ."
97. Ibid.: "Res Deo plane indigna!"
98. Ibid., 68. Johann Christian Döderlein, *Institutio theologi Christiani in capitibus religionus theoreticus nostris temporibus accomodata* (Nuremberg: 1787), 1:602–3.
99. Wecklein, *Momenta,* 67–68; ibid., 69: "Quam praeclare vero providentia divina, per eventus etiam naturales in historia revelationis obvios esse manifestaverit, ex eo apparet, quod ultimato omnes in fine illo collimant, quem per revelationem obtinendum sibi proposuit."
100. Molkenbuhr, *Neue Auslegungsart,* 140–41.

receive the new method as Wecklein outlined it, because it had been invented by Protestants and was not even fully accepted among them.[101] While, for Molkenbuhr, liberal exegesis led to deism and a rationalist flattening of the Bible, Wecklein defended his approach as the most promising way to teach the faith as an option in a changing world, in which more and more people were skeptics. The old theology could only produce wonder and awe but not improve public morals. Once children became able to reason for themselves, they would abandon such theology and declare religion to be suspicious and incredible. Only a renewed, enlightened theology could counter this trend, Wecklein was sure.[102]

There are two things I think contemporary theologians can learn from this episode, apart from the mere historical importance of this case: first of all, it informs us about the unresolved question as to whether exegesis is a theological or a literary discipline. Wecklein seems to think the latter, and thus is inclined to a religious studies approach to scripture, while Molkenbuhr embodies scripture as a theological and ecclesial task. Second, the controversy sheds light on how theologians disseminate their knowledge and how they view tradition. It is stunning how Wecklein dismisses generations of scholars as "ignorant," but is himself unable to communicate his enlightened insights to his students in a way that does not upset them. Thus, for me, this episode raises the question of how a theologian can be humble, yet creative at the same time. Wecklein is certainly not an example of the former, but his bold and creative thinking should be remembered as the attempt of an eighteenth-century priest who desperately tried to remind the church how important rationality was in the teaching and preaching of scripture. Yet, Catholic theology was not yet ready for his comparative approach to other religions.

---

101. Ibid., 5–6.
102. Wecklein, *Momenta*, 58. Molkenbuhr comments in *Neue Auslegungsart*, 108 without any hermeneutic generosity: "Welch eine verworrene unbeiwesene Anklage! . . . Den Sinn des grauen Alters in Betracht der h. Schrift sollen wir aus den blinden Heiden Homer, Herodot und andern erlernen; dann würde aller Aberglaube und Unglaube verschwinden. Allein bei den Heiden war ja der grosse Aberglaube, und bei vielen auch ein gänzlicher Unglaube."

Bibliography

Ackva, Friedhelm. *Johann Jakob Hess (1741-1828) und seine Biblische Geschichte. Leben, Werk und Wirkung des Zürcher Antistes.* Frankfurt: Peter Lang, 1992.

Ages, Arnold. "Voltaire, Calmet and the Old Testament." *Studies on Voltaire and the Eighteenth Century* 41 (1966): 87–187.

Albertan-Coppola, Sylviane. "Counter-Enlightenment." In *Encyclopedia of the Enlightenment.* Edited by Alan Charles Kors. Oxford: Oxford University Press, 2002, 1:307–11.

Albrecht, Michael. *Eklektik. Eine Begriffsgeschichte mit Hinweisen auf die Philosophie- und Wissenschaftsgeschichte.* Stuttgart-Bad Cannstatt: Fromann-Holzboog, 1994.

Alcazar, Luis de. *Vestigatio arcani sensus in Apocalypsin.* Antwerp: 1614.

Alden, Dauril. *The Making of an Enterprise: The Society of Jesus in Portugal, Its Empire, and Beyond, 1540-1750.* Stanford: 1996.

Allgeier, Arthur. "Martin Gerbert and Karl Theodor von Dalberg. Beiträge zu den Schlußkapiteln der Geschichte des Bistum Konstanz." *Freiburger Diözesanarchiv* 69 (1949): 66–91.

_____. "Der Briefwechsel von J. J. Hess mit Martin Gerbert." *Zeitschrift für die Geschichte des Oberrheins* 56 (1943): 504–49.

Altenberend, Johannes. *Leander van Ess (1772-1847): Bibelübersetzer und Bibelverbreiter zwischen katholischer Aufklärung und evangelikaler Erweckungsbewegung.* Paderborn: Bonifatius, 2001.

Altmann, Alexander. *Die trostvolle Aufklärung. Studien zur Metaphysik und politischen Theorie Moses Mendelssohns.* Stuttgart-Bad Cannstatt: Frommann-Holzboog, 1982.

Amort, Eusebius. *Epistola Justiniani Frobenii ad Cl. V. Justinum . . . de legitima potestate summi pontificis.* Augsburg: 1764.

_____. *Theologia eclectia, moralis et scholastica.* Augsburg and Würzburg: 1752.

_____. *Demonstratio Critica Religionis Catholicae Nova, Modesta, Facilis.* Venice: 1744.

Anonymous. *Nachricht, Einrichtung, Rechte und Gesetze der Hoch-Gräflich Neuwiedischen Akademie zur Vereinigung des Glaubens und weiterer Aufnahme der Religion.* Neuwied: 1757.

_____. *Katholische Betrachtungen über die zu Mainz, Heidelberg und Strassburg wider den Isenbiehlischen Versuch vom Emmanuel ausgebrachten Censuren.* Frankfurt and Leipzig: 1778.

_____. "Denkschrift auf den sel. Herrn Alois Sandbichler." *Neue Quartalschrift für katholische Geistliche* 7 (1833): 1–14.

_____. "Von den Exorzismen bei der heiligen Taufe." *Linzer Monatsschrift* 3/2 (1804): 233–51.

_____. "Eine gefälschte Briefsammlung Joseph II." *Historisch-Politische Blätter für das katholische Deutschland* 133 (1904): 786–94.

_____. *Weder die christliche Religion noch die römisch-katholische Kirche ist die Alleinseligmachende: Aus entscheidenden Vernunftgründen erwiesen von einem römisch-katholischen Pfarrer in Schlesien.* Frankfurt: 1791.

_____. *Katholische Betrachtung eines Köllnischen Theologen über die Scriptursätze des P. Thadaeus a S. Adamo.* Erfurt: 1785.

_____. *Zwote katholische Betrachtung . . . die Erwägungen welche Herrn Goldhagen zu Mainz . . . und Herr Pater Feller . . . zu machen beliebten wider die Scriptursätze des P. Thaddäus vom H. Adam.* Frankfurt: 1785.

_____. *Judicium Theologorum Argentinensium de Libro Germanico Vulgato: J. L. Isenbiehl, Neuer Versuch.* Mainz: 1778.

Apel, Max and Peter Ludz, eds. *Philosophisches Wörterbuch.* Berlin, New York: De Gruyter, 1976.

Aquilino, Alexius A. *Pentateuchi Hebraeo-Samaritani praestantia in illustrando et emendando textu masorethico ostensa, una cum aliis subsidiis hermeneutico-critici, ad totum textrum Hebraeum rite intelligendum servientibus.* Heidelberg: 1783.

Aretin, Karl O. von. "Katholische Aufklärung im Heiligen Römischen Reich." In Idem, *Das Reich. Friedensgarantie und europäisches Gleichgewicht 1648-1806.* Stuttgart: Klett-Cotta, 1986, 403–33.

Arigler, Altmann. *Hermeneutica Biblica Generalis.* Vienna: 1813.

____. *De Studio Biblico.* Vienna: 1809.

Armenteros, Carolina. *The French Idea of History: Joseph de Maistre and his Heirs, 1794-1854.* Ithaca: Cornell University Press, 2011.

Armogathe, Jean-Robert. "Per Annos Mille: Cornelius a Lapide and the Interpretation of Revelation 20:2–8." In *Millenarianism and Messianism in Early Modern Europe: Catholic Millenarianism: From Savonarola to the Abbe Gregoire.* Edited by Karl A. Kottman. Dordrecht: Kluwer, 2001, 45–52.

____. "Interpretations of the Revelation of John: 1500–1800." In *Encyclopedia of Apocalypticism.* Edited by John J. Collins and Bernard McGinn. New York: Continuum, 1998, 2:185–203.

Asselt, Willem J. van. *The Federal Theology of Johannes Cocceius (1603-1669).* Leiden: Brill, 2001.

Babor, Johann. *Uebersetzung des Neuen Testaments mit erklärenden Anmerkungen.* Vienna: 1805.

____. *Allgemeine Einleitung in die Schriften des alten Testaments.* Vienna: 1794.

____. *Kritische Untersuchung, ob die sogenannte Weissagung Jakobs 1. Mos. 49, 10 vom Messias handle.* 1789.

Bahrdt, Carl Friedrich. *De eo, an fieri possit, ut sublato pontificis imperio reconcilientur dissidentes in religione Christiani contra Justinum Febronianum dissertatio.* Leipzig: 1763.

Bantle, Franz Xaver. *Unfehlbarkeit der Kirche in Aufklärung und Romantik: eine dogmengeschichtliche Untersuchung für die Zeit der Wende vom 18. zum 19. Jahrhundert.* Freiburg: Herder, 1976.

Barnes, Robin. "Images of Hope and Despair: Western Apocalypticism, 1500–1800." In *The Continuum History of Apocalypticism.* Edited by Bernard McGinn, John J. Collins, and Stephen J. Stein. New York: Continuum, 2003, 143–84.

Bauer, Georg Lorenz. *Entwurf einer Hermeneutik des Alten und Neuen Testaments.* Leipzig: 1799.

____. *Hermeneutica sacra veteris testament.* Leipzig: 1797.

Bäumer, Remigius. "Interpretation und Verbindlichkeit der Konstanzer Dekrete." *Theologisch-Praktische Quartalschrift* 116 (1968): 44–53.

____. "Die Bedeutung des Konstanzer Konzils für die Geschichte der Kirche." *Annuarium Historiae Conciliorum* 4 (1972): 26–45.

Baumgarten, Siegmund Jacob. *Unterricht von Auslegung der heil. Schrift.* Halle: 1759.

Bayer, Josef. "Dr. Philipp Brunner, Ministerialrat in Karlsruhe und Pfarrer in Hofweier." *Freiburger Diözesanarchiv* 92 (1972): 201–22.

Beales, Derek. *Enlightenment and Reform in the 18th Century.* London: Tauris, 2005.

____. *Prosperity and Plunder: European Catholic Monasteries in the Age of Revolution, 1650–1815.* New York: Cambridge University Press, 2003.

Bedouelle, Guy. *The Reform of Catholicism, 1480–1620.* Toronto: Pontifical Institute of Mediaeval Studies, 2008.

Bellarmine, Robert. "Disputationes de controversiis christianiae fideo adversus huius temporis haereticos [1581–1592]." In *Opera Omnia.* Paris: 1870.

Bellinger, Dom Aidan. "Superstitious enemies of the flesh? The Variety of Benedictine Responses to the Enlightenment." In *Religious Change in Europe 1650–1914.* Edited by Nigel Aston, 149–60. Oxford: Clarendon Press, 1997.

Bendel, Rainer. *Der Seelsorger im Dienst der Volkserziehung. Seelsorge im Bistum Breslau im Zeichen der Aufklärung.* Cologne: Böhlau, 1996.

____, and Norbert Spannenberger. *Katholische Aufklärung und Josephinismus: Rezeptionsformen in Ostmittel- und Südosteuropa.* Cologne: Böhlau, 2015.

Bell, David. *Lawyers and Citizens. The Making of a Political Elite in Old Regime France.* Oxford: Oxford University Press, 1994.

Berg, Franz, and Gregor Zirkel. *Predigten über die Pflichten der höhern und aufgeklärten Stände bey den bürgerlichen Unruhen unserer Zeit.* Würzburg: 1793.

Berg, Ursula. *Niklas Vogt (1756–1836): Weltsicht und politische Ordnungsvorstellungen zwischen Aufklärung und Romantik.* Stuttgart: Steiner, 1992.

Berger, Klaus. *Die Bibelfälscher wie wir um die Wahrheit betrogen warden.* Munich: Pattloch, 2013.

Bertelli, Sergio. *Erudizione e storia in Ludovico Antonio Muratori.* Naples: Istituto Italiano per gli Studi Storici, 1960.

Berthold, Jakob. *Nova litteratura de religione Kantii aliorumque in sacram scripturam neo-exegetarum refutata.* Augsburg: 1800.

____. *Orthodoxe Bibelexegese mit den nothwendigen Vorkenntnissen und*

Hülfswissenschaften, Schrift- und Moral-Principien sammt einem allgemeinen Schriftkriterium. Bamberg: 1807.

_____. *Cogitationes Pacis et Unionis inter Religiones Christianas.* Würzburg: 1778.

Bertrand, Regis. "Modelle und Entwürfe zum christlichen Leben. Die katholische Spiritualität und ihre Vermittler." In *Geschichte des Christentums.* Edited by Bernard Plongeron. Freiburg: Herder, 1998, 823–65.

Besange, Hieronymus. *Introductio in Vetus Testamentum critico-hermeneutico historica.* 3 vols. Styra: 1765.

Beutel, Albrecht. *Aufklärung in Deutschland.* Göttingen: Vandenhoeck & Ruprecht, 2006.

Bianco, Bruno. "Wolffianismus und katholische Aufklärung. Storchenaus' Lehre vom Menschen." In *Katholische Aufklärung—Aufklärung im katholischen Deutschland,* Edited by Harm Klueting. Hamburg: Meiner, 1991, 67–103.

Bietenholz, Peter. *Historia and Fabula: Myths and Legends in Historical Thought from Antiquity to the Modern Age.* Leiden: Brill, 1994.

Bischoff, Bruno. *Interpretatio sibi specietenus adversa complurium cum Animadversionibus in Librum Geneseos.* Ulm: 1772.

Blaschke, Olaf. "Das 19. Jahrhundert. Ein zweites konfessionelles Zeitalter?" *Geschichte und Gesellschaft* 26 (2000): 38–75.

Blau, Felix Anton. *De regula fidei Catholicae.* Mainz: 1780.

_____. *Über die Bilderverehrung mit Rücksicht auf das angeblich neue Algesheimer Wunderbild.* Mainz: 1788.

_____. *Über die Wirksamkeit der gottesdienstlichen Gebräuche in der katholischen Kirche.* Frankfurt: 1792.

Blau, Felix Anton, and Anton Dorsch. *Beyträge zur Verbesserung des äussern Gottesdienstes in der katholischen Kirche.* Frankfurt: 1789.

Boeckler, Richard. "Grenzen der Lehraussagen im römisch–katholischen Ökumenismus." *Kerygma und Dogma* 15 (1969): 340–53.

Bolton, Charles. *Church Reform in 18th Century Italy.* The Hague: Nijhoff, 1970.

Bönike, Johann Michael. *Sr. Hochfürstlichen Gnaden des Hw. Herrn Hieronymus Joseph Erzbischofs und des H. R. Reichs Fürsten zu Salzburg . . . Hirtenbriefe gesammelt.* Salzburg: 1782.

Bossuet, Jacques-Bénigne. *L'apocalypse avec une explication.* Paris: 1689.

Brachwitz, Peter. *Die Autorität des Sichtbaren: Religionsgravamina im Reich des 18. Jahrhunderts.* Berlin: de Gruyter, 2011.

Brandl, Manfred. "Bemühungen der Wiener Nuntiatur um die Verbreitung von Hontheims (Febronius') Widerruf (1779)." *Römische Historische Mitteilungen* 20 (1978): 77–108.

____. *Die katholischen Theologen der Neuzeit: Aufklärung.* Salzburg: Neugebauer, 1978.

Brandmüller, Walter. *Das Konzil von Konstanz 1414-1418.* 2 vols. Paderborn: Schöningh, 1991–97.

Brandolini, Luca. "La Pastorale dell'eucaristica di Ludovico A. Muratori." *Ephemerides Liturgicae* 81 (1967): 333–75; 82 (1968): 81–118.

Braun, Heinrich. *Die göttliche heilige Schrift des neuen Testamentes in lateinischer und deutscher Sprache . . . nach dem Sinne der heiligen-römisch-katholischen Kirche.* Vol. 3. Augsburg: 1788.

Bretschneier, Karl Gottlieb. *Historisch-dogmatische Auslegung des N. T.* Leipzig: 1806.

Brenner, Johann Hermann. *Prüfung der neuen Aufrichtung einer Hochgräflich-Neuwiedischen freyen Akademie zur Vereinigung des Glaubens und Aufnahme der Religion.* Giessen: 1758.

____. *Zeugnis über die Neuwiedische Anstalten.* 1758.

Breuer, Dieter. "Einleitung." In *Die Aufklärung in den deutschsprachigen katholischen Ländern 1750-1800. Kulturelle Ausgleichsprozesse im Spiegel von Bibliotheken in Luzern, Eichstätt und Klosterneuburg.* Paderborn: Schöningh, 2001, 1–48.

____. "Katholische Aufklärung und Theologie." *Rottenburger Jahrbuch für Kirchengeschichte* 23 (2004): 75–90.

Brück, Philipp Anton. *Die Mainzer theologische Fakultät im 18. Jahrhundert.* Wiesbaden: F. Steiner, 1955.

Brunner, Philipp. *Christliche Reden, welche von katholischen Predigern in Deutschland seit dem Jahr 1770 bei verschiedenen Gelegenheiten vorgetragen worden sind.* Heidelberg: 1789.

____. *Gebethbuch für aufgeklärte katholische Christen.* Heilbronn: 1801.

____. *Die letzte aktenmäßige Verketzerungsgeschichte unter der Regierung des Herrn*

Bischoffes von Speier August Grafen von Limburg-Stirum: Mit Beilagen. Germanien: 1802.

Bulffer, Gervasius. *Geheime Offenbarung, oder einzige Weissagung des neuen Testamentes.* Augsburg: 1773.

Burkard, Dominik. "Schwierigkeiten bei der Beschäftigung mit der päpstlichen Zensur im ausgehenden 18. Jahrhundert am Beispiel der Causa Isenbiehl." In *Verbotene Bücher. Zur Geschichte des Index im 18. und 19. Jahrhundert.* Edited by Hubert Wolf. Paderborn: Schöningh, 2008, 299–316.

Burkarth, Klaus-Peter. *"Raisonable" Katholiken: Volksaufklärung im katholischen Deutschland um 1800.* PhD dissertation; Essen, 1994.

Calmet, Augustin. *Dictionarium Manuale Biblicum.* Augsburg: 1775.

——. *Dissertationes ac Disquisitiones: Excerptae ex Commentario Literali in Omnes Veteris Testamenti Libros.* 8:83–117. Tyrnau: 1773.

——. *Commentarium Literale in omnes ac singulos tum veteris cum novi testament libros.* Augsburg: 1734.

——. *Commentaire litteral sur tous les livres de l'Ancien et du Nouveau Testament.* Paris: 1724–26.

Carboncini, Sonia. *Transzendentale Wahrheit und Traum. Christian Wolffs Antwort auf die Herausforderung durch den Cartesianischen Zweifel.* Stuttgart–Bad Cannstatt: Frommann-Holzboog, 1991.

Carhart, Michael. *The Science of Culture in Enlightenment Germany.* Cambridge, MA: 2007.

Cartier, Gallus. *Tractatus theologicus de Sacra Scriptura.* Freiburg: 1736.

Castello, Wilhelm Joseph. *Dissertatio de Immoderata Alios Haereseos Insimulandi Libidine. . . .* Trier: 1791.

Chadwick, Owen. *The Popes and European Revolution.* Oxford: Oxford University Press, 1981.

Châtellier, Louis. *The Religion of the Poor: Rural Missions in Europe and the Formation of Modern Catholicism, C.1500–C.1800.* Cambridge: Cambridge University Press, 1997.

Christmann, Franz Xaver. *Roms unglückliche Sechser: Oder Beleuchtung des bekannten Verses "Semper sub sextis perdita Roma fuit."* Constance: 1803.

Cooman, Guido, Maurice van Stiphout, and Bart Wauters, eds. *Zeger-Bernard* van Espen at the Crossroads of Canon Law, History, Theology, and Church-State Relations. Leuven: Leuven University Press, 2003.

Collins, Anthony. A Discourse of the Grounds and Reasons of the Christian Religion [1724]. London: 1741.

Cordier, Philipp. Religio christiana ex prophetis antiquis demonstrate. Trier: 1775.

Coreth, Anna. Pietas Austriaca [1959]. West Lafayette: Purdue Univ. Press, 2004.

Corrodi, Heinrich. Beyträge zur Beförderung des vernünftigen Denkens in der Religion, no. 3. Frankfurt: 1782.

_____. Stromata: eine Unterhaltungsschrift für Theologen, no. 2. Duisburg: 1787.

Cottret, Monique. "Der Jansenistenstreit." In Geschichte des Christentums. Edited by Bernard Plongeron. Freiburg: Herder, 1998, 9:348–408.

Cramer, Winfrid. "Molkenbuhr, Marcellinus." Neue Deutsche Biographie 17 (1994): 731.

Crehan, F. J. "The Bible in the Roman Catholic Church From Trent to the Present Day." In Cambridge History of the Bible. Cambridge: Cambridge University Press, 1963, 3:199–237.

Cremeri, Rezension von Benedict Anton. Neueste Sammlung der auserlesenen Gebethe. Linz: 1791.

Cressener, Drue. A Demonstration of the First Principles of the Protestant Applications of the Apocalypse. London: 1690.

_____. The Judgements of God Upon the Roman-Catholick Church, from Its First Rigid Laws for Universal Conformity to It, Unto Its Last End. . . . In Explication of the Trumpets and Vials of the Apocalypse, Upon Principles Generally Acknowledged by Protestant Interpreters. London: 1689.

Cunningham, Lawrence. "Review of Ulrich Lehner, Enlightened Monks." Commonweal 139 (September 3, 2012): 26–27.

Dalberg, Karl Theodor von. Betrachtungen über das Universum. 3rd ed. Mannheim: 1787.

Dathe, Johann August. Psalterium Syriacum. Halle: 1768.

Dawson, Christopher. The Gods of Revolution. Washington, DC: Catholic University of America Press, 2015.

Dereser, Thaddäus Anton. Entstehung und Einweihungsgeschichte der kurkölnischen Universität zu Bonn. . . . Bonn: 1786.

_____. "Der jüdische und christliche Pharisäismus." In *Allgemeines Magazin für Prediger, Seelsorger und Katecheten* 2 (1793): 329–59.

_____. *Necessitas linguarum orientalium ad S. Scripturam intelligendam, vindicandam ac dogmati fidei inde probanda.* Cologne: 1783.

_____. *Notiones Generales Hermeneuticae Sacris Vetris Testamenti.* Bonn: 1784.

_____. *Scriptursätze aus dem Grundtexte des ersten mosaischen Buches, mit Anmerkungen über etliche Ausdrücke im XIX. Kap.* Bonn: 1784.

_____. *Die Versuchungsgeschichte Christi, erklärt und von Widersprüchen gerettet.* Bonn: 1789.

Didacus a S. Antonio. *Auctuarium Scripturistici.* 4 vols. Brussels: 1748.

_____. *Enchiridion Scripturisticum Tripartitum.* Brussels: 1745.

Dietrich, Thomas. *Die Theologie der Kirche bei Robert Bellarmin (1542-1621): Systematische Voraussetzungen des Kontroverstheologen.* Paderborn: Bonifatius, 1999.

Döderlein, Johann Christian. *Institutio theologi Christiani in capitibus religionus theoreticus nostris temporibus accomodata.* Nuremberg: 1787.

Dompnier, Bernard. "Die Fortdauer der katholischen Reform." In *Geschichte des Christentums.* Edited by Bernard Plongeron. Freiburg: Herder, 1998, 9:211–300.

Drury, John. *Critics of the Bible 1724-1873.* Cambridge: Cambridge University Press, 1989.

Duchon, Robert "De Bossuet a Febronius," *Revue d'histoire ecclesiastique* 65 (1970): 375–422.

Duguet, Jacques Joseph. *Regeln zum Verstande der heiligen Schrift.* Vienna: 1777.

_____. *Regles Pour L'Intelligence Des Stes. Ecritures.* Paris: 1716.

Dumont, Franz. "Wider Freygeister, Protestanten und Glaubensfeger: Hermann Goldhagen und sein 'Religions-Journal,'" in *Von 'Obscuranten' und 'Eudämonisten': gegenaufklärerische und antirevolutionäre Publizistik im späten 18. Jahrhundert*, edited by Christoph Weiss, 35–76. St. Ingbert: Röhrig, 1999.

Düntzer, Heinrich. "Zu Schiller." *Archiv für Literaturgeschichte* 4 (1875): 79–88.

Dupin, Louis Ellies. *Analyse de l'apocalypse, contenant une nouvelle explication simple & littéraire de ce livre, avec dissertations sur les millenaires, sur l'état des ames aprés la mort, sur le purgatoire, sur le jour du jugement, et sur d'autres matieres importantes de la religion.* Paris: 1714.

____. *A compleat history of the canon and writers of the books of the Old and New Testament, by way of dissertation.* . . . London: 1694.

Du Plessis d'Argentré, Charles. *Elementa theologica, in quibus de autoritate ac pondere cujuslibet argumenti theologici . . . disputatur. Postremo etiam accedit, cum de fide divina, tum de summa Ecclesiae authoritate in proscribendis nominatim et damnandis perversis quibuscumque scriptis, tractatio.* Paris: 1702.

Ehrensperger, Alfred. *Die Theorie des Gottesdienstes in der späten deutschen Aufklärung (1770-1815).* Zürich: Theologischer Verlag, 1971.

Eichhorn, Johann Gottfried. *Commentarius in Apocalypsin Joannis.* 2 vols. Göttingen: 1791.

____. "Über die innern Gründe gegen die Aechtheit und Kanonicität der Apokalypse." In *Allgemeine Bibliothek der biblischen Litteratur* 3 (1791): 571–645.

Elliott, Edward. *Horae Apocalypticae.* Vol. 4. London: 3rd ed., 1847.

Endres, Joseph Anton. *Die Korrespondenz der Mauriner mit den Emmeramern und die Beziehungen der letzteren zu den wissenschaftlichen Bewegungen des 18. Jahrhunderts.* Stuttgart: 1899.

Ernesti, Johann August Ernesti. *Institutio Interpretis N. T.* Leipzig: 1761.

Ernesti, Jörg. *Ökumene im Dritten Reich.* Paderborn: Bonifatius, 2007.

Ernst, Harold E. "The Theological Notes and the Interpretation of Doctrine." *Theological Studies* 63 (2002): 813–25.

Färber, Konrad Maria. *Kaiser und Erzkanzler. Carl von Dalberg und Napoleon am Ende des Alten Reiches.* Regensburg: Mittelbayerische Verlagsgesellschaft, 1988.

Faggioli, Massimo. *A Council for the Global Church: Receiving Vatican II in History.* Minneapolis, MN: Fortress Press, 2015.

Fauchet, Claude. *De la religion nationale.* Paris: 1789.

Feder, Johann Heinrich. *Untersuchungen über den menschlichen Willen.* 2nd ed. Göttingen: 1785.

Fehr, James Jakob. *"Ein wunderlicher nexus rerum": Aufklärung und Pietismus in Königsberg unter Franz Albert Schultz.* Hildesheim: Olms, 2005.

Feil, Ernst. *Religio.* Göttingen: Vandenhoeck & Rupprecht, 2007.

Feilmoser, Benedict. *Einleitung in die Bücher des Neuen Bundes [1810],* 2nd ed. Tübingen: 1830.

Feist, Dagmar. "Der Fall von Albini—Rechtsstreitigkeiten um die väterliche Gewalt in konfessionell gemischten Ehen." In *In eigener Sache: Frauen vor den höchsten Gerichten des Alten Reiches*. Edited by Siegrid Westphal. Cologne: Böhlau, 2005, 245–70.

Feldkamp, Michael F. "Das Breve 'Zelo domus Dei' vom 26. November 1648—Edition," *Archivum Historiae Pontificiae* 31 (1993): 293–353.

Feller, Francois. "Review of Dereser, *Scriptursätze*." *Journal historique et littéraire* 159 (1784, October 15): 256–64.

Filthaut, Theodor. *Das Reich Gottes in den katechetischen Unterweisungen*. Freiburg: Herder, 1958.

Fischer, Christoph. *Institutiones Hermeneuticae N. T.* Prague: 1788.

Flammer, Thomas, ed. *Franz von Fürstenberg (1792-1810): Aufklärer und Reformer im Fürstbistum Münster*. Münster: Aschendorff, 2012.

Fleming, John V. *The Dark Side of the Enlightenment: Wizards, Alchemists, and Spiritual Seekers in the Age of Reason*. N.p.: W. W. Norton, 2013.

Fleming, Robert. *Discourses on Several Subjects. The First Containing a New Account of the Rise and Fall of the Papacy. The Second Upon God's Dwelling with Men. The Third Concerning the Ministerial Office. The Fourth Being a Brief Account of Religion As It Centres in the Lord Jesus Christ*. London: 1701.

Forst, Rainer. *Toleranz im Konflikt*. Frankfurt: Suhrkamp, 2003.

Frei, Hans W. *The Eclipse of Biblical Narrative. A Study in Eighteenth and Nineteenth Century Hermeneutics*. New Haven and London: Yale University Press, 1974.

Frey, Alphons. *Erklärung der Offenbarung des hl. Johannes als prophetischer Schlüssel zu den Schicksalen der Kirche und der Staaten. Das ist: Fragmente und Ahnungen einer Universalhistorie der christkatholischen Kirche von der Sendung des heiligen Geistes bis zum Ende der Zeiten*. 2 vols. Ulm: 1822; 2nd ed., 1832.

Freyh, Antje. "Dalbergs schriftstellerische Tätigkeit in Erfurt." In *Aufklärung in der Dalbergzeit*. Edited by Michael Ludscheidt. Erfurt: Ullenspiegel 2006, 21–44.

Friedrich, Franz, and Daniel Wadzeck. *Leben und Schicksale des berüchtigten Franz Rudolph von Grossing, eigentlich Franz Matthäus Grossinger genannt: nebst, der Geschichte und Bekanntmachung der Geheimnisse des Rosen-Ordens*. Frankfurt: 1789.

Fritsch, Matthias. *Religöse Toleranz im Zeitalter der Aufklärung.* Hamburg: Meiner, 2004.

Froom, Edwin LeRoy. *The Prophetic Faith of Our Fathers: The Historical Development of Prophetic Interpretation, 2.* Washington: Review & Herald, 1948.

Frowein, Peter. "Primat und Episkopat." *Römische Quartalschrift für christliche Altertumskunde, und Kirchengeschichte* 69 (1974): 227–29.

____, and Edmund Janson. "Johann Nikolaus von Sontheim—Justinus Febronius. Zum Werk und seinen Gegnern," *Archiv für mittelrheinische Kirchengeschichte* 28 (1976), 129–53.

Füssel, Marian. "Akademische Aufklärung. Die Universitäten im Spannungsfeld von funktionaler Differenzierung, Ökonomie und Habitus," *Geschichte und Gesellschaft. Sonderheft* 23 (2010): 47–73.

Gass, Joseph. *Strassburger Theologen im Aufklärungszeitalter, 1766-1790.* Strasbourg: 1917.

Gay, Peter. *The Enlightenment: An Interpretation.* 2 vols. New York: Knopf, 1966–69.

Geddes, Alexander, and Ildephonsus Schwarz. *De vulgarium Sacrae Scripturae versionum vitiis eorumque remediis libellus.* Bamberg: 1787.

Gerbert, Martin. *De Sublimi in Evangelio Christi, 3.* St. Blasien: 1793.

____. *Ecclesia Militans, 2 vols.* St. Blasien: 1789.

____. *Principia Theologiae Exegeticae.* St. Blasien: 1757.

Gerdil, Sigismond. *The Anti-Emile: Reflections on Theory and Practice of Education against the Principles of Rousseau.* South Bend, IN: St. Augustine Press, 2011.

Gerhards, Albert. "Von der Synode von Pistoia (1786) zum Zweiten Vatikanischen Konzil? Zur Morphologie der Liturgiereform im 20. Jahrhundert." *Liturgisches Jahrbuch* 36 (1986): 28–45.

Goldhagen, Hermann. *Introductio in Sacram Scripturam Veteris ac Novi Testamenti.* Mainz: 1765.

Gratz, Peter Alois. "Meine Ansicht von Kapitel 4-20 der Apokalypse." In *Theologische Quartalschrift* 11 (1829): 3–38.

____. "Reflexionen über die Offenbarung Johannis." In *Theologische Quartalschrift* 8 (1826): 587–605.

____. *Historisch-kritischer Kommentar über das Evangelium des Matthäus.* Tübingen: 1821.

Griesbach, Johann Jacob. *Anleitung zum Studium der popukären Dogmatik.* Jena: 1789.

Groethuysen, Bernhard. *Die Entstehung der bürgerlichen Welt-und Lebensanschauung in Frankreich,* 2 vols. Halle: 1927–1930; Frankfurt: Suhrkamp, 1978. English edition: *The Bourgeois. Catholicism vs. Capitalism in Eighteenth-Century France.* New York: Rinehart and Winston, 1968.

Grossing, Franz Rudolph von [Franz Grossinger]. *Allgemeines Toleranz und Religions System für alle Staaten und Völker der Welt.* Leipzig: 1784.

____. *Der Souverain, oder die ersten Haupt- und Grundsätze einer monarchischen Regierung.* Vienna: 1780.

Gunther, Rudolf. "Die erste deutsche Liturgie der katholischen Kirche der Aufklärung." *Monatschrift für Gottesdienst und kirchliche Kunst* 6 (1901): 333–40; 368–73.

Habermas, Jürgen. "Modernity: An Unfinished Project." In *Habermas and the Unfinished Project of Modernity: Critical Essays on the Philosophical Discourse of Modernity.* Edited by Maurizio Passerin d'Entreves and Seyla Benhabib. Translated by Nicholas Walker. Cambridge: Polity Press, 1996.

Habersaat, Sigrid. *Verteidigung der Aufklärung: Friedrich Nicolai in religiösen und politischen Debatten.* Würzburg: Königshausen & Neumann, 2001.

Habichler, Alfred. *Reich Gottes als Thema des Denkens bei Kant.* Mainz: Grünewald, 1991.

Haefs, Wilhelm. "Reformkatholizismus und Komödien der Religion, Katholische Aufklärung als Gegenstand literaturwissenschaftlicher Forschung." In *Zwischen Aufklärung und Romantik. Neue Perspektiven der Forschung. Festschrift für Roger Paulin.* Edited by Konrad Feilchenfeldt. Würzburg: Echter, 2006, 255–88.

____. *Aufklärung in Bayern. Leben, Werk und Wirkung Lorenz von Westenrieders.* Neuried: Ars Una, 1998.

Haering, Stephan. "Der Salzburger Kirchenrechtler Gregor Zallwein OSB (1712–1766). Ein Beitrag zur Gelehrtengeschichte des kanonischen Rechts im Zeitalter der Aufklärung." In *Studien und Mitteilungen zur Geschichte des Benediktinerordens und seiner Zweige* 103 (1992), 269–312.

Hahn, Thomas. *Staat und Kirche im deutschen Naturrecht.* Tübingen: Mohr Siebeck, 2012.

Hammermayer, Ludwig. *Geschichte der Bayerischen Akademie der Wissenschaften 1759–1807.* 2 vols. Munich: C.H. Beck, 1983.

———. "Die Benediktiner und die Akademiebewegung im katholischen Deutschland (1720–1770)." In *Studien und Mitteilungen des Benediktinerordens und seiner Zweige* 70 (1959): 45–146.

Haquin, Andre. "The Liturgical Movement and Catholic Ritual Revision." In *Oxford History of Christian Worship.* Edited by Geoffrey Wainwright and Karen W. Tucker. Oxford: Oxford University Press, 2006, 696–720.

Hartlich, Christian, and Walter Sachs. *Die Entstehung des Mythosbegriffs in der modernen Bibelwissenschaft.* Tübingen: Mohr Siebeck, 1952.

Hayd, Stefan. *Hermeneutica in Sacros Novi Testamenti libros.* Augsburg: 1777.

Hazart, Cornelius, and Ulrich Dirrhaimer. *Kirchen-Geschicht der gantzen Welt absonderlich der vergangnen und nunmehr verflossnen zwey-hundert Jahren: in welchen enthalten wird die Gelegenheit der Landen Art und Manieren der Religion der Innwohnern.* 4 vols. Vienna: 1678/84; Munich: 1701/02; 1725.

Heckel, Martin. "Itio in partes: Zur Religionsverfassung des Heiligen Römischen Reiches Deutscher Nation." In *Gesammelte Schriften.* Edited by Martin Heckel. Tübingen: Mohr Siebeck, 1989, 2:636–737.

———. "Die Wiedervereinigung der Konfessionen als Ziel und Auftrag der Reichsverfassung im Heiligen Römischen Reich Deutscher Nation." In *Die Reunionsgespräche im Niedersachsen des 17. Jahrhunderts: Rojas y Spinola—Molan—Leibniz.* Edited by Hans Otte and Richard Schenk. Göttingen: Vandenhoeck & Rupprecht, 1999, 15–38.

Hegel, Eduard. *Geschichte der katholisch-theologischen Fakultät Münster.* Münster: Aschendorff, 1966.

Heidenreich, Marianne. *Christian Gottlob Heyne und die alte Geschichte.* Munich: Saur, 2006.

Heinz, Gerhard. *Divinam christianae religionis originem probare: Untersuchung zur Entstehung des fundamentaltheologischen Offenbarungstraktates der katholischen Schultheologie.* Mainz: Matthias-Grünewald-Verlag, 1984.

Hell, Leonhard. *Reich Gottes als Systemidee der Theologie: historisch-systematische Untersuchungen zum theologischen Werk B. Galuras und F. Brenners.* Mainz: M.-Grünewald-Verlag, 1993.

Hellyer, Marcus. *Catholic Physics: Jesuit Natural Philosophy in Early Modern Germany.* Notre Dame, IN: University of Notre Dame Press, 2005.

Hengel, Martin. "Heilsgeschichte," in *Theologische, historische und biographische Skizzen: Kleine Schriften.* Tübingen: Mohr Siebeck, 2010, 7:1–34.

Herder, Johann Gottfried. *Vom Geist der ebräischen (sic!) Poesie.* 2 vols. Dessau: 1782.

Hermon-Belot, R. "God's Will in History: The Abbe Gregoire, the Revolution and the Jews." In *Millenarianism and Messianism in Early Modern Europe: Catholic Millenarianism: From Savonarola to the Abbe Gregoire.* Edited by Karl A. Kottman. Dordrecht: Kluwer, 2001, 91–100.

Herrmann, Erwin. "De reconciliatione Christianorum: Gedanken eines Abtes zur Wiedervereinigung der Konfessionen." In *Glaube und Gesellschaft: FS Wilhelm F. Klasch.* Edited by Klaus D. Wolff. Bayreuth: Fehr, 1981, 177–87.

Hersche, Peter. *Muße und Verschwendung. Europäische Gesellschaft und Kultur im Barockzeitalter.* 2 vols. Freiburg: Herder, 2006.

――. "Lutherisch machen—Rekonfessionalisierung als paradoxe Folge aufgeklärter Religionspolitik." In *Ambivalenzen der Aufklärung.* Edited by Gerhard Ammerer, Ernst Wangermann, and Hans Haas. Vienna and Munich: Verlag für Geschichte und Politik, 1997, 155–68.

Herten, Bart Van der. *Het begin van het einde, Eschatologische interpretaties van de Franse revolutie.* Leuven: Leuven University Press, 1994.

Hess, Johann Jakob. *Die Schriften des Neuen Testamentes.* Lebensgeschichte Jesu, 2. Teil. vol. 3. Zurich: 1828.

――. *Von dem Reiche Gottes. Ein Versuch über den Plan der göttlichen Offenbarungen und Anstalten.* 2 vols. Zurich: 1774; 2nd ed. Zurich: 1781.

――. *Geschichte der drey letzten Lebensjahre Jesu.* 2nd ed. Zurich: 1773.

Hildebrand, Dietrich von. *The Trojan Horse in the City of God.* Chicago: Franciscan Herald Press, 1967.

Hinske, Norbert. "Die Grundideen der deutschen Aufklärung." In *Die Philosophie der deutschen Aufklärung. Texte und Darstellung.* Edited by R. Ciafardone. Stuttgart: Reclam, 1990, 407–58.

Hochbichler, Johann. *P. Beda Mayrs Vertheidigung der katholischen Religion theologisch untersuchet.* Augsburg: 1790.

Hömig, Herbert. *Carl Theodor von Dalberg: Staatsmann und Kirchenfürst im Schatten Napoleons.* Paderborn: Ferdinand Schöningh, 2011.

Hörmann, Joseph. "P. Beda Mayr von Donauwörth. Ein Ireniker der Aufklärungszeit," *Festgabe Alois Knöpfler zur Vollendung des 70. Lebensjahres.* Edited by by Heinrich Gietl and Georg Pfeilschifter. Freiburg: Herder, 1917, 188–209.

Holden, Henry. *Divinae Fidei Analysis [1652].* Paris: 1757.

Hollerweger, Hans. *Die Reform des Gottesdienstes zur Zeit des Josephinismus in Österreich.* Regensburg: Pustet, 1976.

____. "Das Rituale im Bereich des Josephinismus." In *Aufklärungskatholizismus und Liturgie. Reformentwürfe für die Feier von Taufe, Firmung, Busse, Trauung und Krankensalbung.* Edited by Franz Kohlschein. St. Ottilien: EOS, 1989, 181–99.

Holzem, Andreas. *Christentum in Deutschland 1550-1850 Konfessionalisierung - Aufklärung - Pluralisierung.* 2 vols. Paderborn: Schöningh, 2015.

Hontheim, Nikolaus. *Commentarius in Suam Retractationem.* Frankfurt: 1783.

____. *Febronius Abbreviatus.* Frankfurt: 1777.

____. *De Statu Ecclesiae.* 4 vols. Frankfurt and Leipzig: 1770–74.

____. *Vindiciae Febronianae seu refutationes nonullorum opusculorum quae adversus Justini Febronii Jcti tractatum de statu Ecclesiae et potestate Romani Pontificis nuper prodierunt.* Zurich: 1765.

____. *De Statu Ecclesia.* Frankfurt: 1763

Horstmann, Axel. "Mythologie und Altertumsiwssenschaft Der Mythosbegriff bei Christian Gottlob Heyne." *Archiv für Begriffsgeschichte* 16 (1972): 60–85.

Huet, Pierre-Daniel. *Demonstratio Evangelica.* 3rd ed. Paris: 1690.

Hug, Johann Leonhard. *Introduction to the Writings of the New Testament.* London: 1837.

____. *Einleitung in die Schriften des Neuen Testaments.* Tübingen: 1808.

Irvine, Stuart A. *Isaiah, Ahaz, and the Syro-Ephraimitic Crisis.* Atlanta: Scholars Press, 1990.

Isenbiehl, Johann Lorenz. *De Rebus Divinis tractatus.* 2 vols. Mainz: 1787.

____. *Neuer Versuch über die Weissagung vom Emmanuel.* n.p.: 1778.

____. *Beobachtungen von dem Gebrauche des syrischen Punkti diacritici bey den Verbis.* Göttingen: 1773.

Israel, Jonathan. "Enlightenment! Which Enlightenment?." *Journal of the History of Ideas* 67 (2006): 523–45.

———. *Enlightenment Contested. Philosophy, Modernity, and the Emancipation of Man 1670-1752.* Oxford: Oxford University Press, 2006.

———. *Radical Enlightenment: Philosophy and the Making of Modernity 1650-1750.* Oxford: Oxford University Press, 2001.

Jahn, Johann Martin. *Einleitung in die göttlichen Bücher des Alten Bundes.* 2 vols. Vienna: 1793.

———. *Enchiridion Hermeneuticae Generalis.* Vienna: 1812.

———. *Nachträge zu seinen theologischen Werken.* Tübingen: 1821.

Jahns, Sigrid. *Das Reichskammergericht und seine Richter: Verfassung und Sozialstruktur eines höchsten Gerichts im Alten Reich.* Cologne: Böhlau, 2011.

Jansen, Cornelius. *Commentariorum in Suam Concordiam ac totam Historiam Evangelicam.* Leuven: 1606.

Janson, Edmund. *Das Kirchenverständnis des Febronius.* Rome: Gregoriana, 1978.

Joas, Hans. *Faith as an Option: Possible Futures for Christianity.* Stanford: Stanford University Press, 2014.

Johansson, Torbjörn, Robert Kolb, and Johann Anselm Steiger, eds. *Hermeneutica Sacra: Studien zur Auslegung der Heiligen Schrift im 16. und 17. Jahrhundert.* Berlin: De Gruyter, 2010.

Jung, Norbert. *Der Speyerer Weihbischof Andreas Seelmann (1732-1789) im Spannungsfeld von "nachgeholter" Aufklärung und "vorgezogener" Restauration.* Mainz: Verlag für Mittelrheinische Kirchengeschichte, 2001.

———. *Der Speyerer Weihbischof Andreas Seelmann (1732-1789) im Spannungsfeld von "nachgeholter" Aufklärung und "vorgezogener" Restauration.* Mainz: Gesellschaft für mittelrheinische Kirchengeschichte, 2002.

Just, Leo. "Zur Enstehungsgeschichte des Febronius." *Jahrbuch für das Bistum Mainz* 5 (1950): 369–82.

———. "Hontheims Bemühungen um einen Bischofssitz in den österreichischen Niederlanden (1756-62)." *Quellen und Forschungen aus italienischen Archiven und Bibliotheken* 21 (1929/30): 256–90.

Kaczynski, Reiner. "Kommentar zu Sacrosanctum Concilium." In *Herders Theologischer Kommentar zum Zweiten Vatikanischen Konzil.* Freiburg: Herder, 2012, 2:1–227.

____. "Liturgie in der Weite der Catholica? Fortschreitende Mißachtung und endgültige Aufhebung eines Konzilsbeschlusses," in *Was ist heute noch katholisch? Zum Streit um die innere Einheit und Vielfalt der Kirche (QD 192)*. Edited by Albert Franz. Freiburg: Herder, 2001, 160–88.

Kant, Immanuel. *Religion innerhalb der Grenzen der blossen Vernunft*. 1793.

Kaplan, Benjamin. *Divided by Faith: Religious Conflict and the Practice of Toleration in Early Modern Europe*. Cambridge, MA: 2009.

Karniel, Joseph. *Die Toleranzpolitik Joseph II*. Gerlingen: Bleicher, 1985.

Kasper, Walter. *Die Lehre von der Tradition in der Römischen Schule*. Freiburg: Herder 1962.

Katz, David S. "The Occult Bible: Hebraic Millenarianism in Eighteenth-Century England." In *The Millenarian Turn, Millenarian Contexts of Science, Politics and Everyday Anglo-American Life in the Seventeenth and Eighteenth Centuries*. Edited by James E. Force and Richard H. Popkin. Dordrecht: Kluwer, 2001, 119–32.

Keller, Erwin. *Leonhard Hug: Beiträge zu seiner Biographie*. Freiburg: n.p., 1973.

Kerkherdere, Johann Gerard. *Prodromus Danielicus sive Novi Conatus Historici, Critici, in celeberrimas Difficultates Historiae Veteris Testameni, Monarchiarum Asiae &*. Leuven: 1711.

Kistemaker, Johann Hyacinth. *Sendschreiben der Apostel*. Münster: 1823.

Klauck, Hans-Josef. "Die katholische neutestamentliche Exegese zwischen Vatikanum I und Vatikanum II." In *Die katholisch-theologischen Disziplinen in Deutschland, 1870-1962*. Edited by Hubert Wolf. Paderborn: Schöningh, 1999, 39–71.

Klek, Konrad. *Erlebnis Gottesdienst: Die liturgischen Reformbestrebungen um die Jahrhundertwende unter Führung von Friedrich Spitta und Julius Smend*. Göttingen: Vandenhoeck & Ruprecht, 1996.

Kleuker, Johann Friedrich. *Anhang zum Zend-Avesta*. Riga: 1781.

Klüpfel, Engelbert. *Commonitorium S. Vincentii Lerinensis*. Vienna: 1790.

____. *Institutiones theologicae dogmaticae in usum auditorum*. 2 vols. Vienna: 1789.

Klueting, Harm. "Wiedervereinigung der getrennten Konfessionen oder episkopalistische Nationalkirche? Nikolaus von Hontheim (1701–1790), der *Febronius* und die Rückkehr der Protestanten zur katholischen Kirche," in *Irenik und Antikonfessionalismus im 17. und 18. Jahrhundert*. Edited by Harm Klueting. Hildesheim: Olms, 2003, 258–77.

_____. "Der Genius der Zeit hat sie unbrauchbar gemacht. Zum Thema Katholische Aufklärung–Oder: Aufklärung und Katholizismus im Deutschland des 18. Jahrhunderts. Eine Einführung." In *Katholische Aufklärung*. Edited by Harm Klueting. Hamburg: Meiner, 1993, 1–35.

Kluxen, Kurt. "Politik und Heilsgeschehen bei Bossuet. Ein Beitrag zur Geschichte des Konservativismus." *Historische Zeitschrift* 179 (1955): 449–69.

Knowles, David. *Great Historical Enterpises*. London: Nelson, 1963.

Kolbe, Ferdinand. *Die liturgische Bewegung*. Aschaffenburg: Pattloch, 1964.

Koselleck, Reinhart. "Aufklärung und die Grenzen der Toleranz." In *Glaube und Toleranz. Das theologische Erbe der Aufklärung*. Edited by Trutz Rendtorff. Gütersloh: Gütersloher Verlagshaus, 1982, 256–71.

Kremer, Bernd Mathias. *Der Westfälische Friede in der Deutung der Aufklärung. Zur Entwicklung des Verfassungsverständnisses im Hl. Röm. Reich Deutscher Nation vom konfessionellen Zeitalter bis ins späte 18. Jahrhundert*. Tübingen: Mohr Siebeck, 1989.

Kümmeringer, Hans. "Es ist Sache der Kirche, *iudicare de vero sensu et interpretatione scripturarum sanctarum*. Zum Verständnis dieses Satzes auf dem Tridentinum und Vaticanum I." *Theologische Quartalschrift* 149 (1969): 282–96.

Küng, Hans. *Disputed Truth: Memoirs*. New York: Continuum, 2008.

_____. *Erlebte Menschlichkeit*. Munich: Piper, 2013.

Lallement, Jacques-Philippe. *Réflexions morales sur le Nouveau Testament*, 12. Paris: 1725.

Lamy, Bernard. *Apparatus Biblicus. Nova Editio*. Lyon: 1696.

Lapide, Cornelius A. *Commentarius in Apocalypsin Apostoli*. 2nd ed. Venice: 1717.

Leclerc, Gustave. *Zeger-Bernard van Espen (1646-1728) et l'autorité ecclésiastique*. Zurich: Pas, 1964.

Legaspi, Michael C. *The Death of Scripture and the Rise of Biblical Studies*. Oxford: Oxford University Press, 2010.

Lehner, Ulrich L. "Benedict Stattler—Renewal of Catholic Theology with the Help of Wolffian Metaphysics." In *Enlightenment in Catholic Europe. A Transnational History*. Edited by Ulrich L. Lehner and Jeffrey Burson. Notre Dame: University of Notre Dame Press, 2014, 169–92.

_____. *The Catholic Enlightenment: The Forgotten History of a Global Movement*. Oxford: Oxford University Press, 2016.

_____. *Enlightened Monks: The German Benedictines, 1740-1803*. Oxford: Oxford University Press, 2011.

_____. "Jakob Salat." In *Dictionary of Eighteenth-Century German Philosophers*. Edited by Manfred Kuehn and Heiner Klemme. Bristol: Thoemmes, 2010, 972–74.

_____. "Ecumenism and Enlightenment Catholicism." In *Beda Mayr—Vertheidigung der katholischen Religion*. Edited by Ulrich L. Lehner. Leiden: Brill, 2009, i–lxxxix.

_____. "Theologia Benedictina ac Kantiana. Zur Kant-Rezeption der Benediktiner Ildefons Schwarz und Ulrich Peutinger." In *Kant und der Katholizismus*. Edited by Norbert Fischer. Freiburg: Herder, 2005, 234–61.

_____, and Michael Printy, eds. *Brill's Companion to the Catholic Enlightenment in Europe*. Leiden: Brill, 2010.

Lichter, Eduard. "Johann Wilhelm Josef Castello und die Aufklärung im Erzstift Trier." *Archiv für Mittelrheinische Kirchengeschichte* 21 (1969): 179–228.

_____. "Volksfrömmigket und Wissenschaft unter dem Einfluss von Bischof Josef von Hommer im Spiegel der Arbeiten des Trierer Klerus." *Archiv für Mittelrheinische Kirchengeschichte* 30 (1978): 161–90.

Martin-Palma, José. *Gnadenlehre von der Reformation bis zur Gegenwart: Handbuch Der Dogmengeschichte*. Vol. 3. Freiburg: Herder, 1980.

Mathy, Helmut. "Toleranz im Kur-und Erzstift Mainz." In *Toleranz am Mittelrhein*. Edited by Isnard Frank. Mainz: Verein f. MRh. Kirchengeschichte, 1984, 45–77.

Mattei, Roberto de. *The Second Vatican Council: An Unwritten Story*. Fitzwilliam, NH: Loreto, 2012.

May, Georg. *Das Versöhnungswerk des päpstlichen Legaten Giovanni B. Caprara. Die Rekonziliation der Geistlichen und Ordensangehörigen 1801-1808*. Berlin: Duncker & Humblot, 2012.

_____. *Die Auseinandersetzungen zwischen den Mainzer Erzbischöfen und dem Heiligen Stuhl um die Dispensbefugnis im 18. Jahrhundert*. Frankfurt: Peter Lang, 2007.

_____. *Mit Katholiken zu besetzende Professuren von 1817 bis 1945. Ein Beitrag zur Ausbildung der Studierenden katholischer Theologie, zur Verwirklichung der*

Parität an der württembergischen Landesuniversität und zur katholischen Bewegung. Amsterdam: Gruner, 1975.

_____. *Das Recht des Gottesdienstes in der Diözese Mainz zur Zeit von Bischof Joseph Ludwig Colmar (1802-1818).* 2 vols. Amsterdam: Gruner, 1987.

Mayer, Anton. "Liturgie, Aufklärung und Klassizismus." *Archiv für Liturgiewissenschaft* 9 (1929): 67–127.

Mayr, Beda. *Apologie seiner Vertheidigung der katholischen Religion; eine Beylage zu seiner Vertheidigung der natürlichen, christlichen und katholischen Religion.* Augsburg: 1790.

_____. *Vertheidigung der natürlichen, christlichen, und katholischen Religion nach den Bedürfnissen unsrer Zeiten.* 3 vols. Augsburg: 1787-89.

_____. *Prüfung der bejahenden Gründe, welche die Gottesgelehrte anführen, über die Frage, soll man sich in der abendländischen Kirche bey dem Gottesdienst der lateinischen Sprache bedienen.* Frankfurt und Leipzig: 1777.

_____. *Festpredigten und Redem von dem guten Tode für das Landvolk.* Augsburg: 1778.

_____. *Der erste Schritt zur künftigen Vereinigung der katholischen und der evangelischen Kirche, gewagte von—Fast wird man es nicht glauben, gewaget von einem Mönche.* P. F. K. in W.: 1778.

_____. "Brief über den neulich gesehenen Kometen." *Baierische Sammlungen und Auszüge* 17 (1766): 546–66.

_____. *De Copernicano mundi systemate dissertatio.* Dillingen: 1768.

Mayr, Gregor. *Institutio Interpretis Sacri.* Vienna: 1789.

McDonald, John Paul, ed. *Jean Mabillon—Treatise on Monastic Studies (1691).* Lanham, MD: University Press of America, 2004.

McMahon, Darrin M. *Enemies of the Enlightenment: The French Counter-Enlightenment and the Making of Modernity.* Oxford: Oxford University Press, 2001.

Meier, Gerhard. *Die Johannesoffenbarung und die Kirche, WUNT 25.* Tübingen: Mohr Siebeck, 1981.

Meijknecht, Ton. "De Zaak Wecklein 1806." *Nederlands archief voor kerkgeschiedenis* 56 (1976): 450–62; 57 (1977): 62–94; 222–37.

Meiners, Christoph. *Ueber den thierischen Magnetismus.* Lemgo: 1788.

Mejer, Otto. *Febronius. Weihbischof Johann Nikolaus von Hontheim und sein Widerruf.* Tübingen: 1880.

Melton, James V. H. *The Rise of the Public in Enlightenment Europe.* Cambridge: Cambridge University Press, 2001.

Mendelssohn, Moses. *Jerusalem oder über die religiöse Macht und Judentum.* Berlin: 1783.

Merkle, Sebastian. *Die kirchliche Aufklärung im katholischen Deutschland.* Berlin: Reichl, 1910.

_____. *Die katholische Beurteilung des Aufklärungszeitalters.* Berlin: Fredebeul, 1909.

Merz, Aloys. Frag. *Ob die der Schritt, den ein namenloser Projectant, aus Hoffnung die Protestanten mit den Katholiken zu vereinigen, gewagt hat, ein erlaubter und zu seinen Absichten dienlicher Schritt sey. In den heiligen Pfingstfeyertagen beantwortet.* Augsburg: 1778.

Meyer, Gottlob Wilhelm. *Geschichte der Schrifterklärung seit der Wiederherstellung der Wissenschaften.* Göttingen: 1809.

_____. *Versuch einer Hermeneutik des alten Testaments.* 2 vols. Göttingen: 1779–80.

Michaelis, Johann David. *Einleitung in die göttlichen Schriften des Neuen Testaments.* 2nd ed. Göttingen: 1788.

_____. *Entwurf der typischen Gottesgelartheit.* 2nd ed. Göttingen: 1763.

_____. "Briefe von der Schwierigkeit der Religions-Vereinigung, an Herrn Pastor Aurand, Secretaire der Neuwidischen (*sic!*) Unions-Academie." In *Syntagma commentationum.* Edited by Johann David Michaelis. Göttingen: 1759, 1:121–70.

Miller, Samuel J. "Portugal and Utrecht. A Phase of the Catholic Enlightenment." *The Catholic Historical Review* 43 (1977): 225–48.

_____. *Portugal and Rome. An Aspect of the Catholic Enlightenment.* Rome: Universita Gregoriana, 1978.

Möller, Horst. *Vernunft und Kritik. Deutsche Aufklärung im 17. und 18. Jahrhundert.* Frankfurt: Suhrkamp, 1986.

Molkenbuhr, Marcellinus. *Neue Auslegungsart der heiligen Schrift des alten Testaments. Empfohlen von dem Herrn Michael Wecklein. . . .* Dorsten: 1806.

Monod, Paul Kleber. *Solomon's Secret Arts. The Occult in the Age of Enlightenment.* New Haven: Yale University Press, 2013.

Monsperger, Joseph Julius. *Institutiones hermeneutica V. T.: praelectionibus academicis accomodata.* Vienna: 1776/84.

Moser, Jakob. *Unterthänigstes Gutachten wegen der jezigen Religions-Bewegungen, besonders in der Evangelischen Kirche wie auch über das Kayserliche Commissionsdecret in der Bahrtschen Sache.* N.p.: 1780.

Mosheim, Johann Lorenz. *De odio theologico commentatio.* Göttingen: 1748.

Moss, Candida. *The Myth of Persecution: How Early Christians Invented a Story of Martyrdom.* New York: HarperOne, 2013.

Müller, Bonaventura. *Widerlegung einer Schrift, worinn ein seyn sollender römisch-katholischer Pfarrer in Schlessien unternommen hat zu erweisen, dass weder die christliche Religion. . . .* Prague: 1790.

Müller, Johann Kaspar. *Dissertatio de ortu, vero religionis systemate, progressu, statu hodierno sectae unitarie seu Socinianae ac de prono e secta protestantium ad illam transit.* Mainz: 1784.

Müller, Josef. *Der Freiburger Pastoraltheologe Carl Schwarzel (1746–1809) unter besonderer Berücksichtigung seiner Stellung zu Jansenismus und Aufklärung.* Dissertation, University of Freiburg (1959), 2007, accessed July 10, 2015, http://www.freidok.uni-freiburg.de/volltexte/2883/pdf/ mueller_schwarzel.pdf.

Müller, Michael. *Fürstbischof Heinrich von Bibra und die Katholische Aufklärung im Hochstift Fulda (1759–1788).* Fulda: Pazeller, 2005.

Müller, Sascha. *Kritik und Theologie. Christliche Glaubens- und Schrifthermeneutik nach Richard Simon (1638–1712).* St. Ottilien: EOS, 2004.

Müller, Winfried. "Aufklärungstendenzen bei den süddeutschen Jesuiten zur Zeit der Ordensaufhebung." *Zeitschrift für Bayerische Landesgeschichte* 54 (1991): 203–17.

Müller-Goldkuhle, Peter. *Die Eschatologie in der Dogmatik des 19. Jahrhunderts.* Essen: Ludgerus, 1966.

Mulsow, Martin. "Eclecticism or Skepticism? A Problem of the Early Enlightenment." *Journal of the History of Ideas* 58 (1997): 465–77.

Muratori, Ludovico. *Antiquitates Italicae.* Vol. 5. Milan: 1738.

____. *Des hochwürdigen Ludwig Muratori gründliche Auslegung des grossen Geboths von der Liebe des Nächsten.* 2nd ed. Augsburg: 1768.

____. *De ingeniorum moderatione in religionis negotio [1714].* Augsburg: 1779.

____. *De recta hominis devotione.* Venice: 1760.

____. *Della regolata divozione.* Venice: 1747.

____. *Die wahre Andacht des Christen.* Aschaffenburg: 1751.

Murphy, Dennis, ed. *The Church and the Bible. Official Documents of the Catholic Church.* New Delhi: 2007.

Nellen, H. J. M. "Growing Tension between Church Doctrines and Critical Exegesis of the Old Testament." In *The Old Testament. The History of Its Interpretation.* Edited by Magne Saebo. Göttingen: Vandenhoeck & Ruprecht, 2008, 2:802–26.

Neugebauer-Wölk, Monika. "Das Alte Reich und seine Institutionen im Zeichen der Aufklärung: Vergleichende Betrachtungen zum Reichskammergericht und zum Fränkischen Kreistag." *Jahrbuch für fränkische Landesforschung* 58 (1998): 299–326.

Newport, Kenneth G. C. *Apocalypse and Millennium: Studies in Biblical Eisegesis.* Cambridge: Cambridge University Press, 2000.

Niemann, Franz-Josef. *Jesus als Glaubensgrund in der Fundamentaltheologie der Neuzeit.* Innsbruck: Tyrolia, 1983.

Noé, Marc Antoine. *Discours sur l'état futur de l'Église.* N.p. 1788.

Northeast, Christine.*The Parisian Jesuits and the Enlightenment, 1728-1762.* Oxford: Oxford University Press, 1991.

Oakley, Francis. *Conciliarism: Constitutionalism in the Catholic Church, 1300-1870.* Oxford: Oxford University Press, 2003.

____. *The Conciliarist Tradition.* Oxford: Oxford University Press, 2003.

Oberthür, Franz. *Idea Biblica Ecclesiae.* 6 vols. Würzburg: 1790–1821.

____. *Theologische Enzyklopädie.* Augsburg: 1828.

O'Collins, Gerald. *The Second Vatican Council: Message and Meaning.* Collegeville, MN: Michael Glazier, 2014.

Oest, Johann. *Schriften der Ostfriesischen freyen Gesellschaft zur Aufnahme der Religion.* N.p. 1756.

Olechowski, Thomas. "Zur Zensur am Ende des 18. Jahrhunderts: Dichter als Zensoren." In *Jahrbuch der Österreichischen Gesellschaft zur Erforschung des 18. Jahrhunderts.* Bochum: Winkler, 2007, 21:135–43.

Olivade, Pablo de. *Triumph des Evangeliums: Memoiren eines von den Verirrungen der heutigen Philosophie zurückgekommenen Weltmenschen.* Vol. 4. Translated by J. des Echelles. Regensburg, 1848.

Onymus, Adam Joseph. *Entwurf zu einer Geschichte des Bibellesens.* Würzburg: 1786.

Osculati, Roberto. "Hic Romae: Cornelio a Lapide commentator dell' Apocalisse al Collegio Romano." In *Storia e figure dell'Apocalisse fra '500 e '600.* Edited by Roberto Rusconi. Rome: Viella, 1994, 315–29.

Osterwald, Peter von [Franz Grossinger]. *De religiosis ordinibus et eorum reformatione liber singularis quem e Germanico in Latinum traduxit, suisque auxit animadversionibus.* 1781.

Ott, Ludwig. *Fundamentals of Catholic Dogma.* Rockford, IL: Tan, 1974.

Paulus, Heinrich Eberhard Gottlob Paulus. *Philologisch-kritischer und historischer Commentar über das Neue Testament.* 4 vols. Lübeck: 1800–1804.

Pehem, Johann Josef von. *Abhandlung von der Einführung der Volkssprache in den öffentlichen Gottesdienst.* Vienna: 1785.

Picard, Paul. *Zölibatsdiskussion im katholischen Deutschland der Aufklärungszeit. Auseinandersetzung mit der kanonischen Vorschrift im Namen der Vernunft und der Menschenrecht.* Düsseldorf: Patmos, 1975.

Piccolomini, Giovanni Battista, ed. *Merkwürdige Briefe des Pabstes Clemens des XIV (Ganganelli) nebst Reden, Lobreden und andern wichtigen Schriften.* Frankfurt: 1777.

Pieper, Anton. *Die alte Universität Münster 1773-1818.* Regensburg: 1902.

Pitzer, Volker. *Justinus Febronius. Das Ringen eines katholischen Irenikers um die Einheit der Kirche im Zeitalter der Aufklärung.* Göttingen: Vandenhoeck & Rupprecht, 1976.

Plassmann, Engelbert. *Staatskirchenrechtliche Grundgedanken der deutschen Kanonisten an der Wende vom 18. zum 19. Jahrhundert.* Freiburg: Herder, 1968.

Plongeron, Bernard. "Wahre Gottesverehrung und das Problem des Unglaubens. Debatten um Inhalte und Wege von Religiosität und Seelsorge." In *Geschichte des Christentums.* Edited by Bernard Plongeron. Freiburg: Herder, 2000, 10:233–293.

____. "Was ist katholische Aufklärung." In *Katholische. Aufklärung und Josephinismus.* Edited by Elisabeth Kovacz. Munich: Böhlau, 1979, 39–45.

Pocock, J. G. A. *Barbarism and Religion. The Enlightenments of Edward Gibbon.* Cambridge: Cambridge University Press, 1999.

Popkin, Richard H. *The Third Force in Seventeenth-Century Thought.* Leiden: Brill, 1992.

Pothier, Remy. *Die Offenbarung des heiligen Johannes. Der prophetische Schlüssel zu den Schicksalen der Kirchen, und der Staaten bis ans Ende der Zeiten.* Augsburg: 1798.

_____. *Compendium Operis in Apocalypsin, ex quo habetur prophetiae intelligentia.* Augsburg: 1797.

_____. *Ouvrage sur l'apocalypse par un prêtre François.* Cologne: 1776.

Pottmeyer, Hermann. "Die historisch-kritische Methode und die Erklärung zur Schriftauslegung in der dogmatischen Konstitution 'Dei Filius.'" *Annuarium Historiae Conciliorum* 2 (1970): 87–111.

Pracher, Beda. *Neue Liturgie des Pfarres M. in K. im Departement L.* Tübingen: 1802.

_____. *Sendschreiben an den Verfasser der Schrift: Ueber den Entwurf eines neuen katholischen Rituals.* Ulm: 1807.

Prechtl, Maximilian. *Friedensworte an die katholische und protestantische Kirche für ihre Wiedervereinigung.* 2nd ed. Sulzbach: 1820.

_____. *Seitenstück zur Weisheit Martin Luthers.* 1817.

Probst, Manfred. *Der Ritus der Kindertaufe: die Reformversuche der katholischen Aufklärung des deutschen Sprachbereiches: mit einer Bibliographie der gedruckten Ritualien des deutschen Sprachbereiches von 1700 bis 1960.* Trier: Paulinus-Verlag, 1981.

Pruggheim, Carl Prugger von. *Tugendhafte Gesinnungen und Thaten von Heiden, Juden und Türken, in Erzählungen für Leser aus allen Ständen.* 2 vols. Munich: 1802.

Raab, Heribert. "Die katholische Ideenrevolution des 18. Jahrhunderts. Der Einbruch der Geschichte in die Kanonistik und die Auswirkungen in Kirche und Reich bis zum Emser Kongress." In *Katholische Aufklärung—Aufklärung im katholischen Deutschland.* Edited by Harm Klueting. Hamburg: Meiner, 1993, 104–18.

_____. "Das Fürstbistum Fulda (1752–1802/03)." *Archiv für Mittelrheinische Kirchengeschichte* 41 (1989): 173–201.

____. "Toleranz im Kur- und Erzstift Trier." In *Toleranz am Mittelrhein*. Edited by Isnard Frank. Mainz: 1984, 21–43.

____. "Der reichskirchliche Episkopalismus von der Mitte des 17. bis zum Ende des 18. Jahrhunderts." In *Handbuch der Kirchengeschichte*. Edited by Hubert Jedin. Freiburg: Herder, 1970, 6:477–507.

____. *Clemens Wenzeslaus von Sachsen und seine Zeit, 1739-1812*. Freiburg: Herder, 1962.

____. "Das Mainzer Interregnum von 1774." *Archiv für Mittelrheinische Kirchengeschichte* 14 (1962): 168–93.

____. "Damian Friedrich Dumeiz und Kardinal Oddi. Zur Entdeckung des Febronius und zur Aufklärung im Erzstift Mainz und in der Reichsstadt Frankfurt." *Archiv für mittelrheinische Kirchengeschichte* 10 (1958): 217–40.

____. *Die Concordata Nationis Germanicae in der kanonistischen Diskussion des 17. bis 19. Jahrhunderts. Ein Beitrag zur Geschichte der episkopalistischen Theorie in Deutschland*. Wiesbaden: Steiner, 1956.

____. "Johann Kaspar Barthels Stellung in der Diskussion um die Concordata Nationis Germanicae." In *Herbipolis Jubilans*. Würzburg: Echter, 1953, 599–616.

Raggenbass, Niklas. *Harmonie und schwesterliche Einheit zwischen Bibel und Vernunft. Die Benediktiner des Klosters Banz: Publizisten und Wissenschaftler in der Aufklärungszeit*. St. Ottilien: EOS, 2006.

Ratzinger, Joseph / Pope Benedict XVI, *Jesus von Nazareth*. 3 vols. Freiburg: Herder, 2006–2012.

____. *Jesus of Nazareth. The Infancy Narratives*. New York: Image, 2012.

Ratzinger, Joseph. *Milestones: Memoirs, 1927-1977*. San Francisco: 1998.

____. "Schriftauslegung im Widerstreit. Zur Frage nach Grundlagen und Weg der Exegese heute." In *Schriftauslegung im Widerstreit*. Edited by Joseph Ratzinger. Freiburg: Herder, 1989, 15–44.

____. "Ein Versuch zur Frage des Traditionsbegriffes." In *Offenbarung und Geschichte*. Edited by Karl Rahner and Joseph Ratzinger. Freiburg: Herder, 1965, (QD 25), 2569.

Rau, Johann Wilhelm. *Fremüthige Untersuchung über die Typologie*. Erlangen: 1784.

Rauch, Wendelin. *Engelbert Klüpfel. EIn führender Theologe der Aufklärungszeit.* Freiburg: 1922.

Rauwolf, Gerhard J. "P. Beda Mayr OSB (1742-1794): Versuch einer ökumenischen Annäherung." *Jahrbuch des Vereins für Augsburger Bistumsgeschichte* 33 (1999): 317-53.

Rechenmacher, Ludwig. *Der Episkopalismus im 18. Jahrhundert in Deutschland und seine Lehren über das Verhältnis zwischen Kirche und Staat.* Regensburg: 1908.

Reichert, Franz Rudolf. "Das Trierer Priesterseminar zwischen Aufklärung und Revolution (1786-1810)." *Archiv für Mittelrheinische Kirchengeschichte* 38 (1986): 107-44.

_____. "Trier und seine Theologische Fakultät im Isenbiehlschen Streit (1773-1779)." In *Verführung zur Geschichte. Festschrift zum 500. Jahrestag der Eröffnung einer Universität in Trier.* Edited by Georg Droege and Wolfgang Frühwald. Trier: NCO-Verlag, 1973, 276-301.

_____. "Johann Gertz (1744-1824). Ein katholischer Bibelwissenschaftler der Aufklärungszeit im Spiegel seiner Bibliothek." *Archiv für Mittelrheinische Kirchengeschichte* 18 (1966): 41-99.

Reinke, Laurenz. *Die Weissagung von der Jungfrau und vom Immanuel Jes. 7:14-16. Eine exegetisch-historische Untersuchung.* Münster: 1848.

Reiser, Marius. *Bibelkritik und Auslegung der Heiligen Schrift.* Tübingen: Mohr Siebeck, 2007.

_____. "Richard Simons biblische Hermeneutik." In *Bibelkritik und Auslegung der Heiligen Schrift.* Edited by Marius Reiser. Tübingen: Mohr Siebeck, 2007, 185-218.

_____. "The History of Catholic Exegesis, 1600-1800." In *Oxford Handbook of Early Modern Theology.* Edited by Ulrich L. Lehner, A. G. Roeber, and Richard Muller. New York: Oxford University Press, 2016, 185-218.

Repgen, Konrad. "Der päpstliche Protest gegen den Westfälischen Frieden und die Friedenspolitik Urbans VIII." *Historisches Jahrbuch* 75 (1956): 94-122.

Reutemann, Johann T. *Bemerkungen über die von dem Herrn J. Jac. Hess . . . herausgegebene Lebens-Geschichte Jesu.* N. p.: 1802.

Reventlow, Henning Graf. *History of Biblical Interpretation.* Translated by Leo G. Purdue. Houston Mill, GA: Society of Biblical Literature, 2010.

_____. "Katholische Exegese des Alten Testamentes zwischen den

Vatikanischen Konzilien." In *Die katholisch-theologischen Disziplinen in Deutschland, 1870-1962.* Edited by Hubert Wolf. Paderborn: Schöningh, 1999, 15–39.

Ribera, Francisco. *In sacram beati Joannis Apostoli & Evangelistae Apocalypsin Commentarii.* Lyon: 1593.

Robertson, John. *The Case for the Enlightenment: Scotland and Naples, 1680-1760.* New York: Cambridge University Press, 2005.

____. "The Enlightenments of J. G. A. Pocock." *Storia della storiografia—History of Historiography* 39 (2001): 140–51.

____. *Enlightenment: A Very Short Introduction.* Oxford: Oxford University Press, 2015.

Robinson, Robert B. *Roman Catholic Exegesis since Divino Afflante Spiritu. Hermeneutical Implications.* Atlanta: Scholars Press, 1988.

Rösel, Martin. "Die Jungfrauengeburt des endzeitlichen Immanuel." *Jahrbuch für biblische Theologie* 6 (1991): 135–51.

Rogier, Louis. "L'Aufklärung catholique." In *Nouvelle Histoire de l'Église.* Paris: Éditions du Seuil, 1966, 4:137–61.

Rosa, Mario. "Roman Catholicism." *Encyclopedia of the Enlightenment.* Edited by Alan C. Kors. Oxford: Oxford University Press, 2002, 3:468–72.

Rosenmüller, Ernst Friedrich Karl. *Handbuch für die Literatur der biblischen Kritik und Exegese.* Göttingen: 1797–1800.

Rothschild, Emma. *The Inner Life of Empires: An Eighteenth-Century History.* Princeton, NJ: Princeton University Press, 2011.

Sacy, Isaac-Louis de [Maistre]. *Die heilige Schrift erklärt aus den heiligen Vätern . . . des neuen Bundes zwölfter Band.* Augsburg: 1803.

Sailer, Johann Michael. *Sämmtliche Werke.* Sulzbach: 1835.

____. *Vernunftlehre für Menschen wie sie sind. . . .* 2nd ed. Munich: 1795.

Sailhamer, John. *Introduction to Old Testament Theology: A Canonical Approach.* Grand Rapids, MI: Zondervan, 1995.

Sala, Giovanni. "Fallible Teachings and the Assistance of the Holy Spirit." In *Kontroverse Theologie.* Cologne: Nova & Vetera, 2005.

Salat, Jakob. *Auch ein paar Worte über die Frage: Führt die Aufklärung zur Revolution?* München: 1802.

Salmerón, Alfonso. *Disputationum in Epistolas canonicas et Apocalypsin.* Madrid: 1602.

____. *Prolegomena Biblica.* Madrid: 1598.

Sandbichler, Aloysius. *Darstellung der Regeln einer allgemeinen Auslegungskunst von den Büchern des alten und neuen Bundes.* Salzburg: 1813.

____. *Stimme des Rufenden in der Wüste.* 3 vols. Linz: 1805–14.

____. *Erläuterungen der biblischen Geschichte nach Herrn Johann Jakob Heß besonders zum Gebrauche für katholische Leser.* 2 vols. Salzburg: 1794.

____. "Wahre Ursachen der vielfältigen und gräulichen Verketzerungen in unseren Zeiten." In *Revision der Augsburger Kritik über gewisse Kritiker.* Edited by Aloysius Sandbichler. Augsburg: 1792, 2:281–325.

____. *Revision der Augsburger Kritik über gewisse Kritiker. Freymüthige Betrachtungen über wichtige von Obscuranten entstellte Religionsgegenstände nach den Bedürfnissen unserer Zeit.* Salzburg: 1792.

____. *Abhandlung über die zweckmässigen Mittel den hebräischen und griechischen Grundtext dem Wortsinne nach richtig zu verstehen.* Salzburg: 1791.

____. *Lasen die ersten Christen die heilige Schrift? Und wie lasen sie dieselbige?* Salzburg: 1784.

Sashegyi, Oskar. *Zensur und Geistesfreiheit unter Joseph II.* Budapest: Akademie Verlag, 1958.

Schäfer, Christoph. *Staat, Kirche, Individuum: Studie zur süddeutschen Publizistik über religiöse Toleranz von 1648 bis 1819.* Frankfurt: P. Lang, 1992.

Schäfer, Philipp. *Kirche und Vernunft.* Munich: Hueber, 1974.

Schatz, Klaus. *Kirchenbild und Päpstliche Unfehlbarkeit bei den deutschsprachigen Minoritätsbischöfen auf dem I. Vatikanum.* Rome: Universita Gregoriana Editrice, 1975.

Scheib, Otto. *Die innerchristlichen Religionsgespräche im Abendland.* 3 vols. Wiesbaden: Harrassowitz, 2010.

Schindling, Anton. "Theresianismus, Josephinismus, katholische Aufklärung." *Würzburger Diözesangeschichtsblätter* 50 (1988): 215–44.

Schlaich, Klaus. "Maioritas–protestatio–itio in partes–Corpus Evangelicorum: Das Verfahren im Reichstag des Hl. Römischen Reichs Deutscher Nation nach der Reformation." In *Gesammelte Aufsätze: Kirche und Staat von der*

Reformation bis zum Grundgesetz, Ius Ecclesiasticum 57. Edited by Klaus Schlaich. Tübingen: Mohr Siebeck, 1997, 68–134.

Schlögl, Rudolph. "Secularization: German Catholicism at the Eve of Modernity." *German Historical Institute/London Bulletin* 25/1 (2003): 5–21.

———. *Glaube und Religion in der Säkularisierung. Die katholische Stadt—Köln, Aachen, Münster—(1740-1840).* Munich: Oldenbourg 1995.

Schmidt, Bernward. *Die Konzilien und der Papst.* Freiburg: Herder, 2013.

Schneider, Bernhard. "Katholische Aufklärung. Zum Werden und Wert eines Forschunsgbegriffs." *Revue d'Histoire Ecclesiastique* 93 (1998): 354–97.

———. "Armutsdiskurse, Armenfürsorge und Industrialisierung im ‚deutschen' Katholizismus während des langen 19. Jahrhunderts." In *Wirtschaft und Gemeinschaft. Konfessionelle und neureligiöse Gemeinsinnsmodelle im 19. und 20. Jahrhundert.* Edited by Swen Steinberg and Winfried Müller. Bielefeld: Transcript, 2014, 34–61.

Schneider, Eulogius. *Gedichte.* Frankfurt: 1790.

Schneider, Han. *Der Konziliarismus als Problem der neueren katholischen Theologie.* Berlin: De Gruyter, 1976.

Schneiders, Werner. *Die wahre Aufklärung. Zum Selbstverständnis der deutschen Aufklärung.* Freiburg: Alber, 1974.

Schönberg, Matthias von. *Die Wahrheitsgründe des katholischen Hauptgrundsatzes für die Unfehlbarkeit der Kirche wider den sogenannten ersten Schritt.* Munich: 1779.

Schroeckh, Johann Mathias. *Unpartheyische Kirchen-Historie: Alten und Neuen Testaments . . . Vierter Theil, in welchem die Geschichte vom Jahr nach Christi Geburt 1751 bis 1760 enthalten sind.* Jena: 1766.

Schromm, Arnold. "Wissenschaft und Aufklärung im Benediktinerstift Heilig–Kreuz Donauwörth." In *Zeitschrift für Bayerische Landesgeschichte* 54 (1991): 287–98.

Schulze, Winfried. "Majority Decision in the Imperial Diets of the Sixteenth and Seventeenth Centuries." *Journal of Modern* History 58, Supplement (1986): S46–S63.

Schwarz, Ildephons. *Anleitung zur Kenntnis derjenigen Bücher, welche den Candidaten der Theologie . . . wesentlich nothwendig und nützlich sind.* Coburg: 1804.

Schwarzbach, Bertram Eugene. "Dom Augustin Calmet. Man of the Enlightenment Despite Himself." *Archiv für Religionsgeschichte* 3 (2001): 135–48.

———. *Voltaire's Old Testament Criticism.* Geneva: Droz, 1971.

Schwarzhueber, Simpert. *Praktisch-katholisches Religionshandbuch zum Gebrauche des gemeinern Stadt- und Landvolkes, wie auch zum Behufe der Christenlehrer.* Salzburg: 1784.

Schweigard, Jörg. *Felix Anton Blau: Frühdemokrat, Theologe, Menschenfreund.* Obernburg: Logo, 2007.

Second Vatican Council, Documents of the. Accessed via www.vatican.va/ archive/hist_councils/ii_vatican_council/index.htm.

Sedlmeier, Franz. "Jesaja 7, 14. Überlegungen zu einem umstrittenen Vers und zu seiner Auslegungsgeschichte." In *"Geboren aus der Jungfrau." Klarstellungen.* Edited by Anton Ziegenaus. Regensburg: Pustet, 2007, 3–43.

Seidel, Hans Werner. "Bibelwissenschaftliche Arbeit und Forschung an der Katholisch-Theologischen Fakultät der Universität Breslau." *Jahrbuch der Universität Breslau* 10 (1965): 7–45.

Seigfried, Adam. *Vernunft und Offenbarung bei dem Spätaufklärer Jakob Salat: Eine historisch-systematische Untersuchung.* Innsbruck: Tyrolia, 1983.

Seitz, Johann Christian. *Ausführlicher Beweis, daß I. die zween Apoc. XI gedachte Zeugen zwey einzelne Personen, II. daß solche Moses und Elias in Person sehen . . . : von J.C.S. Dienern der großen Gemeinde Ps. 40:10.* N.p.: 1721.

———. *Mathematischer, das ist himmelfester und sonnenclarer Beweiss, daß die 3 1/2 und 1260 Tage der Zeugen Apoc. 2 . . . natürliche Tage seyn.* N.p.: 1735.

Sellert, Wolfgang. "Richterliche Unabhängigkeit am Reichskammergericht und am Reichshofrat." In *Gerechtigkeit und Geschichte: Beiträge eines Symposions zum 65. Geburtstag von Malte Dießelhorst.* Edited by Okko Behrends. Göttingen: Wallstein, 1996, 118–32.

Selmar, Anton. *Die öffentlichen Gottesverehrungen der katholischen Christen waren anfangs anders beschaffen als jetzt, und sollten wieder anders werden: Aus der Geschichte, Religion und Vernunft dargestellt von einem alten, katholischen Pfarrer in Baiern und königl. Bezirksinspektor der Volkschulen.* Landshut: 1810.

Shea, William H. *Selected Studies on Prophetic Interpretation.* Washington: n.p., 1982.

Sieben, Hermann Josef. *Die katholischen Konzilsidee von der Reformation bis zur Aufklärung.* Paderborn: Schöningh: 1988.

_____. *Traktate und Theorien zum Konzil vom Beginn des Grossen Schismas bis zum Vorabend der Reformation (1378-1521).* Frankfurt: Knecht, 1983.

Simon, Richard. *Kritische Historie des Textes des Neuen Testamentes. Herausgegeben von Johann Salomo Semler.* Halle: 1776.

_____. *Historia Critica Commentatorum praecipuorum V. & N. T.* Gosslar: 1713.

_____. *Histoire Critique des principaux commentateurs du Nouveau Testament.* Rotterdam: 1693.

Spaemann, Robert and Reinhard Löw. *Natürliche Ziele: Geschichte und Wiederentdeckung teleologischen Denkens.* Stuttgart: 2005.

Spehr, Christoph. *Aufklärung und Ökumene. Reunionsversuche zwischen Katholiken und Protestanten im deutschsprachigen Raum des späteren 18. Jahrhunderts.* Tübingen: Mohr Siebeck, 2005.

Stahl, Ernst Christian. "Versuch über die Erscheinungen Jehovas." In *Eichhorn's Bibliothek der Biblischen Litteratur* 7:156-80. 1795.

Stargardter, Steven A. *Niklas Vogt, 1756-1836: A Personality of the Late German Enlightenment and Early Romantic Movement.* New York: Taylor and Francis, 1991.

Stattler, Benedict. *Authentische Aktenstücke wegen dem zu Rom theils betriebenen, theils abzuwenden getrachteten Verdammungsurtheil über das Stattlerische Buch: Demonstratio Catholica.* Frankfurt: 1796.

_____. *Plan zu der alleinmöglichen Vereinigung im Glauben der Protestanten mit der katholischen Kirche und den Grenzen der Möglichkeiten.* Munich: 1791.

_____. *Demonstratio Catholica.* Pappenheim: 1775.

_____. *Demonstratio Evangelica.* Eichstätt: 1770.

_____. *De Locis Theologicis.* Weissenburg: 1775.

_____. "Anacaephaleosis ad DD. Protestantes in Germania et Proposition Conditionum sub quibus solis Unio Religionis Exoptata possibilis est." In Idem, *Theologia Christiana Theoretica, De Sacramentis.* Eichstätt: 1780.

_____. *Plan zu der allein möglichen Vereinigung im Glauben der protestanten mit der katholischen Kirche, und den Gränzen dieser Möglichkeit.* Augsburg: 1791.

Steiner, Josef. *Liturgiereform in der Aufklärungszeit: Eine Darstellung am Beispiel Vitus Anton Winters.* Freiburg: Herder, 1974.

Stephan-Kopitzsch, Ursula. *Die Toleranzdiskussion im Spiegel überregionaler Aufklärungszeitschriften.* Frankfurt: Peter Lang, 1999.

Strayer, Brian. *Suffering Saints: Jansenists and Convulsionnaires in France, 1640-1799.* Eastbourne: Sussex Academic Press, 2008.

Stroumsa, Guy. *A New Science: The Discovery of Religion in the Age of Reason.* Cambridge, MA: Harvard University Press, 2010.

Stümper, Franz. *Die kirchenrechtlichen Ideen des Febronius.* Aschaffenburg: Druckerei Dr. G. Werbrun, 1908.

Surer, Thaddäus. *Das Bibellesen in den ältesten Zeiten.* Salzburg: 1784.

____. *Freymüthige Beleuchtung des Glaubensbekenntnisses des Pietro Gianonne und der Mönchsgelübde.* Nuremberg: 1790.

Swidler, Leonard. *Aufklärung Catholicism 1780-1850.* Missoula, MT: Scholars Press, 1978.

Taylor, Charles. *A Secular Age.* Harvard, MA: Belknap Press, 2007.

Teller, Johann F. *Gedanken eines sächsischen Predigers über die Geschichte der drey letzten Lebensjahre Jesu.* Leipzig: 1774.

____. *Nöthige Erinnerungen über Herrn Johann Jakob Hess Geschichte der drey Lebensjahre Jesu.* Frankfurt and Leipzig: 1774.

Theiner, Augustin. *Die katholische Kirche Schlesiens dargestellt von einem katholischen Geistlichen.* Altenburg: 1826.

Thiel, Burchard, *Die Liturgik der Aufklärungszeit.* Breslau: 1926.

Thieme, Traugott. *Ueber die Hindernisse des Selbstdenkens in Deutschland.* Gotha: 1791.

Tiefenthal, Franz S. *Die Apokalypse des Johannes.* Paderborn: 1892.

Trapp, Waldemar. *Vorgeschichte und Ursprung der liturgischen Bewegung vorwiegend in Hinsicht auf das deutsche Sprachgebiet.* Würzburg: 1939.

____. *Vorgeschichte und Ursprung der liturgischen Bewegung: vorwiegend in Hinsicht auf das deutsche Sprachgebiet.* Würzburg: 1939.

Tutor, Gomez. *Die wissenschaftliche Methode bei Christian Wolff.* Stuttgart–Bad Canstatt: Frommann-Holzboog, 2005.

Unterburger, Klaus. *Vom Lehramt der Theologen zum Lehramt der Päpste?: Pius XI., die Apostolische Konstitution "Deus scientiarum Dominus" und die Reform der Universitätstheologie.* Freiburg im Breisgau: Herder, 2010.

Valeske, Ulrich. *Hierarchie Veritatum—Theologiegeschichtliche Hintergründe und mögliche Konsequenzen eines Hinweiss im Ökumenismusdekret des II. Vatikanischen Konzils zum zwischenkirchlichen Gespräch.* Munich: Claudius, 1968.

Van Kley, Dale. *The Religious Origins of the French Revolution.* New Haven: Yale University Press, 1996.

Vanysacker, Dries. "Der Widerruf des 'Febronius' und Kardinal Guiseppe Garampi in Rom. Eine aufklärerische ultramontane Bekämpfung des Febronianismus, 1764–1792." *Kurtrierisches Jahrbuch* 43 (2003), 125–41.

____. *Cardinal Giuseppe Garampi, 1725-1792: An Enlightened Ultramontane.* Bruxelles: Institut historique belge de Rome, 1995.

Venturi, Franco. *Settecento riformatore.* 5 vols. Torino: Einaudi, 1969–90.

Vismara, Paola. "Ludovico Muratori: Enlightenment in a Tridentine Mode." In *Enlightenment and Catholicism in Europe.* Edited by Ulrich L. Lehner and Jeffrey Burson. Notre Dame, IN: University of Notre Dame Press, 2014, 251–70.

Vizer, Adam. *Praenotiones hermeneuticae Novi Testamenti.* Tyrnau: 1777.

Vogl, Franz. *Die heilige Schrift und ihre Interpretation durch die heiligen Väter der Kirche.* Augsburg: 1836.

Vogt, Niklas. *Gedanken über das Allerheiligste im Menschengeschlechte.* Bamberg: 1812.

____. *System der allgemeinen Weltgeschichte.* Mainz: 1785.

Volk, Otto, ed. *Franz Oberthür: Persönlickeit und Werk.* Neustadt: Degener, 1966.

Wallnig, Thomas. *Gasthaus und Gelehrsamkeit.* Vienna: Oldenbourg, 2007.

Walmsley, Charles. *The General History of the Christian Church . . . deduced from the Apocalypse of St. John.* N.p.: 1771.

Walton, Brian. *Biblia Polyglotta Prolegomena.* Leipzig: 1777.

Wangermann, Ernst. *Die Waffen der Publizität.* Vienna: Verlag für Geschichte und Politik, 2004.

Waterworth, James. *Canons and Decrees of the Council of Trent.* London: C. Dolman, 1848.

Weber, Hermann. "Niklas Vogt. Ein aufgeklärter Historiker der alten Mainzer Universität." In *Aufklärung in Mainz,* edited by Hermann Weber. Wiesbaden: Steiner, 1984, 31–46.

Weber, Lothar. *Die Parität der Konfessionen in der Reichsverfassung von den*

Anfängen der Reformation bis zum Untergang des alten Reiches 1806. Bonn: Fuchs, 1961.

Weber, Sascha. "Mainz ist nicht Göttingen. Der Mainzer Kurstaat und die Affäre Isenbiehl (1773–1780)." *Archiv für Mittelrheinische Kirchengeschichte* 61 (2009): 211–28.

Wecklein, Michael. *Momenta praecipua ad liberaliorem V. T. interpretationem.* Essen: 1806.

Weishaupt, Johann Adam. *Geschichte der Vervollkommung des menschlichen Geschlechts.* Frankfurt: 1788.

Weislinger, Nikolaus. *Vogel Friß oder Stirb.* 2nd ed. Oberammergau: 1751.

Weiss, Christoph and Wolfgang Albrecht. *Von "Obscuranten" und "Eudämonisten": gegenaufklärerische, konservative und antirevolutionäre Publizisten im späten 18. Jahrhundert.* St. Ingbert: Röhrig, 1997.

Weitlauff, Manfred. *Der "Fall" des Augsburger Diözesanpriesters und Münchener Theologieprofessors Joseph Schnitzer (1859-1939).* Augsburg: Verlag des Vereins für Bistumsgeschichte, 2011.

____. "Ignaz Heinrich von Wessenberg (1774–1860)." *Jahrbuch des Vereins für Augsburger Bistumsgeschichte* 44 (2010): 1–335.

____. *Kirche zwischen Aufbruch und Verweigerung: Ausgewählte Beiträge zur Kirchen-und Theologiegeschichte des 19. und frühen 20. Jahrhunderts.* Stuttgart: Kohlhammer, 2001.

Welker, Karl. *Rechtsgeschichte als Rechtspolitik. Justus Möser als Jurist und Staatsmann.* 2 vols. Osnabrück: Verein für die Geschichte und Landeskunde von Osnabrück, 1996.

Werkmeister, Benedict. *Beyträge zur Verbeserung der katholischen Liturgie in Deutschland.* Ulm: 1789.

____. *Predigten in den Jahren 1784-1791.* Ulm: 1812.

____. *Thomas Freykirch: oder freymüthige Untersuchungen über die Unfehlbarkeit der katholischen Kirche.* Frankfurt and Leipzig [i.e., Göttingen]: 1792.

____. *Über die deutschen Mess- und Abendmahlsanstalten in der katholischen Hofkapelle zu Stuttgart.* Stuttgart: 1787.

____. *Vertheidigung des von Herrn Pfarrer Brunner herausgegebenen neuen Gebetbuches, für aufgeklärte katholische Christen: Gegen die Obscurenten zu Augsubrg, und ihre Brüder im übrigen katholischen Deutschland.* 1802.

____. "Über den mystischen Sinn." In *Jahrschrift für Theologie und Kirchenrecht der Katholiken* 2/2 (1809): 259–376.

Wessenberg, Ignaz von. *Der Geist des Zeitalters: Ein Denkmal des achtzehnten Jahrhunderts.* Zurich: 1801.

Wetterer, Anton. "Johann Adam Gärtier: Prediger und Kanonikus an der Stiftskirche zu Bruchsal." *Der Katholik* IV-21 (1918): 245–59; 327–41.

Whaley, Joachim. *Germany and the Holy Roman Empire.* 2 vols. Oxford: Oxford University Press, 2012.

Wicks, Jared. "Tridentine Motivations of John XXIII before and during Vatican II." *Theological Studies* 75 (2014): 847–62.

Widman, Meinrad. *Freymüthige Anmerkungen zu der Frage: Wer sind die Aufklärer?* 4 vols. Augsburg: 1789–1790.

____. *Wer sind die Aufklärer? beantwortet nach dem ganzen Alphabet.* 2 vols. Augsburg: 1786.

Williams, John. *A free enquiry into the authenticity of the first and second chapters of St. Matthew's Gospel.* London: 1771.

Wiltgen, Ralph. *The Rhine Flows into the Tiber: The Unknown Council.* New York: Hawthorn, 1967.

Winter, Vitus Anton. *Deutsches, katholisches, ausübendes Ritual.* Frankfurt: 1813.

____. *Erstes deutsches kritisches katholisches Ritual.* Landshut: 1811.

____. *Erstes deutsches kritisches Messbuch.* Munich: 1810.

Wittmann, Georg Michael. *Principia catholica de sacra Scriptura.* Regensburg: 1793.

Wolf, Gerhard Philipp. "Maximilian Prechtl (1757–1832)—Letzter Abt des Benediktinerklosters Michelfeld in der Oberpfalz." *Zeitschrift für Bayerische Kirchengeschichte* 68 (1999): 77–124.

Wolff, Christian. *Discursus Praeliminaris.* Edited by Günter Gawlick. Hildesheim: Olms, 1996.

____. *Vernünftige Gedanken Von Den Kräfften Des Menschlichen Verstandes (Deutsche Logik).* Reprint of the 1754 edition. Edited by Hans Werner Arndt. Hildesheim: Olms, 1965.

Wolff, Fritz. *Corpus Evangelicorum und Corpus Catholicorum auf dem Westfälischen Friedenskongress. Die Einfügung der konfessionellen Städteverbindungen in die Reichsverfassung.* Münster: Aschendorff, 1966.

Wolff, Norbert. *Peter Alois Gratz (1769-1849). Ein Theologe zwischen 'falscher Aufklärung' und 'Obscurantismus.'* Trier: Paulinus-Verlag, 1998.

Zaccaria, Franciscus Antonius, *Antifebronio o sia apologia polemico-storica del primato del Papa.* 2nd ed. 4 vols. Cesena, 1768–70.

Zumkeller, Adolar. "Sandbichler, Aloys." In *Biographisch-Bibliographisches Kirchenlexikon.* Nordhausen: Bautz, 1994, 8:1303.

Publication Credits

Some of the chapters of this book have appeared elsewhere in print. Some were revised and amended for the present publication. I thank the respective publishers for their kind permission to reproduce these texts here:

Chapter 2: What is Catholic Enlightenment?

"What is Catholic Enlightenment?" in *History Compass* 8 (2010): 166–78. © Wiley Publishing.

Chapter 3: The "Heresy-Hunting" of the Obscurantists and the "Martyrdom" of Catholic Enlighteners

"Die Verketzerungssucht der Obskurantisten. Die Feinde der katholischen Aufklärung aus der Sicht ihrer Opfer," in *Fiat Voluntas Tua. Festschrift Harm Klueting*, ed. Raimund Haas. (Munster: Aschendorff, 2014) 415–29. © Aschendorff Verlag.

Chapter 4: Ghosts of Westphalia

"The Ghosts of Westphalia. Fictions and Ideals of Ecclesial Unity in Enlightenment Germany," in *A Man of the Church: The Work and Witness of Ralph del Colle*, ed. Michel R. Barnes. (Eugene, OR: Wipf and Stock, 2012) 283–301. © Wipf and Stock Publishers, www.wipfandstock.com.

Chapter 5: Enlightenment and Ecumenism: Beda Mayr (1742–94)

"Enlightenment and Ecumenism," *Pro Ecclesia. A Journal of Catholic and Evangelical Theology* 18 (2009): 415–35. © Rowman & Littlefield.

Chapter 7: Johann Nikolaus von Hontheim's *Febronius*

"Johann Nikolaus von Hontheim and his Febronius: A Bishop and his Censored Ecclesiology," *Church History and Religious Culture* 88 (2008): 93–121. © Brill Publ.

Chapter 10: The Conundrum of Catholic Biblical Scholarship

"Against the Consensus of the Fathers? The Conundrums of Catholic Biblical Scholarship in the Eighteenth Century," *Pro Ecclesia* 12 (2013): 189–221. © Rowman & Littlefield.

Chapter 11: Apocalypse 2014—Post-Tridentine Catholic Exegesis of Revelation

"Apocalypse 2014? Alphonsus Frey's Futurist Commentary on Revelation (1762)," *Journal of Baroque Studies* 2 (2014): 25–53. © Institute for Baroque Studies, Malta.

Chapter 12: Apocalypse, Enlightenment, and the Beginning of Salvation History

"Apocalypse, Enlightenment and the Beginning of Salvation History: The Ecumenical Friendship between Johann Jakob Hess and Aloysius Sandbichler," *Pro Ecclesia* 13 (2014): 219–37. © Rowman & Littlefield.

Translations of biblical texts follow the *New American Bible, Revised Edition* (NABRE) [2011], online: http://www.usccb.org/bible/books-of-the-bible

Throughout this volume, all books published before 1900 do not carry publisher information.

Magisterial documents of the Catholic Church are cited, unless otherwise noted, according to Heinrich Denzinger and Peter Hünermann, *Compendium of Creeds, Definitions, and Declarations on Matters of Faith and Morals* (San Francisco: Ignatius Press, 2012) (DH).

Index of Names

Eichhorn, Johann Gottfried, 286, 311, 343, 362
Elijah, 282, 284, 303, 304, 324, 343
Enoch, 282, 284, 303
Erichteus, 346
Ernesti, Johann August, 222, 223, 274, 309, 314, 317, 362
Erthal, Friedrich von, 74
Erthal, Karl F., 251
Estius, William, 236
Eugene IV, Pope, 145
Eybel, Valentin, 162

Fagnani, Prospero, 151
Fauchet, Claude, 305, 306, 309, 362
Feder, Johann Heinrich, 47, 362
Feijoo, Benito, 37
Feller, Francois, 219, 363
Fichte, Johann G., 87
Fischer, Christoph, 222, 363
Fischer, Gottlob N., 178
Flacius, Matthias, 341
Fleming, Robert, 287, 363
Fleury, Claude, 144
Foucher, Paul, 252
Francis de Sales, Saint, 1, 296
Francis of Assisi, Saint, 1
Francis, Pope, 1
Franz, Wolfgang, 341
Frederick the Great, 6
Freher, Marquard, 152
Frey, Alphonsus, 14, 279, 289, 290, 299, 302, 303, 363, 392

Fürstenberg, Franz von, 49, 332–33, 337

Galiani, Celestino, 36
Gall, Joseph Anton, 182
Galura, Bernhard, 313, 317
Garampi, Giuseppe, 75
Gärtler, Adam, 56
Gay, Peter, 6, 364
Geddes, Alexander, 193, 364
Gerbert, Martin, 152, 263, 264, 287, 288, 353, 364
Gerdil, Sigismond Hyacinthe, 9, 364
Gerson, Jean, 144, 151, 158
Gerstenberg, Jakob Heinrich, 72, 92
Gertz, Johann, 74, 94, 248, 380
Goldhagen, Hermann, 219, 246, 247, 251, 361, 364
Gratz, Peter Alois, 273, 274, 311
Gregory the Great, Pope, 202
Griesbach, Johann Jakob, 130, 365
Grossing, Franz Rudolph, 125, 126, 127, 363, 365
Grotius, Hugo, 214, 281
Guardini, Romano, 172

Habermas, Jürgen, 5, 365
Häffelin, Johann Kasimir, 74
Hamelius, Jean, 236
Hardts, Hermann von der, 152
Hayd, Stefan, 222
Hazart, Cornelius, 294, 366
Heidegger, Johann H., 314